Brunei – History, Islam, Society and Contemporary Issues

Brunei, although a relatively small state, is disproportionately important on account of its rich resource base. In addition, in recent years the country has endeavoured to play a greater role in regional affairs, especially through ASEAN, holding the chair of the organization in 2013, and also beyond the region, fostering diplomatic, political, economic and educational ties with many nations. This book presents much new research and new thinking on a wide range of issues concerning Brunei. Subjects covered include Brunei's rich history – the sultanate formerly had much more extensive territories and was a key player in regional affairs – the country's economy, politics, society and ethnicities, and resource issues and international relations.

Ooi Keat Gin is Professor of Southeast Asian Studies (History) at Universiti Sains Malaysia.

Routledge Contemporary Southeast Asia Series

Singapore in the Global System
Relationship, structure and change
Peter Preston

Chinese Big Business in Indonesia
The state of the Capital
Christian Chua

Ethno-religious Violence in Indonesia
From soil to God
Chris Wilson

Ethnic Politics in Burma
States of conflict
Ashley South

Democratization in Post-Suharto Indonesia
Edited by Marco Bünte and Andreas Ufen

Party Politics and Democratization in Indonesia
Golkar in the Post-Suharto era
Dirk Tomsa

Community, Environment and Local Governance in Indonesia
Locating the Commonweal
Edited by Carol Warren and John F. McCarthy

Rebellion and Reform in Indonesia
Jakarta's security and autonomy policies in Aceh
Michelle Ann Miller

Hadrami Arabs in Present-day Indonesia
An Indonesia-oriented Group with an Arab Signature
Frode F. Jacobsen

Vietnam's Political Process
How education shapes political decision making
Casey Lucius

Muslims in Singapore
Piety, politics and policies
Kamaludeen Mohamed Nasir, Alexius A. Pereira and Bryan S. Turner

Timor Leste
Politics, history and culture
Andrea Katalin Molnar

Gender and Transitional Justice
The women of East Timor
Susan Harris Rimmer

Environmental Cooperation in Southeast Asia
ASEAN's regime for trans-boundary haze pollution
Paruedee Nguitragool

The Theatre and the State in Singapore
Terence Chong

Ending Forced Labour in Myanmar
Engaging a pariah regime
Richard Horsey

Security, Development and Nation-Building in Timor-Leste
A cross-sectoral assessment
Edited by Vandra Harris and Andrew Goldsmith

The Politics of Religion in Indonesia
Syncretism, orthodoxy, and religious contention in Java and Bali
Edited by Michel Picard and Remy Madinier

Singapore's Ageing Population
Managing healthcare and end of life decisions
Edited by Wing-Cheong Chan

Changing Marriage Patterns in Southeast Asia
Economic and socio-cultural dimensions
Edited by Gavin W. Jones, Terence H. Hull and Maznah Mohamad

Brunei – History, Islam, Society and Contemporary Issues

Edited by Ooi Keat Gin

LONDON AND NEW YORK

First published 2016
by Routledge

2 Park Square, Milton Park, Abingdon, Oxfordshire OX14 4RN
711 Third Avenue, New York, NY 10017

Routledge is an imprint of the Taylor & Francis Group, an informa business

First issued in paperback 2017

British Library Cataloguing in Publication Data
A catalogue record for this book is available from the British Library

Library of Congress Cataloging-in-Publication Data
Brunei : history, Islam, society and contemporary issues / [edited by]
Ooi Keat Gin.
pages cm — (Routledge contemporary Southeast Asia series ; 78)
Includes bibliographical references and index.
1. Brunei—Social conditions. 2. Brunei—Foreign relations. 3. Brunei—
History. I. Ooi, Keat Gin, 1959- editor. II. Druce, Stephen C. Birth of
Brunei. Container of (work): III. Series: Routledge contemporary Southeast
Asia series ; 78.
DS650.3.B795 2016
959.55—dc23
2015024398

ISBN: 978-1-138-78765-0 (hbk)
ISBN: 978-1-138-47712-4 (pbk)

Typeset in Times New Roman
by Swales & Willis Ltd, Exeter, Devon, UK

To Yang Yang
for her unwavering love and devotion

Contents

Figures

Tables

Contributors

Haji Awg Asbol bin Haji Mail, a specialist in Brunei history, has authored numerous books in Malay, such as with Hjh Zuslina Haji Jolkifli, *Politik Brunei (1959–1983: Isu Pertahan dan Keselamatan [Bruneian Politics (1959–1983): Defence and Security Issues]* (2012) and *Sejarah dan Pensejarahan Brunei: Dinamika Pembentukan dan Transformasi [Bruneian History and the Making of History: Formation and Transformation Dynamics]* (2012). He is currently Associate Professor of History and International Studies at the Faculty of Arts and Social Sciences, Universiti Brunei Darussalam.

Ampuan Haji Brahim bin Ampuan Haji Tengah is an Associate Professor and Director of the Academy of Brunei Studies, Universiti Brunei Darussalam. He has published extensively on Malay literature and creative works, and was awarded the SEA Write Award in 2005. His recent publications include *Kesusasteraan Brunei Tradisonal: Pembicaraan Genre dan Tema [Traditional Brunei Literature: A Discussion of Genre and Themes]* (2010) and *Pembicaraan Sastera dan Budaya [Discussion on Literature and Culture]* (2011).

Stephen Charles Druce obtained his PhD from the Centre for South-East Asian Studies, University of Hull, UK. He has carried out historical and archaeological research in Indonesia and Brunei, and has published articles in English- and Indonesian-language journals on pre-modern Southeast Asia, particularly Indonesia. One of his recent major works is *Lands West of the Lakes: A History of the Ajattappareng Kingdoms of South Sulawesi, CE 1200 to 1600* (2009). Currently he is head of the Graduate Programme at the Academy of Brunei Studies, Universiti Brunei Darussalam.

Pengiran Khairul Rijal bin Pengiran Haji Abdul Rahim is a lecturer at the Academy of Brunei Studies, Universiti Brunei Darussalam. His recent publications include *Teknologi Penangkapan Ikan Tradisi Masyarakat Melayu Brunei [Traditional Fishing Technology of Malay Society in Brunei]* (2009) and 'Perusahaan Perikanan dan Teknologi Menangkap Ikan yang digunakan di Negara Brunei Darussalam semasa Zaman Pentadbiran Residen British, 1906–1941' ['The Fisheries Industry and Fishing Technology in Brunei during the British Residency Period, 1906–1941'], *Janang: Jurnal Akademi Pengajian Brunei* (2008). He is one of the foremost authorities on the fisheries industry in Brunei.

Noralipah binti Haji Mohamed is presently a lecturer at the Academy of Brunei Studies, Universiti Brunei Darussalam. Her published works include 'Pasang Surut Pekerja Asing dan Kesannya Terhadap Pembangunan Negara Brunei Darussalam 1906–1959' ['Fluctuation of Foreign Labour and its Effect on the Development of Brunei, 1906–1959'], *Borneo Research Journal* (2007) and 'Perkembangan Kedatangan Pekerja Asing ke Negara Brunei Darussalam' ['The Development of Foreign Labour Immigration to Brunei'], *Janang: Jurnal Akademi Pengajian Brunei* (2008).

Mikio Oishi is an Associate Professor at the Academy of Brunei Studies, Universiti Brunei Darussalam. His current research interests include the new ASEAN approach to conflict management; managing territorial disputes in East Asia; the Shanghai Cooperation Organisation as a conflict management regime, and the *Pax Sinica* (Chinese Peace). His recent publications include *International Conflict in the Asia-Pacific* (2010) and *Managing Conflict in Economic Development* (2011).

Ooi Keat Gin is Professor of History and Coordinator of the Asia Pacific Research Unit at Universiti Sains Malaysia, Penang, Malaysia. His research interests are primarily focused on Borneo, with two recent publications: *The Japanese Occupation of Borneo, 1941–1945* (2011) and *Post-war Borneo, 1945–1950: Nationalism, Empire, and State-building* (2013). As an editor, he has proven his expertise by producing the critically acclaimed and award-winning *Southeast Asia: A Historical Encyclopedia from Angkor Wat to East Timor* (3 vols, 2004).

Datin Hajah Saadiah binti Datu Derma Wijaya Haji Tamit was Senior Lecturer at the Academy of Brunei Studies, Universiti Brunei Darussalam. Her recent publications include: *Tranformasi Undang-undang Islam Brunei* [*Transformation of Islamic Law in Brunei*] (2010), *Institusi Keluarga dan Undang-undang* [*The Family Institution and the Law*] (2012) and *Pembubaran Perkahwinan Dalam Undang-Undang Keluarga Islam Brunei dan Perbandingan Dengan Undang-undang Keluarga Islam Malaysia* [*Dissolution of Marriage in Islamic Family Law in Brunei and the Comparison with Islamic Family Law in Malaysia*] (2012).

Mohd Shahrol Amira bin Abdullah has overseen the teaching of an undergraduate module on Ethnicity, focusing on the various ethnic groups in Brunei, at Universiti Brunei Darussalam since 2004. He is currently involved in research to map ethnic groups throughout contemporary Brunei, with particular attention to recording the genesis of each ethnic community. Between 2012 and 2014 he served as Deputy Director of the Academy of Brunei Studies, Universiti Brunei Darussalam.

Awang Haji Tassim bin Haji Abu Bakar received his PhD from the Department of Southeast Asian Studies, Universiti Malaya, Malaysia. His MA thesis analysed the incorporation of the concept of the Malay Islamic Monarchy in Brunei society through the mass media. His doctoral dissertation evaluated the impact of the transfer of inhabitants of Brunei's iconic Kampong Ayer (Water Village) to land settlements. He is currently Deputy Director of Academy of Brunei Studies, Universiti Brunei Darussalam.

Foreword

Victor T. King

It is with great pleasure that I write this Foreword, in that this volume demonstrates what can be done when a gathering of scholars working on a particular country or site come together from different disciplinary and subject perspectives to focus on a set of issues, processes and characteristics which, in some sense, give definition to the country under scrutiny. The Academy of Brunei Studies has demonstrated the advantages of deploying a multidisciplinary approach to the study of Negara Brunei Darussalam, and Professor Ooi Keat Gin has been helpfully and successfully engaged in this enterprise. This is not a comprehensive view of Brunei, in that some academic disciplines are not represented and some important national and international matters facing the country are not addressed, given that the Academy is a relatively small unit at Universiti Brunei Darussalam and it cannot cover the whole range of issues that need to be discussed. Yet the Academy can show the way, as it has done here, in mobilizing thinking about Brunei and presenting the possibility and opportunity to draw on expertise on Brunei elsewhere in the university; and this expertise and knowledge, whether in the social sciences and humanities or natural sciences, is formidable.

The volume is divided into four parts – 'Genesis, historical ties and contemporary relations', 'Multi-ethnic mosaic and lifestyle', 'Islam' and 'Current concerns' – which seems to me to be an admirable reflection of the content and scope of the collection. Yet the book also raises a number of cross-cutting issues and suggests a number of challenges facing a small country which is seeking to maintain its traditions and institutions while enjoying the advantages of oil and gas resources, but which has to modernize and equip its young people in particular with the skills and knowledge to compete in a globalizing world as hydrocarbon resources diminish. The tensions between what modernization theorists referred to as 'tradition' and 'modernity' – which, though they are social science constructs and have been subsequently heavily criticized – still have some symbolic resonance, and are all too obvious in Brunei. But we should constantly keep in mind that these constructs (which contrast established customs, rituals and genealogies with change, movement and the abandonment of the old) also generate certain kinds of realities, or rather, they come to be perceived as real by those who live by and with them.

The historical chapters add to our store of information on Brunei, which is already ample, but they demonstrate in very direct ways that further reflection and contemplation are required. Brunei's past is a constant source of inspiration for scholars to consider and examine what was happening on the northwest coast of Borneo before the emergence of the Brunei seaborne empire during the sixteenth century, and particularly the links, dynamics and conflicts between the small port states which were active there in the proto-historical period. These early linkages, on a smaller scale and primarily within the Southeast Asian maritime world, bear some similarities to the contemporary period, when Brunei has had to engage with a much wider arena, but one which presents infinite possibilities and dangers: with its immediate Borneo neighbours, with the Muslim states of Malaysia and Indonesia, and other Muslim communities in the region, with ASEAN, and with the wider Muslim world, the Commonwealth and the United Nations.

The chapters on ethnicity and lifestyles and the ways in which identities are maintained, negotiated and transformed provide us with an interesting sociological laboratory in which we find a constant tension between a state-directed and official vision of what identity should be and what the state prescribes in classifications, and what those who experience and live with these categories do, think and feel. These are matters which are not peculiar to Brunei, and are to be found throughout the region, though with much more intensity in such states as Malaysia and Myanmar.

Part III on Islam comprises one chapter on a vitally important issue in Southeast Asia: gender and identity. It raises questions about the rights of Muslim women in relation to family and property, which lead to issues of a much more general and comparative kind with other Muslim nation states.

Finally, we enter the more practical arena of what countries with increasingly porous borders in the era of globalization have to do in response to the need to import labour and other resources to sustain particular economic activities and consumer demands while protecting local employment and national integrity. This is a problem which may have no solution.

Therefore, the volume ranges over several current issues: historical and contemporary development and the processes underlying them; constructed tradition and modernity; globalization and nation statehood; national identity and sub-national ethnicities; religion and gender; cross-national labour migration and employment for local residents, and the problem of coping with the need to import resources (in the case indicated in this volume, there is too much dependence on the import of fishery resources).

In my view, this is a volume which will shape some of the debates and research on the future development of Brunei, drawing on its major purpose, which is to relate the country to its origins, its historical development, its current problems and forthcoming challenges, and its prospects and opportunities.

Preface

The Sultanate of Brunei Darussalam hangs rather precariously on the northeast rump of the island of Borneo. 'Precarious' might appear to be too harsh a term to describe the location of one of the wealthiest nation states of the twenty-first century thanks to its oil and gas resources. But historically, 'precarious' was an appropriate way to describe the position of this ancient sultanate, particularly during the mid-nineteenth century, with the arrival of an English adventurer named James Brooke in 1839, and another visit by him in 1841. During his second visit, the title of rajah, or governor, of the territory of Sarawak, then comprising the valleys between the Lundu and the Samarahan that approximate the present-day Kuching division, was granted to Brooke for successfully suppressing an anti-Brunei revolt (1837–41). Thereafter, Brunei's physical integrity became increasingly threatened in the face of territorial ambitions from both the Brooke regime of Sarawak and, from 1881, the Chartered Company administration of British North Borneo. For the next four decades Brooke Sarawak's borders expanded eastwards. Meanwhile, after its establishment in 1881, the Chartered Company administrators of British North Borneo asserted rights to territories at the expense of Brunei. In order to arrest the complete emaciation of Brunei, Britain accorded protectorate status to the sultanate, Sarawak and British North Borneo in 1888. For a while Brunei appeared to be 'saved'; however, the Limbang (1890) and the Padas (1898) were annexed by Sarawak and British North Borneo respectively, and London was apparently powerless to intervene.

Brunei's body politic was much reduced when the sultanate entered the twentieth century; internally, the prognosis for its political and administrative health was far from acceptable or encouraging. It was then decided by the mandarins of the Colonial Office that Brunei needed a similar advisory mechanism to the rather effective Residency system that had been in place in the western peninsular Malay states since the mid-1870s. Consequently, the Residency system was introduced in 1906, primarily to ensure that Brunei's administrative structure was modernized to keep pace with the times. Since that time, the description 'precarious' was no longer applicable as Brunei embarked on a politico-administrative 'healthy' revival plan. Brunei plodded along with the assistance of a British-staffed bureaucratic machinery with the Resident at the apex of control. Not unduly affected by the First World War (1914–18) apart from some loss of British civil service personnel who were called to the front lines, Brunei gradually advanced in most aspects of governance, and attained and enjoyed reasonable prosperity. Following the discovery of oil at Seria in 1929, Brunei's future was assured, and its prosperity was in sight.

As a British protectorate, Brunei braved the turbulent years of the mid-twentieth century, which brought the intrusion of modern war and military occupation (1941–45), the post-war development of Cold War tensions, an abortive rebellion (1962) and an oil crisis (1970s). Emerging relatively unscathed from trying times, Brunei became an independent nation state in 1984, when the Union Flag and the last Resident left the sultanate. At the same time, Brunei's legacy as a Malay Islamic Monarchy was singularly embraced to reflect the newly independent sultanate's heritage and identity – characteristics that have been nurtured, retained and sustained to the present.

The most recent development in 'the Abode of Peace', a long-standing nickname for the country, was the adoption of *hudud*, 'crimes against God' – a reassertion of the sultanate's Islamic credentials. At first glance, the implementation of *hudud* appears to be retrogressive, but upon closer scrutiny, such a legal development is consistent with the sultanate's trajectory in transforming into an Islamic state, reasserting its Malay Islamic Monarchy concept.

On a personal level, Brunei is an inevitable stopover in my academic involvement with Borneo. My professional relationship with Borneo began with Sarawak in the late 1980s and over the subsequent decades. Then came a short attachment to Sabah (British North Borneo). Brunei featured briefly in the late 1990s and early 2000s when I was working on the Australian military re-occupation of the northern coast of the island in mid-1945. Throughout the one and a half decades of the twenty-first century, my scholastic focus was devoted to Kalimantan. Brunei was seemingly off my academic radar.

Then, out of the blue, an invitation came for a visiting year-long sojourn at the Adobe of Peace. Serendipity was at play. I was in the process of planning my nine-month sabbatical between Universitiet Leiden and the University of Michigan at Ann Arbor. The invitation from Universiti Brunei Darussalam derailed my original plans, hence I opted for Plan B by splitting my sabbatical leave between Bandar Seri Begawan and Ann Arbor.

On reflection, it was indeed a fruitful outing while affiliated as a visiting professor at the Academy of Brunei Studies. Interactions with the academic staff were pleasant encounters, benefiting from the best Brunei Malay culture has to offer. I had first-hand experience of and bore witness to the workings of the Malay Islamic Monarchy, or in Malay, Melayu Islam Beraja (MIB). I left before *hudud* took effect.

As a result of the various workshop sessions with the academics of the Academy, it seemed logical and prudent that the expertise of each of them in their respective disciplines should be showcased to the wider world. Tradition meant that the dissemination of their labours on their beloved sultanate was confined to what little of the literature was available to a wider audience beyond Brunei. Much of this academic work, including the Academy's journal *Janang*, is in Brunei Malay, which is not unlike Bahasa Malaysia or Bahasa Indonesia, the Malay languages of Malaysia and Indonesia respectively, but with slight local differences.

After much encouragement and investment of time and energy, the present volume represents the academic labour of the majority of my colleagues of the Academy. They all come from different disciplines and backgrounds, including history, international relations, sociology, Malay literature, Islamic jurisprudence, social anthropology and economics. Owing to prior commitments, several other individuals from the Academy regretfully had to withdraw their contributions, although they too had exhibited unrelenting enthusiasm from the start of this book project – alas, reality sometimes sets in.

I am indeed very proud that my colleagues at the Academy decided to accompany me on this journey to its conclusion – a personal struggle for many of them, but the fruits of their labours and undertakings will undoubtedly prove beneficial and worthwhile. Others currently not involved may take a cue from this present endeavour to produce a second volume in the foreseeable future.

Brunei is neither a microcosm of Malaysia nor Indonesia, and far from resembling or aping Singapore, Brunei has its own identity derived from an ancient heritage characterized by its ideological basis as a Malay Islamic Monarchy. This volume seeks to showcase recent academic work undertaken by Bruneian scholars themselves and other academics currently working in the sultanate.

Acknowledgements

Any endeavour, academic or otherwise, is a consequence of a collective undertaking by many parties. This present volume relied on the involvement of several individuals and institutions that facilitated its development and completion.

This volume has been realized through the contribution of individuals currently serving in the Academy of Brunei Studies, Universiti Brunei Darussalam. Appreciation is due to Professor Ampuan (Associate Professor Ampuan Dr Haji Brahim bin Ampuan Haji Tengah), who as director of the Academy was most supportive of this undertaking from the very beginning. In his unassuming manner he helped and encouraged his colleagues to deliver their work, and interceded whenever there were problems that might have an adverse impact on the overall undertaking. I am grateful for his understanding and assistance in seeing through this ambitious publication project, as well as for his contribution of a chapter. Shahrol (Mohd Shahrol Amira bin Abdullah), the deputy director of the Academy, was instrumental in arranging the various workshops and seminar sessions during my sojourn, and these interactions gave rise to the concept of this present volume. For all his assistance, friendship and for contribution of a chapter in this volume, I wish to express my thanks to Shahrol. I am indeed also thankful to Steve (Dr Stephen Charles Druce), who was pivotal in arranging for my affiliation with the Academy as visiting professor that presented possibilities and/or opportunities, including the production of this present volume. Steve also contributed a chapter to this volume, and also in his own way assisted in seeing it through to publication. For his friendship and the many lunches together during my sojourn, I am grateful.

Others instrumental as contributors to the present volume have certainly earned my appreciation for supporting this endeavour, namely Associate Professor Dr Mikio Oishi, Associate Professor Dr Haji Awg Asbol bin Haji Mail from the Faculty of Arts and Social Sciences, Dr Haji Tassim bin Haji Abu Bakar, the late Datin Hajah Saadiah binti Datu Derma Wijaya Haj Tamit, Pg. Noralipah binti Haji Mohamed and Pengiran Khairul Rijal Pengiran Hj. Abdul Rahim.

I am grateful to the Academy for its kind invitation to serve as visiting professor and for hosting my sojourn in the first half of 2013 during which this present volume was conceptualized. At the same time, I am also thankful to my home institution, the School of Humanities, Universiti Sains Malaysia, Penang, Malaysia for granting me a sabbatical leave of absence.

Who better than Professor V.T. King, one of the foremost scholars of Borneo, to deliver a Foreword for this volume? My appreciation to him for graciously penning a contribution that points to some pertinent directions and future endeavours for consideration.

Furthermore part of the review and preparation for publication of this volume were undertaken during my sojourn (July–October) as visiting research scholar at the Center for Southeast Asian Studies (CSEAS), Kyoto University hence my gratitude to the latter for the time and opportunity.

To Peter Sowden, Senior Editor at Routledge, my gratitude for his confidence, trust and vision in seeing this project through to fruition. I again express my appreciation to the Routledge team (editorial, production and marketing), whom I had worked with in the past, and who, as usual, displayed professionalism, co-operation and close attention to detail in the realization of this present edited volume.

As always, I thank my family – my mother, Tan Ai Gek, my wife, Beh Swee Im, and sisters, Ooi Saw Lian and Ooi Saw Ean – who have long tolerated my 'away from home syndrome', for their love and support of my scholarly pursuits. This present volume is simply another outcome of my never-ending scholarly quest to adorn their bookshelves and add to their ever-expanding collection. I am eternally grateful to my family, and particularly to Swee Im, to whom this volume is dedicated, for her steadfast love and support regardless of my absence, presence, and other challenges in between.

Abbreviations and acronyms

ADMM	ASEAN Defence Ministers' Meeting
ADMM+HADR & MM Exercise	ASEAN Defence Ministers' Meeting Plus Humanitarian Assistance and Disaster Relief & Military Medicine Exercise
AEC	ASEAN Economic Community
AMM	ASEAN Ministerial Meeting
APSC	ASEAN Political-Security Community
ASCC	ASEAN Socio-Cultural Community
ASEAN	Association of Southeast Asian Nations
BAKER	Barisan Kemerdekaan Rakyat (Brunei People's Independence Front)
BAP	Brunei Alliance Party
BAR	*Brunei Annual Report*
BDEC	Brunei Darussalam Economic Council
BIMP-EAGA	Brunei Darussalam-Indonesia-Malaysia-Philippines East ASEAN Growth Area
BMA	British Military Administration
BMPC	British Malayan Petroleum Company
BND	Brunei dollar
CO (UK)	Colonial Office, London
EDU	Entrepreneurship Development Unit
EEIC	English East India Company
EEZ	Exclusive Economic Zone
EFS	Enterprise Facilitation Scheme
ETF	Employees Trust Fund
FDI	foreign direct investment
GDP	gross domestic product
GPS	Global Positioning System
HADR	Humanitarian Assistance and Disaster Relief
ICLARM	International Coastal Living Aquatic Resources Management
ICT	information and communication technology
IJA	Imperial Japanese Army
ILO	International Labour Organization

IMF	International Monetary Fund
IMT	International Monitoring Team
JAPEM	Jabatan Pembangunan Masyarakat (Department of Community Development)
LNG	liquefied natural gas
MCS	Malayan Civil Service
MFS	Microcredit Finance Scheme
MIB	Melayu Islam Beraja (Malay Islamic Monarchy)
MM	Military Medicine Exercise
MOU	memorandum of understanding
mt	metric ton
NDP	Brunei National Development Plan
NKKU	Negarabagian Kesatuan Kalimantan Utara (Unitary State of North Kalimantan)
nm	nautical mile
OIC	Organisation of Islamic Cooperation
OPEC	Organization of the Petroleum Exporting Countries
PKS	Skim Pembiyaan Pengusaha Kecil dan Sederhana (Payment Scheme for Small and Medium Industries)
PRB	Partai Rakyat Brunei (Brunei People's Party)
PRC	People's Republic of China
R	Indonesian rupiah
RCEP	Regional Comprehensive Economic Partnership
s.a.w.	*ṣallā Allāhu 'alayhi wa-sallam* ('may Allah's peace and blessings be upon Him'; Muslim expression of love and respect for the Prophet)
SCS	South China Sea
Sdn. Bhd.	Sendirian Berhad (designation for incorporated companies)
SEAFDEC	Southeast Asian Fisheries Development Centre
SMEs	small and medium-sized enterprises
SMS	Short Message Service (via mobile phones)
SOAS	School of Oriental African Studies, University of London
s.w.t.	*Subhanahu Wa Ta'ala* ('the most glorified, the most high'; a formula for Muslims to glorify Allah when mentioning His name)
UBD	Universiti Brunei Darussalam
TNI	Tentera Nasional Indonesia (National Armed Forces of Indonesia)
TNKU	Tentera Nasional Kalimantan Utara (National Army of North Kalimantan)
UBD	Universiti Brunei Darussalam
UNIFIL	United Nations Interim Force in Lebanon
UNISSA	Universiti Islam Sultan Sharif Ali (Sultan Sharif Ali Islamic University)
WO	(British) War Office, London
ZOPFAN	Zone of Peace, Freedom and Neutrality

Glossary

adai-adai   one of the famous Bruneian dances, depicting life in the fishing community of Kampong Ayer

akad nikah   marriage ceremony

akhlak   morality and manners, the practice of virtue

alai busak baku   Murut dance to exhibit one's beauty

alai busak pakoi   Murut dance to mark the end of the rice harvesting season

alai karur   Murut wedding dance

alai ngapo lun raya   Murut welcoming dance to honour high-ranking officials

alai nguan   Murut dance during the rice planting season

alai siga   Murut dance to praise women

alai ukui   Murut war dance

alai umak rumak   Murut dance to enter a new house

andang   *andang karan,* a trammel gill net, or *andang jarang,* a bottom-set gill net, both used in deep waters

aqidah   (Islamic) religious faith, monotheistic belief

awargalat   courteousness

Babun Nikah   Bab al-Nikah; the Prophet of Islam has said, 'Marriage is my Sunnah [practice or action of the Prophet] and whoever does not follow my Sunnah is not my true follower' (Ibn Haiah, Babun Nikah)

baju cara Melayu   lit. 'Malay-style dress'; attire of Tutong men, consisting of a collarless loose shirt with a pair of trousers whose legs extend just below the knee

baju kebaya   body-hugging dress of Tutong women, comprising a blouse top and a *sarung*

baju umak ruma   black attire of Murut women decorated with colourful beads at the edges

balai   a purpose-built building as a centre of education, a storage room or space for fishing equipment, an open compound, a space for *silat*, or a workshop for weaving or making fishing gear

bejana-bejana   clay pots for storing water

bejarum-jarum   'proposition'; the second stage of the Bruneian wedding ceremony

belacan   shrimp paste

benang parung upper part of the *takap* that serves as sleeping quarters for children

beraga-agaan visiting one another's homes

beramu the gathering of natural resources from the forest and collecting shell-fish and other sea produce

berbedak blessing ceremony by family members using rice flour; an obligatory custom during weddings

berian wedding gift as required by Islamic law

berpacar decorating the hands using henna; an obligatory custom during weddings

bersanding the bride and bridegroom's sitting in state ceremony on the wedding day

berzikir chanting praises to Allah

besuruh Bruneian engagement ceremony

bubu fish trap

bumiputera lit. 'son of the soil'; indigenous, native

bungsu *amit*; honorific title for the youngest sibling, uncle or aunt

buri puo 'washing of the feet' ceremony; part of Tutong wedding proceedings

ceteria knights, military commanders

dapur kitchen

dastar cloth headgear of red colour

demersal species living mostly on or near the sea bed

dewato spirits

dharar syar'ie from the Islamic family perspective, this is defined as a threat (physically or mentally) towards the wife, particularly to her rights concerning religion, life, physical wellbeing, mental health and property

fahisyah a contemptible act

Faraidh section of Sharia Law that deals with inheritance

Fardh' Ain obligatory practices for individual Muslims

Fardh' Kifayah obligatory practices for the Muslim community as a whole

fasakh annulment of a Muslim marriage

fiqh Islamic jurisprudence; deals with the observance of Islamic rituals, morals and social legislation

fitnah false accusations

gambus folk lute

gendang labik drum made from the skin of an animal such as a buffalo, cow or goat

gerunung a large clay container for storing water

gotong royong mutual assistance, collective effort

gulingtangan percussion musical instrument made from brass

hadanah guardianship (of children)

Hadrah a collective supererogatory ritual performed by Sufi orders; it features various forms of *dhikr*, including sermons, collective study, recitation of the Quran, praise and supplication to God, religious exhortations and praise of the Prophet

hibah gift

hudud   'crimes against God', including religious crimes of adultery, fornication, homosexuality, accusing someone of illicit sex but failing to present four Muslim eyewitnesses, apostasy, consuming intoxicants, transgression, highway robbery and theft; punishable by a class of legally sanctioned punishments dictated by God: public lashing, publicly stoning to death, amputation of the hands or public execution

iddah   grace period following Muslim divorce

ila'   one of three means (the other two are *talaaq* and *zihar*) whereby a Muslim husband can repudiate his marriage; a husband takes an oath to abstain from sexual relations with his wife for a period of four months, after which the marriage is irrevocably dissolved

iraga   season between December and February when the northeast monsoon winds sweep across the South China Sea

ithbat al-nasab   legality of status

jajahan   colonies

jarring   net for snaring animals

Jawi   Arabic letters adapted to the Malay language

kabatan/kabat   intertidal fish trap

kain batik   batik cloth

kain jongsarat   traditional woven cloth

Kampong Ayer   lit. 'Water Village'; Brunei's conglomeration of floating villages

kampung   village

kelong   a wooden offshore platform used to catch or trap fish in deep water or at the mouth of a river

ketua kampung   headman of a village

ketupat   glutinous rice cake wrapped in leaves

kelupis   glutinous rice cake wrapped in leaves; Malay desert and also among Bisaya

khatam Quran   recitation, completion of the Quran

khuluq   divorce

kuih   sweet and savoury dessert snacks

kuih penyaram   a kind of cake; if perfectly made, it symbolizes a girl's virginity

langkah dulang   lit. 'jumping over the tray'; gifts offered to each of the unmarried elder sisters of the bride

langkah sungai/laut   lit. 'to leap across the river/sea'; a requirement (in the form of cash) to be paid if the groom and the bride are not from the same ethnic group

lemang   glutinous rice cooked in bamboo

lemiding   vines

lian   one of the grounds for divorce; if a Muslim husband makes false charges of adultery against his wife, then this amounts to character assassination and the wife has the right to ask for divorce on these grounds

lilit selampit   Bisaya/Dusun; red headgear worn by both men and women

lintau   a bamboo trap for prawns, also used for fish

majlis doa selamat   supplication for safe deliverance

makan bersuap   lit. 'feeding each other food'; ceremony participated in by the bride and bridegroom, part of Tutong wedding proceedings

makan taun   Kedayan festival after each rice harvesting season, a thanksgiving for the success of the rice crop

malam berambil-ambilan   lit. 'the night of taking the husband'; Bruneian wedding ritual performed by the groom's family preparing him prior to entering the wedding chamber (bride's bedroom)

mandi berlawat   baby shower for the first child

marad al-maut   terminal illness

memucang-memucang   working collaboratively and collectively

menghantar berian   Bruneian ceremony involving the bestowal of wedding gifts

menongkat   additional supports that may be added to further strengthen and/or stabilize house posts

menteri   ministers

merisik   'investigation'; initial stage in the Bruneian wedding ceremony

mukim   administrative division below a district; parish

mulih tiga hari   lit. 'the third day return'; ceremony of the Bruneian wedding ritual

mumaiyiz   the age of discernment or discretion; following divorce, a child who has attained 'the age of discernment' shall have the choice of living with either of the parents, unless the Sharia Court instructs otherwise

mutaah/mut'ah   compensation (monetary or in kind) paid to a divorced woman

nahu   grammar, syntax

nakhoda   captain of a ship, skipper; also a merchant

Nihon-go   Japanese language

nusyuz   rebellion

nyiru   bamboo sieve for separating rice from its husk

padian   female trader from Kampong Ayer

pantaran   porch of a house

pata   headgear made of beads worn by Murut women

Pehin Menteri Agama   titled religious minister

pelagic   species living mainly in water columns away from the shore or sea bed

pembuka mulut   lit. 'opening of the mouth'; ritual initiating marriage negotiations among the Bruneis

pengalu   trader from Kampong Ayer

penghulu   headman of a cluster of villages

pengiran/pangeran   nobleman, blood relation to Bruneian royalty

penugu   a tool to catch fish and prawns

puak jati   indigenous ethnic group

Qawaid   principles of grammar

qisas   non-*hudud* crimes, considered to be private disputes between two parties where retaliation as a punishment is allowed

rakyat   subjects, common people, including slaves

Ramadhan   month in the Islamic calendar when a dawn-to-dusk fast is observed

rambat   cast net

rantau   drift gill net; small-scale fishing gear

Ratib Samman   Sufi manuscript

rawai   longline fishing gear

resam   practices and rituals that subsequently become customs

rigid   belt worn by Murut women to accessorize a dress

saikeirei   ritual of mandatory bowing to a portrait of the Imperial Japanese Emperor

sambal   pungent, fiery condiment comprising a mixture of shrimp paste, garlic, chillies and shallots

sampan   *perahu*; small native craft

sang jati   indigenous people

sape   four-string musical instrument exclusive to the Dusun

selambau   lift net; small-scale fishing gear

sembilang   a species of catfish

sharia/syariah   Islamic religious laws

sigar   piece of red fabric worn around the waist by Murut men to cover the lower parts of the body

sikang   common or public space in a Murut longhouse used for social gathering and ritual performances

silat   Malay form of martial arts

silaturahim   fellowship, brotherhood and bonding among the Muslim faithful

sulh   settlements

sultan   Muslim king, ruler

Sungai Kerajaan   non-hereditary land or territory that belonged to the Sultan of Brunei only by virtue of his title and position as ruler

Sungai Kuripan   non-hereditary land in the possession of the Wazir of Brunei only by virtue of his title and position as chief minister

Sungai Tulin   land owned by the Sultan of Brunei, royal family and nobility that could be passed on to their descendants

Sunnah   sayings and practices of the Prophet Muhammad s.a.w.

Syarak   Islamic teachings

syiar   greatness or glory of Islam

tadarus   Quran recitation

tahlil   prayer for the deceased

takap   sleeping room in a Murut longhouse

takliq   dissolution of Muslim marriage

takzir/tazir   non-*hudud* crimes; punishment is left to an Islamic judge's discretion

talaaq   technical legal term when a Muslim husband exercises his unilateral right to pronounce divorce without assigning any reason

talak   divorce

tarawih   additional prayers performed by Sunni Muslims at night during Ramadhan

Tasawuf   Arabic for Sufism; conforming to the path of Islam through direct experience of the Real (God) instead of via word of mouth or learning from books

tauke/towkay   entrepreneur, businessman, proprietor of shop or factory; originally restricted to Chinese entrepreneurs, but nowadays may also refer to other ethnicities, such as Malay businessmen

tawak-tawak   brass percussion musical instrument

temarok   Bisaya religious ritual to seek divine assistance from *dewato*; *tamorok* in Dusun

tengah   honorific for the middle sibling, uncle or aunt

teratak   an open hut or house to accommodate all the villagers during the Kedayan *makan taun* festival

timbaran   attire of Murut men made from the bark of a tree

tua   *nini*; honorific title for the eldest sibling, uncle or aunt

tugu   conical tidal trap; small-scale fishing gear

ubar   plant dye used to colour khaki uniforms

ulama   religious scholar

wajid   sweet cake made from sticky glutinous rice

wakaf   *nazar*; contribution to the community

wazir   chief minister, senior minister

zihar   mode of Muslim divorce occurring when a husband compares or associates his wife with his mother or sister, namely a woman within his prohibited (sexual) relationships; he does not cohabit with his wife for a period of four months, after which the marriage is dissolved

Zikir/dhikr   perpetual remembrance of God; devotional act in Islam in which short phrases or prayers (from the *hadith* or the Quran) are repeatedly recited, either silently within the heart or aloud

Introduction

With an estimated population of 423,000 in 2014, according to the World Bank,[1] Brunei appears to have an appropriate balance of people and land area (5,765 km²). Perched on the northeast hump of the island of Borneo, Negara Brunei Darussalam (Abode of Peace), its official designation, enjoys more than 160 kilometres of coastline along the South China Sea. Physically, it largely comprises a low coastal plain where the elevation progressively increases southwards, reaching a maximum height of 300 metres above sea level. Bukit Pagon (elevation 1,841 metres) in the eastern part of the country is the highest peak. Located merely 4–5° N of the Equator, the hot and humid climate averages around 27°C with more than 2,500 mm of rainfall throughout the year, accounting for a typical equatorial climate. As much as 75 per cent of the land area remains under thick equatorial rainforest.

This Malay Muslim sultanate's rather odd configuration, resembling two teardrops with a comparatively larger western half, is the result of its historical development, which stretches to, at least verifiably, the fourteenth–fifteenth centuries CE. Seemingly cosily lodged between the East Malaysian states of Sabah and Sarawak, Brunei was one of the last footholds of Western colonial domination, only attaining independence from Britain in 1984. Since then, Brunei has sought its fate among the neighbouring nation states of Southeast Asia, joining ASEAN (Association of Southeast Asian Nations) a week after independence.

Nearly 40 per cent of its residents live in the capital, Bandar Seri Begawan.[2] In terms of gross domestic product (GDP) and gross national product (GNP), Brunei is more akin to the city state of Singapore; in comparison, in 2012 Brunei attained a GDP of US$17 billion and enjoyed a per capita GDP of US$41,127,[3] while Singapore attained a GDP of US$276.5 billion and a per capita GDP of US$52,141.[4] The similarities end, however, when lifestyle and pace of living are considered. It is neighbouring Malaysia, particularly the states of Sabah and Sarawak, with which a degree of camaraderie is apparent. Despite the wealth derived substantially from oil and gas, the laid-back *kampung* ambience permeates the sultanate, not dissimilar to the environment in Sabah and Sarawak. A first-time visitor might be surprised or disappointed not to be awed by wealth, luxury or abundance being publicly flaunted – alas, not in this serene, tranquil haven of peaceful bliss aptly styled 'the Abode of Peace'.

Because of the state philosophy of Malay Islamic Monarchy (MIB, Melayu Islam Beraja), Brunei is to all intents and purposes governed by an absolute monarchy. Although rather anachronistic in the twenty-first century, the current ruler, Sultan Haji Hassanal Bolkiah Muizzaddin Waddaulah (b. 1946; r. 1967–), is generally regarded as an exemplary ruler, statesman and gentleman who is much respected and loved by his subjects. Paternalism has been one of the hallmarks of Brunei's monarchy for centuries, and this commendable tradition continues in the present reign. The Islamic faith is all-embracing, with the predominantly ethnic Sunni Malay Muslim population adhering to the Shafi school of Islamic jurisprudence. The traditional Malay belief in undivided loyalty to the monarch remains steadfastly relevant in modern-day Brunei, where the sultan reigns and governs. The present monarch is not only the head of state, but also Brunei's prime minister, finance minister and defence minister.

In accordance with the Brunei Nationality Status Acts 1961, seven ethnic communities in contemporary Brunei are officially designated as indigenous ethnic Malay: Belait, Bisaya, Brunei, Dusun, Kedayan, Murut and Tutong. Being considered ethnic Malay in Brunei includes both Muslims and non-Muslims – a far different conception from neighbouring Malaysia's constitutional (legal) definition of a 'Malay' as 'an individual who professes the religion of, habitually speaks the Malay language, and conforms to Malay customs and traditions'.[5] Nonetheless, as in Malaysia, Malay Muslims predominate (78.8 per cent of the population)[6] in Brunei, both in terms of numbers and composition of the ruling elite.

The 'other indigenous' classification includes non-Muslims (3.4 per cent)[7] Ibans and largely animist nomadic Penan. There are also minority Chinese (10.3 per cent),[8] a sizeable number having been in Brunei for numerous generations. The bulk of the Chinese community are mainly resident in the capital and the oil centre of Seria, and are largely engaged in trade and commerce. Since independence in 1984, Brunei has accommodated a large number of foreigners (20.6 per cent)[9] brought in to serve various sectors of the economy, mainly the oil and gas industry, construction and domestic service. A concerted effort at economic diversification in order to lessen over-dependency on oil and gas resulted in an influx of immigrant labour from neighbouring countries, namely Malaysia, Indonesia and the Philippines. Therefore, an expatriate community ranging from professionals to unskilled menial labourers has continued to fuel contemporary Brunei's economy.

Brunei's genesis as a political entity remains murky in the annals of time. Brunei's purported existence during the Hindu-Buddhist 'classical age' (first to thirteenth centuries CE) related to a sixth-century CE Hindunized entity on the northwestern coast of Borneo, as well as a purported reference from Chinese records, remain unverifiable, perhaps a case of mistaken identity concerning place names and/or oversight.[10] Local Brunei scholarship claims 1363 CE as the year of the conversion to Islam, while another source dates it to 1405, both in contrast to European sources that suggest an early sixteenth-century Islamization.[11] What was apparent was that by the heyday of the Malay Muslim Malaccan sultanate of the fifteenth century, Brunei had evolved into one of the many tributary feeder ports that witnessed the flow of trade from the Straits of Malacca to the northwestern coast of Borneo. But whether Brunei was a Malay Muslim port of call at that time was unclear; its conversion during this period was not an uncommon move, as several secondary ports in insular Southeast Asia that serviced the Malaccan Empire had embraced Islam to curry favour from it. In fact, the *pasisir* (coastal) ports of northern Java had converted to Islam due to trading rice with Malacca. Brunei, on the other hand, supplied Malacca with jungle products (beeswax, camphor, *gaharu* wood, cowries, rattan, hornbill, bezoar stones) and low-assay gold, while cloth from India was imported through Malacca. Brunei was famed for much-prized camphor and cowries. Hence, Brunei's status as a Malay Muslim trading centre during this period was not at all surprising, if not consistent with the regional trend.

Unilaterally, pre-Islamic Brunei carried on sea trade with China in luxury and exotic commodities, for which the latter paid handsomely. Chinese junks ventured to the Bornean coast with Brunei as their major port of call to purchase jungle products, from bezoar stones and high-quality camphor to the celebrated birds' nests and feathers of exotic birds. Later, locally cultivated pepper also featured as a valuable trade commodity for the China market. These trade relations appear to have continued into the late eighteenth century. It is not surprising, then, that the sultanate has a long-settled Chinese community.

The Portuguese seizure of Malacca in 1511 and the imposition of rather onerous dues thereafter encouraged many Muslim traders to bring their custom to other Muslim-ruled ports such as Aceh and Brunei. Brunei was a Muslim port that clearly prospered from the 1520s onwards. European eyewitness accounts of the time reported that Brunei reputedly held sway as far north as Luzon and southwards to the Kapuas delta. This Malay Muslim trading entity had its royal court and administrative centre built on water, a kind of 'water city', referring to present-day Kampong Ayer (lit. 'Water Village').

Brunei was a maritime trading power akin to Buddhist Srivijaya (*c.* seventh to thirteenth centuries CE) where there was no actual direct political or administrative control, but rather economic relations with far-flung trading centres. Brunei was in fact a thalassocracy: it controlled trade, not territory, hence trade relations were prioritized over territorial occupation.[12] On the island of Borneo itself, Brunei's sway was similarly enforcing economic control; the *modus operandi* simply consisted of a *pangeran* (nobleman, official) and his entourage stationing themselves strategically at a river mouth or confluence to impose tax on the incoming and outgoing traffic. Brunei's military force (on land and sea) was at best modest in manpower, weaponry and prowess, no match for the formidable Acehnese armada, the Portuguese Malacca naval force or the Malay Johor fleet.

The sixteenth century witnessed the European challenge to Brunei. The Portuguese regarded Brunei in strategic terms: it was a half-way post between Malacca and Maluku, the fabulous Spice Islands of the Moluccas. Control of Brunei would facilitate the flow of spices to Malacca, and thence to Lisbon. But Portuguese ambitions were dashed with the unification of Portugal and Spain under Philip II that saw the assertion of Spanish power over the Philippines, and Luzon in particular. Then in mid-1578 Brunei itself was sacked by the Spanish fleet; the Spanish returned a year later, but more as a show of force rather than with any intention of conquest and/or occupation. Consequently, Brunei lost control over Sulu, and trading relations with Manila (Luzon) deteriorated.

The early decades of the seventeenth century marked a high point in Brunei's assertion of power. Both Sambas and Sulu returned to Brunei's fold. But the second half of the century saw Sulu successfully unshackled from Brunei. The tables were turned when Sulu, a one-time dependency, imposed domination over the northern and northeastern parts of Borneo (territories that largely comprise present-day Sabah) at the expense of Brunei, but failed to subjugate Brunei proper. Throughout the century, succession disputes factionalized and weakened the Brunei court, thereby adversely affecting the sultanate's sway over its outer limits.

The passing of Sultan Muhammad Aliuddin in 1690 sparked a controversy and quarrel over the rightful, legitimate heir to the Brunei throne. Apparently, the illegitimate son of the deceased monarch seized the throne, eliminated contenders, and secured power and ascension, thereby establishing a line of usurpers. It appears that the coming to the throne of Sultan Omar Ali Saifuddin I (r. 1762–95) marked the end of the so-called illegitimate or usurper rule and a reinstatement of the Bendahara line.[13] On the other hand, Brunei sources – *Silsilah Raja-Raja Brunei*[14] and *Batu Tarsilah*[15] – claim that Sultan Omar Ali Saifuddin I was the heir, while Spanish reports maintained that the deceased apparently had no legitimate son.[16]

Eighteenth-century Brunei, then, was marked by civil wars and internal strife, along with external interference – notably Bugis involvement in court affairs and piratical activities on the coast – and overall instability. The Bugis, famed for their martial prowess, were recruited by factions in the court to champion their royal aspirations. Furthermore Sulus, Bajau Laut and others embarked on piratical raids along the north and northeastern Bornean coasts, undoubtedly a thorn in the side and a challenge to Brunei's political and naval strength.

The English East India Company (EEIC) came onto the scene in the last quarter of the eighteenth century. The EEIC viewed north Borneo as a possible alternative route to China in anticipation of the closure of the Straits of Malacca due to protracted conflict. Trade agreements and alliances were contracted with Sulu, including the cession of Balambangan (1763). This barren island off northern Borneo was supposed to be the base for an Anglo-Chinese trade that in a single ambitious stroke sought to divert trade from Spanish Manila and Dutch Batavia.

In mid-1774 the EEIC approached Brunei with an offer whereby, in return for the former's protection against Sulu, the EEIC was promised the monopoly of locally cultivated pepper and a site on Labuan identified as a trading settlement. Brunei needed protection against the ever-aggressive Sulu. But Brunei's would-be protector could not even protect its own settlement on Balambangan, which was sacked by Sulus in 1775. Disaster at Balambangan convinced the EEIC directors in London to abort all plans involving northern Borneo; Labuan was abandoned in late 1775.[17]

Brunei entered the nineteenth century beset with perennial succession disputes. The situation beyond its borders was rapidly changing: the EEIC established an outpost on Singapore in 1819 to oversee its increasingly profitable China trade in luxuries (tea, silk, china), and an individual with grandiose ambitions arrived on the stage – James Brooke. The second half of the century saw the systematic dismemberment of Brunei, so that by 1888 the sultanate's configuration and borders resembled what they are today.

Chinese gold miners had settled and were prospering in southwestern Borneo, in Mempawah, Mandor, Monterado (Montrado) and Sambas since the 1740s. Initially invited by Malay rulers, the Chinese gold-mining communities grew larger and became self-governing entities (*kongsi*), bowing to no authority but themselves. Economic rivalry and quarrels over gold-bearing sites pitted one *kongsi* against another, which subsequently led to all-out war. Defeated groups fled across from Sambas to upper Sarawak.[18] The auriferous area around present-day Bau enabled the Chinese gold miners to continue their livelihood. Pengiran Mahkota, the Brunei noble who had authority over the fiefdom of Sarawak, proved ineffectual, and the Chinese were left to their own devices.

Then, in the 1820s, antimony was discovered in the Sarawak valley. Newly established Singapore facilitated the trade in this mineral on the international market. Pengiran Mahkota was eager to exploit the antimony, which he did through forced labour recruited from the native Malays and Bidayuhs (Land Dayaks). Establishing himself at Kuching on the lower course of the Sarawak river, Mahkota oversaw the mining and export of antimony. An anti-Brunei revolt (1836–41) broke out due to the exploitative treatment of the native miners. Pengiran Bendahara Pengiran Muda Hashim (d. 1846), Brunei's heir apparent and uncle to the reigning sultan, was sent to Kuching to put down the rebellion that was disrupting mining and earnings. It was at this juncture, in 1839, that Brooke appeared in Kuching bearing gifts.[19]

James Brooke utilized his inheritance to purchase a schooner, christened *Royalist*, to embark on an adventure to the East. His scientific expedition went to Marudu Bay in northern Borneo, the Celebes (Sulawesi) and New Guinea to collect samples of fauna and flora for study. While he and his crew transited at Singapore, the governor requested Brooke to deliver a letter of commendation and gifts to the 'ruler' of Sarawak in gratitude for his assistance in helping shipwrecked British sailors.

Brooke dutifully delivered the letter and gifts to Hashim, and the two men established a friendship. Sarawak was in the midst of a revolt, hence Brooke was discouraged from venturing inland and only managed to visit longhouses in Lundu on the coast. Thereafter, the *Royalist* continued its original expedition.

On the return journey, Brooke decided to visit his friend Hashim. It was then that a fateful decision was made: if Brooke could help in ending the revolt, he would be granted the title Rajah (Governor) of Sarawak. Brooke and his crew took up the challenge and managed to defeat the rebels, but pleaded with Hashim to spare their lives, which was reluctantly granted. Visiting Brunei in 1841, Brooke was officially conferred as the first white rajah of Sarawak by Sultan Omar Ali Saifuddin II (d. 1852).

Brooke was deeply inspired by the Rafflesian vision of a British commercial empire in the Malay Archipelago where free trade is practised, in contrast to the hitherto monopolistic imposition of the Dutch. In this connection, he engineered the cession of Labuan to Britain in 1846. But the massacre of the pro-British Hashim, his brother Bedruddin and their family in a palace coup in 1846 forced Brooke to abort his plans for Brunei and instead to turn inward to his fiefdom of Sarawak.

During the last quarter of the nineteenth century, Brunei found itself sandwiched not only between Sarawak and British North Borneo, but also the ambitious and expansionist tendencies of both regimes, the Brooke Raj and the Chartered Company.[20] By the mid-1880s the eastern borders of Sarawak had reached the Baram river and Chartered Company rule had extended to the Putatan river (May 1884), the Padas district (November 1884), the Kawang river (February 1885) and the Mantanani Islands (April 1885) – all at the expense of Brunei, which lost massive territories to the predatory ambitions of the two neighbouring regimes. In order to arrest the further loss of territory and to maintain the integrity of a rather emaciated Brunei, in 1888 the British Colonial Office (CO) intervened to create protectorates over the three northern Bornean territories, Brunei, Sarawak and British North Borneo. This created British Borneo, as opposed to Dutch Borneo which comprised the island's southern and western portions. Notwithstanding London's efforts to preserve Brunei, Rajah Charles Brooke, the second white rajah of Sarawak, annexed the Limbang (1890), while the Chartered Company added Padas (1898).

By the first decade of the twentieth century, the mandarins at the CO decided that in order to ensure Brunei's political survival and sustainability, a Residency system similar to the one in practice in the western peninsular Malay states since the mid-1870s should be established, and this was done in 1905–1906. By then the sultanate had settled into its contemporary odd configuration, like two dissociated teardrops separated by Sarawak's Limbang district.

The appointment of a British Resident to the Brunei court who served the sultanate on the basis of proffering advice managed to transform practically all sectors of administration and governance in line with up-to-date practices.[21] The responsibility of the Resident to offer advice was all-encompassing, including legislation and taxation, except for matters relating to Islam and Malay traditions and practices. Reform was Brunei's salvation, both governmentally and economically. As with the situation in the peninsular Malay states (increasingly being referred as British Malaya), the residential system relied on the premise that the Resident worked with a co-operative sultan and the ruling class. In fact, the Resident to Brunei was seconded from the Malayan Civil Service (MCS), comprising British officers who were well versed and experienced with the Malay monarchy and sociocultural practices.

British Resident Sir Geoffrey Cator (r. 1916–21), writing in 1939, credited a large measure of the success of the Residency system to the goodwill and appreciation of those governed:

> But accept [change] they [Brunei aristocracy] did, not with the resignation of despair but with unfailing goodwill and appreciation that our [British officers] activities, crude though they might seem, were inspired by a genuine wish to help and serve their state.[22]

Economic salvation came in the form of oil. The Seria oil field became operational from 1929, which resolved most of Brunei's pecuniary woes. With financial sustainability, Brunei was on even keel both politically and economically. Progress and developments in terms of infrastructure and social services remained modest. In the 1930s, more oil fields were discovered, the most celebrated being in the remote Belait district; towards the end of the decade, oil from Belait accounted for some 84 per cent of exports by value, and royalties from oil comprised half of total government revenue.[23]

When the clouds of war begin to gather from the mid-1930s and actual hostilities broke out in September 1939, Brunei profited through trade in oil, a strategic commodity, and demand for khaki dye for military attire that boosted its cutch industry. But on the downside, war preparations by the British War Office (WO) focused on Singapore and Malaya, while the British Bornean territories of Sarawak, Brunei and British North Borneo were left to defend themselves.[24] Scorched-earth tactics were planned to disable the oil installations (the refinery at Lutong), set fire to the oil wells (Miri-Seria) and destroy airfields (Miri, Kuching), and these were executed following the attack on Pearl Harbor on 7 December 1941.

In less than a week (16–22 December 1941) Brunei was overrun and militarily occupied by the Imperial Japanese Army (IJA). Administratively, Brunei together with Baram, Labuan, Lawas and Limbang came under Miri-shu, one of five newly created prefectures. There were no radical changes in the administrative structure: Japanese military officers simply replaced the Europeans. The Resident, E.E. Pengilly, and his handful of European officers were incarcerated at the Batu Lintang Prisoner of War and Internment Camp in Kuching. Malay government officers remained in their posts, but now served a Japanese superior. Likewise, Sultan Ahmad Tajuddin (r. 1924–50), who was bestowed with Japanese medals and honours and a pension, retained his throne, but without any political and/or executive power. Awang Ibrahim bin Muhammad Jaafar, Secretary to the Resident, now became Chief Administrative Officer to the Japanese Governor who replaced the Resident.

Wartime Brunei was not an unduly harsh place. Scarcity of daily necessities such as foodstuffs, including rice, clothing, cooking oil, matches and Western medicines meant that the people, particularly those in towns, suffered prolonged deprivation. Rural farming communities fared favourably, with better access to rice and other foodstuffs that they themselves produced. Even the low-profile small Chinese community escaped the wrath of the IJA; no witch-hunt or *sook ching* (lit. 'purification') confronted Chinese residents. Overall, nothing dramatic or horrific occurred during this trying wartime period.

IJA engineers not only managed to sink 16 new oil wells at Miri-Seria, but also attained half the pre-war levels of output despite the dire conditions.[25] *Nihon-go* (language) classes catered for both children and adults. Japanese sociocultural traditions and values were imposed on the local people, in particular performing *saikeirei*, the ritual of bowing, paying homage to the portrait of the Imperial Japanese Emperor.

Within three days of the Australian landings on 10 June 1945 at Brunei Bay and Labuan, Brunei Town was recaptured. By August, the official Japanese surrender ended the war and occupation. The subsequent brief tenure of the British Military Administration (BMA) addressed pressing issues such as food supply and distribution; reconstruction matters were left to the incoming civilian government. The second phase of the Residency administration period commenced in September 1946 with Resident W.J. Peel at the helm, assisting Sultan Ahmad Tajuddin.

The post-war British Labour government had decided that following a period of political tutelage, eventual political independence under indigenous governments was to be granted to British Bornean territories.[26] While Brunei retained its status as a protectorate, Sarawak and British North Borneo became Crown Colonies. The Governor of Sarawak also served as High Commissioner for Brunei; senior British officials were seconded from the Sarawak Service rather than the MCS. By the 1950s, it was a clear-cut policy objective that Brunei's Malay Muslim Sultanate be maintained, with political independence as the ultimate goal.[27]

Reconstruction was on track thanks to oil revenue that was boosted by increased production and exports and the Korean War (1950–53). Rubber also enjoyed a boom as a result of the conflict. The First Development Plans (1953–58) realized efforts to develop transport and communications, deep-water ports, infrastructure, schools, hospitals and a public sanitation system.

Apart from the physical rebuilding, the peoples of Brunei came through the wartime period largely unscathed physically, but mentally, to some extent, they were transformed. A return to the pre-war era was no longer tenable; expectations of moving forward were increasingly heard. But Bruneians were apparently split in their nationalism: the sultan and the ruling elite favoured a progressive paternalism; in contrast, the general populace looked toward some form of popular democracy that the general public could participate in through the ballot box.

On the political and constitutional front, one daunting issue – the road to self-determination and independence (*merdeka*) – confronted the sultanate, specifically the sultan and Sheikh Ahmad M. Azahari bin Sheikh Mahmud (1928–2002). Sultan Omar Ali Saifuddin III (1914–1986), who came to the throne in 1950, was not only clear about what he intended for the throne (himself) and the sultanate, but also mindful and determined about the means to attain his ambition – political independence for Brunei as a Malay Islamic Monarchy with supreme executive power invested in the sultan.[28]

Azahari, undoubtedly one of the most charismatic political figures of Brunei and founder president of Partai Raykat Brunei (PRB, Brunei People's Party), was equally forceful and determined, but lacked focus and direction in terms of what exactly his ultimate goals were, both for himself and/or for Brunei. He subscribed to Indonesian President Achmat Sukarno's 'Indonesia Raya', a pan-Malay state comprising the entire Malay Archipelago, literally insular Southeast Asia. At the same time, Azahari was drawn, albeit briefly, to Malayan prime minister Tunku Abdul Rahman Putra Al-Haj's wider federation of 'Malaysia' that encompassed Malaya, Singapore, Sarawak, Brunei and British North Borneo. Then his ambition turned to a revival of the ancient empire of Brunei that allegedly claimed suzerainty over the island of Borneo and the Philippines.

The British for their part, particularly the governors of Sarawak and British North Borneo, favoured a federation of the Borneo territories as an interim step to independence. Federation of the three Bornean states was thought of as a logical progression towards eventual independence.[29] The concept of closer union followed up the idea initially mooted in 1930 by Sir Cecil Clementi, Governor of the Straits Settlements and High Commissioner to the Malay States and Brunei. Its revival could be discerned in the so-called Inter-Territorial Conference (1953–61). Arguments for some form of closer ties emphasized the benefits of greater co-ordination in policies and administration, reducing costs and unnecessary duplication.

Reflecting the rather radical approach of Azahari, within a year of its establishment the PRB sent a three-man delegation on a Merdeka Mission to London to demand from Whitehall a specific date for independence, which the latter rejected.[30] This radical approach was anathema to Sultan Omar; in fact, this confrontational manner was simply not the Malay way of pursuing a cause. A subtle, step-by-step approach was favoured by the palace and the Brunei ruling elite.

Sultan Omar rejected a closer union of the Bornean territories. It was rather unpalatable, even demeaning, to equate Brunei, a sovereign state, with the two British Crown Colonies of Sarawak and British North Borneo. Instead, the Brunei ruler favoured Malaya, intending to foster closer ties following the latter's independence from Britain in 1957.

To gain both support and consensus from within and legitimacy and respectability from without, Sultan Omar decreed that unofficial members of district councils who had hitherto been appointed were henceforth to be elected. The second step was that in the proposed new constitution of Brunei, the Legislative Council was to have a majority of the elected members. The third development was the formulation and promulgation of a new constitution. Meanwhile, the sultan prepared to hold discussions with London for a new Anglo-Brunei agreement. Sultan Omar was practical in laying the constitutional steps towards eventual independence for Brunei.

In March 1959, Sultan Omar held talks with the British government that resulted in the Brunei Agreement, wholly replacing the 1906 treaty. It was seen as a first step towards political independence for the sultanate: Britain granted self-government, but retained power over internal security, defence and foreign relations (external affairs). The Resident was replaced by a High Commissioner to advise the sultan and his government. This 1959 Brunei Agreement not only put Brunei on a progressive road towards independence, but also unshackled the country from its uneasy relations with neighbouring Sarawak that the sultan and most Bruneians viewed with suspicion and trepidation.

In September 1959, Sultan Omar presented a new Constitution.[31] The State Council was abolished, and in its place were the Executive Council and Legislative Council, more in line with post-war democratic governments. The Executive Council was presided over by the sultan himself, and comprised the High Commissioner, seven *ex officio* members and seven sultan-nominated unofficial members. It was apparent that the sultan remained the predominant power in the Executive Council, as the monarch could summon its meetings, set the agenda, approve the annual budget and disregard all advice (in writing) if he wished. The Legislative Council's membership comprised eight *ex officio* members, six sultan-nominated official members, three sultan-nominated non-official members and 16 elected members drawn from district councils. Elections to the district councils were to be held within two years of the promulgation of the Constitution, in 1961. The Legislative Council was to oversee financial expenditure and pass laws. Day-to-day administration was to be conducted by the Menteri Besar (chief/prime minister), the state secretary, the attorney general and the state financial controller. Two other councils – the Privy Council and Religious, Succession, and Regency Council – were also created, the former to advise the sultan in exercising his prerogative of mercy, the latter focusing on Islamic issues, the royal succession and regency matters. A Public Service Commission was to oversee public service appointments; however, all appointments needed approval from the palace.

The new Constitution to all intents and purposes entrenched the sultan's powers as the supreme executive authority: 'The British [government] had granted internal self-government to the Sultan, not to the people [and/or Brunei]. There was no elective majority on the Legislative Council and no direct elections to that Council.'[32]

The next decade, the 1960s, particularly the first half, was to be one of the most challenging periods to face Brunei, and it was Sultan Omar's action at a critical moment that decided the sultanate's ultimate fate. A coalescence of overlapping developments finally reached a climax in a revolt in December 1962 – an unprecedented outbreak in this serenely tropical state.

The Tunku was expecting that Brunei would join the wider federation when he publicly announced his 'Malaysia' proposal in May 1961. There was no immediate reaction from the palace, but Azahari's PRB openly opposed this proposal. Azahari had other plans for Brunei, namely the creation of Negarabagian Kesatuan Kalimantan Utara (NKKU, Unitary State of North Kalimantan), comprising Brunei, Sarawak and North Borneo, with Sultan Omar as head of state and himself as prime minister. The NKKU, it seemed, would eventually join Sukarno's Republik Indonesia. An armed revolt was the alternative if constitutional means to realize the NKKU failed.[33]

The year-long delay in holding the pledged elections to the district councils that would see 16 elected representatives on the Legislative Council frustrated the PRB. Furthermore, when the elections were finally held in late August 1962, the PRB confidently won 54 out of 55 contested seats. In the Legislative Council's inaugural sitting on 5 December 1962, the PRB presented three written motions for the agenda:

(1) a motion rejecting the concepts of the Federation of Malaysia; (2) a motion asking the British Government to restore the sovereignty of the Sultanate of Brunei over the former territories of Sarawak and North Borneo; and (3) a motion urging the British Government to federate the three territories

of Sarawak, Brunei and North Borneo under the Unitary State of Kalimantan Utara with Sultan Omar Ali Saifuddin [III] as its constitutional and parliamentary Head of State and the granting of complete and absolute Independence to this new State not later than 1963.[34]

All three motions were turned down, as it was beyond the jurisdiction of the State Legislative Council to discuss and/or sanction such demands. It appears that 'constitutional means in realizing the NKKU [had] failed', and the alternative was '[a]n armed revolt'. The uprising was launched by the PRB's armed wing, Tentera Nasional Kalimantan Utara (TNKU, National Army of North Kalimantan), which received military training from Tentera Nasional Indonesia (TNI, National Armed Forces of Indonesia).[35]

It appears that the date set for the revolt, 24 December, had to be brought forward to 8 December owing to the chance discovery of two military training camps in Sarawak's Lawas district with a cache of 35 TNKU uniforms, during which ten people were apprehended.[36]

In a drama that played out over a week, Brunei appeared to be at a crossroads:

By the first evening [8 December 1962] of the insurrection, most of the country was in rebel hands, as were neighbouring parts of Sarawak and North Borneo. However, the government still controlled the capital [Brunei Town], including the telecommunications network, the radio station, and, crucially, the airport. Meanwhile, a message had been received in Singapore through the chief minister, saying that the sultan [Omar Ali] wished to invoke the protection of the British as enshrined in the 1959 agreements between Brunei and the United Kingdom.[37]

The signal for help from Sultan Omar led to the arrival of police personnel from British North Borneo and British troops airlifted from Singapore. Within a week, all was over, with a total of 47 fatalities (40 TNKU, 7 British).[38] The sultan also broadcast a denunciation of the revolt that led to many rebels surrendering, as many had thought they were fighting in the name of their monarch. Mass arrests ensued, followed by detention, but no one was ever charged or brought to court; the last detainee was released in 1990. The 'Brunei Rebellion' remains a taboo event within the sultanate even after more than five decades.[39]

Numerous factors brought forth this armed outbreak, in particular frustrations about the unfulfilled democratic aspirations of the PRB, perceived economic uncertainties resulting from the interim period between the end of the first national development plan (1953–58) and the implementation of the second (1962–66), and the peaking of the Seria oil field (1956) and the discovery of offshore fields (1963). Moreover, the dominance of British officials (from Malaya) in senior positions in the bureaucracy while non-royal Bruneians were in the lower echelons of the government machinery was a bone of contention among Bruneians.[40]

The 'Malaysia' proposal created regional uncertainty about the status of Brunei itself *vis-à-vis* this wider federation.[41] The PRB opposed the 'Malaysia' proposal, but the sultan appeared to favour such a new setup, in particular as a means of bolstering Brunei's security. But by mid-1963, two outstanding issues remained unresolved: petroleum revenues, and perhaps more importantly, the sultan's status and precedence over the nine peninsular Malay rulers. Two face-to-face meetings between Sultan Omar and the Tunku failed to resolve the notable issues, hence Brunei did not join when Malaysia came into being in September 1963. Consequently, relations soured between Brunei and Kuala Lumpur. At the same time, when the revolt was linked to support from Indonesia, relations deteriorated between Brunei and Jakarta. It was a low ebb for Brunei and its immediate neighbours.

The failed revolt resulted in mistrust of political organizations; the PRB was proscribed, and others gravitated to the Brunei Alliance Party (BAP), which supported entry into Malaysia. The BAP's insistence on a fully elected legislature was rejected. As a compromise, Sultan Omar agreed to allow some elected seats in the legislature, and replaced the Executive Council with a Council of Ministers, resembling a cabinet-style executive. Mistrust of political parties continued. In 1966, the call by the Barisan Kemerdekaan Rakyat (BAKER, Brunei People's Independence Front) for a fully elected legislature and full ministerial system was turned down.

Meanwhile, Britain was unhappy and impatient at the sluggish pace of Sultan Omar's constitutional reform. By early 1968, the British government had decided to withdraw troops and its military commitment from Southeast Asia and the Indian Ocean, hence the phrase 'East of Suez'.[42] A year earlier, in 1967, Sultan Omar had decided to abdicate in favour of his son, Hassanal Bolkiah, who ascended to the throne in October. Sultan Hassanal negotiated a new agreement: signed in 1971, the new arrangement saw an amendment to the Constitution of 1959 whereby the sultan assumed full responsibility for internal governance, and Britain only handled foreign relations of the sultanate. A battalion of Gurkhas drawn from the British army was stationed at Brunei for internal security.

While London was anxious to sever ties with Brunei, Brunei was reluctant owing to fear of its predatory neighbours, Malaysia and Indonesia. Apart from the threat from without, there were also concerns about opposition and secessionist groups within. In fact, Sultan Hassanal and his father, the Seri Begawan Sultan (title adopted from 1967), held a series of meetings in London in 1978 and 1979, and in 1979 an agreement was signed whereby Brunei was to attain independence on 1 January 1984. In September 1983, a defence agreement was made whereby the Gurkha battalion under British command was retained at the sultanate's expense.

Upon attaining independence, Sultan Hassanal presided over a seven-member cabinet that included the Seri Begawan Sultan and two of his brothers in lieu of the Council of Ministers. The state ideology of Melayu Islam Beraja was officially proclaimed.[43] The MIB upheld ethnic Malay language, culture, traditions and practices as the predominant sociocultural heritage and identity of the sultanate. Islam, the official religion, is also the dominant religion, and the Malay monarchical system the unquestioned mode of governance. All three components – Malay, Islam, monarchy – collectively portray the national identity, values, image and heritage of this Malay Muslim sultanate.

Brunei citizens benefited from free medical care, education (to the tertiary level) and housing loans, were excluded from paying income tax, and enjoyed subsidies for many essential commodities, including fuel and housing. Ethnic Malays, increasingly referred to as *bumiputera* (lit. 'son of the soil'), enjoyed preferential treatment in all fields. The 1970s and 1980s posed few serious issues, but the 1990s witnessed the increasing emergence of social problems. The young population (half the population in the early 1990s were below 20 years of age) and exposure to the currents of modernity, particularly from without, brought about societal issues and challenges that hitherto had not been apparent, notably drug abuse and alcoholism among the youth. Rising unemployment, and in particular the dire shortage of menial labour that relied heavily on immigrant workers, caused grave concerns.[44] In response, the 1990s saw a greater emphasis on the tenets of the MIB in schools and workplaces. Islamic teachings were emphasized, religious holidays like the Prophet's birthday were marked on a grander scale, and mosques, religious schools and colleges were built. The importation of alcohol was banned from January 1991, and public celebration of Christmas was proscribed.[45]

The passing of the Seri Begawan Sultan in 1986 saw the re-strengthening of the royal family's grip on power with a dominant role in government. Key ministries such as defence, finance and foreign affairs were in royal hands, with Sultan Hassanal himself serving as prime minister and minister of defence, and later (from 1998) minister of finance as well. There was little semblance of political concessions and/or free democratic elections to public office. Sultan Hassanal increasingly portrayed himself as a paternal figure, the 'People's Sultan', eschewing the extravagant lifestyle of the royalty of old. In 1998, Prince Al-Muhtadee Billah Bolkiah, eldest son of Sultan Hassanal, was installed as heir apparent to the Brunei throne. This consolidated the Malay Muslim monarchy beyond any doubt.

Concern about the misappropriation and mismanagement of funds (apparent in the late 1990s) led to the establishment of the Brunei Darussalam Economic Council (BDEC) in September 1998. A BDEC report in the year 2000 warned of the unsustainability of the economy. This spurred the creation of a long-term development planning body that would lay plans for the next three decades from 2006. There was also a national aspiration to be a regional financial hub and a safe haven for international financial services, but compatible with Islamic tenets. However, there was no compatible political reform to match the forward-looking economic transformation.

The programme of Islamization continued throughout the 2000s. Islamic teachings to ensure adherence to social and moral values were to go hand in hand with economic development. The Islamic Development Bank of Brunei opened in 2000, and the International Islamic Exposition, attracting 25 participating countries, was held in 2001. In 2007, the Seri Begawan Training College for Teachers of Islamic Religion was upgraded to become the Seri Begawan University College for Teachers of Islamic Religion. The Sultan Sharif Ali Islamic University (UNISSA), the country's second university (after Universiti Brunei Darussalam, set up in 1985) was established in 2007.

The media, both broadcast and print, remained closely monitored. Besides the state-owned television station, a commercial television channel made its debut in 1999. The press exercised self-censorship, and all media refrained from criticizing the sultanate or the MIB. The Local Newspapers (Amendment) Order 2001 imposed a yearly permit for publication, allowing the government to suspend without appeal any recalcitrant newspaper and to ban foreign newspapers from entering the country.

Contemporary Brunei's economy derived the bulk of its revenue from oil and natural gas. This enormous reliance had existed since the 1930s, and continued into the post-independence period. Brunei is currently the fourth largest producer of crude petroleum in Southeast Asia, and globally the fourth largest producer of liquefied natural gas (LNG). The major importers of Brunei's LNG and crude petroleum products are Japan, South Korea, Indonesia and Australia. Owing to the capital-intensive nature of the oil and gas sector, the labour requirements do not exceed 4,000, and a quarter of the professional and specialist workers are foreigners. Over-dependence on oil and gas as revenue earners is a major concern. Moreover, world petroleum prices are notoriously volatile, making such over-reliance an unsustainable option. Economic diversification is therefore a priority in the economic policy of the sultanate.[46] Efforts are being made to promote wholesale and retail trade, manufacturing and construction, and other sectors of the economy that are increasingly contributing to national revenue and employment.

Subsistence rice farming and the collection of jungle produce were once significant activities as well as sources of livelihood. By 1947, half the population remained agriculture-based, but from the 1970s less than 10 per cent were involved, and present-day farming activities are mostly on a part-time basis to provide subsidiary sources of income. Consequently, Brunei is a net importer of more than 80 per cent of its foodstuff needs – undoubtedly an unhealthy state in terms of long-term food security. This concern is addressed in economic and development policy in terms of improvements in basic infrastructure, capital and materials inputs, marketing processes and strategies, all aimed at meeting local demand, and secondarily, to explore the export potential of Brunei's agricultural sector.

Brunei has long faced the perennial problem of shortage of labour, both skilled and unskilled. The oil and gas industries from the outset engaged foreign expertise in the professional and specialist fields; non-Bruneians continue to the present day to dominate this highly capital-intensive, specialized sector. Unskilled immigrant labour continues to be needed in other sectors of the economy, particularly in construction. The presence of foreign labour remains a necessary phenomenon in contemporary Brunei.

However, from the 1980s, unemployment among Bruneians, particularly among the youth, was increasingly apparent and a worrying concern. Youth unemployment appears to be one of the major causes of nascent social problems in present-day Brunei. Apart from this, increasing unemployment reflects imbalances in the economy and impairs its long-term viability. Brunei Malays in particular, and to a lesser extent other local ethnic groups, tend to prefer public sector positions where perceived higher status and job security are the primary motivations. Moreover, as improvements have been made in education, Bruneians increasingly hold high academic qualifications that dissuade them from taking up floor-level and/or menial jobs in the private sector. Blue-collar workers are apparently lacking among the citizenry, hence the inflow of immigrant labour. The private sector relies heavily on foreign labour, mainly drawn from neighbouring ASEAN nations, and also from South Asia, Australasia and the United Kingdom. To counteract this, provision for vocational and technical education is being prioritized to facilitate the Bruneianization programme in both white-collar and blue-collar positions, although it appears that the former – senior management, supervisory and specialist jobs – are given greater emphasis.

This present volume, comprising eight chapters, presents an overview of Brunei spread across four themes, as befits its title: history, Islam, society and contemporary issues.

The first part, 'Genesis, historical ties and contemporary relations', consists of three chapters. Pre-tenth-century Borneo, the rather obscure proto-historic period, appears to harbour several polities of complex societies along its northwest coast – in and around present-day Brunei, the Limbang, Santubong and Gedung areas of Sarawak. The genesis of the polities is explored by Stephen Charles Druce (Chapter 1), who attempts to ascertain the antecedence of contemporary Brunei by drawing on a host of source materials, including archaeological and linguistic data, recorded oral traditions, indigenous written sources and information gleaned from Chinese records.

The *Silsilah Raja-Raja Brunei*, translated as the 'Genealogical History of the Sultans of Brunei', is available in three versions: two manuscripts are held in London, at the School of Oriental and African Studies (SOAS) library, University of London, and the Royal Asiatic Society of London library; a second version, referred to as 'Dari Hal Tarsilah Raja Di Dalam Brunei' ('From the Royal Stone Inscription of Brunei') is in the collection of the Brunei Historical Centre, Bandar Seri Begawan; the third is *Sejarah Brunei* (*History of Brunei*), by Datuk Imam Aminuddin ibnu Orang Kaya Di Gadong Lewadin and subsequently copied by Abdul Ghafar bin Abdul Mumin. As Ampuan Dr Haji Brahim bin Ampuan Haji Tengah points out (Chapter 2), the *Silsilah Raja-Raja Brunei* not only details the royal genealogy, but also contains a wealth of information on the sociocultural and socioeconomic characteristics, royal customary practices and court rituals, and foreign relations. Drawing on the various versions, the chapter examines the relationship between Brunei and other contemporaneous polities, and the implications of such linkages.

Turning to the contemporary scene, Mikio Oishi (Chapter 3) utilizes Small State Diplomacy theory and insights provided by Constructivism to evaluate several aspects of Brunei's foreign relations that are relevant to its state identity, and its struggle to ascertain, establish and maintain its place in an increasingly complex world.

The second part, 'Multi-ethnic mosaic and lifestyle', features two chapters. The Brunei Nationality Status Acts 1961 designated seven native ethnic groups in Brunei as indigenous Malay: Belait, Bisaya, Brunei, Dusun, Kedayan, Murut and Tutong. Over time, interactions between communities and the acculturation process blurred the once clearly defined boundaries between these ethnic groups. Mohd Shahrol Amira bin Abdullah (Chapter 4) attempts to delineate 'being "Malay"' in present-day Brunei, relying on qualitative analysis from observations of ethnic Malays' cultural attributes. In their contribution (Chapter 5), Haji Awg Asbol Bin Haji Mail and Haji Tassim Haji Abu Bakar offer an insightful portrayal of what daily life and goings-on in Brunei's famed Kampong Ayer were like during the British Residency Period, 1906–41. The authors argue that despite a programme to relocate the residents of Kampong Ayer to land, the latter remained loyal to their traditional lifestyle, characteristics, and in turn their identity and heritage – to remain afloat, 'to live on water' – that to some extent remain conspicuous to the present.

The third part, 'Islam', focuses on the rights of Muslim women under Islamic jurisprudence, particularly relating to owning property during marriage and after its dissolution. Datin Dr Hajah Saadiah binti Datu Derma Wijaya Haji Tamit (Chapter 6) examines whether the implementation in Brunei of the Emergency Order (Islamic Family Law) 1999 has maintained the status of the family institution and safeguarded women's rights, especially in marriage. Islamic law notwithstanding, there remained weaknesses where legal rights of women in marriage and following divorce had not been protected and injustices perpetrated. The chapter makes some recommendations to alleviate Brunei Muslim women's plight.

The final part, 'Current concerns', looks at two contemporary issues facing modern-day Brunei. Noralipah binti Haji Mohamed (Chapter 7) raises the problem of the sultanate's over-dependence on foreign labour as a consequence of its economic diversification programme to non-oil sectors of the economy. The presence of foreign workers has undeniably contributed significantly to sustaining Brunei's development in the past, and continues to do so in the present, but on the other hand, their overwhelming presence has created economic, social, cultural and political issues and implications. Pengiran Khairul Rijal Pengiran Hj. Abdul Rahim (Chapter 8) addresses the issue of food security, notably the over-dependence on imports of fishery resources. This insightful overview of the fishing industry, including the various government-driven programmes, weaknesses of the local processing sector and the marketing aspects of fisheries resources, much needs to be addressed to alleviate Brunei's high dependency on the importation of fishery resources.

Notes

1 http://data.worldbank.org/indicator/SP.POP.TOTL. Accessed 22 August 2015. Another source gave a lower estimate of 416,000 for 2014: http://worldpopulationreview.com/countries/brunei-darussalam-population/. Accessed 22 August 2015.

2 http://worldpopulationreview.com/countries/brunei-darussalam-population/. Accessed 22 August 2015.

3 http://kushnirs.org/macroeconomics/gdp/gdp_brunei.html. Accessed 22 August 2015.

4 http://kushnirs.org/macroeconomics/gdp/gdp_singapore.html. Accessed 22 August 2015.

5 Ooi Keat Gin, *Historical Dictionary of Malaysia* (Lanham, MD: Scarecrow Press, 2009), p. 181.

6 https://www.cia.gov/library/publications/the-world-factbook/geos/bx.html#People. Accessed 22 August 2015.

7 Ibid.

8 Ibid.

9 Ibid.

10 See Johannes L. Kurz in two recent articles: 'Pre-modern Chinese Sources in the National History of Brunei: The Case of Poli', *Bijdragen tot de Taal-, Land- en Volkenkunde*, 169 (2013): 213–43, and 'Boni in Chinese Sources from the Tenth to the Eighteenth Century', *International Journal of Asia-Pacific Studies*, 10(1) (2014): 1–32. See also Chapter 3 in this volume.

11 See Jamil al-Sufri, *History of Brunei in Brief*, 2nd edn (Bandar Seri Begawan: Brunei History Centre, Ministry of Culture, Youth and Sports, 2000); Robert Nicholl, *European Sources for the History of the Sultanate of Brunei in the Sixteenth Century* (Bandar Seri Begawan: Muzium Brunei, 1973).

12 See Bala Bilcher, *Thalassocracy: A History of the Medieval Sultanate of Brunei Darussalam* (Kota Kinabalu: School of Social Science, University of Malaysia Sabah, 2005).

13 See Graham Saunders, *A History of Brunei* (Kuala Lumpur: Oxford University Press, 1994), p. 65.

14 P.L. Amin Sweeney, 'Silsilah Raja-Raja Berunai', *Journal of the Malaysian Branch of the Royal Asiatic Society*, 41(2) (1968): 1–82.

15 P.M. Sharifuddin and Abdul Latif bin Haji Ibrahim, 'The Genealogical Tablet (Batu Tarsilah) of the Sultans of Brunei', *Brunei Museum Journal*, 3(2) (1974): 253–64.

16 See Robert Nicholl, 'Some Problems in Brunei Chronology', *Journal of Southeast Asian Studies*, 20(2) (1989): 175–95.

17 See Nicholas Tarling, *Britain, the Brookes and Brunei* (Kuala Lumpur: Oxford University Press, 1971), pp. 10–16.

18 Ooi Keat Gin, *Of Free Trade and Native Interests: The Brookes and the Economic Development of Sarawak* (Kuala Lumpur: Oxford University Press, 1997), pp. 121–3.

19 Ibid., pp. 12–13.

20 See Tarling, *Britain, the Brookes and Brunei*; L.R. Wright, *The Making of British Borneo* (Hong Kong: Hong Kong University Press, 1988).

21 See A.V.M. Horton, *The British Residency in Brunei, 1906–1959*, University of Hull, Centre for South-East Asian Studies, Occasional Paper no. 6, 1984.

22 G.E. Cator, 'Brunei', *Asiatic Review*, 35 (1939): 736–44, at 744.

23 Saunders, *A History of Brunei*, p. 119.

24 Ooi Keat Gin, *The Japanese Occupation of Borneo* (London: Routledge, 2011), pp. 30–34.

25 Ibid., pp. 55–6.

26 See Ooi Keat Gin, *Post-war Borneo, 1945–1950: Nationalism, Empire, and State-building* (London: Routledge, 2013).

27 *Borneo Bulletin*, 13 July 1957.

28 B.A. Hussainmiya, *Sultan Omar Ali Saifuddin III and Britain: The Making of Brunei Darussalam* (Singapore: Oxford University Press, 1995).

29 Vernon L. Porritt, *British Colonial Rule in Sarawak, 1946–1963* (Kuala Lumpur: Oxford University Press, 1997), pp. 58–61.

30 Haji Zaini Haji Ahmad, ed., *Partai Rakyat Brunei/The People's Party of Brunei: Selected Documents/Dokumen Terpilih* (Petaling Jaya: Institute of Social Analysis, n.d. [1987?]).

31 See Horton, *The British Residency in Brunei*, pp. 60–61.

32 Saunders, *A History of Brunei*, p. 138.
33 See Ooi Keat Gin, 'The Cold War and British Borneo: Impact and Legacy 1945–63', in *Southeast Asia and the Cold War*, edited by Albert Lau (London: Routledge, 2012), pp. 102–32.
34 'Proclamation of Independence 8 December, 1962', reproduced in *Partai Rakyat Brunei/The People's Party of Brunei: Selected Documents/Dokumen Terpilih*, p. 198.
35 Ooi, 'The Cold War and British Borneo', p. 117.
36 *Sarawak Tribune*, 10 December 1962; J.A.C. Mackie, *Konfrontasi: The Indonesia–Malaysia Dispute, 1963–1966* (Kuala Lumpur: Oxford University Press, 1974), p. 120; Vernon L. Porritt, *The Rise and Fall of Communism in Sarawak 1940–1990* (Clayton, Australia: Monash Asia Institute, 2004), p. 85.
37 A.V.M. Horton, 'Brunei Rebellion (December 1962): A Cry for Change', in *Southeast Asia: A Historical Encyclopedia, from Angkor Wat to East Timor*, vol. I, edited by Ooi Keat Gin (Santa Barbara, CA: ABC-CLIO, 2004), pp. 278–9 at 278.
38 Harold James and D. Sheil-Small, *The Undeclared War: The Story of Indonesian Confrontation, 1962–1966* (London: Leo Cooper, 1971), pp. 42–3.
39 In recent years, there have been numerous studies on this revolt. See Harun Abdul Majid, *Rebellion in Brunei: The 1962 Revolt, Imperialism, Confrontation, and Oil* (London: I.B. Tauris, 2007); Roger Kershaw, 'The Last Brunei Revolt? A Case Study of Microstate (In)security', *Internationales Asienforum*, 42(1–2) (2011): 107–34; Nicholas Van der Bijl, *The Brunei Revolt, 1962–1963* (Barnsley: Pen & Sword Military, 2012).
40 Horton, 'Brunei Rebellion', p. 278.
41 See Matthew Jones, *Conflict and Confrontation in South East Asia, 1961–1965: Britain, the United States, and the Creation of Malaysia* (Cambridge: Cambridge University Press, 2001).
42 See P.L. Pham, *Ending 'East of Suez': The British Decision to Withdraw from Malaysia and Singapore* 1964–1968 (Oxford: Oxford University Press, 2010).
43 See Shukri Zain et al., *The Malay Islamic Monarchy: A Closer Understanding* (Bandar Seri Begawan: National Supreme Council of the Malay Islamic Monarchy Brunei Darussalam, 2013); Haji Duraman Tuah, *Brunei Darussalam: Nation Building Based on Melayu Islam Beraja (Malay Islamic Monarchy Philosophy)* (Gadong, Negara Brunei Darussalam: Civil Service Institute, Prime Minister's Office, n.d. [2002?]); Sven Alexander Schottmann, '"Melayu Islam Beraja": The Politics of Legitimisation in a Malay Islamic Monarchy', *RIMA: Review of Indonesian and Malaysian Affairs*, 40(2) (2006): 111–39.
44 The unemployment issue has remained unresolved until recent times. For instance, see 'Unemployment Issues in Brunei (1)', *Brunei Times*, 27 December 2013. http://www.bt.com.bn/2013/05/27/unemployment-issues-brunei-1. Accessed 22 August 2015.
45 Prashanth Parameswaran, 'Brunei Explains its Christmas Celebration Ban', *The Diplomat*, 31 December 2014. http://thediplomat.com/2014/12/brunei-explains-its-christmas-celebration-ban/. Accessed 22 August 2015.
46 See P.M. Yakub Othman, *Brunei Darussalam – Challenges for Economic Diversification: Economic Diversification within the Context of National Development Planning in Brunei* (Saarbrücken, Germany: Lambert Academic Publishing, 2012).

Part I

Genesis, historical ties and contemporary relations

1 The 'birth' of Brunei

Early polities of the northwest coast of Borneo and the origins of Brunei, tenth to mid-fourteenth centuries

Stephen Charles Druce

This chapter explores the appearance of early polities and development of complex societies between the tenth and mid-fourteenth centuries along the north-west coast of Borneo, a region encompassing present-day Sarawak, Brunei and Sabah. Archaeological data from this region provides evidence for the existence of a number of coastal or semi-coastal complex societies in the first decade of the second millennium CE on the northwest coast, with the most significant in Brunei and the Limbang, Santubong and Gedong areas of Sarawak. The development of these early polities in this northwest region as well as in the island as a whole remains obscure, and it is fair to surmise that we know more about the prehistory of Borneo than its proto-historical period.[1]

Several writers have argued that two of the polities that arose along the northwest coast were established by peoples from outside Borneo.[2] The focus, then, of this chapter is to examine this possibility within a broad historical and archaeological framework, working on the premise that there are three possibilities for the origin of the said polities. The first possibility is that the polities emerged as a consequence of a gradual development in complexity among indigenous groups located in riverine regions, stimulated by the advent of regular and sustained external trade and the introduction of elite imported goods in exchange for local forest and sea produce. The second is the likelihood that Malay-speaking trading groups from polities in the western part of the Malay Archipelago established trading polities based on political systems similar to theirs, and thereafter developed riverine trading networks with inland indigenous groups, presumably to obtain forest produce for the international market.[3] The third possibility is a combination of the first and second, where external Malay-speaking trading groups settled in, or close to, existing indigenous polities that subsequently became the dominant political and cultural force.

Support for advancing these possibilities is drawn from archaeological and linguistic data, recorded oral traditions and indigenous written sources, and information found in Chinese records. This investigation opens with an overview of data relating to before the tenth century, including the problematic associations that some of the source materials have made between the northwest coast of Borneo and early toponyms mentioned in Chinese sources.

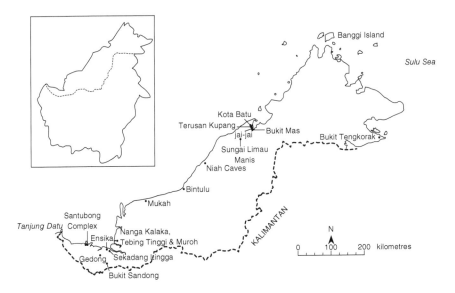

Figure 1.1 Early polities of the northwest coast of Borneo, *c.* tenth to mid-fourteenth
centuries

The paucity of evidence for pre-tenth-century developments

The earliest evidence of external trade along the northwest coast of Borneo comes
from Bukit Tengkorak in northern Sabah, where Bellwood and Koon found evidence of trade in obsidian between early Austronesian settlers of this region and the
Bismarck Archipelago dating to about 3,000 years ago.[4] Fragments of an approximately 2,000-year old Dong Son drum have also been found in Banggi Island, which
lies off the north coast of Sabah – presumably the only such example known in
northwest Borneo.[5] For the first millennium CE, there is little evidence in northwest
Borneo of any external trade or development in political complexity *vis-à-vis* Java
and Sumatra. The region appears to have been marginal. There is evidence, however,
of significant Indic influence in the early first millennium, but this is uncovered in the
island's southeast at Kutai, where stood seven stone pillars (*yūpa*, sacrificial posts)
inscribed with the early Pallava script and Sanskrit language that date to about the
early or mid-fourth century CE.[6] One of the inscriptions, inscribed during the reign of
King Mūlawarman (referred to as the 'lord of kings') lists the names of three generations of kings. Another ruler called Aśwawarman is attributed as 'the founder of the
dynasty'. The Kutai inscriptions appear to have been written within the context of
'state formation' and illustrate the earliest evidence for the development of a complex polity in Borneo, however short-lived, that used Indic Hindu concepts.

Very different and unrelated Sanskrit inscriptions, dated a century or more later
than those of Kutai, have been found in West Kalimantan, near the Kapaus river
at Batu Pahat, and in Brunei and Limbang. The Batu Pahat inscription, the most

extensive of the three, is on a massive boulder that is inscribed with seven stupas and eight Buddhist inscriptions that relate to rebirth and karma.[7] Two brief Buddhist inscriptions written in Sanskrit script and language have also been found in Brunei. Although the context is somewhat different to that of Batu Pahat, they too relate to karma and rebirth. One of the brief Brunei inscriptions is inscribed on one side of a lotus-shaped stone situated in a small Islamic cemetery known as Ujong Tanjong. The other side of the stone is inscribed in Jawi script, informing that Sulaiman bin Abdul Rahman bin Abdullah Nurullah died in the year 821 (1418–19).[8] Shariffuddin and Nicholl suggested that the Sanskrit and Jawi inscriptions may be contemporaneous with one another, perhaps the 'work of the same artist', which appears unlikely.[9] The second short Sanskrit inscription found in Brunei, at the Islamic Dagang Cemetery, is inscribed on what may have been a sandstone stupa of slightly over a metre in height; it is again Buddhist, and makes brief reference to karma.[10] The 'stupa' probably came to be used as a tombstone before being replaced by another stone.[11] The Limbang inscription found at Buang Abai is similar to the Dagang 'stupa' in that it too refers to karma and is engraved on a similar structure ('stupa'?) that had become an Islamic gravestone.[12] Like the more extensive and permanent inscription of Batu Pahat in West Kalimantan, the three northwest Borneo inscriptions lack archaeological context, and hence are difficult to date. Furthermore, they also appear to have been transported to the locations where they were discovered from other locations in order to be used as Islamic gravestones.

Jan Christie has argued that these Borneo Buddhist inscriptions are related to the various Buddhist inscriptions of the Muda-Merbok estuary of Kedah on the Malay Peninsula that dates from the fifth century. The script and Buddhist content are similar, and the karma formula of the inscriptions appears to have been popular for a brief period then. Christie further argues that the 'communities or individuals' who produced these inscriptions were linked in some way to a Buddhist traders' cult based on a central cult site in Kedah.[13]

Are the short Brunei and Limbang inscriptions evidence of a link, probably short-lived, to a Buddhist traders' cult some time in the mid-first millennium? While this is a possibility, the fact that the stones with the inscriptions were brought to their present locations for use as Islamic gravestones makes it problematic to draw such a conclusion without supporting archaeological data and supplementary evidence. What is clear is that the Buddhist inscriptions at Batu Pahat, Brunei and Limbang are wholly dissimilar in nature to the fourth-century Hindu inscriptions of Kutai. Unlike Kutai, they were not created in the context of 'state formation', and on their own would provide no evidence of a polity even if the locations for the Brunei and Limbang inscriptions were fixed. Furthermore, given the very specific nature of the inscriptions, they do not appear to be related to other and more substantial evidence of Indic influence found in northwest Borneo dating to the second millennium, mainly in the Santubong and Limbang areas (see below).

That there is no archaeological evidence for the development of any complex societies along the northwest coast of Borneo before the tenth century, or of external trade in the first millennium, is consistent with Wang Gungwu's detailed account of the Nanhai trade during the Tang (618–907) and earlier periods, which suggests that Borneo, the Philippines and Sulawesi played little or no role in this trade.[14] Some writers have, however, attempted to identify pre-tenth-century toponyms mentioned in Chinese sources with parts of Borneo, including the northwest coast. Such identifications are at best speculative, not supported by archaeological data, and the toponyms have, and continue to be, associated with numerous places throughout Island Southeast Asia.[15]

As Munoz points out, many historians who have attempted to locate early toponyms in Chinese sources have used the highly unreliable method of trying to identify locations by analysing the length of time it took to sail from one place to another. The problem with this method is that journey times contain many variables: different captains, different types and sizes of ship travelling at different speeds, the seasons and 'meteorological conditions'.[16]

Poli, which Robert Nicholl attempted to identify as a precursor of Brunei, is a particularly good example of the confusion and controversy surrounding the identification of places in Chinese sources.[17] Wolters briefly reviews the numerous identifications that had been made by 1967:

> P'o-li has been located in Borneo by Bretschneider, on the southern coast of Sumatra by Groeneveldt, and at Asahan on the north-east coast of Sumatra by Schlegel. Pelliot identified it with Bali, Gerini with the west coast of the Malay Peninsula, Moens with southern Sumatra and also with Java, Obdeijn with Bangka off the South-eastern coast of Sumatra, and Hsü Yün-ts'iao with Panei on the north-eastern coast of Sumatra. Sir Roland Braddell identified it with Borneo and thus completed the cycle of identifications where Brestchneider began as long ago as 1871.[18]

Wolters himself considered that Poli 'could not have been anywhere but in Java', and probably east Java.[19] Since then, different scholars have continued to make similar or different guesses as to the location of Poli.[20] Not surprisingly, Wang Gungwu tells us that the island the sources are referring to in relation to Poli cannot really be identified, although he himself favours Bali.[21] Similarly, Kurz has recently shown that the Chinese court officials themselves who compiled the accounts clearly had no idea where Poli was located.[22]

As opposed to Poli and other toponyms, the case of Boni, as it appeared in Chinese sources from the latter part of the tenth century, is somewhat different.[23] There is broad agreement among writers that Boni was located in western Borneo, and the majority have sited it along the northwest coast.[24] Unlike the earlier toponyms in Chinese sources, there is considerable supporting archaeological evidence from several places along the northwest coast dating from the tenth century to support identification. Nicholl, Mohammed Jamil Al-Sufri, and Pengiran Karim associate Boni with Brunei.[25] Pengiran Karim supports his argument with archaeological data, concluding that results from Brunei 'fit well with the problematical historical references to the locality called P'o-ni in Chinese records'.[26] While his archaeological data do support the identification of Boni as Brunei, similar data from other sites along the northwest coast have likewise been used to support a different location. Christie, based on the extensive archaeological evidence and iron industry found around the Sarawak river delta, associates Boni with Santubong.[27] Heng also considers that Boni was probably located at Santubong.[28] Hall, however, does not fix Boni at any specific location, simply placing it along the northwest coast. He points out that: 'Chinese literary references to place were coastline-inclusive rather than specific to a single and continuous port.'[29] Similarly, McKinnon doubts that references to Boni relate to a single precise location along the northwest coast.[30] Kurz, who presents a detailed analysis and modern accurate translations of the sources relating to Boni, is of the opinion that: 'Boni meant different localities with probably shifting centres in most likely Borneo, during different Chinese dynasties; one or several of these may have been precursors of modern day Brunei.'[31]

While some of the references in Chinese sources may therefore not specifically refer to Brunei, there is, however, good reason to believe that any mention of Boni in Chinese sources that relates to contact with China in the fourteenth century, especially from the beginning of the Ming period, does refer to Brunei. This inference is premised on archaeological data (discussed below) which shows that by the mid-fourteenth century, other major polities along the northwest coast appear to have declined, and from this period, Brunei emerges as the dominant trading polity, then probably located at Kota Batu, the water city described by Pigafetta in 1521.[32] Also of note in the context of associating some of the references to Boni with Brunei is the existence of a number of early tombstones found in Brunei that indicate connections with the important trading city of Quanzhou in China. The earliest of these is that of Master Pu, which is believed to date to about 1264, as the Chinese inscription tells us that it was set in the last year of Ching-ting's reign, the Southern Song emperor (1255–64). The tombstone is made of granite, and it has been argued that it was engraved in Quanzhou before being brought to Brunei and that Master Pu was a Muslim.[33] Another Chinese connection appears to be the undated tombstone belonging to a sultan called 'Maharaja Bruni', which, unlike that of Brunei rulers whose tombstones are written in Jawi except for verses from the Quran, is inscribed solely in Arabic. The stone is made of diabase (dolerite), which is not found in Brunei, and Chen Da-sheng argues that it was carved in Quanzhou before being brought to Brunei. Through palaeographic study, he dates the inscription to 1301.[34] There are no other tombstones of comparable antiquity found at other sites along the northwest coast, and these tangible links to the important trading city of Quanzhou found in Brunei do at least suggest the existence of a significant relationship.

The case for an external origin of northwest coast polities

In 1969, Cheng Te-k'un argued that the large iron-smelting industry that Harrisson and others had found at Santubong and the development of Santubong as a large and major trading centre were predominantly the work of Chinese immigrants during the eighth to thirteenth centuries.[35] He accepts that there was probably a small trading post at Songei Jaong at Santubong when Chinese traders, and perhaps a few Indians, first arrived, but it was these traders who by chance discovered iron ore and began the iron-smelting industry. He believed that the means of iron-smelting was the Chinese cast-iron method, and associates this with what were thought to be crucibles identified by Harrisson and O'Connor. He contends that Santubong grew and expanded into a major Chinese industrial town and port. The underlying reason for this development, he claims, was that there was a shortage of iron in China, particularly during the Southern Song dynasty (1127–79), when the northern industrial parts of the county had been lost to the Mongols.

Cheng's argument that the large and complex society that flourished at Santubong prior to its demise was not of Borneo but Chinese origin is, however, unconvincing. He appears to assume that the presence of Chinese ceramics at Santubong is sufficient evidence to indicate that the area was inhabited by Chinese. Furthermore, Harrisson and O'Connor, who excavated the site, proposed that the means of smelting used was the Indian 'Wootz' method, not the Chinese cast-iron method, and associated their crucible identifications with the former.[36] Subsequent research shows that neither of these methods appears to have been used, and that the iron-working technology employed at Santubong was in fact indigenous to Borneo and other parts of Southeast Asia,[37] while the crucibles that Harrisson and O'Connor identified were in fact tuyères (clay nozzles for the piston bellows).[38]

Equally unconvincing is Cheng's contention of a major shortage of iron in China during this period that dictated a need to find Southeast Asian imports. As far as can be ascertained, no Chinese source ever claims iron as an important imported trade good from anywhere in Island Southeast Asia, and as Christie points out, Chinese records show that at this time China was in fact exporting significant quantities of iron goods to Southeast Asia.[39]

In relation to the origins of Brunei, Robert Nicholl set out in two main articles published in 1980 and 1990 his theory that the Brunei rulers and their followers had been expelled from Funan around 680 CE and fled to Borneo, where they founded a new empire, originally located at Lawas, on the northern part of Brunei Bay.[40] Central to Nicholl's argument is a garbled tradition mentioned by the Arab scholar Ibn Sa'id in his *Bast al-Ard*, which he compiled from various sources in the second half of the thirteenth century.

The gist of the tradition, following Nicholl's translation from a French source, states that '[the Khmer] lived with the Chinese in the eastern ends of the earth', but after a conflict broke out, the Chinese chased the Khmer towards the island, where they stayed with their king, named Kamrun. Further conflict broke out, and a non-royal group left for Madagascar while the others stayed in the city of Komorriya.

There appears to be no reference to any particular place in the tradition, and somewhat speculatively, Nicholl reinterprets it to mean that rather than the Khmer being driven out by the Chinese, it was the Khmer themselves who drove out the people of Funan. Nicholl's perception of Funan appears to have derived from older speculative theories that have long since been discarded for lack of supporting evidence. These include the notion of Funan rulers being related to the

Sailendras and that they fled to Java, 'king of the mountain' titles for Funan rulers, and that the inhabitants may have spoken Austronesian languages.

Currently we now know more about Funan than when Nicholl espoused his theory in 1980. The previously held idea that Funan was some kind of large unitary state or empire appears to be inaccurate. It was a flawed assumption based largely on misleading references in Chinese sources that often assumed that Southeast Asian polities were inferior versions of imperial China and thus shared similar features.[41] Funan appears to have been a collection of smaller polities that were culturally very similar, and their demise was a consequence of shifting trade routes during the sixth and seventh centuries leading to a movement northwards to present-day southeastern and central Cambodia. Research on sixth- to eighth-century Khmer and Sanskrit inscriptions strongly suggests that the population of Funan were mainly Khmer, although Mon people may also have been present. There was also clear cultural continuity from the Funan period through to that of the Khmer empire.[42]

Sanib Said also sees the origins of Brunei as external, and presents a theory of a mid-ninth-century Sumatran origin. He partly drew on Nicholl's mistaken ideas that the Sribuza mentioned in Arabic texts may have been in Borneo and variants in the spelling of Srivijaya found in different Chinese sources may also refer to a polity somewhere in Borneo.[43] Sanib suggests that the arrival of the Sailendra dynasty from Java to Srivijaya in the mid-ninth century must have met with opposition from some Srivijaya nobles; consequently, they decided to move to another location, eventually Brunei Bay, where they founded a kingdom similar to Srivijaya. This too is apparently speculative. What we know about the Sailendras is gleaned from a small number of inscriptions that have seen numerous and often conflicting interpretations over the years. What does seem clear is that the Sailendras and Srivijaya had close marital and commercial ties, and their relationship does not appear to have been one of antagonism, conflict or conquest. Furthermore, the wide prestige the Sailendras had among Buddhists was probably an attraction for the Srivijaya rulers.[44]

A more likely period for any exodus from Srivijaya ports is the eleventh century, following a series of successful attacks by the south Indian Cola kingdom which severely weakened Srivijaya. Alternatively, the exodus could have occurred towards the long-drawn demise of Srivijaya from the thirteenth to fourteenth centuries. Sanib also links his theory to movements set out in the Brunei origin tradition, as in the Syair Awang Semaun, as well as similarities between some place names in Borneo and Sumatra. But many of the place names mentioned can be found throughout Island Southeast Asia, and are probably a consequence of the region's inhabitants speaking numerous related Austronesian languages. Furthermore, linguistic data suggest that any similarities in place names are more likely a result of Proto-Malay speakers moving from Borneo to Sumatra, perhaps dating from about 2,500 years ago, when Sumatra and the Malay Peninsula were colonized by Austronesian speakers. Nevertheless, Sanib's idea of a Sumatran origin for Brunei does have support from some linguistic studies that argue that there was a back-migration from Sumatra to Borneo.

Overview of archaeological sites along the northwest coast

Professional archaeological work in northwest Borneo began in 1948, when Tom Harrisson and the Sarawak Museum began to carry out a series of systematic excavations at several sites in the Sarawak river delta around Santubong. Harrisson was the leading archaeological figure in the region, and largely set the archaeological agenda with his pioneering work. Likewise in Brunei, he led the first preliminary investigations at the Kota Batu site in 1952.

Tom Harrisson's article 'The Ming Gap and Kota Batu, Brunei', published in 1958,[45] is apparently the first study that attempts to apply ceramic[46] data in relation to the history of northwest Borneo. This and his other publications, as well as those he wrote with Zainie and O'Connor, are especially important as the identifications and dates applied to ceramics were often used and referred to in later studies, in particular the identification of Tang dynasty (618–907) wares.[47] At the time when Harrisson and others wrote, knowledge of Chinese and Mainland Southeast Asian and Chinese ceramic trade wares, and their production and export dates, was largely rudimentary, and dates applied were based on the limited data available then. Current knowledge of dates and classifications is far different to Harrisson's.

Harrisson and others identified a number of the ceramics as 'Yueh-type' wares dating to the seventh to tenth centuries, during the Tang dynasty, and assigned early dates to other wares. This Tang label continues to persist in some contemporary publications despite subsequent reassessment that discarded this early dating by archaeologists, giving the mistaken impression that the northwest coast polities developed as trading centres as early as the seventh century.[48] Writing in the mid-1980s, Christie considered that none of the sherds found at Santubong sites dated to before the Song period.[49] Thereafter, Lucas Chin, who also reassessed ceramics found in Sarawak, stated that the 'Tang' identifications are more accurately assigned to the tenth to twelfth centuries.[50]

Similarly, at several sites in Brunei, ceramics recovered by archaeologists once thought to date to the Tang dynasty, following Harrisson's early classifications, have been reassessed. Matussin Omar and P.M. Shariffuddin noted that while Tang sherds were thought to have been found at Kota Batu in Brunei, they now believed that these sherds were made after the demise of the Tang dynasty.[51] Bellwood and Omar also noted that no Tang identifications could be made from the Terusan Kupang site in Brunei.[52] Pengiran Karim similarly dates nothing at any Brunei site to before the tenth century, but considers that a few of the earliest wares may date to the early tenth century, towards the close of the Tang period.[53]

The present author's observations of ceramics from Sarawak and Brunei broadly concur with these studies: namely, none can be assigned to before the tenth century. Similarly, dates for Thai and Vietnamese wares given in some earlier publications relating to this region are often too early. Sawankhalok and Sukhothai Thai wares can be dated to the fifteenth and sixteenth centuries, while in the light of the late Roxanna Brown's meticulous work on shipwreck data, in most cases Vietnamese export wares date to the fifteenth century.[54]

The Santubong sites of the Sarawak river delta

Santubong is a complex of mainly port sites strategically located for both external and internal trade. Standing at 800 metres, Mount Santubong acted as a visible marker for traders along the northwest coast, while its rivers extended far into the interior, providing vital access to a wide range of valuable forest produce in demand on the international market. Long before professional archaeological work began, the Santubong area was well known for its 'ancient pottery, obsolete beads and gold ornaments' that were sought by local people; James Brooke is said to have amassed a collection that was apparently lost when his residence was sacked during the so-called Chinese rebellion in 1857.[55]

The Santubong complex consists of six sites, which include the important iron-smelting industry that remains the largest known metal working site in pre-modern Borneo. Initial and later surveys and excavations recovered huge quantities of ceramic sherds dating from the tenth to the early fourteenth century, including some 'Yueh-type'. Large quantities of earthenware, various beads, other jewellery and numerous gold items, and Chinese coins were also recovered.[56] There was also evidence of some Buddhist influence and practice in the discovery of the so-called Tantric shrine located on Bukit Mara, within which was found a silver box with deposits of about 140 gold objects and semi-precious stones. A stone Buddha figure about 26 centimetres in height, probably of the Gupta tradition, was also found.[57]

The iron industry was one of the most important discoveries at Santubong, which Harrisson and O'Connor believed to have developed into a major industry during the tenth to fourteenth centuries and was exporting to the Chinese market. Local people working the iron presumably adopted the South Indian 'Wootz' steel method. They further suggested that the iron ore was imported from various other places throughout Borneo by boat.[58] Christie, on the other hand, has been highly critical of Harrisson and O'Connor's conclusions, arguing that the Santubong iron industry was in fact moderate in size, the sources of ore were local, as was the market, and what were thought to be crucibles were in fact tuyères, indicating indigenous technology. But more recent investigations into the Santubong iron industry, while confirming the tuyères, suggests that this industry was larger than Christie's assertion, and further smelting sites have been discovered.[59]

In Santubong's development as a polity, the earliest site appears to be at Songei Jaong in the tenth century and its nearby burial ground at Tanjong Kubor. During the following centuries, the complex expanded to Bongkissam and Songei Buah. It was perhaps in the twelfth century that the Tantric shrine on Bukit Mara, which is adjacent to Bongkissam, was used, and another burial ground was established at its foot, presumably a response to population growth.

Harrisson and O'Connor report that no sherds dating to later than around 1370 (the beginning of the Ming period) could be identified, and the complex appears to have reached its peak in the late twelfth to early thirteenth century.[60] By the second half of the fourteenth century, the sites had been abandoned. In the conspicuous absence of Ming blue and white wares in Santubong, or at the time from other sites in Sarawak, Harrisson hypothesized that there had been a localized shift in trade from Santubong to Brunei at Kota Batu around the fourteenth century, where he and others had found an abundance of Ming blue and white sherds, but very few from earlier periods in comparison to Santubong. Since then, later ceramics, including Ming blue and white, have been found in other parts of Sarawak, namely further inland and towards the east of the Santubong sites.

Gedong and Bukit Sandong

About 65 km to the east of the Sarawak river delta are several sites that were excavated after Harrisson had left Sarawak that may represent a separate development to Santubong. One of the largest and most important is located around Batang Karang at Gedong, which Chin considered to be as early as Santubong, initially suggesting it was a large burial ground despite the absence of human remains.[61] Christie's subsequent assessment is that Gedong was a large habitation site that developed a century or so later than the earliest of the Santubong sites.[62] While Gedong is located considerably inland, it was connected to the River Sadong and perhaps linked to a port closer to the coast, although Chin believed that trading boats could have sailed far inland.[63] By the fourteenth century, as with Santubong, Gedong declined, and the lack of later ceramics suggests it was abandoned by at least the mid-fourteenth century.

   About 25 km further inland from Gedong is the smaller site of Bukit Sandong. While ceramic sherds of slightly later dates than Gedong were found, the site differs significantly from those hitherto discussed, as Ming blue and white sherds dating from the fifteenth, and mainly the sixteenth and early seventeenth century, were also recovered, together with a small number of Thai wares. Bukit Sandong's main phase of occupation appears to date from about the fifteenth to seventeenth century.

Sekadang Lingga and Ensika

Northeast of Gedong and closer to the coast are two further sites that appear to be early, Sekadang Lingga and Ensika. They are located close to the Batang Lupar river, one of the widest in Borneo, and ideally situated for internal and external trade. However, little is known of these sites, and Chin merely states that Song ceramics were found at Ensika and Lingga, and Song and Ming ceramics at Sekadang.

Nanga Kalaka, Tebing Tinggi and Muroh

In the Kabong region of Sarawak, several other sites where some early ceramics have been found include Nanga Kalaka, Tebing Tinggi and Muroh.[64] The earliest appear to have been at Kalaka, perhaps dating to the tenth or eleventh century,[65] while Tebing Tinggi and Muroh perhaps date from the thirteenth.[66]

The Brunei sites

Kota Batu

The Kota Batu (stone fort) site is located on Brunei Bay, which at its widest points is nearly 50 km across. The bay itself would have been a strategic location for trade, offering protection from winds for large ships. Around Kota Batu, the estuary narrows, becoming the Brunei river, which suggests defence may have been a concern for its inhabitants as access to Kota Batu could be blockaded by boats. The Brunei river also provided significant access to the interior.

Initial results from the Tom Harrison-led excavations in 1952–53 showed that Kota Batu's participation in international trade was continuous from the tenth to seventeenth century.[67] However, early ceramics found were small in number, which was confirmed by later research.[68] While Kota Batu was an early trade centre, it is conclusive that its main growth period dates to the beginning of the Ming dynasty, in the second half of the fourteenth century, and attained its zenith in the fifteenth and sixteenth centuries.[69] Also found at Kota Batu were the remains of what has been called a 'stone wall', which can perhaps be equated with the name Kota Batu.[70]

Terusan Kupang

Terusan Kupang is located about 4 km upriver from Kota Batu via the River Mendaun, a tributary of the Brunei river. Its location is strategic, as it not only connects to river systems that provide access to various valuable forest produce from the interior, but also has two outlets to Brunei Bay, one leading to Kota Batu, and the other to Limbang. Following excavations by Omar and Bellwood, it became evident in the late 1970s that Terusan Kupang was the most important Song period site in Brunei.[71] Much early research focused on earthenware, but it was nevertheless evident that most of the imported ceramics dated from before the Ming period, as few Ming or Thai sherds were present, suggesting that the site was largely depopulated by the Ming period.[72]

Further work, particularly the surface surveys carried out by Pengiran Karim, have revealed a similar pattern in terms of dates and occupation, with large quantities of early sherds, including 'Yueh-type', dating from the tenth to fourteenth century comprising almost 90 per cent of ceramic finds with only a fraction dating to the fifteenth and sixteenth centuries or later.[73] Given the growth of Kota Batu in the fourteenth century and the decline of Terusan Kupang at this time, it has been argued that Terusan Kupang was the centre of Brunei until the fourteenth century, when there was a major population shift to Kota Batu.[74]

The true extent of the Terusan Kupang site is, however, not fully understood, and it may be linked to the adjacent Jai-jai site in Limbang, as suggested by Pengiran Karim, constituting a single territory.[75]

Sungai Limau Manis

The Sungai Limau Manis site is located some distance inland, about 30 km upriver from Kota Batu along the Limau Manis river. This is a tributary of the Brunei river, and the location would thus have provided a river connection to Brunei Bay and both Kota Batu and Terusan Kupang. The site was discovered inadvertently in 2002 as the river was being widened and deepened, leading to a salvage archaeological operation by the Brunei Museum.

The Sungai Limau Manis site was clearly a large and important urban centre that thrived on trade. The impressive finds from this site include nearly 50,000 sherds from imported wares that are predominantly pre-Ming, dating from the tenth to fourteenth century, with hardly any later Ming, Thai or Vietnamese sherds found.[76] In fact, several hundreds of the early Chinese wares were found either in perfect condition or almost wholly intact. Also salvaged were a large number of Chinese copper cash coins, parts of the hulls of several wooden riverine boats, various house posts, kitchen implements, wooden artefacts including a face mask, beads, glass bracelets, stone tools, shells, animal bones, and a small amount of gold jewellery in the form of rings and bracelets. There was also evidence of small-scale iron-working.

Similarly to the Santubong sites and Terusan Kupang, Songai Limau Manis appears to have experienced a sudden decline in the mid-fourteenth century. The hundreds of intact ceramic wares, gold jewellery and over 1,000 Chinese coins that were left at the site suggest that this abandonment was abrupt and there had been a major upheaval. Reasons suggested for this rapid abandonment include war, possibly disease, or the emergence of a new power at Kota Batu.[77] All are valid suggestions. As Kota Batu, which appears to have been a much smaller site before the mid-fourteenth century, and Terusan Kupang were in positions to restrict access to Brunei Bay, the large site at Songai Limau Manis was probably linked to one or both of these coastal trading centres, and it seems unlikely that non-Borneo traders came directly to the site because of this and its inland location. Given that Terusan Kupang and Songai Limau Manis appear to have declined at about the same time, coinciding with the expansion of Kota Batu, a possibility is that the population of the latter was forcibly relocated to Kota Batu.

Other smaller sites in Brunei include Pulau Chermin, which was linked to Kota Batu, and Sungai Limut, which dates to the fifteenth to sixteenth centuries and may have been a burial, or at least a ritual, area. Ceramics have also been found in small numbers at other sites, including Tanjong Batu at Muara, although this is not strictly a site, but where ceramics have been washed ashore from a shipwreck.

Limbang sites

JAI-JAI

The Jai-jai site is located close to the Limbang river, giving direct access to Brunei Bay. In addition to being well situated for external trade, as with many other sites along the northwest coast, it was well connected to the interior through river systems, allowing it to draw on the rich forest resources of its hinterland.

Jai-jai is a potentially important site, but little data is available. Pengiran Karim has suggested that it was linked to the Terusan Kupang site and that they were perhaps a single polity. However, he considered Jai-jai to be richer in archaeological remains than Terusan Kupang, particularly in imported ceramics.[78] A small selection of sherds from Jai-jai is held at the Limbang Museum. A closer examination of the exhibits by the present author revealed tenth-century 'Yue-type', northern and southern Song and a thirteenth- to fourteenth-century Yuan sherd. According to information presented at the Limbang Museum, sixteenth-century ceramics have also been found.

Two important finds have come from Bukit Mas, which is located in the modern town of Limbang that overlooks the Limbang river. The first was in 1899, when a landslide revealed about 25 gold objects, which included beads, buckles, rings chains, a phallic pendant, ear and nose ornaments, and a small gold bar.[79] Secondly, in 1912, a stone Ganesa (elephant-headed Hindu God) was found at the base of the hill during building work.[80] At the time of writing, Harrisson noted that further building work on the hill revealed no evidence of occupation or a religious, shrine and suggested that the objects found may simply have been hidden there.[81] Both the gold hoard and the Ganesa are believed to be of Javanese influence, and possibly made in Java. The Ganesa's provenance dated to the thirteenth–fourteenth century, while the gold items dated from 1200–1500.[82]

Melanau areas, Niah caves and Sabah

No serious archaeological work in areas inhabited by coastal Melanau people, around the Rajang river, Mukah and Bintulu, has been undertaken. Nevertheless, these areas were clearly important, and Chin notes that the Melanau living in coastal areas seem to have been engaged in maritime activities from the tenth century and the only people of Sarawak to possess ceramics that range from the tenth century through to the nineteenth century.[83]

A small number of tenth-century and later ceramics have been found at the Niah caves, which have long been a valuable source of swiftlet bird nests for the Chinese market. Most of the ceramics are associated with burials. Only a few early ceramics have currently been found in Sabah, too. Some early wares, as early as the tenth century, have been found, but most appear to date to the fifteenth century or later.[84]

Discussion

From about the early tenth century to about 1300, Southeast Asia was part of a major trade boom encompassing India, the Middle East, and in particular China. Geoff Wade argues that the consequences of this major expansion of trade were far-reaching in these regions and Southeast Asia, leading to the emergence of new ports and urban centres, population growth and movements of people towards coastal areas, increased interaction between trading communities, the development of new industries, trade-related warfare, a growth in monetization, and the expansion of Theravada Buddhism and Islam.[85] A number of these consequences are visible along the northwest coast of Borneo, in particular the emergence of ports, development of urban centres and population growth. Perhaps, too, there was a development of Buddhism, as suggested by evidence from Santubong and Limbang, and there is the possibility that trade-related warfare led to the demise of Sungai Limau Manis. It was during this period that the northwest coast of Borneo and the Philippines, which had been areas of peripheral interest in earlier periods, became incorporated into major trade networks and emerged as prominent players in commerce during the Song and Yuan periods.[86]

This boom in trade, which can be seen all along the northwest coast of Borneo, was linked to the large-scale commercial growth in China during the Northern and Southern Song periods (960–1127, 1127–1279), which saw a major expansion of Song maritime trade, new policies in relation to foreign trade and liberalized shipping regulations.[87] Increased trade with Southeast Asia and other regions further increased demand for Chinese ceramics, creating new production centres in China and product diversity to meet growing demand.[88] Particularly important in trade with Southeast Asia was the city of Quanzhou, which rose to prominence in the twelfth century. From that time, relations between its traders and those of Southeast Asia accelerated. Quanzhou was a cosmopolitan and religiously diverse city where the most prosperous traders were Muslims of both Chinese and non-Chinese ethnicity.[89]

Thereafter, during the succeeding Yuan dynasty (1271–1368), similar policies of maritime trade with Southeast Asia continued. Much of the maritime trade during this Mongol-ruled period was in the hands of non-Chinese allied with officials or noble families, particularly in southern ports such as Quanzhou, where Muslim traders continued to dominate.[90] Given the importance of Quanzhou from the twelfth century, a trade relationship with northwest coastal areas of Borneo is undoubtedly apparent, and the tombstones found in Brunei suggest that this relationship was particularly important.

But just how dependent on trade with Quanzhou were the Borneo northwest coast polities? There is presently insufficient data to identify what other trade networks were linked to this region of Borneo and what their extent was. The evident collapse of numerous polities along the northwest coast of Borneo around the later Yuan period suggests that the Quanzhou trade was of fundamental importance to their existence. Quanzhou's decline as a major trading centre began in the mid-1350s, and came to an end in 1366 following a ten-year war that began when Muslim traders launched the Ipsah Rebellion. Their defeat led to a massacre of Muslims and marked the end of Quanzhou as a major trading centre.[91] Shortly after, the Ming Hongwu emperor (1368–98) imposed restrictions on Chinese foreign trade and merchants, leading to a major reduction in the quantity of Chinese ceramics exported to Southeast Asia.[92] As the Quanzhou trade came to an end, so did many of the trading partners/clients along the northwest coast. Unlike Java and South Sulawesi, the Bornean polities had no agrarian base, and without the lifeblood of trade, their demise was inevitable. At Kota Batu, Brunei emerged in the early Ming period as the northwest coast's leading trade centre – one of numerous other Borneo coastal polities over which the Javanese Majapahit kingdom claimed nominal suzerainty.

Traditions, origins and languages

A major factor in the emergence of polities along the northwest coast of Borneo was the development of trade, but were they established and developed by foreigners, as Cheng, Nicholl and Sanib Said have argued, or by indigenous communities? It is undoubted, despite the lack of archaeological data, that any trading centre in Melanau-speaking areas was founded by indigenous non-Malay speakers, as they continue to inhabit many of these areas to the present day. But for Santubong and the Brunei Bay area, the origins of the founders are less clear.

One problem in identifying the founders and inhabitants of Santubong is that the site was abandoned by the early to mid-fourteenth century and has no connection to the nearby present-day Malay settlement. Harrisson, however, believed the burials at Santubong were characteristic of the Melanau, who he believed formerly occupied the area.[93] Other non-Malay-speaking Borneo peoples had similar burial traditions, and this at least suggests that the bulk of the population were indigenous, likewise the reassessed iron-working data.

In this connection, the well-known Datu Merpati traditions should be briefly considered. Datu Merpati's arrival in Sarawak is linked to Tanjung Datu, about 75 km east of Santubong. Harrisson collected numerous versions of this tradition, and notes that this folk tale often had different meanings for different ethnic groups.[94] In many versions, Datu Merpati's ancestry is pedigreed and prestigious: a Minangkabau noble and grandson of a Raja Jawa, who came to Sarawak from Sumatra together with his wife, a daughter of the ruler of Johor. In some versions, the couple's offspring are said to have become rulers of places around the Sarawak river and eastwards to the Rejang river. The best-known of the traditions are the Malay versions that claim Datu Merpati as the first Muslim immigrant to the region, thereby suggesting they post-date Santubong. A link to Islam is also common in traditions propagated by other groups.

The tradition of Brunei's origin is of an entirely different nature to the Datu Merpati traditions. Brunei's provenance is set out in the *Syair Awang Semaun*, a long epic poem written in Jawi that recounts the origin and development of Brunei. There are various versions of the *Syair* which are collations from earlier oral accounts. To date no full-length versions of the *Syair* have been published, although various partial summaries and related oral accounts that have been collected and are available.[95]

There are several features of the *Syair* that will be briefly highlighted in relation to the origins of Brunei (and Limbang). These include the association of the father of the first ruler with the upper Limbang valley, and various movements by his 14 sons prior to the establishment of Brunei that can be identified with the Brunei Bay area and its immediate hinterland. Although nothing is said regarding the ethnicity of the 14 children, they are commonly believed to be Murut. Oral Murut traditions also claim that Awang Alak Betatar, the son who became the first ruler of Brunei, was a Murut. Traditions of the Bisaya, who inhabit the Limbang region today, contend that he was Bisaya.[96] A particularly Borneo feature found in a number of parts of the *Syair* that has been highlighted by Maxwell, is the large amount of head-taking executed following victory in battles.[97] Interestingly, however, when the followers offer the severed heads to Awang Alak Betatar, he declines to accept them, suggesting that he may be culturally different.

Overall, the *Syair* presents an indigenous Borneo account of Brunei's origins by people who appear to have lived in the vicinity of Brunei Bay and its hinterland, some of whom may have been Murut or Bisaya. As both these ethnic groups speak non-Malay languages, the obvious question that needs to be addressed is how we account for the large, sophisticated Malay sultanate that developed in Brunei, as described by Pigafetta in 1521. It has been well documented that the majority of the peoples in Borneo who identify themselves as Malay are, in fact, descendants of various Dayak groups who, following conversion to Islam, adopted Malay language and culture,[98] a process that continues to the present that began several centuries after polities along the northwest coast were founded. Can linguistic studies shed light on this matter?

Linguistic and archaeological evidence shows that speakers of Austronesian languages began moving into Island Southeast Asia from Taiwan about 4,500 years ago, initially into the Philippines, and thereafter Borneo and Sulawesi, later colonizing the remaining parts of Island Southeast Asia, southern Vietnam, the Pacific Islands and Madagascar.[99] One of the numerous proto-languages that developed in Island Southeast Asia from Proto-Austronesian was Proto-Malay. There is broad agreement among linguists that this development took place in Borneo 2,000–3,000 years ago, and that Proto-Malay is the ancestor of all languages within the Malayic-Dayak family, including Malay proper and its dialects.

Adelaar and Blust have argued that while the ancestral origins of the Malay language lie in Borneo, the development of the modern Malay language and culture took place in southeast Sumatra.[100] In support of this, they refer to the epigraphical data in the form of various Sanskrit inscriptions in old Malay that are associated with Srivijaya and the reference to a place called 'Melayu' in this region of Sumatra by the Chinese Buddhist monk I Ching. Adelaar and Blust are thus of the opinion that while Borneo is the home of Proto-Malay, the existence of the Malay language and culture in Borneo is a consequence of a 'back-migration' of Malay speakers from Sumatra to Borneo that took place as Srivijayan trade networks began to expand.

Still seen as controversial, Bernd Nothofer and James Collins have argued that Borneo is not simply the homeland of Proto-Malay, but also where the Malay language and, to some degree, culture developed, although their supporting arguments based on archaeological data are weak.[101] They also argued that the Brunei-Malay dialect developed solely in Borneo, but was later subject to some external influence. Of potential importance in the possible autonomous development of the Malay language in the Brunei region are the Kedayan people, who in 1991

shared 80 per cent cognates with Standard Malay.[102] The Kedayan were traditionally inland farming people living in the immediate hinterland of Brunei Bay, and
while closely linked with the Brunei Malays at Kampong Ayer, were culturally
very different. Of particular significance is that Kedayan has retained the Proto-
Malay *h*,[103] which suggests that the Kedayan and their dialect of Malay developed in Borneo, probably in the hinterland of Brunei Bay. While Brunei Malay
has not retained this feature, its speakers had a long period of direct interaction
with external traders, Malay being used as a lingua franca, which may account
for this. There is also the probability of linguistic and cultural influence in later
periods, such as after the decline of Srivijaya and later in the early sixteenth century following the fall of Melaka and dispersal of traders to other ports in Island
Southeast Asia such as Brunei. Further linguistic research is needed in this region,
and Borneo as a whole, before more confident conclusions can be drawn.

A major stimulus for the rise and development of the northwest coast polities
was the incorporation of the region into a major international trading network from
the tenth century onward. These polities probably comprised various Borneo ethnic groups that were supplemented by transient foreign traders. There is no evidence to suggest any were founded by people from outside Borneo, and in the case
of Brunei, there is clearly the possibility that some of its founders were indigenous
Borneo Malay speakers. Indic influences in this period also appear to have been of
marginal importance, visible only in the limited finds at Santubong, particularly the
small twelfth-century Tantric shrine, and the Bukit Mas objects of obscure provenance. Unless evidence to the contrary emerges, the origins and development of
Borneo's northwest coast polities should be seen as inherently local.

Notes

1 See, for example, Graeme Barker et al., 'Foraging–farming Transitions at the Niah
   Caves, Sarawak, Borneo', *Antiquity*, 85 (2011): 492–509.
2 For example, Cheng Te-k'un, *Archaeology in Sarawak* (Cambridge: W. Heffer and
   Sons for University of Toronto Press, 1969); Robert Nicholl, 'Brunei Rediscovered:
   A Survey of Early Times', *Brunei Museum Journal*, 4 (1980): 219–37; Robert Nicholl,
   'A Study of the Origins of Brunei', *Brunei Museum Journal*, 7 (1990): 20–31; Sanib
   Said, 'Pembentukan kerajaan Brunei lama: Teori Penghijrahan dari Sumatera' ['The
   Establishment of Old Brunei Government: Migration Theory from Sumatra'], *Jurnal
   Darussalam*, 1 (1992): 88–100.
3 In this chapter, the term 'Malay' refers to people who spoke Malay, or one of its dia-
   lects, as a first language in the past, not to speakers of other Austronesian languages in
   Island Southeast Asia.
4 Peter Bellwood and Peter Koon, 'Lapita Colonists Leave Boats Unburned!' The
   Question of Lapita Links with Island Southeast Asia', *Antiquity*, 63 (1989): 613–22.
5 Stephen Chia, 'Archaeological Evidence of Early Human Occupation in Malaysia',
   in *Austronesian Diaspora and the Ethnogenesis of People in [the] Indonesian
   Archipelago: Proceedings of the International Symposium*, edited by Truman
   Simanjuntak et al. (Jakarta: LIPI, 2006), p. 249. Two other Dongson drums about
   2,000 years old were found at Bukit Selindung in Sambas, Kalimantan in the early

1990s; see E. Edwards McKinnon, 'The Sambas Hoard: Bronze Drums and Gold Ornaments Found in Kalimantan in 1991', *Journal of the Malaysian Branch of the Royal Asiatic Society*, 67 (1994): 9–28.

6 B.C. Chhabra, *Expansion of Indo-Aryan Culture during Pallava Rule (as Evidenced by Inscriptions)* (Delhi: Munshi Ram Manohar Lal, 1965), pp. 50–52, 85–92; J.G. de Casparis, *Indonesian Palaeography: A History of Writing in Indonesia from the Beginning to c. A.D. 1500* (Leiden: E.J. Brill, 1975), pp. 14–18.

7 Jan Wisseman Christie, 'The Sanskrit Inscriptions Recently Discovered in Kedah, Malaysia', in *Modern Quaternary Research in Southeast Asia*, edited by Jan Bartstra and Willem Arnold Casparie (Rotterdam: A.A. Balkeme, 1990), p. 49.

8 P.M. Shariffuddin and Robert Nicholl, 'A Possible Example of Ancient Brunei Script', *Brunei Museum Journal*, 3 (1975): 116–22; Arvind Sharma, 'The Interpretation of a Sanskrit Inscription in the Ancient Script of Brunei', *Journal of the Malaysian Branch of the Royal Asiatic Society*, 52 (1979): 99–101.

9 Shariffuddin and Nicholl, 'A Possible Example', p. 117.

10 Matassim bin Haji Jibah, 'Notes on Tombstones Recently Found in Brunei', *Brunei Museum Journal*, 5 (1982): 19–36.

11 Ibid, p. 23.

12 Ibid, pp. 24–5. A copy of this stone can be seen in Limbang Museum. Sanib Said et al. appear to assume that the Buang Abai stone is connected to the 25 gold pieces and Ganesa found at Limbang hill and that these are all a consequence of Javanese influence in the twelfth and thirteenth century; see Sanib bin Haji Said et al., *Dahulu Terasing Kini Terjalin: Bahagian Limbang-Daerah Limbang dan Lawas* [*Divided in the Past, Enjoined at the Present: Limbang Division-Limbang and Lawas District*] (Sarawak: Pejabat Residen Bahagian Limbang, 2009), p. 3.

13 Jan Wisseman Christie, 'State Formation in Early Maritime Southeast Asia: A Consideration of the Theories and the Data', *Bijdragen tot de Taal-, Land- en Volkenkunde*, 151 (1995): 235–88 at 257–62.

14 Wang Gungwu, 'The Nanhai Trade: A Study of the Early History of Chinese Trade in the South China Sea', *Journal of the Malaysian Branch of the Royal Asiatic Society*, 31 (1958): 1–135.

15 These toponyms include Yeh-po-ti, Vijayapura, Poli, Poluo, and even the Sribuza referred to in Arabic texts. It is beyond the scope of this chapter to give a brief summary of studies that have attempted to associate these toponyms with numerous localities in Island Southeast Asia. It should, however, be noted that Sribuza is clearly a reference to Srivijaya in Sumatra. See Kenneth R. Hall, *A History of Early Southeast Asia: Maritime Trade and Societal Development, 100–1500* (New York: Rowman & Littlefield, 2011), pp. 129–30. See also G.R. Tibbetts, *A Study of the Arabic Texts Containing Material on South-East Asia* (Leiden: Brill, 1979), p. 113, and R.E. Jordaan and B.E. Colless, *The Mahārājas of the Isles: The Śailendras and the Problem of Śrīvijaya* (Leiden: Department of Languages and Cultures of Southeast Asia and Oceania, University of Leiden, 2009), p. 66. Possibly the earliest references to Borneo in Chinese sources are brief mentions to two places, c. 250 CE: P'u-lo-chung and Chu-po. Chu-po has been associated with the northern coast of Kalimantan/Sabah, and P'u-lo-chung, where the Chinese claimed there were cannibals with tails, around the Sarawak river delta. Hitherto, there is no reference to these toponyms in later sources.

16 Paul M. Munoz, *Early Kingdoms of the Indonesian Archipelago and the Malay Peninsula* (Singapore: Editions Didier Millet, 2006), p. 84. Other problems relating to the identification of Southeast Asian toponyms in Chinese sources and the

shortcomings of the sources themselves have been highlighted by Johannes L. Kurz in two recent articles: 'Pre-modern Chinese Sources in the National History of Brunei: The Case of Poli', *Bijdragen tot de Taal-, Land- en Volkenkunde*, 169 (2013): 213–43, and 'Boni in Chinese Sources from the Tenth to the Eighteenth Century', *International Journal of Asia-Pacific Studies*, 10(1) (2014): 1–32.

17 Poli disappears from Chinese records after 630 CE, and its trade with China belongs to an earlier period. Wang, 'The Nanhai Trade', p. 95.

18 O.W. Wolters, *Early Indonesian Commerce: A Study of the Origins of Srivijaya* (Ithaca, NY: Cornell University Press, 1967), p. 169.

19 Ibid, p. 201.

20 Nicholl's assertion that Poli was a precursor to Brunei is partly based on Braddell's flawed work that attempted to identify Poli as situated in southwest Borneo and inadvertently conflated Poli with Poluo. Geoff Wade, 'Po-luo and Borneo – a Re-examination', *Brunei Museum Journal*, 6 (1986): 13–35, demonstrates that the Poluo in question was connected neither to Poli nor Borneo; see also Nicholl, 'Brunei Rediscovered', p. 221; Roland Braddell, 'A Note on Sambas and Borneo', *Journal of the Malayan Branch of the Royal Asiatic Society*, 22(4) (1949): 1–15. Poli is most commonly associated by scholars with east Java and Bali. The admittedly vague Chinese sources claim that rice was planted twice a year in Poli, which, if correctly reported, is highly unlikely to refer to Borneo, with its infertile soils. Java and Bali are more likely locations.

21 Wang, 'The Nanhai Trade', p. 57.

22 Kurz, 'Pre-modern Chinese Sources'.

23 In many publications, Boni has been rendered as P'o-ni, Po-ni, or B'o-ni. In the old Wade-Giles transliteration system, only Po-ni is correct. In the modern Chinese Hanyu pinyin system, Boni is the correct transcription. See Kurz, 'Boni in Chinese Sources', p. 2.

24 Pelliot (first published in French in 1904) assumed that the first mention of 'Boni' was in the late ninth-century *Manshu* work. Kurz refuted this assumption, as this is not a reference to a place, but to an ethnic group. He translates the sentence mentioning Boni as: 'And then there are several peoples living in the foreign regions to the south, such as the Poluomen, Bosi, Shepo, *Boni*, and Kunlun' (my emphasis). From his examination of the sources, Kurz concludes that the Chinese court had no knowledge of Boni before the year 977; Kurz, 'Boni in Chinese Sources', p. 4.

25 Robert Nicholl, 'Notes on the Early Toponymy of Brunei', *Brunei Museum Journal*, 3 (1975): 123–30 (as one example); Pehin Mohammed Jamil Al-Sufri, *Tarsilah Brunei: Sejarah Awal dan Perkembangan Islam* [*Brunei Inscriptions: Early History and the Development of Islam*], rev. edn (Bandar Seri Begawan: Pusat Sejarah Brunei, 2001), pp. 8–13; Pengiran Karim bin Pengiran Haji Osman, 'The Evidence of Oriental Ceramics and Earthenware Distributions in Brunei Darussalam as an Aid in Understanding Protohistoric Brunei' (PhD thesis, University of Southampton, 1997).

26 Pengiran Karim, 'The Evidence of Oriental Ceramics', p. 327.

27 Jan Wisseman Christie, 'On Po-ni: The Santubong Sites of Sarawak', *Sarawak Museum Journal*, 34 (1985): 77–89, and 'Trade and the Santubong Iron Industry', in *Southeast Asian Archaeology 1986: Proceedings of the First Conference of the Association of Southeast Asian Archaeologists in Western Europe*, edited by Ian Glover and Emily Glover (Oxford: British Archaeological Reports, International Series 561, 1986).

28 Derek Heng, *Sino-Malay Trade and Diplomacy from the Tenth through the Fourteenth Century* (Athens, OH: Ohio University Press, 2009), p. 39.

29 Kenneth R. Hall, 'Sojourning Communities, Ports-of-trade, and Commercial Networking in Southeast Asia's Eastern Regions, c. 1000–1400', in *New Perspectives on the History and Historiography of Southeast Asia: Continuing Explorations*, edited by Michael Arthur Aung-Thwin and Kenneth R. Hall (London: Routledge, 2011), pp. 57, 60.

30 E. Edwards McKinnon, 'Buddhism and the Pre-Islamic Archaeology of Kutei', in *Studies in Southeast Asian Art: Essays in Honor of Stanley J. O'Connor*, edited by Nora A. Taylor (Ithaca, NY: Southeast Asia Program, Cornell University, 2000), p. 222.

31 Kurz, 'Boni in Chinese Sources', p. 3.

32 For Pigafetta's account of Brunei, see Antonio Pigafetta, *First Voyage Round the World by Magellan, Translated from the Accounts of Pigafetta, and Other Contemporary Writers* (London: Hakluyt Society, 1874), pp. 111–18.

33 Wolfgang Franke and Ch'en T'ien-fan, 'A Chinese Inscription of A.D. 1264, Discovered Recently in Brunei: A Preliminary Report', *Brunei Museum Journal*, 3 (1973): 91–9; Chen Da-sheng, 'A Brunei Sultan in the Early 14th Century: Study of an Arabic Tombstone', *Journal of Southeast Asian Studies*, 23 (1992): 1–13; Pengiran Karim bin Pengiran Haji Osman, 'Further Notes on a Chinese Tombstone Inscription of A.D. 1264', *Brunei Museum Journal*, 8 (1993): 1–10. Kurz, however, cautions about the lack of proof regarding a Quanzhou connection and the apparent lack of evidence for the conclusions drawn regarding Master Pu's identity, ancestry and religion; Kurz, 'Boni in Chinese Sources', p. 10.

34 Chen Da-sheng, 'A Brunei Sultan'.

35 Cheng Te-k'un, *Archaeology in Sarawak*.

36 Tom Harrisson and Stanley J. O'Connor Jr, *Excavations of the Prehistoric Iron Industry in West Borneo*, Data Paper no. 72, 2 vols (Ithaca, NY: Cornell University Southeast Asia Program, 1969), vol. 1, p. 164.

37 Christie, 'On Po-ni', pp. 83–5; Christie, 'Trade and the Santubong Iron Industry', pp. 235–6.

38 F.E. Treloar, 'Chemical Analysis of Iron, Iron Slag and Pottery Remains of the Prehistoric Iron Industry of the Sarawak River Delta', *Sarawak Museum Journal*, 26 (1978): 125–33 at 131; Christie, 'On Po-ni', p. 84; C. Doherty et al., 'Archaeological Investigations at Songai Santubong, Kuching, Sarawak 2006', *Sarawak Museum Journal*, 63 (2007): 65–94 at 73–4. O'Connor himself also reconsidered the identification of crucibles, acknowledging that they were probably tuyères. See Stanley J. O'Connor, 'Tom Harrisson and the Ancient Iron Industry of the Sarawak River Delta', *Journal of the Malaysian Branch of the Royal Asiatic Society*, 50 (1977): 4–7.

39 Christie, 'Trade and the Santubong Iron Industry', p. 236.

40 Nicholl, 'Brunei Rediscovered', and Robert Nicholl, 'A Study of the Origins of Brunei', *Brunei Museum Journal*, 7 (1990): 20–31.

41 Or, as Lieberman puts it: 'Chinese sources awarded this area, known as "Funan", an exaggerated political solidity, for in truth what Chinese writers, eager to flatter their emperor, described as a substantial tributary kingdom seems to have been no more than an unstable network of superficially Indianized ports and small principalities'; Victor Lieberman, *Strange Parallels: Southeast Asia in Global Context, c. 800–1830*, vol. 1, *Integration of the Mainland* (Cambridge: Cambridge University Press, 2003).

42 Claude Jacques, '"Funan", "Zhenla": The Reality Concealed by These Chinese Views of Indochina', in *Early South East Asia: Essays in Archaeology, History, and Historical Geography*, edited by R.B. Smith and W. Watson (New York: Oxford University Press, 1979), pp. 371–9; Michael D. Coe, 'Winds of Change: The Early

Kingdoms Period', in *Angkor and the Khmer Civilization (Ancient Peoples and Places)* (New York: Thames and Hudson, 2003), pp. 57–96; Michael Vickery, 'Funan Reviewed: Deconstructing the Ancients', *Bulletin de l'Ecole française d'Extrême-Orient*, 90 (2003): 101–43.; Miriam Stark, 'From Funan to Angkor: Collapse and Regeneration in Ancient Cambodia', in *After Collapse: The Regeneration of Complex Societies*, edited by G. Schwartz and J. Nichols (Tucson, AZ: University of Arizona Press, 2006).

43 Sanib Said, 'Pembentukan kerajaan Brunei lama'.

44 William A. Southworth, 'Sailendras: A Javanese Buddhist Dynasty', in *Southeast Asia: A Historical Encyclopedia, from Angkor Wat to East Timor*, vol. 3, edited by Ooi Keat Gin (Santa Barbara, CA: ABC Clio, 2004), pp. 1,167–8.

45 Tom Harrisson, 'The Ming Gap and Kota Batu, Brunei', *Sarawak Museum Journal*, 8 (1958): 273–7.

46 In this chapter, the term 'ceramics' includes imported stoneware, but excludes earthenware.

47 Harrisson, 'The Ming Gap'; Carla Zainie and Tom Harrisson, 'Early Chinese Stonewares Excavated in Sarawak, 1947–67' *Sarawak Museum Journal*, 15 (1967): 30–90; Harrisson and O'Connor, *Excavations*.

48 Two examples of this persistent reference to Tang are found in Geoffrey C. Gunn, *History Without Borders: The Making of an Asian World Region, 1000–1800* (Hong Kong: Hong Kong University Press, 2011), p. 91, and Wan Kong Ann, 'Examining the Connection between Ancient China and Borneo through Santubong Archaeological Sites', *Sino-Platonic Papers*, 236 (2013): 1–18.

49 Christie, 'On Po-ni', pp. 80–81.

50 Lucas Chin, *Ceramics in the Sarawak Museum* (Kuching: Sarawak Museum, 1988), pp. 1–2.

51 Matussin Omar and P.M. Shariffuddin, 'Distribution of Chinese and Siamese Ceramics in Brunei', *Brunei Museum Journal*, 4 (1978): 59–65 at 65.

52 Peter Bellwood and Matussin bin Omar, 'Trade Patterns and Political Developments in Brunei and Adjacent Areas, A.D. 700–1500', *Brunei Museum Journal*, 4 (1980): 155–79 at 161.

53 Pengiran Karim, 'The Evidence of Oriental Ceramics'.

54 Roxanna Brown, 'The Ming Gap and Shipwreck Ceramics in Southeast Asia' (PhD thesis, University of California, Los Angeles, 2004).

55 Harold H. Everett and John Hewitt, 'A History of Santubong, an Island Off the Coast of Sarawak', *Journal of the Straits Branch of the Royal Asiatic Society*, 51 (1909): 1–30 at 6.

56 The coins dated from the eighth to twelfth century, and were used to support the early dates given to ceramics. However, Chinese coins remained in circulation for centuries after being made, and consequently cannot be used for dating. Furthermore, old Chinese coins appear to have been exported to Southeast Asia up to 900 years after they were made. The Rang Kwien wreck off Thailand carried several tonnes of Chinese coins, an analysis of which showed that ages ranged from the fourth century through to the reign of Hongwu (1368–98). See Jeremy Green and Rosemary Harper, 'Maritime Archaeology in Thailand: Seven Wrecksites', in *Proceedings of the Second Southern Hemisphere Conference on Maritime Archaeology 1983*, edited by W. Jeffery and J. Amess (Adelaide: South Australia Department of Environment and Planning and the Commonwealth Department of Home Affairs and Environment, 1983), pp. 153–74.

57 Griswold could not date the image, which he believed was not of Borneo origin, but from photographs the British Museum dated it to *c.* eighth–ninth century. See A.B. Griswold 'The Santubong Buddha and its Context', *Sarawak Museum Journal*, 11 (1962): 363–71. Associated archaeological evidence suggests it may date to some time in the early second millennium.

58 Harrisson and O'Connor, *Excavations*, p. 164.

59 Doherty et al., 'Archaeological Investigations'.

60 Harrisson and O'Connor, *Excavations*, p. 19.

61 Lucas Chin, 'Trade Pottery Discovered in Sarawak from 1948 to 1976', *Sarawak Museum Journal*, 25 (1977), 1–7; *Archaeological Work in Sarawak: With Special Reference to Niah Caves*, Sarawak Museum Occasional Paper no. 1 (Kuching: Vanguard Press, 1980).

62 Christie, 'On Po-ni', p. 82.

63 Chin, 'Trade Pottery', p. 6.

64 At present, these sites, as with the two previously mentioned, are not regarded as significant in relation to Santubong and Gedong; see Christie, 'On Po-ni', p. 82. However, data remain limited, and it is possible they are of greater significance than currently thought.

65 Chin, 'Archaeological Work', p. 29.

66 Christie, 'On Po-ni', p. 82.

67 Tom Harrisson and Barbara Harrisson, 'Kota Batu in Brunei', *Sarawak Museum Journal*, 7 (1956): 283–319 at 290.

68 Barbara Harrisson, 'A Classification of Archaeological Trade Ceramics from Kota Batu, Brunei', *Brunei Museum Journal*, 2 (1970): 114–88. Pengiran Karim provides a summary of later research, including his own in 'The Evidence of Oriental Ceramics', pp. 117–32.

69 It was the large number of Ming sherds, which were not found by Harrisson in Sarawak, that led him to coin the phrase 'Ming Gap', a term which today has a different meaning. Following Brown's work, a small number of these Ming sherds date to the latter part of the fourteenth century, and the majority to the sixteenth. The fifteenth century would have been compensated by Thai and Vietnamese wares.

70 See Matussin Omar, 'A Note on the Stone Wall and Earthen Causeway at Kota Batu', *Brunei Museum Journal*, 5 (1983): 27–50.

71 Matussin Omar and Shariffuddin, 'Distribution of Chinese and Siamese Ceramics', p. 64; Bellwood and Omar, 'Trade Patterns'.

72 Cf. Matussin Omar, *Archaeological Excavations in Protohistoric Brunei* (Bandar Seri Begawan: Muzium Brunei, 1981); Bellwood and Omar, 'Trade Patterns', p. 161.

73 Pengiran Karim, 'The Evidence of Oriental Ceramics', pp. 109–14.

74 Ibid, p. 325.

75 Ibid, p. 106.

76 Pengiran Karim bin Pengiran Haji Osman, ed., *Songai Limau Manis: Tapak arkeologi abad ke 10–13 Mashih [Songai Limau Manis: Archaeological Site of the 10th–13th Century AD]*, (Bandar Seri Begawan: Muzium Brunei, 2004), pp. 18–19.

77 Ibid, p. 167.

78 Ibid, p. 94.

79 Tom Harrisson, 'The Golden Hoard of Limbang', *Brunei Museum Journal*, 1 (1969): 57–71.

80 Ibid, p. 60.

81 Ibid, pp. 60, 70.

82 Ibid, p. 70.

83 Chin, *Ceramics in the Sarawak Museum*, p. 3.

84 See Tom Harrisson and Barbara Harrisson, *The Prehistory of Sabah*, Sabah Society *Journal*, 4 (special monograph) (1971).

85 Geoff Wade, 'An Earlier Age of Commerce in Southeast Asia, 900–1300 CE', *Journal of Southeast Asian Studies*, 40 (2009): 221–65. Wade is also referring to other places outside Southeast Asia. See also Jan Wisseman Christie, 'Javanese Markets and the Asian Sea Trade Boom of the Tenth to Thirteenth Centuries A.D.', *Journal of the Economic and Social History of the Orient*, 41 (1998): 344–81.

86 During this period, China was the major market for Borneo camphor and was no longer dependent on Sumatra camphor; Hall, 'Sojourning Communities', p. 57. See also Wai Toon Han, 'Notes on Bornean Camphor Imported to China', *Brunei Museum Journal*, 6 (1985): 1–31.

87 Wade, 'An Earlier Age', p. 225; Hall, *A History of Early Southeast Asia*, p. 33.

88 Wade, 'An Earlier Age', p. 226.

89 Also linked to the development and expansion of ports along the northwest coast was a change in trading patterns as a consequence of successful attacks on Srivijayan ports by the South Indian Cola kingdom in 1024–25 that to some extent coincided with the Song commercial expansion. Traders then began to seek out other markets in Southeast Asia as well as the source of the trade goods. See Hall, *A History of Early Southeast Asia*, p. 33.

90 Wade, 'An Earlier Age' p. 228.

91 See Richard Pearson, Li Min and Li Guo, 'Quanzhou Archaeology: A Brief Review', *International Journal of Historical Archaeology*, 6 (2002): 23–59 at 28–9, and John Chaffee, 'Muslim Merchants and Quanzhou in the Late Yuan–Early Ming: Conjectures on the Ending of the Medieval Muslim Trade Diaspora', in *The East Asian Mediterranean: Maritime Crossroads of Culture, Commerce and Human Migration*, edited by Angela Schottenhammer (Wiesbaden: Otto Harrassowitz, 2008), pp. 115–32.

92 Roxanna Brown's detailed analysis of ceramic data from shipwrecks in Southeast Asia shows that before Hongwu's reign, ceramic cargoes were made up of 100 per cent Chinese wares. In the Hongwu period, this share declined to 30–40 per cent and from 1424/30 to 1487, Chinese ceramics made up just 5 per cent of ceramic cargoes. This suggests that most of the blue and white Ming ceramics found at Kota Batu date to the late fifteenth and sixteenth centuries; Brown, 'The Ming Gap'.

93 Tom Harrisson, *The Malays of South-west Sarawak before Malaysia: A Socio-ecological Survey* (London: Macmillan, 1970), p. 133.

94 Ibid, pp. 120–30. See also Mohammad Tahir bin Abdul Ghani, *Hikayat Datuk Merpati* (Kuala Lumpur: Dewan Bahasa dan Pustaka, 1989).

95 For example, see D.E. Brown, *Brunei: The Structure and History of a Bornean Malay Sultanate*, *Brunei Museum Journal*, 2(2) (special monograph) (1970): 134–5, and 'Hiranyagarbha – the Hindu Cosmic Egg – and Brunei's Royal Line', *Brunei Museum Journal*, 4 (1980): 30–37; Alan Maxwell, 'Headtaking and the Consolidation of Political Power in the Early Brunei State', in *Headhunting and the Social Imagination in Southeast Asia*, edited by Janet Hoskins (Stanford, CA: Stanford University Press, 1996), pp. 90–126; Mohammed Jamil Al-Sufri, *Tarsilah Brunei*, pp. 33–6; Ampuan Haji Brahim bin Ampuan Haji Tengah, 'Manuskrip Syair Awang Semaun: Kajian dan manfaatnya kepada orang Brunei', *Jurnal Darussalam*, 10 (2010): 73–83.

96 Mohammed Jamil Al-Sufri, *Tarsilah Brunei*, pp. 36; Benedict Sandin, 'The Bisayah of Limbang', *Sarawak Museum Journal*, 19 (1971): 1–19 at 1–6.

97   Maxwell, 'Headtaking'. Interestingly, Pigafetta reports that he and others were shown the heads of people recently defeated in battle by a returning ship; Pigafetta, *First Voyage*, p. 115.

98   Victor T. King, *The Peoples of Borneo* (Oxford: Blackwell, 1993), pp. 130–34.

99   The literature on this evidence-based model is immense. Two standard sources are Robert Blust, 'The Austronesian Homeland: A Linguistic Perspective', *Asian Perspectives*, 26 (1984–85): 45–68, and Peter Bellwood, *Prehistory of the Indo-Malaysian Archipelago*, rev. edn (Honolulu, HI: University of Hawai'i Press, 1997).

100 Alexander K. Adelaar, 'Where Does Malay Come From? Twenty Years of Discussions about Homeland, Migrations and Classifications', *Bijdragen tot de Taal-, Land- en Volkenkunde*, 160 (2004): 1–30; Robert Blust, *The Austronesian Languages*, rev. ed. (Canberra: Asia-Pacific Linguistics Research School of Pacific and Asian Studies, Australian National University, 2013), pp. 64–7.

101 James T. Collins, 'Sumbangan Dialek Brunei dalam Pengkajian Sejarah Bahasa Melayu' ['The Contribution of the Brunei Dialect in the Study of the History of Malay Language'], in *Tinggal Landas ke Abad 21* [*Takeoff to the 21st Century*] (Bandar Seri Begawan: Dewan Bahasa dan Pustaka, 1994), pp. 62–75; Bernd Nothofer, 'The Network of Malay Isolects in Borneo: A Preliminary Analysis', in *Proceedings of the International Seminar on Brunei Malay Sultanate 13–17 November 1994*, edited by Hj. Mohd. Taib Osman and Hj. Abdul Latif Hj. Ibrahim (Tungku Link: Academy Pengajian Brunei, Universiti Brunei Darussalam, 1996), pp. 460–71.

102 Bernd Nothofer, 'The Languages of Brunei Darussalam', in *Papers in Austronesian Linguistics*, vol. 1, edited by in H. Steinhauer (Canberra: Australian National University, 1991), pp. 151–76.

103 Adrian Clynes, *Brunei Malay: An Overview*, Occasional Papers in Language Studies, col. 7, (Tungku Link: Department of English Language and Applied Linguistics, Universiti Brunei Darussalam, 2001), p. 12.

2 *Silsilah Raja-Raja Brunei*

The Brunei Sultanate and its relationship with other countries

Ampuan Haji Brahim bin Ampuan Haji Tengah

There exist at least three available versions of the *Silsilah Raja-Raja Brunei* (*Genealogical History of the Sultans of Brunei*), one of which is located in the School of Oriental and African Studies (SOAS) library (hereafter referred to as manuscript A) and another in the Royal Asiatic Society of London library (hereafter referred to as manuscript B), which were transliterated and published by Amin Sweeney. Manuscripts A and B, both penned by Dato Imam Yaakub, appear to be the only published copies thus far that have been referred to by most scholars and researchers of the culture and history of Brunei. Secondly, there is a version of the *Silsilah Raja-Raja Brunei* manuscript in the Brunei Historical Centre, Bandar Seri Begawan (hereafter referred to as 'Dari Hal Tarsilah Raja Di Dalam Brunei' ['From the Royal Stone Inscription of Brunei']). The name of the author of this manuscript is not mentioned anywhere in the text, but the name of the owner is stated as Awang Abas bin Ampuan Mumin, who could possibly be the editor or copyist as well. The third manuscript is the *Sejarah Brunei* (*History of Brunei*) written by Datuk Imam Aminuddin ibnu Orang Kaya Di Gadong Lewadin and later copied by Abdul Ghafar bin Abdul Mumin. The first line of this *Sejarah Brunei* manuscript announces in Arabic script: 'This is the family history of the sultans that rule the state of Brunei Darussalam', thus it could be regarded as the 'family history of the sultans of Brunei'. This chapter is not intended to digress on the similarities and differences between the three manuscripts, but aims to examine the relationship between the Brunei Sultanate and other contemporaneous neighbouring polities and beyond, and to draw implications from such connections.

Historical aspects of the family history of the sultans of Brunei

The existence of these three versions illustrates the popularity and importance of the *Silsilah Raja-Raja Brunei* in the development of literature and culture in Brunei and its relationship with other Malay historiographic literature. In the history and development of Malay literature, the *Silsilah Raja-Raja Brunei* is considered an example of historiographic literature that showcases local expertise. One of the characteristics of Malay historiographic literature is that it narrates the lineage of kings in a mythical style. However, the *Silsilah Raja-Raja Brunei* does not recount the ancestry of the sultans in mythical terms, but instead begins with an account of the first Sultan of Brunei, Awang Alak Betatar:

The first to become king in the state of Berunai is Awang Khalak Betatar, car-rying the title Sultan Muhammad, who first brought Islam in accordance with the shari'at of our prophet Muhammad s.a.w. Hence, his Highness had a child with his queen, the Emperor of China's sister, who hailed from Kinabatangan. In commencing the reign as the king of Berunai, Awang Alak Betatar was an atheist; and at that time was colonised by Betara Majapahit and Pateh Gajah Mada, and presented a drum of drink from young betel nut as a tribute to Majapahit annually. When Majapahit collapsed, he no longer presented the tribute as Berunai became sovereign and ruled the domain.[1]

The *Silsilah Raja-Raja Brunei* did not relate the ancestry of the sultans as a con-sequence of the influence of religious education and the literary atmosphere of the time. The text was written by Datuk Imam Yakub in AH 1148 (1735 CE), improved by Khatib Abdul Latif in AH 1221 (1807 CE), and later continued by Haji Abdul Ghafar bin Mumin in AH 1355 (1936 CE). In the excerpt above, Sultan Muhammad proceeded to spread Islam throughout Brunei following his conver-sion. The development of Islam heightened in tandem with its strong develop-ment in the region, especially in Aceh, which produced numerous clerics who wrote several religious books, such as *Siratul-Mustaqim*. This phenomenon gave rise to literature that was influenced by writers from Aceh, such as Nuruddin al-Raniri's *Bustanus-Salatin* about the family history of the first sultans, which contained no mythical accounts.

Teuku Iskandar divided the *Silsilah Raja-Raja Brunei* into two sections: firstly, the family history, which recounts the lineage of the sultans of Brunei from Awang Alak Betatar, and secondly, the *Risalat Al-Marhum fi Adati Al-Marhum*, on the customs of Brunei[2] and also the customs related to trading with seafarers.

The lineage of the sultans of Brunei is stated clearly in the *Silsilah Raja-Raja Brunei*[3] as follows:

1 Sultan Muhammad Shah
2 Sultan Ahmad
3 Sultan Sharif 'Ali Bilfakih
4 Sultan Sulaiman
5 Sultan Bolkiah
6 Sultan 'Abdul Kahar
7 Sultan Saiful Rijal
8 Sultan Shah Berunai
9 Sultan Hasan
10 Sultan 'Abdul Jalilul Akbar
11 Sultan 'Abdul Jalilul Jabbar
12 Sultan Muhammad 'Ali
13 Sultan Muhiuddin
14 Sultan 'Abdul Mubin
15 Sultan Nasruddin

16   Sultan Kamaluddin
17   Sultan 'Alauddin
18   Sultan 'Omar 'Ali Saifuddin
19   Sultan Muhammad Tajuddin
20   Sultan Muhammad Jamalul 'Alam
21   Sultan Muhammad Kanzul 'Alam
22   Sultan Muhammad 'Alam
23   Sultan 'Omar 'Ali Saifuddin
24   Sultan 'Abdul Mu'min
25   Sultan Hashim Jalilul 'Alam Akamuddin
26   Sultan Muhammad Jamalul 'Alam
27   Sultan Ahmad Tajuddin 'Akadzul Khairu Waddin.

Apart from stating the family history of the sultans, the *Silsilah Raja-Raja Brunei* also includes the *Risalat Al-Marhum fi' Adati'l-Marhum*, which details the royal customs of Brunei during the reign of Sultan Hassan. These customs comprise mainly the procedures and policies utilized by the sultans in the appointment of dignitaries, and it also describes the customs of the royal court, complete with regalia used for specific occasions such as for the *berchiri* custom, the coronation, the demise of a sultan and royal weddings. The *Silsilah Raja-Raja Brunei* describes the preparations for the coronation of Sultan Muhammad Jamalul 'Alam, and the accompanying set of customs that are still practised today. During the coronation of Sultan Muhammad Jamalul 'Alam, flags and decorations were put up in the palace, in the *lapau* (ceremonial hall) and in offices. The doors of the ceremonial hall were decorated with yellow royal banners and parasols. On the day of the ceremony, kings, dignitaries of the royal court and subjects were invited to attend.[4]

For the passing of a sultan, preparations are undertaken according to full customary procedures:

> Hence, when a great king departs to his maker, his body will be carried to the mosque. The imam, khatib, mudim, 'ulamas' (religious leaders) and fakirs (the poor) will pray for the king, there is no limit in the number of the congregation that pray for him. Thus is the beginning of the customs for the great kings that depart, and when they have been buried and prayers have been read, thus all the khatib, mudim, 'ulama' and fakir in the country will recite the Quran for the king.[5]

Besides the royal customs, the manuscripts also detail the protocols related to trade and commerce. Trading customs dictated that a tax was imposed on all ships that entered Brunei to trade. However, if a merchant of a ship wished to be excluded from the tax, he could do this by presenting tribute to the king and dignitaries.[6] Although the manuscripts do not elaborate much about the origins of the early Sultanate of Brunei, their contents do illustrate and prove the existence of relationships between the Brunei Sultanate and other polities.

Brunci Darussalam: one of the oldest polities

Negara Brunei Darussalam, one of the oldest polities in the Malay World,[7] has been in existence since the fifth century CE, according to Chinese and Arabic sources, and has a history equal to other Malay states in the region. It is alleged to be as old as, or even older than, Srivijaya in Sumatra. In terms of the expanse of empire and glory of the royal court customs, it is equal to Majapahit in Java and Malacca in the Malay Peninsula.[8] Chinese sources associated Brunei with such place names as Ye Po Ti (411 CE), Po-li (518 CE). Po-lo (669 CE) and Puni (997 CE and 1370 CE).[9] But such attributions have at best remained problematic.[10]

Brunei was also called 'Varuni', 'Bhurni', 'Baru nah' and 'Waruni'. In the case of 'Varuni', the Sanskrit refers to the sea or coastal people. 'Varunai' derives from *varunadvipa*, which symbolizes the island of Borneo.[11] Yet Muller stated that 'Bhurni' means land or state. On the other hand, the older Brunei generation state that 'Baru nah' means 'good' and befits aspirations,[12] and was a customary saying of the followers of Pateh Berbai when they found suitable land to establish a new country. However, 'Waruni' means 'containing everything' or 'the goddess of the sea'.[13] The Indians called Brunei 'Kapuradivipa', which means 'the country that produces camphor'. The Javanese called Brunei 'Buruneng'.[14] Then, some pronunciation changes occurred from Varunai to Bruni, Porni, Po-ni, Po-li, Burney, Burni, and finally to Borneo (which is also known as Brunei) because the Brunei Sultanate once ruled over Borneo, especially at the height of the empire under the reign of Sultan Bolkiah (1485–1524 CE).[15]

The existence of the old Brunei kingdom has given rise to multiple theories, viewpoints and speculations in determining its genesis. Robert Nicholl proposed his theory of immigration, whereby the Brunei Sultanate came into being following the Khmer attack on Funan in the Mekong delta in 680 CE. Seeking refuge, the Funans fled to Borneo landing, in the Brunei Bay area, thus establishing the kingdom of Brunei.

Both Pehin Haji Mohd Jamil Al-Sufri and Sanib Said support this theory of immigration, albeit from another vantage point. According to them, Brunei Malays came from Pagar Ruyong in Sumatra, and migrated to Borneo around the ninth century to form the Brunei kingdom. Moreover, Sanib Saib substantiated this immigration theory by drawing similarities between place names between northwest Borneo and Sumatra: Serawai with Sarawak, Sibao-Sibu and Pelimbang-Limbang. Early settlements appeared to be concentrated in the Brunei Bay area, as it was a strategic location for settlement and defence.[16]

The Brunei Sultanate and its relationship with other countries

Most of the researchers on the history of the Brunei Malay Sultanate have opined that Brunei is one of the oldest kingdoms in Southeast Asia, contemporaneous with empires such as Majapahit, Aceh, Johor and China.[17] This fact is implied in the *Silsilah Raja-Raja Brunei*, which illustrates how the Brunei kingdom forged relations with other countries, through diplomacy, political marriages, trade or conquests. According to the text, countries that had ties with Brunei include Aceh, Johor, Majapahit, China and Sulu.

Brunei and Majapahit

The relationship between Brunei and Majapahit has been likened to that between an imperial state and one of its colonies. During the reign of Awang Alak Betatar, Brunei as a country had not yet embraced Islam and was under the power of the Majapahit kingdom. The Majapahit kingdom which was founded by Raden Wijaya (who later ascended to the throne as King Shril Kertarajasha Jayawardhana) in 1293 CE was powerful and revered throughout Asia, on a par with Tiongkok (China). The Majapahit kingdom, based in East Java, attained its zenith in 1350–89 CE, during the reign of Prabhu Hayam Wuruk with his prime or senior minister, Patih Gadjah Mada. As a small country, Brunei was impelled to forge relations with more powerful states. Brunei, it seems, paid tribute to Majapahit to ensure its political security.

The *Silsilah Raja-Raja Brunei* mentions the tribute the Brunei kingdom presented to Majapahit and Patih Gadjah Mada because it was a colony of the latter:

> In commencing the reign as the king of Berunai, Awang Alak Betatar was an atheist; and at that time was colonised by Betara Majapahit and Pateh Gajah Mada, and presented a drum of drink from young betel nut as a tribute to Majapahit annually. When Majapahit collapsed, he no longer presented the tribute as Berunai became sovereign and ruled the domain.[18]

According to Majapahit sources, Brunei was recorded as one of its colonies, as is also mentioned in the *Silsilah Raja-Raja Brunei*. This proves that Majapahit was a powerful and influential country at that time, and many countries received its protection, including Brunei.

The poem *Nagarakretagama*, written in Kawi by Prapanca in 1365 CE, mentioned 'Buruneng', possibly referring to Brunei, indicating that Majapahit had long known of Brunei. This awareness allowed for a relationship between the two nations, either directly or indirectly: 'Kadangdangan, Landa, on the other hand Samedang. Tirem unseparated, Sedu, Buruneng, Kalka, Saludung, Solot, Pasir, Baritu, Sawako, also Tabulung, Tanjung Kutei, with Malano, having for principal town then: Tanjung Puri.'[19]

According to oral traditions, one of the incidents that was said to have created the ties between Brunei and Majapahit concerned a cock-fighting expert named Awang Sinuai, whose fame reached the Majapahit court. In order to test the strength of his fighting cock, the Majapahit queen issued Awang Sinuai a challenge. Awang Sinuai's cockerel, Mutiara, defeated the queen's cockerel, Asmara. Shamed by the defeat, the queen became angry and cursed the two cockerels. Awang Sinuai's cockerel flew to the ocean and became a *pilung-pilungan* rock, whereas the queen's cockerel flew to the Brunei river and became a rock called Lumut Lunting. Although this tale is merely an oral account that has been passed from generation to generation, it is retold in Awang Semaun's poem, which possibly reflects some truth about the relationship between Brunei and Majapahit.

Brunei and China

The relationship between Brunei and China began during the Liang dynasty, *c.* 502–566 CE. According to Chinese historians, the king of Brunei at the time was 'Pinka', and his family called him 'Kaundinya'. He was a Hindu-Buddhist. Raja Pinka was said to be handsome, rich and brave. In the audience hall of his royal court in the presence of the lords, the king sat on a golden throne, with a silver foot stool and chairs bearing gold carvings.[20]

Sino–Brunei relations appear to be evident even before the reign of Sultan Muhammad Shah in 518 CE. Raja Pinka (the king of Brunei) sent an envoy to China to establish diplomatic and trade ties. Chinese traders who frequented the Malay Archipelago mentioned having sojourned at a place called P'o-li whose king was Pin-ka or Vingka. The Brunei envoy presented a letter and offerings from the land, one of which was a golden mat, to the emperor of China.[21] The letter included the statement:

> I am the king of the country Po-li and now reverently prostrate myself and do homage at the feet of my holy Lord, only hoping that since Your Majesty may know my feelings, which I have harboured since long and which are not of today. Mountains and seas separates us and I cannot have the happiness of coming myself to you, but I now send an envoy to present golden mats and other things.[22]

Nonetheless, the lineage of the early Brunei kings cannot be ascertained. According to Chinese historical records, Brunei was a monarchic nation that had good ties with China. After Sultan Muhammad Shah (Awang Alak Betatar), the first Muslim ruler, ascended the throne, succeeding his grandfather, Sang Aji Brunei, more certainty is ascribed to the royal lineage up to the present.[23] According to Ming dynasty (1368–1644 CE) records, around 1370 CE, during the reign of Hung-wu (1368–98 CE), a Chinese emissary to Java sojourned in Brunei. The party was led by Chang Ching Tze and Sin Tze. They recounted that the king of Brunei at this point was 'Mahamosha', a Chinese rendition of Muhammad Shah.[24]

In the *Silsilah Raja-Raja Brunei* (Amin Sweeney), formal ties between Brunei and China began when the Chinese Emperor ordered two of his envoys, Ong Sum Peng and Ong Bong Kong, to acquire a piece of jade that was jealously guarded by a dragon from the China Balu or Kinabalu (Chinese Widow) mountain. Several attempts were in vain until Ong Sum Peng pitted his wits and finally succeeded in slaying the dragon and securing the jade. However, Ong Bong Kong seized the jade, and claimed credit for the treasure's recovery. Disheartened, Ong Sum Peng refused to return to China and fled to Brunei, where he married the sultan's daughter.

Through political marriages, Brunei forged relations with China. The *Silsilah Raja-Raja Brunei* records that Sultan Muhammad Shah's daughter was married to a Chinese dignitary named Ong Sum Peng:

At that time, Awang Khalak Betatar became sultan, and assumed the name Sultan Muhammad. Henceforth, the sultan had a daughter who was very beautiful indeed. Soon after, Ong Sum Peng asked for the princess's hand in marriage. Thus, Sultan Muhammad accepted Ong Sum Peng's proposal, and they were married in a traditional royal ceremony.[25]

In 'Dari Hal Tarsilah Raja Di Dalam Brunei',[26] Sultan Muhammad Shah's daughter was Puteri Ratna Dewi, who was married to Ong Sum Peng. Thereafter, Ong Sum Peng was bestowed with the title Pengiran Maharaja Lela by Sultan Muhammad Shah.[27] Ong's sister, Princess Kinabatangan, married Pengiran Bendahara Patih Berbai (later Sultan Ahmad).

The *Silsilah Raja-Raja Brunei* (Amin Sweeney) and *Sejarah Brunei* (Datu Imam Aminuddin version) allude to the fact that Ong Sum Peng was Sultan Ahmad after he was appointed a king by Sultan Muhammad.[28] On the other hand, the *Silsilah Raja-Raja Brunei* in Datu Imam Yaakub's version states that Sultan Ahmad was Sultan Muhammad's brother, and was known as Patih Berbai or Pengiran Bendahara. This contradictory account whereby Ong Sum Peng was regarded as Sultan Ahmad is refuted by the Adat Istiadat Mengangkat Raja (Customs of the Coronation of a King) as stated in the *Silsilah Raja-Raja Brunei* (Amin Sweeney).[29] It declares that when a king does not have an heir to the throne, his brother must become sultan. The precise status of Ong Sum Peng might be difficult to ascertain, but his purported presence at the royal court and in the history of Brunei proves that there existed a form of relationship between Brunei and China centuries ago.

The Sino-Brunei relationship is also evident in the *Batu Tarsilah di Makam Diraja*, Bandar Seri Begawan, written by Khatib Haji Abdul Latif in AH 1221 (1807 CE), which mentions relations with China through political marriages:

> Thus the first in the kingdom of Brunei and brought Islam as Prophet Muhammad s.a.w. had summoned was Paduka Seri Sultan Muhammad and his brother Sultan Ahmad. Hence, his Highness had a child with his queen, the Emperor of China's sister, who hailed from Kinabatangan, and henceforth the princess was taken by Sharif Ali who hailed from Taif. Thus Sharif Ali became king and assumed the title Paduka Seri Sultan Berkat who upheld the Prophet's s.a.w. will and built a mosque and the people of China built a city of stone. Tuan Sharif Ali was a descendant of Amirul-Mu'minin Hasan, the Prophet's grandson.[30]

This excerpt from the *Silsilah Raja-Raja Brunei* and inscriptions on Batu Tarsilah prove the relationship between the two countries through Sultan Ahmad's marriage to the Chinese princess from Kinabatangan who was said to be Ong Sum Peng's sister.

Moreover, China also forged ties with Brunei through the channels of trade and commerce. The *Silsilah Raja-Raja Brunei* recounts a Chinese sea captain, Kusi, who went to Brunei with a cargo of *basi* (iron/groundwork/construction materials). The captain sought exemption from taxes for his cargo by paying tribute to Pengiran Bendahara, Pengiran Di Gadong, Pengiran Temenggong, Pengiran Pemanca, Pengiran Shahbandar and Cheteria with some of his trade merchandise. Subsequently, the captain also sought exemption from taxes from the sultan by presenting tribute. If one did not seek exemption, Brunei imposed customs tax in monetary form, for example a 1,000 riyal ingot or a 700 riyal *damit* ingot. Traders who wished to be exempted from taxes had to pay tribute.[31] The establishment and implementation of such customs taxes illustrate that trading had long been carried out in Brunei, and such trading activities and channels fostered relations not only with China, but also with several other countries. Robust trading activities owed much to the sultan's vigilant attentiveness to the welfare of the merchants:

> In that era Datu Imam Ya'akub was the trade representative; his Majesty ordered for all trading merchandise, hence after the completion of a year's trading; thus sailed a Chinese sea captain, named Si Lut, a China [*sic.* read Chinese man] from Jakatra, and he sailed henceforth to China and Manila, only then he did learn of Brunei; its king took a keen interest in the welfare of the merchants and assisted in delivering the trade merchandise throughout the land. Thus it was an endless greetings' of king's name and was made known to all the foreign lands, until the time of his Majesty Seri Sultan Kamaluddin.[32]

The practice of trade dues/customs as mentioned in the *Silsilah Raja-Raja Brunei* was verified by Chau Ju-Kua, a Chinese historian who reported that when merchant ships entered port, they were warmly welcomed by the king and royal dignitaries.[33] Then, according to Brunei's trade customs, merchants and ship captains had to present tribute to the king, royal dignitaries and the king's escorts according to their ranks.

Historical records have also proved Sino–Brunei relations through artefacts such as 'pitis' or 'kue' coins. Earlier, trading between Chinese merchants and the people of Brunei was through the exchange of goods such as cloth, sugar, salt, oil, silk, fish, cups and tableware for rice, sago, vegetables, fruit, camphor, spices, sandalwood, aloes, birds' nests, wax, honey, resin, ivory, tortoise shell, pearls, or as agreed by both parties.[34] Because this barter system was regarded as inefficient or wasteful due to the unequal value of the items exchanged, Brunei took the initiative to adopt the usage of Chinese currency, locally known as 'pitis' or 'kue'. Previously, Brunei had used seashells and tin coins as currency for trade. Finally, Brunei minted its own currency from tin imprinted with a seal bearing the words 'Al-Adil' ('fair') once it realized the importance of currency in commercial transactions.

Brunei and Aceh

Being Muslim kingdoms, Brunei and Aceh forged relations in the field of religious knowledge whereby contacts were established as early as 1524 CE. It is believed that clerics and poets from various parts of the region, including from Brunei, congregated at Aceh to teach and learn:

After the fall of Malacca to the Portuguese in 1511, traders, and with them Muslim clerics and poets, went to Aceh. Sultan Ali Mughayat Syah defeated Pasai in 1524 and with that, the centre for trade and Malay culture shifted to the Aceh capital, Bandar Aceh Darussalam. Starting from there, clerics and poets, whether from the Middle East or from all parts of the South East Asian region, went there to teach and learn.[35]

Aceh in the sixteenth century ruled over a large expanse of territory, and also directly and indirectly clarified Aceh's relationship with Brunei. Dato Imam Yakub compared Sultan Mahrum di Tanjung (Paduka Seri Sultan Hassan) of Brunei and Sultan Iskandar Muda Mahkota Alam of Aceh in terms of the size of the kingdom and ruling style:

> This is the custom from the time of Mahrum di Tanjung, titled as Paduka Seri Sultan Hasan, whose kingdom was vast and ruled strictly . . . was the incomparable Brunei Sultan, but was the equal of Sultan Mahkota Alam in Aceh; a king who had no equal, of king or man, and was a king of royal customs and his kingdom in Berunai did as he please.[36]

One of the greatest rulers of Aceh was Sultan Iskandar Muda Mahkota Alam (r. 1607–36 CE), who ruled with an iron hand and attained success in imperial expansion from conquests that brought increases in wealth and prosperity. Aceh at this time was internationally recognized as a centre for trade and Islamic learning, and the latter motivated Brunei to send clerics and students. The strict style of governance influenced Sultan Hassan, as stated in the comparison by Dato Imam Yakub in manuscript A of the *Silsilah Raja-Raja Brunei*, and in an excerpt from manuscript B:

> Thus, his Majesty Sultan Hasan's kingdom was vast and he ruled strictly, and his four wives, all of royal blood, and a few tens of concubines, and two palaces, and a city of four square miles, and fortified land. And his many children, and his fastidiousness in upholding customs, and his bravery was comparable to Seri Sultan Mahkota 'Alam of Aceh; who had no equal amongst all the kings of Berunai and was known for his bravery throughout the lands, and the whole region feared him.[37]

The comparison between these two rulers meant that Sultan Hassan was a contemporary of Sultan Iskandar Mahkota 'Alam. It suggests that in the early seventeenth century, there were at least two Muslim countries in Southeast Asia that were strong and influential: Brunei and Aceh.[38] The strategic location of Aceh, which made it the port of choice for Muslim merchants from Persia, Arabia and India, promoted it as a centre for Islamic education. Brunei grasped the opportunity to learn from and gain inspiration from Aceh, including knowledge of royal customs and practices. This gave rise to comparisons between Sultan Hassan and Sultan Iskandar Mahkota 'Alam owing to similarities in their styles of governance.

Brunei and Johor

The relationship between Brunei and Johor was established through the conferment of honorary titles, arrangement of political marriages and presentation of gifts. The Brunei–Johor relationship was forged when Sultan Bahteri of Johor bestowed honorary titles on Awang Khalak Betatar (or Sultan Muhammad) and Pateh Merbai of Brunei:

> Hence, was mentioned of the state of Johor. At the dawn of the era, Sultan Bahteri ascended the throne in Johor, thus was the time he invited Awang Alak Betatar and Pateh Merbai of Brunei to Johor. When he reached Johor, Awang Khalak Betatar, titled Sultan Muhammad, became the first king of Berunai, and pateh became Pengeran Bendahara Seri Maharaja. Thus, the sultan was bestowed by the Yang Di Pertuan Johor a ceremonial drum, a warning bell and five colonies, which were the states of Kalaka and Saribas and Semarahan and Serawak and Mukah. Hence, not long after his audience . . . [Sultan Muhammad] took leave to Berunai . . . [39]

Johor at this point was an established and well-developed centre for trade and culture. The prosperity and might of the Johor kingdom at that time can be seen from the excerpt above. Also, a weak kingdom would certainly not have invited and bestowed honours upon rulers and officials from another kingdom. Conversely, as the ruler of a country that is said to have existed since the fifth century, the sultan of Brunei would not have gone to a weak country. On the other hand, the sultan of Brunei might have felt respected and safe in visiting and forging ties with a country that was stronger and larger than his own.

Brunei's direct ties with Johor were apparent when Raja Tengah's sister, Raja Bendahara, the daughter of Marhum Tua (Sultan 'Abdul Jalilul Akbar), was betrothed to the Yang Di Pertuan (Head of State) Johor. This marriage brought the two kingdoms closer, albeit in a relationship between an overlord and a form of dependency for a small country like Brunei. Raja Tengah exemplified the relationship when he went to visit his sister, Raja Bendahara, in Johor.

The *Silsilah Raja-Raja Brunei* recounts that Sultan Muhiuddin (the son of Sultan Muhammad 'Ali) appointed his cousin, Raja Tengah (the son of 'Abdul Jalilul Akbar), as the ruler in Serawak. Raja Tengah was charismatic, and Sultan Muhiuddin did not want his cousin's presence in Brunei, as he might become a threat. After a passage of time, Raja Tengah wanted to visit his sister, who was married to the Yang di Pertuan Johor. On his arrival in Johor, Raja Tengah was welcomed by his brother-in-law, Raja Abdul Jalil, with a dance festivity:

> thus the Maharaja of Johor cordially invited his royal subjects according to the traditional customs of old. Hence, Raja Tengah was honored by his sister the Maharaja Adinda Johor, for the visit with a fine feast . . . thus the Maharaja of Johor himself rose to dance in the festivities, because he wanted to ask Raja Tengah to dance along. . . . Thus said Raja Tengah, 'Do not ask me to dance

because this Berunaian does not know how to dance.' Alas, he was forced to dance by the Maharaja of Johor who was dancing with his handkerchief, two, three times. Hence, Raja Tengah was angered by the Maharaja of Johor's pajal (prank). He thought, 'This Johorean must be a prankster.'[40]

Following this incident, his sister advised Raja Tengah to return to Sarawak immediately. Raja Tengah had angered the Maharaja of Johor, who resolved to kill him. This incident illustrates that Johor and Brunei, each with their own sets of customs despite their ties through marriage, acknowledged each other's sovereignty. The Maharaja of Johor believed that his act of forcing Raja Tengah to dance was honouring him for his presence, whereas Raja Tengah misunderstood the intention as an attempt to make a fool out of him.

History also records ties between Brunei and Johor through the marriage of Sultan Muhammad Shah with a princess from Johor. However, this marriage was not recorded in the *Silsilah Raja-Raja Brunei*. According to Brunei historical records, Sultan Muhammad Shah was the first Sultan of Brunei who embraced Islam after he married the Johorean (Temasek) princess titled Tuan Puteri Pingai. The strong relationship between the two countries was established, and proved that Brunei was recognized by the Johor Sultanate, a great power at the time with a vast empire, and a staunch adherent of Islam. In other words, the bond that was forged between these two countries had a clear motive of Islamization, recognition of sovereignty, and political marriages.

The relationship between Brunei and Johor is also seen in the presence of material culture, as mentioned in the *Silsilah Raja-Raja Brunei*, such as 'the ceremonial drum and warning bell from the state of Johor'[41] and the golden keris (dagger) sheath[42] – artefacts that are highly regarded heirlooms of the Brunei Sultanate. The same could also be said of the relationship between Brunei and Majapahit, which is clearly indicated through material culture as recorded in the *Silsilah Raja-Raja Brunei*: 'and took the ceremonial drum and warning bell from Minangkabau, which is Andalas State'.[43] As a consequence, Brunei acquired ceremonial and material culture from these foreign countries, and also indirectly received recognition from these countries for its sovereignty as a Malay Islamic sultanate.

Brunei and Sulu

According to historical records, Sulu launched an attack on the Poni kingdom (the Old Brunei kingdom) while the latter was under the protection of Majapahit. It was Sulu's strategy to strengthen its defence and economy. According to Sung Lien's (1371 CE) report, Sulu attacked Poni in 1369 CE. This attack would have destroyed the Poni kingdom had it not been for Majapahit's assistance. But the Poni kingdom became weak and impoverished. Sung Lien recorded Brunei's state of distress.[44] It could be seen that the Sulu attack occurred in the reign of Sultan Muhammad Shah (1363–1402 CE), but seemingly was not recorded in the *Silsilah Raja-Raja Brunei*. Instead, what was recorded was the civil war between Sultan Muhiuddin and Sultan 'Abdul Mubin, whereby the former called for Betara Suluk's assistance. This illustrates that Betara Suluk had long since had ties with Brunei, as verified in other places in the *Silsilah Raja-Raja Brunei*, for instance when Sultan Bolkiah (the fifth king) defeated Suluk,[45] and likewise, when Sultan Hassan (the ninth king) conquered Betara Suluk and demanded an annual tribute.[46]

In this civil war, Sultan Muhiuddin appealed for assistance from the Betara Suluk because he felt that he would be unable to defeat Sultan 'Abdul Mubin, who was based on Cermin Island, a strategic location in controlling the move-ment of ships entering Brunei waters. All the necessary food and equipment for war were barred from entering Brunei, forcing Sultan Muhiuddin to seek assistance from Betara Suluk. Betara Suluk agreed to Sultan Muhiuddin's plea for assistance because of the long-standing relationship between Sulu and Brunei. It is also possible that Betara Suluk agreed to help because he sym-pathized with Sultan Muhiuddin, whose father, Sultan Muhammad 'Ali (the twelfth king) was killed by Bendahara Abdul Hak (later Sultan 'Abdul Mubin, the fourteenth king). Or it could be the result of the disgust he felt towards the foolishness of Bendahara Abdul Hak, who appointed Pengiran Bongsu (later Sultan Muhiuddin, the thirteenth king), who had killed his own son. Whatever the reason, Betara Suluk's readiness to assist Sultan Muhiuddin was revealed when the former went to visit Sultan Muhiuddin, who bestowed land on him: 'Oh Betara, if only you would defeat Sultan Mubin in Chermin Island, hence I would bestow upon you the land beside Saba which is Kimanis.'[47] This illus-trates that in difficult times, Brunei bartered territories in return for assistance, lost territories, then when it regained its strength, would conquer and extend its political powers over other regions.

Brunei's Sultan Bolkiah also had ties that were forged through conquest of the Sulu kingdom; consequently, he became known as Adipati Suluk.[48] He success-fully defeated Suluk and Saludang, and thereafter married Puteri Lela Menchanai (Sultan Suluk's daughter) and Puteri Datu Gamban. These unions were not only a strategy to expand settlements, improve influence, increase trading opportunities and spread Islam in the region, but were also an effective method to transform feelings of distrust to those of co-operation and tolerance based on *silaturahim* (fellowship), brotherhood and bonding between conqueror and conquered.[49]

Brunei and other countries and regions

There were also relations between Brunei and other surrounding territories through marriage and blood ties. These ties with other regions extended across the island of Borneo. At the height of Sultan Bolkiah's reign in the sixteenth century, his domain covered the entire island of Borneo and the northern Philippines.[50] Brunei's vast domain was verified by Antonio Pigafetta, an explorer in Magellan's expedi-tion around the world. When Pigafetta reached Brunei in 1521 CE, he reported that the Brunei Malay Sultanate was a vast, powerful and rich kingdom. Brunei then played an important role as a propagation centre of Islam throughout Borneo and beyond into the Philippines.[51] In 1280 CE, according to the Chinese *Nan Hai*

Chih report, Brunei's colonies included Sarawak, territories in North Borneo, the Philippines and Sulu. As early as the thirteenth century, it appeared that Brunei was successful in establishing an empire.[52]

Furthermore, the *Silsilah Raja-Raja Brunei* also mentions that of the brothers Paduka Seri Sultan Saiful Rizal (or Raja Seri, the seventh king) and Pengiran Bendara Raja Sekam, the former was born to a Javanese mother while the latter was born to a Bajau mother. This indirectly demonstrates that Brunei's relationship also bonded the Javanese and Bajau through marriage:

> Paduka Seri Sultan Saiful Rizal has appointed his two cousins to be Pengiran Bendahara. The eldest cousin was known as Pengiran Bendahara Raja Seri and his mother is a Javanese. The other cousin was known as Pengiran Bendahara Raja Sekam, his mother is a Bajau and also the daughter of the head of Bajau. Raja Sekam owned all the land of Bajau.[53]

Other lands that had matrimonial ties with Brunei were Matan and Sambas. The *Silsilah Raja-Raja Brunei* recounts the marriage of Raja Tengah, who once landed in Matan, and proceeded with the nuptials with these consequences:

> And not long after being in Matan, thus Raja Tengah was given by the Sultan of Matan a wife. Hence soon after, Raja Tengah's wife gave birth, a son. Thus when Raja Tengah's son came of age, the Sultan of Matan bestowed him the title Pengeran Mangkunegara.[54]

Thereafter, Raja Tengah landed in Sambas:

> Hence Raja Tengah went to Sambas not long after, and was thus given a wife by the queen of Sambas to Raja Tengah of royal blood, equal for a royal. Thus not long after, Raja Tengah's wife gave birth to a son. Thus when Raja Tengah's son came of age, the queen of Sambas bestowed him the title Radin Bilam.[55]

Besides Matan and Sambas, Raja Tengah also acted as king of Sarawak. Sultan Muhiuddin himself appointed Raja Tengah as king, as he wanted to grant his brother some land:

> Thus Raja Tengah had an audience with Sultan Muhiuddin. His Majesty thus said to his brother Raja Tengah, 'My brother, it is my destiny to be in Berunai as it is. For you, it is in my opinion that I crown you king in the state of Sarawak because we are both the sons of Marhum.'[56]

In the Brunei Empire, colonies included regions in Sarawak, from Tanjung Datu to the Rejang river, which consisted of Simatan, Sadung, Kalaka and others. This is evident in the *Silsilah Raja-Raja Brunei* when Raja Tengah dies and Sultan Muhiuddin orders Raja Tengah's heirs in Matan and Sambas to take their father's place:

Thus after some time Raja Tengah ruled the land and its coasts, henceforth the world turned, and as Allah Subhanahu wa Ta'ala has destined, Raja Tengah died in the state of Serawak and was thus buried there.[57]

Thus whilst in Berunai, Pengeran Mangkunegara was bestowed the title Sultan Anum by Sultan Muhiuddin. And Radin Bilam was summoned back to Sambas to rule the land and was granted by Sultan Muhiuddin the land which bordered between Tanjong Datu' and Batu Belat, and that was the expanse of Sambas; henceforth land under the rule of Matan.[58]

Brunei's domain must have been large for Sultan Saiful Rizal to be able to afford to grant his daughter six of his colonies: 'Thus the dim-witted daughter was granted an inheritance by Sultan Saiful Rijal, six states: the first, Maruda and second, Banggi and third Mempakul, and fourth Lawas and fifth Bukua and sixth Membakut.'[59]

These various relationships demonstrate that Brunei was a strong kingdom with vast territories and many colonies. Granting territories to princes and princesses had long been practised by kings. Consequently, each region had its own king, leader or representative who ruled on behalf of the emperor; and consequently fostered inter-state relations

During the reigns of Sultan Muhiuddin, Sultan Nasruddin/Nassaruddin (The 15th Sultan of Brunei) and Sultan Kamaluddin, the *Silsilah Raja-Raja Brunei* recorded that there were trade ties between Brunei and Manila that had maintained diplomatic relations with the Philippine kingdom since Sultan Bolkiah's reign. Trade relations were further strengthened with diplomatic gifts or tributes (material culture) that were presented by the kingdom in Manila to Brunei, such as cannon, precious stone rings and cloth:

> And it is stated that trade customs came to Berunai in the era of Marhum Di Tanjong cheteria Paduka Seri Sultan Muhiuddin, and Paduka Seri Sultan Nasruddin and Paduka Seri Sultan Kamaluddin. A ship landed in Berunai from Manila with an envoy carrying four iron canons called Si Bendong Lara and two green emerald rings and a red ruby ring and a few silver tablewares and gharip cloth.[60]

Pengiran Bendahara also played an important role as a military leader. The *Silsilah Raja-Raja Brunei* manuscript B recorded that during the reign of Sultan Saiful Rijal, the appointment of Pengiran Bendahara was always held by Pengiran Bendahara Sakam. He was appointed to lead the Brunei army to conquer the lands between Sabah and Luzon. Pengiran Bendahara Sakam with the Brunei army was said to have been successful in defeating the Spanish army, which had earlier been successful in occupying Brunei after the Castila War in 1578 CE:

> And when Sultan Saiful Rijal ruled the kingdom, he appointed one of his brothers, Pengeran Bendahara, from a Javanese mother, and another brother whom he appointed as Pengeran Bendahara/Seri Maharaja Sekam, whose mother was Bajau. Bendahara conquered the entire Bajau lands from Saba' until Lusong, where he ruled.[61]

Brunei proved its strength and power when it conquered the lands between Sabah and Luzon. Religion, wealth and power motivated Spain to wage war on Brunei. Nevertheless, the loyalty of the Brunei people and the firm belief in Islam resulted in the people of Brunei successfully resisting Spanish conquest.

Diplomatic ties were forged between Brunei and the British during the reign of Sultan Muhammad Jamalul 'Alam. The final section of the *Silsilah Raja-Raja Brunei* manuscript B contains the memoirs of Al-Haj Gaffar bin 'Abdul Momin. He records that on 31 October 1914, His Majesty Sultan Muhammad Jamalul 'Alam received the Cross of St Michael and St George, bestowed by His Majesty King George.[62] This medal was brought over by King George's envoy, the governor of Singapore, and Sir F.W. Douglas, the British Resident in Brunei. Then, during the coronation of Sultan Muhammad Jamalul 'Alam in 1918, the ceremony was witnessed by British colonial dignitaries:

> And the sultan ascended on the ceremonial dais, and was seated on the throne. On the left, facing the throne, seated in a chair, was the Secretary of Kuala Lumpur, M.S.H. McArthur and the Berunai British Resident, Sir [Geoffrey Edmund] Cator. On the sand, were the other sirs and madams, and Sir Resident of Jesselton, and Sir Resident of Serawak, and other white sirs.[63]

The above coronation demonstrates the close ties between Brunei, then a British protectorate, and other territories under British colonial influence, such as Sarawak, Malaya (Kuala Lumpur) and British North Borneo (Jesselton). Such records not only showcase Brunei's diplomatic network, but also contribute to the uniqueness of the *Silsilah Raja-Raja Brunei* as a historiographic text *vis-à-vis* other Malay texts of the same genre.

Conclusion

The *Silsilah Raja-Raja Brunei* records the lineage of the Brunei kings and royal customs as well as indicating the relations that were forged between Brunei and other countries, both regionally and internationally. Majapahit, China, Johor and Aceh were the key and significant powers within the orbit of the Brunei Sultanate's external relations. In essence, the Brunei kingdom was once great and powerful, with colonies spread across Borneo and the region. Marriage, Islamization, war, colonization, trade and diplomacy, and possession of material culture (gifts, tributes) fostered relations between Brunei and other polities. The relationships that were forged proved the power and glory of Brunei as a Malay Muslim monarchy that was once a strong country, with vast powers and strong rule under charismatic rulers, notably Sultan Muhammad, Sultan Ahmad, Sultan Saiful Rijal, Sultan Hasan, Sultan Bolkiah and Bendahara Pengiran Sakam. The *Silsilah Raja-Raja Brunei* records and recollects Brunei's zenith of imperial power – its golden age, when it stood among the great and powerful.

Notes

1 P.L. Amin Sweeney, 'Silsilah Raja-Raja Berunai', *Journal of the Malaysian Branch of the Royal Asiatic Society*, 41(2) (1968): 1–82 at 51–2.
2 Ampuan bin Haji Brahim bin Ampuan Haji Tengah, *Traditional Brunei Literature: A Discussion of Genre and Theme* (Bandar Seri Begawan: Dewan Bahasa dan Pustaka, 2010), p. 184.
3 Sweeney, 'Silsilah Raja-Raja Berunai', pp. 70–71.
4 Brahim bin Ampuan Haji Tengah, *Traditional Brunei Literature*, p. 102.
5 Sweeney, 'Silsilah Raja-Raja Berunai', pp. 29–30.
6 Brahim bin Ampuan Haji Tengah, *Traditional Brunei Literature*, p. 100.
7 The Malay World comprised the greater part of insular Southeast Asia or the Malay Archipelago, comprising the modern nation states of Malaysia, Singapore, Brunei, Indonesia and the Philippines. The term 'Malay World' also covers areas where Malay people had migrated and settled, hence stretching as far westwards as East and South Africa and eastwards as the southwest Pacific and northern Australasia.
8 Sanib Said, 'The Establishment of the Old Brunei Government: A Migration Theory from Sumatra', *Jurnal Darussalam*, 1 (1992): 88–100 at 89.
9 Awang Othman bin Haji Mat Don, 'Brunei KM XVII–XIX: An Analysis of the History of its Decline', *Jurnal Darussalam*, 10 (2010): 84–105 at 84.
10 See Chapter 3 in this volume.
11 Haji Hashim Haji Abdul Hamid, 'Malay Islamic Monarchy: An Extension of Brunei History', *Jurnal Darussalam*, 1 (1992): 77–87 at 79.
12 Pehin Jawatan Dalam Seri Maharaja Dato Seri Utama Dr Haji Awang Mohd Jamil Al-Sufri, *Brunei Darussalam: A Malay Islamic Monarchic Country* (Bandar Seri Begawan: Pusat Sejarah Brunei, 2007), p. 3.
13 Haji Awg Asbol bin Haji Mail, *Kesultanan Melayu Brunei Abad ke 19 Politik and Struktur Pentadbiran* [*The Brunei Malay Sultanate in the 19th Century: Politics and Governing Structure*] (Bandar Seri Begawan: Dewan Bahasa dan Pustaka, 2011), p. 2.
14 Mohd. Jamil Al-Sufri, *Brunei Darussalam*, p. 3.
15 Hashim Haji Abdul Hamid, 'Malay Muslim Monarchy', p. 79.
16 Asbol bin Haji Mail, *Brunei Malay Sultanate in the 19th Century*, p. 3.
17 Ibid., p. 1.
18 Sweeney, 'Silsilah Raja-Raja Berunai', p. 52.
19 Yura Halim and Jamil Umar, *Sejarah Berunai* [*History of Brunei*] (Kuala Belait: Brunei Press, 1958), p. 13.
20 See Mohd. Jamil Al-Sufri, *Brunei Darussalam*, p. 6.
21 Ibid., p. 8.
22 Awang Haji Zainuddin bin Haji Hassan, 'Old Brunei: An Early Analysis', *Jurnal Darussalam*, 7 (2007): 114–36 at 122.
23 Mohd. Jamil Al-Sufri, *Brunei Darussalam*, p. 6.
24 Ibid., p. 24.
25 Sweeney, 'Silsilah Raja-Raja Berunai', p. 53.
26 For the early genealogy of the Sultans of Brunei, see Awang Haji Zainuddin bin Haji Hassan, 'Old Brunei: An Early Analysis', *Jurnal Darussalam*, 7 (2007): 14–36 at 15.
27 Mohd. Jamil Al-Sufri, *Brunei Darussalam*, p. 26.
28 Sweeney, 'Silsilah Raja-Raja Berunai', pp. 53–4.
29 Ibid., p. 23.
30 Mohd Jamil Al-Sufri, 'Sultan Sharif Ali', *Jurnal Darussalam*, 1 (1992): 6–33 at 7.

31 Sweeney, 'Silsilah Raja-Raja Berunai', p. 43.
32 Ibid., pp. 42–3.
33 Mohd. Jamil Al-Sufri, *Brunei Darussalam*, p. 15.
34 Ibid., p. 17.
35 Teuku Iskandar, *Malay Classical Literature Throughout the Century* (Bandar Seri Begawan: Universiti Brunei Darussalam, 1995), p. 318.
36 Sweeney, 'Silsilah Raja-Raja Berunai', p. 20.
37 Ibid., p. 56.
38 Pengiran Haji Mohammad bin Pengiran Haji Abd. Rahman, *Islam in Brunei Darussalam* (Bandar Seri Begawan: Dewan Bahasa dan Pustaka, 1992), p. 112.
39 Sweeney, 'Silsilah Raja-Raja Berunai', p. 52.
40 Ibid., pp. 66–7.
41 Ibid., p. 11.
42 'Thus Pengiran Shahbandar asked to take the Pahang-forged golden hilt of a keris (dagger) along with its sheath, a gift from the Di Pertuan Johor'; ibid., pp. 38, 14.
43 Ibid., p. 38.
44 Takong Amit, 'A Discussion on Vital Information about the Existence of the Old Brunei Government Based on Local, Arabic and Chinese Sources', *Beriga*, 19 (April–June 1988): 64.
45 Sweeney, 'Silsilah Raja-Raja Berunai', p. 54.
46 Ibid., pp. 21, 56.
47 Ibid., p. 64.
48 Mohd Jamil Al-Sufri, *Brunei Darussalam*, p. 37.
49 Ibid., p. 39.
50 Asbol bin Haji Mail, *Brunei Malay Sultanate in the 19th Century*, p. 5.
51 Ibid., p. 5.
52 Ibid., pp. 3–4.
53 Sweeney, 'Silsilah Raja-Raja Berunai', p. 49.
54 Ibid., p. 67.
55 Ibid.
56 Ibid., p. 65.
57 Ibid., p. 68.
58 Ibid., p. 68.
59 Ibid., p. 55.
60 Ibid., p. 39.
61 Ibid., p. 54. See also ibid., p. 49.
62 Ibid., p. 77.
63 Ibid., p. 81.

3 Brunei's foreign relations

Maintaining and developing its identity in a rapidly changing world

Mikio Oishi

Although Brunei achieved independence in January 1984, its foreign relations date back to at least 1958, when the prime minister of newly independent Malaya, Tunku Abdul Rahman Putra Al-Haj, proposed the 'Malaysia Plan'.[1] Included in this plan, Brunei, a tiny British protectorate on the northern coast of Borneo island, was inexorably pushed onto the volatile sea of Southeast Asian politics at that time. Suddenly, this sultanate found itself to be the bone of contention among various parties in the region, and its response to the Malaysia plan set the trajectory of a post-independence Brunei within the region and beyond.

A major challenge that Brunei has faced since then has been shared by all small states: that is, maintaining their independence and sovereignty in the state of so-called 'international anarchy'. However, Brunei's specific requirement has been that its independence and sovereignty should be maintained, together with its unique Malay Muslim sultanate system. Given that after thirty years of independence it enjoys peace and prosperity with its national philosophy of Melayu Islam Beraja (MIB, Malay Islamic Monarchy) firmly embedded in the country's polity, this challenge appears to have been met fairly well. Thus, to understand contemporary Brunei's foreign relations, it is necessary to know how Brunei has responded to challenges in historical times and in the regional context.

Moreover, it is not sufficient to dwell on what may be termed as 'passive existence' of a state as represented by maintaining independence and sovereignty. The reason is that a state is not only on a receiving end, but also acts as a giving side, thereby impacting on regional and international politics with its behaviour. Consequently, this chapter also looks at the 'active existence' of Brunei: namely, its contribution to the international community, particularly to the Association of Southeast Asian Nations (ASEAN). The debts small states owe to regional organizations in fulfilling their interests have frequently been discussed.[2] But less frequently addressed has been the contribution of states to these organizations. Brunei undoubtedly has much to offer to ASEAN and its regionalism.

This chapter examines several important aspects of Brunei's foreign relations: Brunei's historical ties with Britain and early relations with its neighbours, its commitment to ASEAN, its relations with extra-regional great powers, Islamic diplomacy as part of identity diplomacy, and external disputes, their management and the role of peacemaker. Prior to addressing these five aspects, it seems prudent to provide a theoretical framework for analysis.

Small state/microstate foreign relations and Brunei: a theoretical framework

There has been a conventional understanding on the problems or predicaments of small states arising from their size: vulnerability to external pressure, the tendency to become sidelined in international politics and the danger of being used as pawns by powerful states in their international strategy, as happened frequently during the Cold War period. Small states have developed strategies specific to their characteristics in order to address these perceived threats and weaknesses. As a result, they demonstrate a high tendency to:

1   rely on international law, which guarantees their own security, independence and sovereignty;
2   join regional, international or value-oriented organizations for recognition, legitimacy, protection and equal status with larger or more powerful states;
3   focus on specific issue areas in international behaviour rather than engaging in world affairs comprehensively, in an effort to create for themselves niche areas that reflect their relative advantages;
4   adopt an ideal stance on global issues such as global warming and anti-personnel mines, being relatively free from vested interests embedded globally;
5   establish close relations with extra-regional great powers in order to enhance external balancing in regional politics.

Among the small states, Brunei Darussalam can be classified further as one of those microstates that are defined as sovereign states with a very small population or very small land area, which largely means a population of less than one million or 10,000 km² of land area.[3] Coupled with the problems and predicaments common to all small states, in addition microstates have to cope with their own specific peculiarities, namely the permanent lack of resources to ensure their own long-term viability, and the everlasting threat of being swallowed up by a larger neighbouring state. The latter eventuality may occur when they fail to establish a strong state identity that would differentiate themselves from large cities or districts of neighbouring states. These factors make microstates even more vulnerable to external forces than other small states.

However, contrary to such a conventional view, microstates have in many cases proven their viability and sustainability, and some of them have even been faring better than ordinary small states, enjoying among the world's highest per capita incomes, as demonstrated by the likes of Luxemburg, Singapore, Bermuda and Brunei. At least two reasons have contributed to this unexpected good performance of microstates. Firstly, a guarantee for the independence and sovereignty of microstates has been firmly embedded in the international system of the early twenty-first century whereby international law stipulates the inviolability of sovereign states, and in acquiring membership of inter-governmental organizations that are regional, functional or identity-oriented. Such organizations treat microstates as equal to other states, and provide them with opportunities to act in important roles, such as chairmanship. The United Nations Security Council in particular possesses the means to ensure the sovereignty of microstates, if necessary, by coercion. A dramatic demonstration of this could be witnessed in the aftermath of the 1990 Iraqi invasion of Kuwait, a quasi-microstate.[4]

Secondly, the global economy in the post-Cold War era provides microstates with niches in which they can prosper. As Ozay Mehmet and M. Tahiroglu explain, 'small states [meaning microstates] may develop comparative advantages in such sectors as tourism, financial services and specialised education on the way to sustainability'.[5] The increasingly borderless economy makes resources available across the world, thus helping resource-poor microstates to overcome their own constraints through appropriate state-led development strategies, mainly focusing on the export of services.[6]

According to the perspective of Constructivism, state identity[7] is of particular significance in understanding the behaviour of a microstate in the international arena. While state identity satisfies the need of a microstate to differentiate itself as a sovereign state from municipalities or districts of neighbouring states, it also serves as an important source of a country's foreign policy by defining the role that a microstate assumes in the regional and international community. Thus, mediated by the state's role, there is a nexus between state identity and foreign policy, in which they impact on each other: while the former leads to the latter, the latter in turn affects the former.

Against the backdrop of the foreign relations of small states, and microstates in particular, Brunei's foreign relations and diplomacy possess the following characteristics. Firstly, the leadership of Sultan Hassanal Bolkiah, and of royal family members Prince Mohamed Bolkiah (as foreign minister) and Princess Masna Bolkiah (as ambassador-at-large) in particular, play prominent roles in the country's diplomacy. Sultan Hassanal Bolkiah, as the longest serving head of state within ASEAN, coupled with his personal successful diplomatic track record, commands high respect within the region as well as on the international stage that in turn has boosted the country's profile. Likewise, Prince Mohamed, who has held the Foreign Ministry portfolio since Brunei's independence in 1984, has remained in office for more than three decades. Secondly, Brunei is in a good position to utilize its wealth from petroleum and natural gas as a powerful diplomatic instrument. The United Nations Convention of the Law of the Sea (1982) grants Brunei 25,340 km^2 of an Exclusive Economic Zone (EEZ),[8] which is nearly 4.5 times the country's land area. Such a vast and rich EEZ provides the microstate of less than 0.5 million population with financial power incommensurate with its size to be deployed within the region and beyond, and sufficient funds to diversify its economy to enable continuous and sustainable prosperity.

Thirdly, Brunei seeks to project its Islamic sultanate identity, as manifested by the MIB, regionally and internationally through various activities in the international arena, such as in disaster relief and restoration works in post-tsunami Aceh, participation in the peace process of the Southern Philippines sectarian conflict, and in Islam-related projects carried out bilaterally with other Islamic states or under the auspices of the Organisation of Islamic Cooperation (OIC). These endeavours stemming from the country's state identity in turn strengthened this identity in a positive boomerang effect.

Lastly, Brunei's historical ties with Britain and the developments leading to its independence in 1984 and the early post-independence period had a strong impact on the trajectory of the country, both within the region and beyond.

These four characteristics will be explored by investigating several significant aspects of Brunei's foreign relations and diplomacy with its basic goal in mind: to maintain its independence and sovereignty as well as its unique sultanate system within the region and in the wider world.

Historical ties with Britain and early relations with its neighbours

There have been long-term historical ties between Brunei and Britain. The latter came to the former's rescue when it faced more and more encroachment on its land by Western non-state entities, specifically the White Rajah of Sarawak and the British North Borneo Chartered Company of Sabah in the late nineteenth century. To maintain its territorial integrity, the sultanate eventually became a British protectorate (1888), followed by the introduction of a British Residency system (1906) over its traditional polity of a Malay sultanate. Under the Residency system, the institutional foundation of a modern Bruneian state was laid, together with public services, a health service and resource and infrastructural development. After the Second World War, decolonization was initiated by Britain, which by the 1960s had realized that independence was inevitable for most of its colonial territories.[9] Thus, the process of independence of Brunei was advanced in an orderly manner in terms of bilateral co-operation. However, differences in vision among Bruneians about the form of the newly independent state prompted Partai Rakyat Brunei (PRB, Brunei People's Party) into an open revolt in 1962 that was swiftly suppressed by the British military, specifically its Ghurkha contingents.

The involvement of Indonesia and Malaysia in Brunei's domestic turmoil from opposite directions as part of their confrontation over the territories of British Borneo left a bitter memory among Bruneians. Jakarta, under President Sukarno's policy of 'liberating North Borneo from Western powers', openly aided the Tentera Nasional Kalimantan Utara (TNKU, North Kalimantan National Army), the military wing of the PRB,[10] while Brunei suffered from the retaliatory policy of Kuala Lumpur's Prime Minister Tunku Abdul Rahman Putra Al-Haj for non-participation in the formation of Malaysia. Only when Singapore under Chief Minister Lee Kwan Yew was expelled from Malaysia in August 1965 by Tunku did Brunei finally find a regional peer with which it shared a number of strategic interests.[11] Since then, the two microstates, one of them having yet to achieve full independence, quickly forged close ties with each other, as reflected in defence co-operation including mutual training programmes and the Currency Interchangeability Agreement.[12] Thus, Brunei's enmity towards and suspicion of Malaysia and Indonesia and, in contrast, its solidarity and co-operation with Singapore – a structure mediated and stabilized by Britain in political and military terms, including the latter's prolonged military presence – defined the sub-regional political environment for most of the 1960s.

This structure began to transform in the late 1960s with the change of leadership in each of these countries that had experienced constant domestic turmoil. Indonesian President Sukarno lost power and was replaced by Suharto in March 1967 after a nationwide upheaval following the abortive coup of the 30 September Movement in 1965; Sultan Omar Ali Saifuddien III of Brunei abdicated in favour of his eldest son, Hassanal Bolkiah, in October 1967, and Prime Minister Tunku Abdul Rahman Al-Haj was marginalized in the aftermath of the 13 May Race Riots in 1969 and eventually handed over power to his long-time deputy, Abdul Razak Hussein, in September 1970. These changes in political leadership ushered in a new era in the relationship of the three countries. ASEAN was finally formed in August 1967 following the downfall of Sukarno, the initiator of Konfrantasi (Confrontation), resulting in the conclusion of the bitter dispute, and brought Indonesia within a non-communist constellation of states in Southeast Asia. Indeed, the regional organization ASEAN could be considered as part of a reconciliation process between post-Sukarno Indonesia and Malaysia. On the other hand, rapprochement in the remaining two sets of troubled bilateral relations – Indonesia–Brunei and Malaysia–Brunei – moved sluggishly. After a period of residual tension, especially in Malaysia–Brunei relations, the late 1970s saw Kuala Lumpur and Jakarta making gestures of reconciliation towards Brunei. Initial informal high-level social exchanges were followed up by bilateral visits of the top leaders.[13] By the time Brunei finally achieved independence in January 1984, its relationship with Malaysia and Indonesia had improved considerably, with both countries establishing diplomatic ties immediately. However, Brunei had not sufficiently overcome a sense of vulnerability from without as well as from within, which made the continued post-independence retention of British military personnel indispensable.

Commitment to ASEAN

Joining international organizations is one of the most effective means for small states or microstates to gain international legitimacy and recognition and enhance their chances of survival. For Brunei, such needs were met through membership of ASEAN with its numerous official meetings, holding positions of responsibility such as ASEAN Chair that are available to all member states, and not least, ASEAN's norms and principles which are beneficial to weak or small states that are explicitly demonstrated in such official documents as the ASEAN Declaration (1967), the Zone of Peace, Freedom and Neutrality (ZOPFAN) (1971) and the Treaty of Amity and Cooperation in Southeast Asia (1976).[14]

Therefore, joining ASEAN was one of the immediate moves of newly independent Brunei, taking place just six days after independence. Singapore played a leading role in the admission of Brunei into the regional organization, which was warmly welcomed by other member states, as well as Indonesia and Malaysia in particular. In fact, Brunei joined regional politics as a sovereign state at an opportune time: disputes among ASEAN members were largely under control, and they were forging solidarity among themselves, especially through regional efforts to settle the Cambodian civil war.[15] Brunei was poised and stood in good stead to quickly fit into the ongoing collective endeavour. This conducive environment in the region is another determinant of the trajectory of Brunei's regional and international behaviour, as reflected by the five guiding principles of its official foreign policy:

1 mutual respect for the territorial integrity, sovereignty, independence and national identity of all nations;
2 recognizing the equality of all nations, large and small;
3 adherence to the principle of non-interference in the internal affairs of other nations;
4 advocating peaceful settlement of disputes;
5 co-operating for mutual benefit.[16]

These guiding principles overlap with those of ASEAN, bringing about the convergence of goals between Brunei and ASEAN and making it even easier for the former to be committed to the latter.

Besides, gaining ASEAN membership has specific significance for Brunei as a microstate. The 1975 Indonesian invasion of East Timor in the wake of the territory's declaration of independence from Portugal was a reminder to the international community that some of ASEAN's principles, such as respect for national sovereignty and non-use of force, could be conveniently set aside for non-member states in the region. At that time, the threat posed by Malaysia, which might have taken a cue from the East Timorese example, was seriously felt by Bruneian leaders. In contrast, Singapore's independence and sovereignty were maintained, to a considerable degree, due to its membership of ASEAN.[17] This regional organization has played the role of an 'incubator' of newly independent states with its non-interference principle and the policy of avoidance of inter-state conflict,[18] protectively nourishing the regimes of these young states. Since its admission to ASEAN in 1984, Brunei has benefited tremendously from this incubation function of the organization, which has drastically reduced its lingering sense of threat from Malaysia and, to a lesser degree, Indonesia.

Moreover, ASEAN has provided Brunei with numerous venues in which its representatives, including its foreign minister, senior officials from other ministries and, increasingly, the sultan as the head of state and government of Brunei, interact with counterparts from other member states. Over time, the mutual recognition, respect and assurance forged by these interactions, including fulfilling obligations and duties as ASEAN members, convinced Brunei to discard its sense of vulnerability. Brunei's three successful stints as ASEAN Chair, in 1989, 1995 and 2013,[19] which involved organizing hundreds of official ASEAN meetings on a wide range of issues within a one-year tenure, have enhanced its regional and international standing. ASEAN, on its part, has benefited from Brunei's contribution as a strong upholder of its constitutive and regulatory norms and principles and as a reliable sponsor of projects under the aegis of ASEAN. The latter role was played out to the gratitude of other ASEAN members when the 1997 East Asian financial and economic crisis hit the region. Sultan Hassanal Bolkiah personally visited Indonesia and Thailand, and was instrumental in extending rescue loans to affected countries through International Monetary Fund (IMF) schemes. In addition, the sultan and the Brunei Investment Agency sought to fill the financial void after hot money moved out of the region in the midst of the crisis.

The current ASEAN endeavour to create an ASEAN Community by the end of 2015[20] has expanded the areas in which Brunei and the regional organization co-operate with each other to mutual benefit. The ASEAN Community will consist of three pillars, the ASEAN Political-Security Community (APSC), the ASEAN Economic Community (AEC) and the ASEAN Socio-Cultural Community (ASCC), each of which will open up potential for Brunei–ASEAN collaboration. Firstly, the APSC envisages that 'countries in the region live at peace with one another and with the world at large in a just, democratic and harmonious environment', and could provide Brunei with the role of regional peacemaker.

Secondly, the AEC projects ASEAN 'as a single market and production base' that may generate opportunities for Bruneian business concerns, particularly small and medium-sized enterprises (SMEs) if they provide high-quality products, whereby demand would be inelastic against price.[21] The Bruneian authorities aim to nurture such SMEs in the field of information and communication technology (ICT), eco-tourism, halal food, and possibly consultancy, under Brunei's economic diversification policy. In this regard, the Brunei-Indonesia-Malaysia-Philippines East ASEAN Growth Area (BIMP-EAGA)[22] appears to be particularly promising. By participating with its entire territory in the scheme and by virtue of its strategic location in a sub-region that is considered the economic backwaters of the other three countries, if Brunei can establish a cluster of high-technology, high-value-added, export-oriented and environmentally friendly businesses, it will stand to reap tremendous gains by effectively exploiting rich agricultural, forest, fishery, tourist and human resources for mutual benefit.[23]

Thirdly, the ASCC envisions 'a Southeast Asia bonded together in partnership as a community of caring societies' and 'fostering regional identity'. Here, the linkage between caring societies and regional identity is significant, in that helping the victims of poverty, natural disaster and other calamities may be conducive to the formation of ASEAN's common identity. In other words, each caring society – that is, each country – can maintain and/or enhance its state identity through such humanitarian and mercy engagements. An example involving Brunei was the disaster relief activities in Aceh, which was badly hit by the Indian Ocean earthquake and tsunami of December 2004. Brunei was among the first to respond to Indonesian President Bambang Yudhoyono's appeal for international assistance for the Aceh disaster. Brunei then extended material relief, including medical aid and personnel, far out of proportion to the country's size. Also, the Sultan was the first foreign head of state to visit Aceh, himself piloting a Black Hawk helicopter to assess the situation at first hand.[24] Furthermore, as part of a disaster restoration package totalling US$2.4 million, Brunei donated to Banda Aceh a 'Brunei Village', equipped with a mosque, called the Brunei Darussalam Mosque, a clinic, a school, an Islamic boarding school and an orphanage for the displaced children. Another mosque, called the Sultan Haji Hassanal Bolkiah Baiturrahim Mosque, together with an Islamic boarding school were also erected in a different part of Aceh.[25] Although Brunei's contribution to Aceh, which was historically a location of an Islamic sultanate, may not be unduly conspicuous, its actions can be construed as the exercise of Islamic virtues and values, extended to the borderless Islamic Ummah across the world.

Relations with extra-regional great powers: the US, China and Japan

Microstates as part of the small state category tend to forge close ties with extra-regional great powers to achieve external balancing towards regional neighbours that are larger or more powerful than themselves. Brunei has traditionally looked to Britain for this function by maintaining close defence ties with the latter, even after independence. In addition, there are three extra-regional powers, the United States, Japan and China, that have been influential over Southeast Asia, including Brunei. In a post-Cold War Southeast Asia, this triumvirate have often been rivals, with a US-Japan alliance facing a 'rising China', while all of them are increasingly interdependent economically. ASEAN's relationship strategy towards such great powers has been one of 'hedging' – maintaining good relations with both sides, rather than committing to one, while obtaining from both sides the best possible economic, political and defence deals.

Brunei, as a member state of ASEAN, largely follows this hedging strategy towards these extra-regional powers, albeit with its own flavour. Firstly, Brunei has regarded Japan as the main and most stable source of its national wealth. As of 2012, Japan was Brunei's largest trade partner, accounting for 44 per cent of Brunei's total exports and 87 per cent of Brunei's natural gas exports.[26] Since 1972, both counties have been parties to a long-term natural gas procurement contract, which was renewed for the third time for another ten years in April 2013.[27] Given that oil and gas account for 90 per cent of the country's total exports and 70 per cent of its GDP, Brunei's economic dependence on Japan is extreme and undoubted.

Besides contributing to Brunei's affluence, Japan is increasingly eager to transfer its technologies to Brunei in response to the latter's efforts in economic diversification. One of these technological transfers concerns renewable energy. Brunei's first photovoltaic power generation plant was built in Seria, a township to the west of Bandar Seri Begawan, the national capital, and came into operation in May 2011, albeit only for demonstration purposes. This project was fully funded by Japan's Mitsubishi Corporation, a major player in the development of Brunei's natural gas resources since early 1972.[28] Mitsubishi Corporation has also been involved in agricultural projects to enhance crop production through improved farm management and, jointly with Japan's Itochu Corporation, in developing a world-class petrochemical hub in Liang, another township in western Brunei. Other areas of potential technological co-operation between Brunei and Japan are ICT, intellectual property and halal food. Through these activities, Japan is helping to transform Brunei from dependence on resource-rich industries to reliance on knowledge-based industries.

Secondly, Brunei–United States relations have been characterized by strategic and security interests, in contrast to the economic and technology-based Brunei–Japan relations. During the Cold War period, the US found Brunei useful as it was strategically located on the routes connecting American bases in the Philippines, Thailand, Singapore and Australia. In addition to utilizing Brunei as a logistical and supply base, the US was granted access to the country's pristine tropical jungle in order to train American troops for anti-guerrilla warfare in Vietnam. For Brunei, the US and Britain have been ultimate guarantors of its independence and sovereignty against larger and more powerful neighbouring states.

What is specific about Brunei's diplomacy with the US is that its leaders have forged close personal ties with many of their American counterparts, who have sought mutual benefit. From Washington's perspective, Brunei is invaluable because of the standing and influence within ASEAN of Sultan Hassanal Bolkiah, whose support is crucial for the smooth implementation of US policy in the region. Also, personal ties have been exploited by US administrations to finance enterprises or operations that US presidents have been involved in or initiated personally, by accepting Brunei's offer from its estimated US$30 billion of financial reserves. On the part of Brunei, such financing is politically cost-effective, targeting the needs of US presidents.[29]

Since the declaration of the 'American pivot to Asia' in 2010, Brunei–United States relations have apparently entered a new era. Since January 2008, Brunei has already been an important US partner in the Trans-Pacific Partnership (TPP) negotiations, which the USA is using as a powerful instrument to enhance its economic interests in the Pacific Rim, perhaps in rivalry with the China-dominated Regional Comprehensive Economic Partnership (RCEP). Brunei appears to have prudently adopted a hedging strategy by participating in both mechanisms. Currently, two schemes involving Brunei and the US act as platforms for both countries to further enhance their bilateral relations: Brunei-US English-Language Enrichment Programme for ASEAN, and the US-Asia Pacific Comprehensive Energy Partnership. The former, funded by Brunei, aims to enhance the proficiency of English within the ASEAN region by offering training programmes involving American and Bruneian English experts and attended by government officials and teachers from member states of ASEAN. The latter is actually a trilateral scheme initiated by Brunei, the US and Indonesia to address 'energy poverty and energy access' in the Asia-Pacific region.[30] The significance the US has attached to these two non-military projects reflects the Obama administration's new Southeast Asian strategy, which seems to create for small states in the region like Brunei a wider manoeuvring space than the conventional alliance approach of the US in the past.

Thirdly, Brunei–China bilateral relations date back to the period of the Han dynasty, some 2,000 years ago. The tomb of Sultan Abdul Majid Hassan of Brunei in Nanjing, China, erected during the Ming dynasty in the early fifteenth century, has been a symbol of long-lasting friendship between the two countries. Later, such ties were eclipsed under the British protectorate of Brunei, which then faced the decades-long threat of Communist China. Only with the conclusion of the Cold

War did bilateral relations greatly improve, culminating in the establishment of official relations in September 1991.[31] As China expanded its economic activities in Southeast Asia, economic interdependence between China and ASEAN countries was forged and expanded. But in contrast with other ASEAN countries, Brunei's economic exchanges (trade and investment) with China remained stagnant, and have jump-started only recently. Bilateral trade stood at US$1.3 billion in 2011, having quadrupled since 2008. Brunei's economic ties with China largely follow the same pattern as those with Japan, albeit at a much faster pace and marked by China's vigorous engagement in joint projects to develop hydrocarbon resources.[32] The year 2013 proved to be epochal for Brunei–China bilateral relations. The sultan made a state visit to China in April 2013 to meet President Xi Jinping; this was reciprocated by the attendance of Prime Minister Li Keqiang at the 8th East Asia Summit in Bandar Seri Begawan, chaired by the sultan. Under numerous agreements signed on these occasions, Brunei–China co-operation, which hitherto had been largely limited to hydrocarbon resource development, has risen to a new level, encompassing not only energy, but trade, infrastructure, agriculture, culture and defence.[33]

Given that Brunei and China have overlapping claims over sovereignty in the South China Sea (SCS), signing agreements on bilateral joint exploration in the disputed area is remarkable in contrast to the incessant bickering and stand-offs in similar situations between China and the Philippines and between China and Vietnam. Among the disputants on the SCS, Brunei is the only state that has yet to occupy any island in the area. Nor does Brunei insist loudly on its claim to Luisa Reef, which is within its Exclusive Economic Zone as defined by the United Nations Convention of the Law of the Sea. Apparently, the successful management of the Brunei–China territorial dispute has been helped by Brunei's approach of maintaining a low profile as a SCS disputant while enhancing goodwill with China. Such a non-confrontational approach defines Brunei's basic strategy for dispute management.

Islamic diplomacy as part of identity diplomacy

State identity constitutes the *raison d'état* for a country, perhaps even more so for a microstate. It may often occur that a microstate alone cannot cater to its own need for national identity, due to constraints on the resources at its command. Identity diplomacy, or Islamic diplomacy in the case of Brunei, becomes relevant as the latter may strengthen itself through sustenance from without. Islamic diplomacy can be conducted multilaterally or bilaterally.

The OIC provides Brunei's Islamic diplomacy with a multilateral venue to 'work closely with the other members in promoting Islamic interests and values for the benefit of the Islamic Ummah'.[34] The OIC's triennial Islamic Summit Conference, annual Council of Foreign Ministers and various subsidiary bodies and expert groups enable Brunei to participate and contribute in addressing current issues pertaining to the worldwide Muslim community. Among the pertinent issues deliberated at the Fourth Islamic Extraordinary Summit of August 2012 in Saudi Arabia were the civil war in Syria, the plight of Rohingya Muslims in Myanmar and the worsening situation in Mali.[35] Brunei is also an important contributor to the OIC's Islamic Solidarity Fund as well as other country-specific funds, including those for Afghanistan, Somalia, Sierra Leone and Niger. Besides, Brunei's involvement in peacekeeping operations and disaster relief activities can be viewed in terms of multilateral Islamic diplomacy. These endeavours are the manifestation and outright demonstration of Islamic values and virtues such as peace, justice, compassion, forgiveness and faith in God, benefiting both providers and recipients. In addition to disaster relief and restoration works in Aceh, Brunei has participated in two peacekeeping operations. Since 2003, Brunei has dispatched a contingent of police and military personnel to the peace process in the southern Philippine conflict as part of a six-party International Monitoring Team (IMT). In showcasing Islamic solidarity with Muslims in the region, Brunei also donated the Sultan Haji Hassanal Bolkiah Mosque, or the Grand Mosque, the largest mosque in the Philippines, situated in a suburb of Cotabato City, as well as extending a host of assistance for peace and development.[36] Brunei has also taken part in the United Nations Interim Force in Lebanon (UNIFIL), sending peacekeepers since 2008.[37]

In bilateral Islamic diplomacy, Brunei has established special ties with certain Islamic countries, contributing again to the enhancement of its state identity. For example, Brunei and the Sultanate of Oman have much in common: both are Islamic absolute monarchies in the category of small states, and both primarily rely on oil and natural gas in their national economies but are not members of the Organisation of the Petroleum Exporting Countries (OPEC). Since establishing diplomatic ties in March 1984, they have forged close relations with each other, with a number of co-operative agreements and memoranda of understanding (MOUs). Starting with co-operation in Islamic affairs, the scope of bilateral co-operation has expanded to cover the areas of trade and commerce, reciprocal protection of foreign investment, education, avoidance of double taxation and health care. Both countries face the common problem of relying too much on oil and natural gas and have every intention to diversify their economies. In 1993, the Bilateral Consultative Meeting was institutionalized between Brunei and Oman to further their bilateral relations, with sessions held alternately in the capitals of both states.[38] The bilateral ties are firmly embedded in an Islamic foundation while strengthening each other's state identity in the international arena.

In April 2014, Brunei began to implement Sharia criminal law in phases. Prior to implementation, representatives of Brunei visited Riyadh and Jeddah in Saudi Arabia to study at first hand how Islamic law was administered in the country's public life. This fact-finding delegation had an audience with one of the country's rulers, discussion sessions with chief justices and Islamic scholars, and courtroom visits to witness trials. Brunei and Saudi Arabia are poised to forge closer relations with each other through the former's ongoing Islamization.[39] At the same time, Brunei has sent a number of students to Egypt to pursue Islamic studies at the famed Al-Azhar University in Cairo.[40] Consequently, there are currently hundreds of Al-Azhar graduates in Brunei serving in various departments of the government and in a position to inspire and inculcate Islamic values in the administrative machinery and in public life.

External disputes, their management and the role of peacemaker

Post-independence Southeast Asia has been fraught with conflicts and disputes, reflecting the ethnic, cultural and ideological diversity of the region and the so-called 'colonial legacy' of disputable or ambiguous demarcation lines among the erstwhile colonial states. It is crucial for newly independent states to handle these conflicts in such a manner that these disputes do not present existential threats. Thus, conflict management is an important part of a state's foreign relations. Brunei has had its own share of conflicts to manage, namely territorial issues with Malaysia, and the South China Sea dispute.

Firstly, Brunei's disputes with Malaysia concern the territorial issue of Limbang and the maritime boundaries between the two countries. The Limbang dispute carries historical baggage. Brunei has never officially acknowledged that the Limbang district was ceded to Sarawak, but saw this as a consequence of Charles Brooke, the second White Rajah, forcefully annexing it in 1890. With the lost territory dividing Brunei into two separate parts like a wedge, there has been a general feeling among Bruneians that their nationhood is incomplete as long as Limbang remains outside the Bruneian fold. After a long dormant period, Brunei revived this dispute against Malaysia in the 1960s and 1970s, bringing a further chill to the already cold Brunei–Malaysia relations of the time. The fact that Limbang provided the rebels of the 1962 revolt with a safe haven gave a new dimension to Brunei's national security concerns. Given the fact that conflict avoidance has been ASEAN's common practice, the 'Limbang Question' has continued to simmer.

Another bilateral dispute on maritime boundaries involves the Exclusive Economic Zones of both countries. Seeds of the dispute were sown when Malaysia published a map in 1979 depicting its EEZs. To the dismay of Bruneians, it totally neglected the Bruneian portion of EEZs, a large part of which fall under the Malaysian EEZ. The particular bone of contention was two oil-rich blocks which Brunei referred as Blocks J and K, while Malaysia labelled them Blocks L and M. The March–April 2003 incidents in these blocks involving a boat from an oil company and naval ships of both countries revived the Limbang Question, prompting a series of bilateral negotiations. Eventually, the historic exchange of letters signed by Brunei Sultan Hassanal Bolkiah and Malaysian Prime Minister Abdullah Ahmad Badawi in March 2009 settled the dispute. Malaysia agreed to drop its claim to the two oil blocks in exchange for its own participation in jointly exploiting resources in the blocks. On the other hand, a tacit understanding was reached between the two sides that Brunei would no longer raise the Limbang issue, which was thus left to eventually lapse.[41]

With these two long-standing thorns in the flesh removed, Brunei–Malaysia bilateral ties improved substantially, almost with a vengeance. This was symbolized by the opening of a Friendship Bridge in December 2013[42] connecting three districts: Brunei's Brunei-Muara, Malaysia's Limbang and Brunei's Temburong. The bridge forms part of the Sarawak–Brunei–Sabah Pan Borneo Highway that has greatly enhanced connectivity in this part of the ASEAN region and fulfilled one of the important agendas of the AEC and the BIMP-EAGA scheme. These improved relations also seem to be reflected in a significant increase in Brunei–Malaysia bilateral trade over the past few years.

Secondly, Brunei participated in the SCS dispute as a disputant and, increasingly, as a mediator. The above-mentioned dispute with Malaysia and another one with China are part of the overall SCS dispute. As a disputant, Brunei has generally been performing fairly well. With China, Brunei has downplayed the fact that both countries possess overlapping sovereignty claims, and has managed to embark on joint exploration and extraction projects. This has certainly been an extraordinary feat on the part of Brunei. Apparently, China is secretly and realistically reassessing the 'nine dotted line' that it utilized to claim sovereignty over most parts of the SCS. Moreover, Brunei's diplomacy towards China has shown the effectiveness of developing comprehensive co-operative relations branching out into more specific co-operative projects, resulting in an effective confidence-building system. With Malaysia, on the other hand, Brunei has explicitly acknowledged the existence of incompatible claims. However, in a show of skilful diplomatic acumen, Brunei successfully convinced Malaysia of the benefit of withdrawing its long-standing maritime claim in exchange for Brunei's tacit acceptance of the status quo in Limbang.

These successful examples of Brunei's conflict management as a disputant appear to frame it as a competent peacemaker in the SCS dispute in general. This role materialized when Brunei assumed the 2013 ASEAN Chair. As ASEAN Chair, Brunei avoided a repeat of the debacle in Cambodia's capital a year before, when the ASEAN Ministerial Meeting (AMM) in Phnom Penh failed to issue a joint communiqué – an unprecedented break in tradition in the history of the AMM due to serious internal differences relating to the handling of the SCS dispute. In 2013, Brunei rescued ASEAN from the danger of a probable break-up by issuing an AMM communiqué which referred to the SCS dispute. Brunei also managed to elicit China's consent to expedite the process of drawing up a Code of Conduct in the SCS which would make the principles and rules of managing the SCS dispute as proclaimed in the 2002 Declaration on the Conduct of Parties binding on signatory states. These achievements were considered triumphs for Brunei-style quiet diplomacy, characterized by frequent behind-the-scenes negotiations and persuasion at the highest level.[43]

Brunei once again demonstrated such a diplomatic capability in successfully hosting the ASEAN Defence Ministers' Meeting Plus Humanitarian Assistance and Disaster Relief & Military Medicine Exercise (ADMM+HADR & MM Exercise) in June 2013, which was its brainchild. It was indeed an impressive feat to organize together the armed forces from ASEAN's ten member states and its eight dialogue partners – Australia, China, India, Japan, New Zealand, Russia, South Korea and the US – involving over 3,000 uniformed personnel in a four-day joint military exercise in Brunei, the ASEAN Chair country, following a year of preparation.[44] The most conspicuous achievement of the ADMM+HADR & MM Exercise was that Brunei successfully persuaded the US, China and Japan, the three most formidable rivals in the region, to work together for the first time in the history of East Asia. The exercise included an element of each country showing its forces to one another, but more important was the confidence-building among the armed forces that was forged by working together. By enhancing understanding and preventing misunderstanding and miscommunication among the relevant armed forces, the joint exercise contributed to more effective dispute management among the disputants to the SCS and those that seek to intervene from outside, such as the US and possibly Japan.

Needless to say, successful conduct of such a joint exercise has not immediately resulted in the settlement of the SCS dispute. Indeed, there have been several incidents in the SCS since the exercise, involving China, Vietnam and the Philippines. Brunei, on its part, has continued in the role of an effective regional peacemaker even after it handed over the ASEAN Chair to Myanmar towards the close of 2013.

Conclusion

This chapter has looked at how Brunei has conducted several significant aspects of its foreign relations as a microstate. Firstly, its regional and international behaviour has been historically contextualized, revealing the crucial roles of Britain, Malaysia, Indonesia and Singapore towards Brunei, especially during its infancy, influencing Brunei's future course in the regional and international arenas. Secondly, ASEAN has been indispensable to Brunei, both as its incubator when it was still young, and later as a platform for its regional and international actions, including its identity diplomacy. Both Brunei and ASEAN have benefited tremendously from these interactions. Thirdly, in its dealing with extra-regional great powers, Brunei has forged mutually prosperous relations with each of them. Thus far, Brunei appears to have been successful in maintaining a balance in two sets of great power rivalry – between the USA and China and between China and Japan – and has found its own benefits in continuing stability in these sets of relations. Fourthly, Islamic diplomacy, conducted multilaterally and bilaterally as part of Brunei's identity diplomacy, has continued to provide sustenance to its *raison d'état*. Lastly, there seems to be an increasingly prominent role for Brunei as a regional peacemaker, which adds a new element to its state identity. This role was performed by bridging the gaps among ASEAN members through quiet diplomacy. Brunei has achieved this capacity through skilful management of two disputes that it was drawn into: the territorial disputes with Malaysia over a land territory and a maritime zone, and the South China Sea dispute with China. The ways these disputes have been managed may provide models to emulate for other disputes in the ASEAN region. The expertise acquired through handling these disputes will contribute to Brunei's abilities to perform its new roles as mediator and peacemaker.

Notes

1 David Easter, *Britain and the Confrontation with Indonesia, 1960–66* (London: Tauris Academic Studies, 2004), p. 6.
2 See, for example, Pushpa Thambipillai, 'Brunei Darussalam and ASEAN: Regionalism for a Small State', *Asian Journal of Political Science*, 6(1) (1998): 80–94 at 86–7;

Jeanne A.K. Hey, 'Introducing Small State Foreign Policy', in *Small States in World Politics*, edited by Jeanne A.K. Hey (Boulder, CO: Lynne Rienner, 2003), pp. 4–5; Jacqueline Anne Braveboy-Wagner, 'The English-speaking Caribbean States: A Triad of Foreign Policy', in *Small States in World Politics*, edited by Jeanne A.K. Hey (Boulder, CO: Lynne Rienner, 2003), p. 37.

3 Ozay Mehmet and M. Tahiroglu, 'Globalization and Sustainability of Small States', *Humanomics*, 19(1) (2003): 45–58 at 46; Hey, 'Introducing Small State Foreign Policy', p. 2.

4 Hey, 'Introducing Small State Foreign Policy', p. 1.

5 Mehmet and Tahiroglu, 'Globalization and Sustainability of Small States', p. 45.

6 Ibid., pp. 48–51.

7 This chapter adopts Marc Lynch's definition of 'state identity', whereby state identity is comprised of 'the set of beliefs about the nature and purpose of the state expressed in public articulations of state actions and ideals'; Marc Lynch, 'Abandoning Iraq: Jordan's Alliances and the Politics of State Identity', *Security Studies*, 8(2–3) (1999): 347–88 at 349.

8 Sea Around Us Project, 'EEZ Waters of Brunei Darussalam'. http://www.seaaroundus.org/eez/96.aspx. Accessed 22 August 2015.

9 C.M Turnbull, *A Short History of Malaysia, Singapore and Brunei* (Singapore: Graham Brash, 1981), p. 278.

10 J.A.C. Mackie, *Konfrontasi: The Indonesia–Malaysia Dispute, 1963–1966* (Kuala Lumpur: Oxford University Press, 1974), p. 211.

11 Abdul Malik Omar, 'How Singapore and Brunei Became Friends', *The AMO Times*, 15 May 2014. http://amotimes.com/tag/brunei-and-singapore-abiding-ties-of-close-neighbours. Accessed 22 August 2015.

12 This was a tripartite agreement between Brunei, Singapore and Malaysia, until Malaysia opted out in 1973. The remaining two countries have continued the agreement to date. See Monetary Authority of Singapore, 'Currency Interchangeability Agreement – Brunei Notes and Coins'. http://www.mas.gov.sg/currency/currency-interchangeability-agreement-with-brunei.aspx. Accessed 22 August 2015.

13 Ralf Emmers, *Cooperative Security and the Balance of Power in ASEAN and the ARF* (London: RoutledgeCurzon, 2003), pp. 76–8.

14 Thambipillai, 'Brunei Darussalam and ASEAN', p. 82.

15 Ibid, p. 77.

16 Ministry of Foreign Affairs and Trade of Brunei Darussalam, 'Brunei Darussalam Country Brief', n.d. http://dfat.gov.au/geo/brunei-darussalam/pages/brunei-darussalam-country-brief.aspx. Accessed 22 August 2015.

17 Emmers, *Cooperative Security*, pp. 73–4.

18 For ASEAN's policy of conflict avoidance in inter-state conflicts as part of the ASEAN Way of conflict management, see Kamarulzaman Askandar, Jacob Bercovitch and Mikio Oishi, 'ASEAN Way of Conflict Management: Old Patterns and New Trends', *Asian Journal of Political Science*, 10(2) (2002): 21–42 at 24–6, 32.

19 Thambipillai, 'Brunei Darussalam and ASEAN', p. 85.

20 The plan to establish an ASEAN Community was included in the Declaration of ASEAN Concord II (the Bali Concord II), signed in October 2003. See ASEAN Secretariat, 'Declaration of ASEAN Concord II (Bali Concord II)', 7 October 2003. http://www.asean.org/news/asean-statement-communiques/item/declaration-of-asean-concord-ii-bali-concord-ii-3. Accessed 22 August 2015.

21 Lim Jock Hoi, 'Achieving the AEC 2015: Challenges for Brunei Darussalam', in *Achieving the ASEAN Economic Community 2015: Challenges for Member Countries and Businesses*, edited by Sanchita Basu Das (Singapore: Institute of Southeast Asian Studies, 2012), p. 24.

22 On the BIMP-EAGA scheme and its potential, see Mohd Yaakub Hj. Johari, Bison Kurus and Janiah Zaini, eds, *BIMP-EAGA Integration: Issues and Challenges* (Kota Kinabalu: Institute for Development Studies, 1997).

23 Lim, 'Achieving the AEC 2015', p. 24.

24 Azlan Othman, 'His Majesty Visits Tsunami-hit Aceh', *The Borneo Bulletin*, 2 February 2005.

25 Zareena Amiruddin, 'Brunei's Financial Aid to Tsunami Victims is Well Spent', *The Brunei Times*, 25 December 2010.

26 Ministry of Foreign Affairs of Japan, 'Japan and Brunei: 30 Years of Diplomatic Relations', p. 6, January 2014. http://www.bn.emb-japan.go.jp/jbyear2014/jb2014_brochure.pdf. Accessed 22 August 2015.

27 'Japan to Provide Energy Tech Aid to Brunei', *Jiji Press*, 13 May 2013.

28 Mitsubishi Corporation, 'Brunei LNG Project Strengthening Ties with a Resource-rich Country to Ensure Stable, Long-term Energy Supplies'. http://www.mitsubishicorp.com/jp/en/mclibrary/evolving/vol01/page3.html. Accessed 22 August 2015.

29 Nicholas D. Swain, 'The Foreign Policy of Small States: A Comparison of Bhutan and Brunei' (MA thesis, University of Hong Kong, 1991), pp. 80–81, 96.

30 Daniel L. Shields, 'Working with Brunei to Get the Rebalance Right', *TheAmbassadors Review*, Spring 2014. http://s3.amazonaws.com/caa-production/attachments/462/C_Pages20to22_Shields.pdf?1399575078. Accessed 22 August 2015.

31 Prashanth Parameswaran, 'China, Brunei: Ties that Bind', *Asia Times Online*, 9 November 2012. http://www.atimes.com/atimes/China_Business/NK09Cb01.html. Accessed 22 August 2015.

32 Ibid.

33 Ministry of Foreign Affairs of the People's Republic of China, 'Premier Li Keqiang Holds Talks with Sultan Haji Hassanal Bolkiah of Brunei, Stressing to Further Uplift Level of China-Brunei Strategic Cooperation', 11 October 2013. http://www.fmprc.gov.cn/mfa_eng/topics_665678/lkqzlcxdyldrxlhy_665684/t1088909.shtml. Accessed 22 August 2015.

34 Waleed P.D. Mahdini. 'Brunei Joins OIC Call for Conflict Resolution', 16 May 2007. http://www.bt.com.bn/classification/frontpage/2007/05/16/brunei_joins_oic_call_for_conflict_resolution. Accessed 22 August 2015.

35 Embassy of Brunei Darussalam and Mission to the European Union, Belgium, 'Sultan to Attend OIC Summit', 14 August 2012. http://bruneiembassy.be/sultan-to-attend-oic-summit/. Accessed 22 August 2015.

36 Edwin Fernandez, 'Brunei Military Official Visits Troops Monitoring Ceasefire of PH Gov't, MILF', *Inquirer Global Nation*, 14 July 2014. http://globalnation.inquirer.net/107908/brunei-military-official-visits-troops-monitoring-ceasefire-of-ph-govt-milf. Accessed 22 August 2015.

37 Wardi Buntar, 'Brunei 8th UNIFIL Team Off to Lebanon', *Brunei Times*, 5 July 2012. http://www.bt.com.bn/news-national/2012/07/05/brunei-8th-unifil-team-lebanon. Accessed 22 August 2015.

38 Asia Economic Institute, 'Brunei and Oman: Strengthening Bilateral Relations', n.d. http://www.asiaecon.org/special_articles/read_sp/12237. Accessed 22 August 2015.

39 Irfan Mohammed, 'Brunei Studying Kingdom's Implementation of Shariah', *Arab News*, 14 February 2014. http://www.arabnews.com/news/525641. Accessed 22 August 2015.

40 Ministry of Foreign Affairs, Arab Republic of Egypt, 'Egypt's Relations with ASEAN Countries', 4 March 2006. http://www.mfa.gov.eg/English/EgyptianForeignPolicy/EgyptianAsianRelation/News/Pages/NewsDetails.aspx?Source=6781921f-3993-444a-859e-ee26ce851de8&newsID=b81c8bfc-cae6-46ff-9efb-d46d90870230. Accessed 20 August 2014.

41 Goh De No, 'Brunei Owns Blocks J and K, Says Abudullah', *The Brunei Times*, 1 May 2010; Leong Shen-li, 'A Tale of Two Blocks', *The Star Online*, 2 May 2010. http://www.thestar.com.my/story.aspx/?file=%2f2010%2f5%2f9%2fnation%2f6188182. Accessed 22 August 2015.

42 'Friendship Bridge a Symbol of Close M'sia-Brunei Ties', *Borneo Post Online*, 9 December 2013. http://www.theborneopost.com/2013/12/09/friendship-bridge-a-symbol-of-close-msia-brunei-ties/. Accessed 22 August 2015.

43 Shields, 'Working with Brunei to Get the Rebalance Right'.

44 Ministry of Defence, Singapore, 'SAF and Other Militaries Conclude the ADMM-Plus HADR/MM Exercise', 20 June 2013. http://www.mindef.gov.sg/imindef/press_room/official_releases/nr/2013/jun/20jun13_nr.html#.U8T6Jq2KDoY. Accessed 22 August 2015.

Part II

Multi-ethnic mosaic and lifestyle

4 Being 'Malay' in modern Brunei

Mohd Shahrol Amira bin Abdullah

'Typically,' as Joseph E. Trimble and Ryan Dickson define it, 'ethnic identity is an affiliative construct, where an individual is viewed by themselves and by others as belonging to a particular ethnic or cultural group', and 'An individual can choose to associate with a [particular] group especially if other choices are available (i.e., the person is of mixed ethnic or racial heritage).'[1] In this context, this chapter attempts to examine ethnic identity in modern Brunei, focusing mainly on the sultanate's seven ethnic groups that in 1961 were designated as indigenous Malay by the Brunei Nationality Status Acts of 1961, namely the Belait, Bisaya, Brunei, Dusun, Kedayan, Murut and Tutong.

I will begin with a general definition of the problematic term 'Malay' before elaborating further on what constitutes being Malay in modern Brunei Darussalam. The term 'Malay' is both culturally and authoritatively defined, both of which are adopted to serve specific objectives and may not imply the same interpretation. The generally accepted definition is the culture-based one, while the authority-based definition is more country-specific. Thus, the so-called 'Malay' in Brunei may not exhibit what it takes to be a contemporary Brunei Darussalam Malay. Various measures taken by both the ethnic groups and the government to preserve Malay ethnic identity and heritage will be highlighted to facilitate greater understanding of Brunei's seven indigenous ethnic groups that are categorized as Malay in the sultanate's contemporary context.

'Malay' and Malays in Southeast Asia

Defining what or who is Malay is problematic. Various anthropologists and historians, as well as modern nation states such as Brunei, Indonesia and Malaysia, all present different definitions or criteria. Certainly, the modern Bruneian definition differs from that of neighbouring countries such as Malaysia. The term has been used by some in reference to the whole of insular Southeast Asia and its peoples, who have also used the terms 'Malay World' (*Alam Melayu*) or 'the Malay Archipelago'. Many others use the term in a more restricted sense to refer to those people who have acknowledged themselves as being culturally and linguistically ethnic Malays.[2] Used in this sense, the flexibility and assimilative nature of Malay ethnicity should be noted, as in Borneo, for example, the majority of those who today refer to themselves as Malay are of Dayak descent and have embraced Islam and adopted Malay culture.[3]

The wealth of archaeological and linguistic data clearly inform us that the antecedents of those who today speak Malay were part of a migration of Austronesian-speaking people into Island Southeast Asia from Taiwan, beginning from about 4,500 years ago and spreading through the Philippines, Borneo and Sulawesi before settling throughout Island Southeast Asia.[4] Prior to the presence of Austronesian speakers in insular Southeast Asia, the region appears to have been inhabited by small numbers of Austroloid hunter-gathers. Linguists agree that Borneo was where the Malay language begun to develop from the broader Austronesian language family in the form of a proto-Malay language that is the progenitor of all languages within the Malayic-Dayak language family.[5] However, Sumatra is seen by many as the cultural and political homeland of the language, and is where the term 'Melayu' was first recorded in the seventh century.[6] Malays, then, have long established themselves in the so-called 'Malay World', some of whom later migrated westwards and settled in South Africa and Sri Lanka.[7]

The term 'Melayu' appears to have been used locally in the fifteenth century in the entrepôt of Melaka in order to differentiate Malays from Thais and Javanese, who had their own cultural preferences.[8] In terms of etymology, the word 'Melayu' is believed to have been derived from various words such as *Mo-Lo-Yu*, *Malauir*, *Ma-li-yu-er*, *Malaiur*, *Malayadvipa*, *Malayapura* and *Sungai Melayu*.[9] These terms were used by indigenes as well as by foreigners, including Chinese, Indians and Europeans, to refer to the historical kingdoms and geographical parts of the Malay Archipelago prior to the fifteenth century.[10] However, during the period of European colonization, the word 'Malay' was adopted into English via the Dutch *Malayo*.

The ethnic Malays are categorized as Austronesian people and speak various Malay dialects drawn from the Austronesian family of languages. Brunei, Malaysia, Singapore and Indonesia use different variants of Malay dialects as their official languages. Apart from having their own distinctive languages, the ethnic Malays are also culturally, socially and genetically diverse due to the long series of immigration and assimilation processes. Malay is one of the major languages of the world, and is today spoken by an estimated 280 million people, either natively or as a second language, with speakers found in as far as the Cocos Islands, Christmas Island, Sri Lanka and Southern Thailand.

Generally, the ethnic Malay cultural and social fabric have been greatly influenced by Indians, with whom Malays began interacting over 2,000 years ago. Relations with Indians through trade and marriages led to ethnic Malays adopting and adapting some forms of the Indian way of life and traditions that were useful to them and taking on Indic religions such as Hinduism and Buddhism, mixing them with their own indigenous beliefs. The Sanskrit language has also influenced Malays, and Indic terms are still used to refer to important Malay institutions, such as *raja* (king) and *dewa* (deities). The arrival of Islam from the end of the thirteenth century CE from West Asia via Indian Muslim traders (and later missionaries, political marriages and empire) literally transformed the Malay World into a 'Malay Muslim World'.

During the early modern period (from the thirteenth/fourteenth to the eighteenth centuries CE), Malays began to feel the impact of the Chinese and European influences as trade, imperialism and colonization gradually manifested in the region. The Spanish, Portuguese and the Dutch, and later the British, brought with them their different brands of Christianity, which drew adherents from a large number of people in the region alongside their social and economic systems. Equally important was the Japanese military occupation (1941–45), which had a significant impact on the ethnic Malays, particularly in fanning the embers of their burgeoning 'national' spirit.

The ethnic Malays of contemporary Southeast Asia are largely Muslims, and have been identified with the orthodox Sunni sect since the epoch of the Melaka Sultanate. But this does not mean that elements of animism, Hinduism, Buddhism, Christianity and other beliefs and practices that contravene Islamic teachings have been totally discarded by Malay Muslims. A large number of those designated as ethnic Malays, especially those in Brunei, have remained pagan or adherents of other beliefs besides Islam. Even though ethnic Malays have been separated by the boundaries of their respective nation states, they are to a large extent closely connected due to ties of proximity, common language, shared socio-cultural practices and history that bind them. The Association of Southeast Asian Nations (ASEAN) contributed to the continuous integration of ethnic Malays and serves as a significant platform for economic, social, religious and cultural forums.

Ethnic Malays in Brunei Darussalam

Brunei Darussalam is a small nation state in Southeast Asia, on the island of Borneo, which only regained its independence from Britain in 1984. With an area of 5,769 km², in 2011 Brunei had a population of 393,372, comprising 65.7 per cent (258,446) Malays, 10.3 per cent (40,534) Chinese and 24 per cent (94,392) other ethnicities.[11]

Administratively, Brunei Darussalam is divided into four districts, Brunei Muara, Tutong, Belait and Temburong, each headed by a district officer. Each district is further divided into *mukim* (parish) headed by a *penghulu* (headman), and each *mukim* consists of several villages (*kampung*) headed by a *ketua kampung* (village chief). Bandar Seri Begawan, the capital city, is situated in Brunei Muara District, which despite being the smallest in terms of land area, is where the majority of the population is concentrated, particularly in and around the capital. The least populated district is Temburong – ironically, the largest of the districts.

Brunei Darussalam is a Malay Muslim sultanate with Sultan Haji Hassanal Bolkiah Muizzaddin Waddaulah as the head of state, prime minister, and finance and defence minister. Constitutionally, he is also the head of Islam and custodian of Malay customs and traditions. In announcing the independence of Brunei Darussalam on 1 January 1984, he declared that Brunei Darussalam would be an independent Malay Islamic Monarchy state. Islam is the official religion, and Malay culture the prominent cultural identity of the state. The official language is Standard Malay; on a daily basis, however, Brunei Malay, a dialect of Malay that is significantly different to Standard Malay, is the *lingua franca*.[12]

The precursor to modern Brunei may have been a polity called Boni that is first mentioned in Chinese sources in the year 977 CE.[13] Accordingly, in that year three non-native envoys from Boni – Shinu, Puyali and Gexin – travelled to China for trade-related activities.[14] Both Chen Da-sheng and Pehin Jamil contended that these envoys were Muslims.[15] However, Brunei only became a Malay Muslim sultanate in 1386 CE, when its ruler, Awang Alak Betatar, is said to have embraced Islam and taken the Muslim name Muhammad Shah.[16] Since then, Brunei Darussalam has been a Malay Muslim monarchic state, with 29 Muslim sultans to date.

According to local oral tradition, Brunei was founded by 14 brothers, the sons of Dewa Emas Kayang who descended from heaven. He married 14 local women who then each gave birth to a son. One of the sons was Awang Alak Betatar, who became the first Muslim ruler of Brunei. His conversion was to enable him to marry Dayang Sri Alam, a princess of Johor, hence securing good relations with the Malay Johor Empire.

Ethnic Malays had been responsible for the foundation of early Brunei, and played important roles in the social, administration, defence, economic and Islamic development of the country. Likewise, a line of Malay sultans and officials had played important roles in shaping the history, civilization and identity of the state.

'Malay' by Brunei definition

The Report of the Population and Housing Census in Brunei (2011) indicated that there were about 258,446 Malays residing in Brunei Darussalam. The majority of them (189,168) lived in the Brunei Muara District. As mentioned, the Brunei Nationality Status Acts 1961 designated only seven ethnic groups as Malay, the Belait, Bisaya, Brunei, Dusun, Kedayan, Murut and Tutong, officially termed *puak jati* (indigenous ethnic group). Other ethnic groups native to Borneo and resident in Brunei such as the Iban and the Punan are excluded and not considered indigenous to Brunei. They were believed to have migrated relatively recently to Brunei, around 1900, compared to the seven ethnic groups designated as Malay.[17] By Brunei's definition, the word 'Malay' encompasses Muslims and non-Muslims. In contrast, the Federal Constitution of Malaysia uses the term 'Malay' to refer to a person who practises Islam and Malay culture, speaks the Malay language and whose ancestors are Malays, while in Indonesia the term 'Malay' simply refers to one of approximately 300 ethnic groups. Thus, the word 'Malay', by state-designated definition, is confined in scope and nature; the general usage of the term, however, has a broader and wide-ranging meaning.

The majority of ethnic Malays in Brunei are Muslims. The Kedayan, Bruneis, Tutong and Belait have long been Muslims, and while some Murut, Dusun and Bisaya have accepted the Islamic faith, a substantial number converted to Christianity and others remained pagan. The State of Brunei Constitution allows freedom of religion, hence non-Muslim Malays are not obliged to embrace Islam. By Malaysian definition, Murut, Dusun and Bisaya could not be categorized as

Malay unless they converted to Islam and spoke Malay as their first language; however, they would be referred to as *bumiputera* (natives of the land).

While it is true that, by authoritative definition, the Murut, Dusun and Bisaya are regarded as Malay, they do not normally refer to themselves as Malay. Nor do any of their languages belong to the Malayic-Dayak sub-family. The Murut are traditionally known as Lun Bawang, while the Dusun call themselves *sang jati* (indigenous people) The reference to these three ethnic groups as Malay is a recent phenomenon following the Brunei Citizenship Status Acts 1961.

Bisaya and Dusun

While the Bisaya and Dusun are officially regarded as two separate ethnic groups, there are many linguistic and cultural similarities between them, hence they will be treated together in this section. Some scholars even view them as a single ethnic group, and in relation to Brunei, V.T. King uses the terms 'Bisaya and 'Dusun' interchangeably, as does Yabit Alas.[18] According to Alas, Bisaya numbers decreased because in the past, parents often registered their children as Dusun rather than Bisaya as they did not want them to be thought of as Malaysians from Limbang in Sarawak, where the majority of Borneo's Bisaya live.[19] Such actions have clearly eroded and clouded what differences existed between the Bisaya and Dusun, making it increasingly difficult to differentiate between them culturally. Lexico-statistical data also indicate that linguistically, there is little difference between the two: based on the Swadesh list, Bisaya and Dusun share 82 per cent of their basic vocabulary, which suggests that rather than being two separate languages, Bisaya and Dusun are in fact two dialects of the same language.[20]

Interestingly, while the term 'Bisaya' appears to be an autonym, the term 'Dusun' is an exonym that in Malay means 'people of the orchards' or 'gardens' and was probably used by the Bruneis on account of their proclivity to own and manage fruit orchards in Tutong and Belait Districts. But the term does not appear in the Dusun/Bisaya language. The Dusun autonym is *sang jati*, meaning 'our race/ethnic group', which remains widely used among the Dusun.[21] However, the term 'Dusun' is used officially and by other ethnic groups, and has become widely accepted in society and also by the Dusun themselves when conversing with other groups. During British colonial rule, the Dusun, then known as *sang jati*, were classified as similar to Dusun living in British North Borneo (present-day Sabah).

In 2011, those in Brunei Darussalam calling themselves Bisaya numbered just 711, while 13,485 called themselves Dusun.[22] Most of the Bisaya (508) resided in the Brunei Muara District, others in Tutong (128), Belait (63) and Temburong (12). Most Dusun lived in Tutong (7,364) with smaller numbers in Brunei Muara (3,689), Belait (2,356) and Temburong (76). Villages in Brunei Darussalam associated with the Dusun are Kampung Sungai Mau, Kampung Kagu Baru, Kampung Bukit Sawat, Kampung Sukang, Kampung Sugai Liang-Lumut, Kampung Rambai, Kampung Ukong, Kampung Lamunin, Kampung Kiudang and Kampung Telisai. The main, *kampung* inhabited by the Bisaya is Kampung Bebuloh. Both groups are also scattered throughout Brunei due to their participation in government resettlement and housing programmes, the need for work, and inter-marriage

In terms of physical appearance, the Bisaya and Dusun are very similar to the other Brunei ethnic groups designated as Malay. Their occupations, material culture and social life have also been similar to most of those other Brunei ethnic groups which traditionally lived on the land. Most were in the past agriculturalists practising shifting rice cultivation as well as planting a variety of fruit and vegetables. In the past, they also kept pigs, buffalo and other livestock that were mainly used as sacrificial animals in various pagan ceremonies.[23] Because of major changes in the socio-economics of Brunei over the last century or so, very few contemporary Brunei Bisaya and Dusun are today engaged in agricultural activities.

Bisaya and Dusun were traditionally animists, and while some have embraced Islam or Christianity, others have maintained their traditional practices.[24] One of the most important of their religious rituals/festivals is called the *temarok* (Bisaya) or *tamorok* (Dusun), of which there are various types, invariably led by a female. The ritual is primarily to seek assistance in all aspects of daily life from the *dewato* (spirits), including curing sickness and ensuring a good rice harvest. Examples of *tamorok* are Tamarok Bulan (monthly ceremony to pray for health and prosperity), Tamarok Parai (annual ceremony after rice harvesting), Tamarok Barayo (crocodile ceremony to begin consuming new rice), Tamarok Bua (fruit season ceremony), Tamarok Nguru Panyakit (curing illness ceremony) and Tamarok Ngirang Alai (ceremony to ward off evil spirits in the house). These *tamorok* rituals collectively form an important part of cultural identity for the Dusun and Bisaya.

Traditional dress is normally worn specifically for certain ceremonies and cultural performances. Black is the official colour for the traditional attire. Dusun and Bisaya traditional dresses are differentiated from other ethnic groups by the nature of accessories. Some elements of red are added to the dress, and colourful beads line its edges. Red headgear, called *lilit selampit*, is worn by men as part of the traditional attire. Females wear the black dress with a blue piece of cloth called *selampai* placed across the chest. The women, like the men, wear *lilit selampit* as headgear, while the Brunei traditional woven cloth *kain jongsarat* is worn as a skirt to cover the lower part of the body. Traditional dress is also worn by the bride and groom during their wedding. Overall, Bisaya and Dusun attire appear to be similar, the only significant difference being the use of coloured stripes. Bisaya dress uses more white and red stripes compared to the Dusun, which generally has more yellow stripes and fewer white ones. Dusun female dress also tends to feature more accessories of beads.

Dusun and Bisaya marriages, just like those of other ethnic Brunei Malay groups, commence with an investigation process. In this first stage, the prospective groom's family will send someone to find out whether the prospective bride is single and ready for marriage. If so, then the groom's family will arrange for the engagement ceremony. Thereafter, the wedding ceremony itself takes place, after the groom has fulfilled all the bride's family's requirements. Shortly before the wedding ceremony, the bride will be required by the groom's family to prepare a traditional dish called *kuih penyaram*, a kind of cake. It is essential for the bride to be able to make a perfect *kuih penyaram* as a sign of her virginity. If she fails because the *kuih penyaram* is incorrectly or poorly prepared, it is taken to indicate that she is no longer a virgin, and the wedding is abandoned.

Three gunshots are fired to mark the start of the wedding ceremony. The new-lywed couple are forbidden to leave the house for three days lest they are harmed by evil spirits.

The Dusun in particular are famous for being rich in cultural performances, a means of preserving their cultural heritage that is passed from one generation to another. Of the many traditional dances of the Dusun, *tarian anchayau* (a festival dance), *tarian tamarok* (a dance to please the rice spirits) and *tarian tog tong genawong* (a dance performed while processing rice) are popular and frequently performed.

The Bruneis

The Bruneis traditionally reside in Kampong Ayer, the former capital and administrative centre of Brunei. In 2011, there were 194,289 ethnic Bruneis in Brunei Darussalam, of which 82,302 lived in Brunei Muara, 18,014 in Belait, 10,278 in Tutong and 2,522 in Temburong. The Bruneis are fairly well distributed throughout the country as a result of population movements, inter-marriages, work requirements, and government resettlement and housing programmes. However, the majority still continue to live in their traditional homes in Kampong Ayer. Those who have resettled on land may apply for modern houses in Kampong Ayer replete with modern amenities, where living conditions are greatly improved. Traditionally, the Bruneis were highly reluctant to settle on land, as their life revolved around water and the sea, being involved in trade and/or fishing.

All Bruneis are Muslims, hence their life cycle is very much influenced and dictated by Islamic principles and teachings. Traditionally, fishing was their main occupation, as their settlements were dominated by water; in present times, many are civil servants and others are engaged in the private sector. Living on the water has helped the Bruneis to maintain close relations among themselves. Several buildings (*balai* or hall) have been especially built in the river city as gathering and meeting places for the community and for religious teaching.

The Bruneis were, and still are, well-known for their elaborate wedding cer-emonies. The process starts with the *merisik* (investigation) activity, where the parents of a groom-to-be, without revealing their actual intentions, will visit a prospective bride's house to investigate. While there, they secretly observe the prospective bride's behaviour, and if her behaviour and character appear favour-able and she has no other suitor, then the next step is the *bejarum-jarum* (propo-sition) ceremony. As the Bruneis are Muslims, they are not allowed to propose marriage to any maiden who has already been proposed to or who is already engaged. Hence, the official proposal ceremony will normally be conducted by elder persons from the male side, usually not involving the parents of the groom-to-be. If the proposal is accepted, then both sides will arrange for the engagement date, *besuruh*, which will be attended by members of both families. Another big event is the *menghantar berian* (sending the gifts), and thereafter the male side meets all the requests and requirements of the bride's side before the actual wedding. On the wedding day, called *bersanding* (sitting in state), all members of both families and their friends will be invited to attend the two ceremonies, which are held separately at the groom's and bride's houses. During the night of the wedding, there is a small ceremony among the family members in the groom's house called the *malam berambil-ambilan* (the night of taking the husband). The groom will normally officially enter his wife's bedroom after this ceremony, witnessed by the members of both families. The final matrimonial ceremony is the *mulih tiga hari* (the third day return) ceremony. Three days after the wedding, the bride and groom, accompanied by some members from the groom's family, will escort the newly married couple back to the wife's house.

The main wedding ceremony itself is divided into various functions, such as the cosmetic powder bath, marriage ceremony (*akad nikah*), cosmetic powdering night, henna night, sitting on the dice and the taking the groom night (as mentioned above). These functions may take place within a day or night or extend over several days and several nights, depending on the family. The following is a list of requests, requirements or gifts expected from the groom's side in an ethnic Bruneian wedding:

- *pembuka mulut* (opening negotiations), often presented in the form of cash (BND50) – a requirement to start a conversation or negotiation during the initial meeting concerning the marriage;
- mark of engagement, either in the form of cash or a gold ring or a piece of traditionally woven cloth;
- *berian* (wedding gift as required by Islamic law), normally in the form of cash, kitchen money or wedding expenditure on the part of the bride's family;
- *langkah dulang* (lit. 'jumping over the tray'), in the form of a gold ring, clothing or cash paid to the elder sister(s) of the bride if she or they are not yet married;
- *langkah sungai/laut* (lit. 'to leap across the river/sea'), in the form of cash, a requirement to be paid if the groom and the bride are not of the same ethnic group; believed to originate from the Kedayan;
- race compensation, normally applicable to a lower-ranking groom wishing to marry a bride of higher status, especially of the noble family;
- additional gifts as a sign of love, which can be in any form, such as foods, household utensils, clothes or toiletries.

Today, the matrimonial ceremonies remain elaborate, but more often are shortened due to time constraints, and they are no longer confined to the houses of the bride and groom, but are commonly held in community halls and hotels.

One of the famous dances which is derived from the Bruneis Malay ethnic group is the *adai-adai*. The dance portrays the life of people in Kampong Ayer, especially the life of the fishing community in the past. The movements in the dance imitate the movement of a person paddling a boat. The song of *adai-adai* itself carries a message about a parent trying to get their child to sleep before they head out to sea to fish. To perform the dance, male dancers will wear traditional dress, *cara Melayu*, the *sinjang* hat along with a woven cloth wrapped around their waists, while female dancers don *baju kurung* and cover their heads with *batik* cloths.

Murut

There are about 1,661 Murut living in contemporary Brunei Darussalam, distributed as follows: 797 live in Brunei Muara, 102 in Belait, 147 in Tutong and 615 in Temburong. Villages normally associated with the Murut in Temburong, reputedly their ancestral home, are Kampung Parit, Kampung Senukoh, Kampung Negalang, Kampung Selapon, Kampung Batu Apoi, Kampung Amo, Kampung Rataie and Pekan Bangar. Murut often have a lighter complexion and are of a shorter stature that differentiates them from other ethnic Brunei Malay groups.

Murut society used to be closed to outsiders, and they lived in groups of about 20 families in a single longhouse. In the past, a longhouse might comprise up to 120 families. Their longhouses were often situated in the interior highlands in locations that could be well defended against enemies, including other sub-Malay groups. These longhouses were normally built near rivers. The Murut refer to themselves as Lun Bawang, which means 'people of the (up)country'. In neighbouring Sarawak, the Murut are referred to as Orang Ulu, or 'upriver people', whereas in Sabah they are known as Lun Dayeh.

A Murut longhouse was divided into three sections. The *sikang* (common space) was used as a place for social gathering and ritual performances. It was also where they kept house tools, musical instruments, swords, spears, shields, and enemy skulls that they had taken. The second section was the *takap* (sleeping room), where family members slept, and was equipped with a fireplace, jars and woven mats. The upper part of the *takap* had a dual purpose, as a place for younger children to sleep (called *benang parung*) and for storing various household belongings. The third main division of the Murut longhouse was the *dapur*, or kitchen, where cooking utensils were kept, preparation and cooking took place, and a dining area for both family and guests.

In Brunei, the Murut language has been influenced by the Brunei Malay dialect as a consequence of inter-marriages and assimilation.

Murut traditional dress, dances, wedding and death rituals

Traditionally, Murut male attire is made from the bark of a tree called *timbaran*. The dress is usually decorated with some red and black patterns and stripes. A piece of red cloth called a *sigar* is worn around the waist to cover the lower parts of the body, while the head is covered by red headgear called the *dastar*. Female dress is called the *baju umak ruma*, which is black in colour and decorated with colourful beads at the edges, worn with a belt known as *rigid*, and headgear made of beads called a *pata*.

The Murut have eight main dances: *alai ukui* (war dance), *alai siga* (dance to praise women), *alai ngapo lun raya* (welcoming dance to honour high-ranking officials), *alai busak baku* (dance to exhibit one's beauty), *alai umak rumak* (dance to enter a new house), *alai busak pakoi* (dance to mark the end of the harvesting season), *alai nguan* (dance during the planting season) and *alai karur* (wedding dance).

The Murut celebrate a special festival after the rice harvest called *irau pengeh ngeranih*. In this festival, rice wine called *burak* is served in large quantities and consumed until everyone is intoxicated – an expression of gratitude for the good harvest and a prayer for a better harvest in the future. Since 2011, an annual cultural festival has been staged to provide an opportunity for the community to gather and interact.

Murut wedding processes are as elaborate as those of other ethnic groups in Brunei Darussalam. Primarily, the three main phases are investigation, engagement and the wedding day, similar to other ethnic groups. The wedding ceremony is normally held in the morning. In the past, the ceremony began with a gunshot to indicate that the bridegroom is approaching the bride's house. The groom's entourage are received with traditional musical instruments.

The Murut death ritual begins with a three-night wake, during which the deceased is kept in a coffin. Thereafter, the coffin is buried in the graveyard. The corpse is left in the coffin to decay, then the bones are transferred into an expensive jar. The jar may be buried or kept in the house. The dead person's family will mourn for about a year, and a widow will only be allowed to remarry after five years.

Tutong

Currently in Brunei, there are 16,958 ethnic Tutong, and the majority (10,974) live in the Tutong District, apparently their place of origin, 4,161 in Brunei Muara, 1,781 in Belait and 42 in Temburong. The term 'Tutong' is said to have originated from a Murut named Tutong who lived by a river later named after him. Tutong was a famous Murut warrior who had helped the people of Lurah Saban against Kayan headhunters. In honour of him, the people he had helped called themselves 'the followers of Tutong'.

The Tutong originally lived in the coastal areas of Tutong District. Later, they moved inland to take up subsistence farming and rubber cultivation. Physically, the Tutong look like other Brunei Malays, but they possess a distinctively different language from the other Malay ethnic sub-groups.

Traditional dress, handicrafts and weddings

White and black are the basic colours of Tutong traditional dress. Black, however, is widely preferred for more formal occasions. For everyday usage, Tutong men wear *baju cara Melayu*, Malay-style dress without a collar, and a pair of trousers extending to just below the knee. Women wear *baju kebaya* and *kain batik*. A piece of cloth of any colour is worn to cover the head.

An important handicraft product for the Tutong people is *takiding*, which is a type of carrier strapped to the back. Other handicrafts include mats made from *pandan* leaves, a bamboo *bubu* (trap) for catching freshwater fish, and a *nyiru* made from bamboo for separating rice from its husk.

A Tutong wedding starts with the *begangai*, a process whereby the parents of the prospective groom pay a visit to the prospective bride's house to observe the attitudes of their proposed future daughter-in-law. If during the visit the prospective bride proves to be well-mannered, diligent and industrious, then the groom's parents will openly declare their real intention. If the bride's parents and the bride herself agree to the marriage proposal, then the official proposal ceremony, the *bedudun* or *berjarum-jarum*, will be the next stage.

During the *bedudun* process, it is usual for the prospective groom's parents not to be involved. A few representatives from the prospective groom's side will negotiate with the bride-to-be's family over the bride price as well as other requirements and requests from the bride-to-be's family. Once all issues are satisfactorily agreed by both parties, a formal engagement ceremony will be held.

The Tutong are the only ethnic group in Brunei in which the bride and groom must provide some services, or duties, to their future in-laws before marriage. Traditionally, at any time during the engagement period, the groom is required to spend at least three nights in his fiancé's house. In return, the bride is also required to spend three or seven nights in her fiancé's house. Today, however, these services to in-laws before marriage are no longer practised, as it is now considered inappropriate to allow an unmarried couple to stay in the same house before the official marriage.

During the day of the wedding ceremony, upon arrival at the bride's house the groom is required to smash a piece of bamboo with his foot. The groom will only be allowed to enter after he has managed to achieve this. Then, after all the Islamic religious obligations have been fulfilled, the newlywed couple will undergo a *buri puo* (washing of the feet) ceremony. Family members will take turns to pour water onto the bride and groom's feet, after which they have to give a certain amount of money or some form of present to the couple. After the *buri puo* ceremony, the bride and groom take turns to feed each other food in a *makan bersuap* (feeding each other food) ceremony.

The wedding ceremony is normally held in the bride's house. For three days after the wedding takes place, the newlywed couple are not allowed to leave the house. They can only leave during the *balik tiga hari* (returning after three days) ceremony has taken place, in which the husband has to bring his wife back to his house to meet his family. The couple's return will be accompanied by some members of the wife's family.

Kedayan

The Kedayan speak a language that is very similar to that of the Bruneis of Kampong Ayer and is categorized as a Malay dialect. Most of the words they use are similar except for certain variants in pronunciation; the Kedayan language does not have the 'r' sound, while the Bruneis put a stress on it.[25] For instance, the Malay word for house is *rumah* in ethnic Brunei, while the Kedayan word for it is *umah*; the word for 'new' in Brunei Malay is *baru*, while the Kedayan word is *bahau*.

Physically, it is almost impossible to differentiate between the Kedayan and other ethnic Malay groups in Brunei. They share the same skin and hair complexion as well as the colour of their eyes. However, while the Bruneis are closely associated with Kampong Ayer, the Kedayan are traditionally identified with inland dry rice agriculture, and their traditional occupation was shifting rice cultivation. Present-day Brunei has about 23,720 Kedayan, of which 15,333 live in Brunei Muara, 1,532 in Belait, 4,569 in Tutong and 2,286 in Temburong District.

The Kedayan appear to have converted to Islam fairly early in history, perhaps a consequence of their interaction with the Bruneis. Traditionally, they preferred traditional occupations, such as agriculture and hunting. Today, like other Malay groups of Brunei, due to changes in economics, education and modern technology, they live a modern life. It had become increasingly difficult to find Kedayan working in any kind of rice field, and the majority, especially the younger generation, work in the government or private sector as the main source of their livelihood. However, many Kedayan still own fruit orchards, either inherited from family members or purchased themselves, or at least continue to grow fruit trees around their homes.

The Kedayan appear to have originated around the Kampung Jerudong area of Brunei, where they planted dry rice. Initially, they grew hill rice, and later, probably in the twentieth century, began to cultivate the more productive wet rice. The Kedayan were also known as expert animal hunters and inland fishermen. To hunt wild animals such as mousedeer and other deer, they used spears, traps and a special net called a *jarring*. For fishing, they used nets, casting nets, fishing hooks and homemade fish traps called *bubu*, an oblong bamboo contraption with an opening at the front. The front opening has a special valve which prevents the fish from swimming out once they have entered.

Every year, the Kedayan hold an annual festival called *makan taun*. In the past, this festival was celebrated on a grand scale after each rice harvesting season in thanksgiving for the success of the rice crop. Today, however, only certain villages continue to organize the festival, largely due to the diminishing number of farmers who are still active agriculturalists. For the *makan taun*, an open hut called a *teratak* is built to accommodate all the villagers. The people gather in the hut during the festival, and each family member will bring food to share with other villagers. The raw foodstuff will be cooked on the spot during the day of the festival or even a few days before. The festival provides an opportunity for villagers to meet each other after a hectic period in the rice fields, get to know each other and enjoy themselves. Any food left after the festival will be shared among the villagers for them to take home.

Belait

According to the 2011 census, a total of 7,622 Belait resided in Brunei. The vast majority (5,866) lived in the Belait District, 1,205 in Brunei Muara, 538 in Tutong and 13 in Temburong. The Belait appear to have originally lived in Kampung Kuala Balai, in the middle section of the Belait river. Later, some of them migrated to Kampung Labi, Mukim Kuala Belait and Kampung Mumong to plant rice and serve in the government sectors, petroleum companies and private firms. Others live in their traditional dwelling places and get married in other villages.

The Belait marriage processes are similar to other ethnic Malay Muslim wedding proceedings. All couples undergo the Islamic wedding rituals before being officially pronounced as husband and wife. Traditionally, the bride price was in the form about 5 kilograms of rice, which had to be kept in a woven container called an *aluk berujut* (a cannon of a quarter ton in weight), and a piece of cloth sufficient to make clothing. Nowadays, these items are no longer in the list of requests from the bride's side; instead, cash, handbags and perfumes comprise the modern-day bride price.

The Belait play their traditional musical instruments not only in times of joy such as weddings, but also in times of sorrow during a passing. Musical instruments are played during the wedding to prevent the matrimonial couple hearing other sounds, in particular those that may bring sorrow. When someone dies, musical instruments are played loudly in order to inform surrounding villagers of the loss and as a medium of connection with the spirits of the dead. In contemporary times, telephones, invitation cards and emails are commonplace mediums of communication among the Belait as with other ethnic peoples in Brunei. The Belait language is now virtually extinct.

Commonalities and differences among Malay ethnic groups

All seven ethnic Malay communities in Brunei share some common characteristics that to some extent are the bonds that bind them. Commonalities are bridged in cuisines, musical instruments, Islam, physical attributes, socio-cultural traditions and practices, and language.

In terms of food, all the ethnic Malays of Brunei have several dishes in common. Their staple food is rice, sometimes cooked in bamboo or wrapped in leaves. Their main sources of protein are from fish and meat. Spices are also used in cooking, as is coconut milk to provide a creamy taste. An important ingredient in their cooking is *belacan* (shrimp paste), which is used for *sambal*, a mixture of shrimp paste, garlic, chillies and shallots. For those who are Muslim, both ingredients and food preparation adhere to Islamic dietary laws. As in many other parts of Southeast Asia, it is taboo to consume food with one's left hand.

Utilizing rice, including glutinous rice, the Malays of Brunei create a variety of traditional cakes, biscuits and desserts such as *kelupis* and *ketupat* (both contain rice wrapped in leaves), *lemang* (rice cooked in bamboo) and *wajid* (sweet cake made from sticky glutinous rice). The origins of most of the traditional foods consumed by the Malays of Brunei are unclear, but they certainly share similarities with the other Austronesian-speaking groups of Island Southeast Asia.

Apart from the differences in the music played for different dances, the ethnic Malays share similar musical instruments, such as the gong, *tawak-tawak* and *gulingtangan* (percussion instruments made from brass) and *gendang labik* (a drum made from the skin of animals such as buffalo, cow or goat). However, the Kedayan and the Brunei also have a *gambus* (folk lute) as part of their traditional orchestra that is similar to other *gambus* found in Island Southeast Asia. The Dusun alone have the *sape* (a four-string instrument). The Kedayan also made two other exclusive musical instruments, the *tangkong* (a plucked instrument made of bamboo), and the *guriding* (a jaw harp made from wild palm).

As the majority of the Malays of Brunei are Muslims, it is an obligation to perform the mandatory prayers five times a day. Muslim parents send their children to religious schools in addition to general schooling until they complete their mandatory religious education at year six after 12 years of conventional formal education.

With regards to physical and physiological attributes, it is clear that the seven ethnic Malay groups of Brunei share the same physical attributes with scant differences, and all are of Southern Mongoloid stock, as are the vast majority of other Southeast Asians today. Their socio-cultural traditions and practices that are currently observed and preserved have been inherited from past generations. Most of the communities each hold fast to the belief that their socio-cultural traditions and practices are exclusive to their community, and *not* the result of emulation of the cultural attributes of other ethnic groups. If there are commonalities or similarities, they are often attributed to accidents or coincidences, and not any conscious attempt at cultural borrowing. However, given the interaction of the various groups over time, some cultural borrowing is inevitable, while some similarities are surely derived from their common Austronesian origin.

While there are numerous binding similarities between the Brunei Malay ethnic groups, there are also a number of contrasts and differences. With regard to the languages spoken, it is evident that the Murut, Tutong, Belait and the Dusun/ Bisaya languages are quite different to that of the Bruneis and the Kedayan. Indeed, unlike the language spoken by the Bruneis and Kedayan, the languages of the other five ethnic groups are not Malay or Malay dialects. Nor do their languages belong to the Malayic-Dayak subgroup of Austronesian languages from which the Malay language and its dialects emerged, but instead to other branches of the Austronesian language family.

Important contrasts also exist between the Bruneis on the one hand and other six ethnic groups on the other. The most visible, at least in traditional society, is that the Bruneis lived on water at Kampong Ayer and did not practise agriculture, while the other six groups were land-orientated and practised shifting cultivation. The land-based groups appear to have had no hereditary leadership and their societies were not stratified, and similarly to the Iban, appear to have been more egalitarian in nature. The position of the chief in these societies was not inherited, but appears to have been based on personal attributes. By contrast, the Bruneis of Kampong Ayer had a highly stratified hierarchical social system with a complex system of ranks and classes.[26]

In modern Brunei, the traditionally land-based groups have to some extent been incorporated into this hierarchical system. Social stratification has been closely bound up with recruitment to or qualification for offices, but this has become largely accepted throughout Brunei over time by the indigenous subjects of the sultanate. Increasing modernization has lessened this phenomenon, and traditional offices have been replaced by ministers and officials in the ministries. However the social stratification is more relevant and visible in the royal court and at official national functions especially those that involve the sultan and the royal family. Nowadays, as in the past, some outsiders, such as the Chinese, Indians and Europeans, have received traditional offices and honorific titles that in terms of rank are equal to those held by non-noble Bruneians.

The social strata, in roughly descending order, are as follows:[27]

- core nobility (*raja-raja bertaras*);
- nobility (*raja-raja, pengiran-pengiran*);
- doubtful nobility (*ampuan-ampuan*);
- aristocrats (internally divided into named strata) (*awang-awang*);
- commoners (*rakyat*);
- subjects, followers (*sakai*);
- servant or dependent, slave (certain dependents or 'slaves' may have been of high rank – *hamba/ulun*).

Main concerns of ethnic Malays

The first and foremost concern of those classed as Malays in Brunei, particularly among the older generation, is the erosion and disappearance of their ethnic cultural heritage, about which the younger generation appear increasingly less interested. Fewer and fewer young people are able to speak their own language fluently, and even when they do speak it, the tendency is to mix it with words from other languages such as English and Malay. The Brunei language is perhaps the most widely spoken in the country. It is even used by some educators in schools as the medium of instruction, even though Standard Malay should officially be used. Thus, most Bruneians communicate in Standard Malay and tend to forget and use less of their own ethnic languages. The modern education system, which puts greater weight on the use of the English language, has also contributed to the decreasing usage of ethnic languages in Brunei. However, the Malay language itself has also contributed to the decline in usage of non-Malay languages and has now become much more widely spoken as a first language among Brunei Malay groups. This issue has been addressed by Noor Azam, who states that before the Second World War, most people living in Brunei were monolingual and spoke their own language.[28] The post-war years up to around 1980 witnessed a shift to bilingualism as many non-Malay speaking groups started to speak Malay as a second language. The subsequent bilingual education system led to widespread use of English as well as Malay, and a decline in the use of other Brunei languages. Today, the Belait language is on the verge of extinction, while the Tutong language struggles to survive.

Other forms of cultural heritage such as dances, food, herbal and healing knowledge and music have not successfully been passed down to the younger generation, partly because of declining interest, but also because only a handful of the younger generation have access to them. Moreover, as older people themselves are often too busy with their modern lifestyle and have less time to spend with the younger generation on matters relating to cultural heritage, such legacies are sadly lost to the latter.

As in many other parts of the world, modernization and new communication technologies have seriously impacted on the community. In the sultanate today, many children possess mobile phones, personal computers and tablets which draw them away from traditional culture. Modern technology is a double-edged sword: it has helped to enhance communication, but at the same time causes defragmentation within the community, especially among the younger generation, with individuals becoming anti-social and avoiding interaction with others. Social gatherings are increasingly participated in only by the older generation who are actively involved, while the younger generation choose to stay away, sometimes simply because they do not want to miss an episode of a popular soap series on television.

Another important factor in cultural change is that rice fields have largely disappeared from Brunei's landscape. Farming has become unpopular, especially among the young, even though rice is still the main staple food in the country. The government is taking some steps to ensure food security in the country by introducing a rice-planting scheme and other agricultural initiatives whereby the government prepares land for the farmers for free and it is left to the farmers to embark on a project, but the response has not been very encouraging. Some have taken up the challenge, but the yields have not been very favourable. If this trend is not reversed, the rice-planting heritage, especially among the Kedayan, will be lost and the country will continue to rely heavily on imported rice to meet domestic demand.

Since the early twentieth century, firstly under the initiative of the British Residential System, followed by the five-year development plans of the Brunei government, the National Housing Scheme and National Resettlement Programmes have been implemented. As a result, there has been a significant movement of the population from rural areas to more urban ones. This affects the people from Kampong Ayer and their culture, as many have to live on land, detached from the water-orientated culture and economy. Moving from their traditional dwelling places means that people leave their traditional activities behind and take up a new life and surroundings. In the new environment, the older generation have limited opportunities to continue their traditional skills and activities. Not only can they not continue their past professions, but the changed environment makes it difficult to pass down certain knowledge to the younger generation.

The Brunei government is taking steps to ensure that ethnic cultures are preserved and inherited by the younger generation, but whether such measures will succeed remains to be seen. The Brunei Handicraft Training Centre has responsibility for preserving the national heritage by providing training to the young in the arts and skills of traditional handicrafts such as weaving clothes, carpentry and blacksmithing. As a result, a significant number of trainees have graduated from the centre and some have taken up handicrafts as their professions. Village Consultative Committees are working with the government to realize the vision of 'one village, one product'. There are also initiatives to produce and revive as many local traditions as possible that can then be commercialized.

If ethnic communities do not consider the above issues seriously and resort to ways and means to overcome them, inevitably cultural attributes will increasingly become homogenous as the younger generation become more comfortable with global cultures and trends. Then boundaries between Brunei's various cultures will disappear and we will no longer be able to recognize the special cultural identities of the specific ethnic groups. Ethnic Malays, like other ethnic communities, will lose their uniqueness and identity.

Conclusion

Prompt and immediate actions need to be taken to preserve the ethnic and cultural identity of ethnic Malays and other ethnic communities while there are still knowledgeable senior members of society who can disseminate their wisdom to the younger generation. The younger generation need to be motivated to be more proactive with regard to undertaking research into their ethnic and cultural heritage, and their history. Every aspect of this cultural heritage needs to be preserved, and modern technology can play a role in this process, along with more traditional forms of media, in order to preserve and make accessible the sultanate's cultural heritage to future generations and other interested parties.

One suggestion that has been put forward is that the cultural heritage of Brunei's ethnic Malays be incorporated into the school curriculum, but thus far nothing has been realized. Currently in schools, in the Malay Islamic Monarchy module, certain components of Brunei's culture are taught, such as traditional foods and games. Schools and government agencies and institutions are constantly encouraged to organize exhibitions on Brunei culture and tradition, including traditional handicrafts, clothes, musical instruments, dishes and locally based products, to help preserve local traditions and pass the knowledge on to the wider public.

There have also been numerous attempts to revive local languages and cultures by individuals, organizations and government sectors through organizing seminars, workshops and symposiums on a more consistent and regular basis. Universiti Brunei Darussalam, for example, offers courses in local ethnic languages to undergraduates as part of the effort to preserve some of the local languages. The challenge, however, is to present the information in such a way that it can attract and stimulate the interest of the younger generation. The mass media should also play roles in documenting and disseminating information of the socio-cultural heritage of Brunei's ethnic Malay groups.

It is pertinent to note that Brunei Darussalam has played significant roles in the Malay World. Being a Malay Islamic Monarchy state since its conversion to Islam, Brunei Darussalam has proved itself capable of preserving and empowering its national heritage. By adopting Melayu Islam Beraja as the national philosophy and way of life, all aspects related to Malay, Islam and the monarchy can be preserved, practised, documented and disseminated. The country is fully committed to the Malay language in particular, which continues to be the official language of the state, and Malay culture remains the predominant culture. However one must realize that Standard Malay language should not be positioned in such a way at the expense of other local ethnic languages on the national stage. Local ethnic languages are much different from the Standard Malay language, and while they may not be important in the international setting, they are a vital part of local ethnic identity and socio-cultural heritage.

It is evident that the seven Brunei ethnic Malay communities in general are supportive of the nation's aspirations with regard to the preservation of their cultural heritage. A concerted effort between the government and the community can ensure the maintenance of the unique cultural attributes of the ethnic Malays. Furthermore, it is crucial for all communities, Malays and non-Malays, to continue to play prominent roles in shaping the history and diversity of the nation. The younger generation should be proactive in this endeavour and work closely alongside the older generation.

Thus, being 'Malay' in modern Brunei will be challenging, with significant and demanding roles to play for the benefit of the country in general and future generations in particular. While being a homogenous nation might be beneficial, being heterogeneous, despite the challenges, is of great value and reflects the diverse cultural heritage of the sultanate. Brunei's ethnic Malays need to choose between preserving their ethnic boundaries and diverse heritage, or continuing to assimilate and integrate with other ethnic groups within the country.

Notes

1 Joseph E. Trimble and Ryan Dickson, 'Ethnic Identity', in *Encyclopedia of Applied Developmental Science*, edited by Celia B. Fisher and Richard M. Lerner (Thousand Oaks, CA: Sage, 2005), p. 417.

2 For a detailed discussion on what constitutes Malay and 'Malayness', see Anthony Milner, 'Thinking about "the Malays" and "Malayness"', in *The Malays* (Oxford: Wiley-Blackwell, 2008), pp. 1–17.

3 Ibid, p. 10.

4 See Peter Bellwood, 'Formosan Prehistory and Austronesian Dispersal', in *Austronesian Taiwan: Linguistics, History, Ethnology, Prehistory*, rev. edn, edited by David Blundell (Taipei: Shung Ye Museum, Berkeley: Phoebe A. Hearst Museum, University of California, 2009), pp. 336–64, and Robert Blust, 'Austronesian Culture History: The Window of Language', in *Prehistoric Settlement of the Pacific*, edited by W.H. Goodenough (Philadelphia, PA: American Philosophical Society, 1996), pp. 28–35. This is a well-established theory supported by a huge body of archaeological and linguistic data. Older theories, such as the flawed notion that there were waves of Proto- and later Deutero-Malays into Island Southeast Asia, have long been discarded due to lack of any supporting evidence.

5 See James T. Collins and Awang Sariyan, eds, *Borneo and the Homeland of the Malays: Four Essays* (Kuala Lumpur: Dewan Bahasa dan Pustaka, 2006).

6 See Chapter 1 in this volume.

7 B.A. Hussainmiya, 'The Malays of Brunei Darussalam and Sri Lanka', *Southeast Asia: A Multidisciplinary Journal*, 10 (2010): 65–78.

8 See Timothy Bernard, ed., *Contesting Malayness: Malay Identity across Boundaries* (Singapore: Singapore University Press, 2004), p. 4.

9 See Thomas Wright, *The Travels of Marco Polo, the Venetian: The Translation of Marsden Revised, with a Selection of His Notes* (Whitefish, MT: Kessinger Publishing, 2004), pp. 364–5.

10 Before the Song period, the Chinese appear to have used the term *kunlun* to refer to people of the Malay ethnic group; see Johannes L. Kurz, 'Boni in Chinese Sources from the Tenth to the Eighteenth Century', *International Journal of Asia-Pacific Studies*, 10(1) (2014): 1–32 at 11.

11 *Population and Housing Census (BPP) 2011 Report*, Bandar Seri Begawan: Department of Economic Planning and Development, 2012.

12 Adrian Clynes, *Brunei Malay: An Overview*, Occasional Papers in Language Studies, vol. 7 (Tugu Link: Department of English Language and Applied Linguistics, Universiti Brunei Darussalam, 2001), pp. 11–43.

13 See Chapter 1 in this volume.

14 The transcriptions of their names from the Chinese texts is as presented in the modern and accurate translations of Chinese sources relating to Boni by Kurz, 'Boni in Chinese Sources', p. 4.

15 Chen Da-sheng, 'A Brunei Sultan in the Early 14th Century: Study of an Arabic Tombstone', *Journal of Southeast Asian Studies*, 23 (1992): 1–13 at 11; Pehin Mohammed Jamil Al-Sufri, *Tarsilah Brunei: Sejarah Awal dan Perkembangan Islam* [*The Early History of Brunei and the Development of Islam*], rev. edn (Bandar Seri Begawan: Pusat Sejarah Brunei, 2001), p. xxi.

16 Mohammed Jamil Al-Sufri, *Tarsilah Brunei*.

17 D.E. Brown, *Brunei: The Structure and History of a Bornean Malay Sultanate, Brunei Museum Journal*, 2(2) (special monograph) (1970), p. 6.

18 V.T. King, 'What is Brunei Society? Reflections on a Conceptual and Ethnographic Issue', *South East Asia Research*, 2 (1994): 176–98; Yabit Alas, 'The Reconstruction of Pre-Dusun and the Classification of its Descendants' (MA thesis, University of Hawai'i, 1994).

19 Alas, 'The Reconstruction of Pre-Dusun', p. 6.

20 Bernd Nothofer, 'The Languages of Brunei Darussalam', in *Papers in Austronesian Linguistics*, vol. 1, edited by H. Steinhauer (Canberra: Australian National University, 1991), pp. 151–76.

21 Alas, 'The Reconstruction of Pre-Dusun', p. 10.

22 *Population and Housing Census (BPP) 2011 Report*.

23 Mustaffa Omar, 'Bisaya: Suatu Tinjauan Ringkas' ['Bisaya: A Brief Overview'], *Brunei Museum Journal*, 9 (1993): 17–28.

24 According to Sarnagi Punchak, many of the Bisaya of Limbang in Sarawak have converted to Christianity; see 'Bisaya Ethnography: A Brief Report', *Sarawak Museum Journal*, 40 (1989): 37–46.

25 Clynes, *Brunei Malay*, pp. 11–12.

26 See Brown, *Brunei*, pp. 11–34.

27 The following is based on ibid., p. 11.

28 Noor Azam Haji-Othman, 'English and the Bilingual Bruneian', in *English in South East Asia: Challenges and Changes*, edited by Katie Dunworth (Perth, Australia: Curtin University of Technology, 2007), pp. 59–70.

5 To live on water

Lifestyle of the Kampong Ayer community during the British Residency period, 1906–1941

Haji Awg Asbol bin Haji Mail and
Awang Haji Tassim bin Haji Abu Bakar

The lifestyle of the Kampong Ayer community from the economic and social aspects in the first phase of administration under the British Resident (1906–41) is the focus of this chapter. Kampong Ayer, literally 'Water Village', is Brunei's unique conglomeration of floating villages located within sight of the shores of the capital city of Bandar Seri Begawan. This chapter will explain and evaluate its economic activities, such as fishing, handcrafting and trading, and social issues such as relationships, education and the relocation to land programme. Economically, the lifestyle of the Kampong Ayer community has seemed more traditional as their activities and livelihood have been more localized. The influences of economic modernization brought forth by the British Resident in terms of economic production for foreign markets, such as rubber plantations and petroleum industries, had scant impact on the Kampong Ayer community and its education. The Kampong Ayer community continued to seek knowledge in religious education through traditional methods, learning in mosques and *balai* (a purpose-built building as a centre of education) institutions. However, after the establishment of Malay schools from 1914 onward, modernization influences inevitably seeped through the community. On the other hand, in the programme to relocate the Kampong Ayer community to settle on land, the Resident was in an unenviable situation and faced various challenges. Nevertheless, the Residential administration finally succeeded in creating a new Brunei township on land, which also became the centre of government administration to replace the role hitherto played by Kampong Ayer. As a result of prioritizing development on land, Kampong Ayer was not able to enjoy the developmental and modernization initiatives that were introduced under the Residential administration, merely remaining a part of the identity of Brunei Town (present-day Bandar Seri Begawan). Today, many members of the community remain permanent residents, and Kampong Ayer maintains its traditional characteristics, which in turn comprise part of the identity of Bandar Seri Begawan and Brunei itself.

This chapter will analyse the lifestyle of the Kampong Ayer community during the British Residency period. There are two phases of this form of quasi-colonial governance. The first phase, 1906–41, ended abruptly on 16 December 1941 on the arrival of the Imperial Japanese Army (IJA). The IJA effortlessly occupied Brunei because there was no resistance, and took over Brunei Town on 22 December; it remained until 17 June 1945, when Brunei was re-occupied by Allied forces. Martial law was enforced by the British Military Administration (BMA). After peace was regained, martial law was replaced by a civil administration headed by the British Resident; the pre-war British Residency system was reintroduced in 1946.[1] This second-phase era of governance under the British Resident continued until 1959, with the proclamation of the written Constitution of Brunei. The Residency was abolished, and the Resident was replaced by a British High Commissioner; unlike the former's wide-ranging authority, the latter's role was limited to advising the sultan on issues of national security. From 1959 onward, the reins of government were in the hands of the chief minister and the secretary of state.[2] This chapter concerns only the first phase of the British Residency, 1906–41, emphasizing the economic and social aspects of the Kampong Ayer community. It attempts to illustrate the depth of the traditional way of life within the community, and examines whether this community was able to withstand modern influences after the introduction of the British Residential administration.

Kampong Ayer as the seat of governance

Before the establishment of the British Residential administration in 1906, the seat of governance in Brunei was located in Kampong Ayer, considered then as the capital and the most important centre, the location of the sultan's palace, residences of the *pengiran* (nobleman), *ulama* (religious scholar), and traders and merchants. Kampong Ayer also oversaw administration of other territories under Brunei's suzerainty, such as Sulu and the western parts of the Philippines. Early evidence of the existence of Kampong Ayer was recorded in the sixteenth century by Antonio Pigafetta, a transcriber on Magellan's circumnavigation of the world. It was undoubtedly the largest settlement in Brunei prior to the British Residency period. Besides serving as the centre of administration, Kampong Ayer also functioned as the centre of economic activities, particularly in fisheries, trading and handicrafts. Moreover, this knot of floating villages was also a centre for Islamic learning and the propagation of Islam, with many scholars and Pehin-Pehin Menteri Agama (religious ministers) gathering and residing there.

Western travellers who visited Brunei mentioned Kampong Ayer as 'resembling Venice, with many water lanes'.[3] Others considered it 'this greatest ever of Malay cities'.[4] Kampong Ayer's original location was in Kota Batu; it was relocated to where it stands today. Pigafetta, who visited in 1521, reported that Kampong Ayer was home to 25,000 families, but only the sultan and the ruling elite resided on land.[5] It could be roughly estimated that the population of Kampong Ayer at the time was 25,000–30,000 – relatively large.

Brunei has been a sultanate since the fourteenth century, when Awang Alak Betatar embraced Islam following his marriage to a Johor princess in 1386. He adopted the title Sultan Muhammad Shah. In the administration of the Bruneian kingdom, the sultan possessed supreme political and socioeconomic power. In socioeconomic terms, the power of the sultan included control over lands and peoples throughout the Bruneian realm, trade, traditions and customs, law, the appointment of civil officials, and he served as the head of Islam. By right, the lands throughout the Bruneian Empire were the possessions of the sultan and the royal family. These lands were classified as Sungai Kerajaan, Sungai Kuripan and Sungai Tulin. Land having the status of Sungai Kerajaan belonged directly to the sultan, whereas that with the status Sungai Kuripan belonged to the *wazir* (senior minister). Title to these lands was non-hereditary, ownership relying on the owner's title, such as sultan, *wazir* or *pengiran*, and would be passed to the successor to the title. In contrast, lands that had the status of Sungai Tulin could be inherited by subsequent owners, who were strictly the sultan and the royal family. Kampong Ayer had the status of Sungai Kerajaan, and hence was a fiefdom of the sultan.[6]

In executing the administration of the country, the sultan was assisted by several dignitaries: the *wazir*, *ceteria* (knights), *menteri* (ministers) and village heads. The group of *wazir* consisted of four dignitaries with the titles Pengiran Bendahara, Pengiran Pemanca, Pengiran Digadong and Pengiran Temenggung. The *ceteria* consisted of the Ceteria Empat (Four Knights), Ceteria Lapan (Eight Knights), Ceteria Enam Belas (Sixteen Knights) and Ceteria Tiga Puluh Dua (Thirty-two Knights). Of the Ceteria Empat, the highest-ranked four knights are titled Pengiran Shah Bandar, Pengiran Maharaja Lela, Pengiran Paduka Tuan and Pengiran Maharaja Adinda. The *menteri*, on the other hand, were elected from among the common people, individuals who were charismatic in their leadership and influential in society. Often candidates were from privileged and wealthy backgrounds. The group of *menteri* consisted of the Menteri Empat (Four Ministers), Menteri Lapan (Eight Ministers), Menteri Enam Belas (Sixteen Ministers) and Menteri Tiga Puluh Dua (Thirty-two Ministers). The highest-ranking menteri were the Dato Perdana Menteri, Orang Kaya Digadong Seri Nara Indera and Orang Kaya Digadong Seri Laila.[7] Other Bruneian dignitaries were appointed as the kingdom's representatives to the *jajahan* (colonies), and were regarded as rulers, enjoying high social status by virtue of their political power and strong standing in the economy. The *rakyat* (subjects) consisted of common people and slaves who were scattered in villages located on land, river banks and on the sea.

Introduction of the British Residency administration

Governance under the British Resident was introduced following the decline in the number of Bruneian colonies as a result of cessions and annexations from neighbouring Sarawak and British North Borneo in the nineteenth century. In 1841, the Brooke family took control over Bruneian colonies in Sarawak, pioneered by James Brooke (r. 1841–68) and succeeded by Charles Brooke (r. 1868–1917). The British North Borneo Chartered Company gained control over North Borneo (present-day Sabah) from the 1880s onward. These territories were controlled by Western powers through leases, grants or outright cession by the Sultan of Brunei. Towards the end of the fifteenth and sixteenth centuries, Brunei attained glory under the reigns of Sultan Bolkiah (1485–1524) and Sultan Muhammad Hassan (1582–1598), and apparently had control over the entire island of Borneo to the north in the Philippines, including Sulu.

The shrinking of Bruneian territories began in the reign of Sultan Omar Ali Saifuddin II (1828–52), when James Brooke was appointed as *rajah* (governor) of Sarawak in 1841 in return for his assistance in ending the anti-Brunei revolt (1836–41). There were further losses of colonies during Sultan Abdul Momin's reign (1852–85) that forced him to make a vow, 'Umanah' (mandate), on 20 February 1885 with the support of the ruling elite and a few dignitaries. This declaration forbade any owner of land with the status of Sungai Kerajaan, Sungai Kuripan or Sungai Tulin to either lease or cede it to any other parties.[8] On 29 May 1885, Pengiran Temenggung Hashim ascended to the throne as Sultan Hashim Jalilul Alam Aqamaddin (1885–1906).[9] The newly appointed sultan vacated his previous office of Pengiran Temenggung. This depleted the office of *wazir*, so that of the original four officers, there were now only three: Pengiran Bendahara, Pengiran Digadong and Pengiran Pemanca.[10] This decision not to appoint a new Pengiran Temenggung not only improved the new sultan's income and finances, but also forestalled the continual loss of Bruneian territories. Sultan Hashim had one less dignitary to prevent from leasing his lands to foreign powers.

Nevertheless, Sultan Hashim himself leased Trusan, of Sungai Tulin status, to Sarawak's rajah, Charles Brooke, in the hope of fostering better relations, and that Brooke would help settle the conflict in Limbang, which had been protracted and unresolved since the 1850s.[11] In agreement to lease Trusan, Brooke promised assistance, but it was to no avail. Instead, not only did Brooke betray his word, but he himself was a threat to the further annexation of Brunei territories.

The Limbang conflict was reignited following the murders of several Bruneian Malays who had visited the area in November 1885. The people of Limbang denied involvement, but offered two men alleged to be the culprits to be handed over to Sultan Hashim. This offer was declined because they were not the guilty parties. In reaction to Sultan Hashim's decision, the people of Limbang severed their ties and ceased paying taxes to Brunei.[12] Meanwhile, British Consul General Peter Leys in Labuan and Rajah Charles Brooke continued to persuade Sultan Hashim to lease Limbang to Sarawak. Brooke levied 6,000 Sarawak dollars[13] a year for the lease of Limbang, arguing that the sultan was no longer capable of governing this colony.[14] The British government apparently acceded to Brooke's persuasive thesis, and Limbang came under Sarawak's rule.

In November 1886, Sultan Hashim, the group of *wazir* and the people of Bandar Brunei demanded the rescinding of the lease of Limbang to Sarawak despite its approval by the British government. They asserted that Limbang and Brunei were one with the protest cry, 'Brunei is the spirit of Limbang and Limbang is the (physical) body of Brunei.' Moreover, the people of Brunei's livelihood depended on this region. Also, they wanted to defend Sultan Abdul Momin's 'Umanah' that had called to a halt to the loss of territories. Brunei forwarded an appeal to the British government to intervene and accede to its demands.[15]

In order to prevent the further loss of Bruneian territories, on 17 September 1888, Sultan Hashim signed a treaty that placed Brunei under the protection of Britain. However, this treaty also failed to prevent the further shrinking of Brunei. Article III of the treaty was evidently unfair to Brunei, because whenever there was a dispute with any state, including with British North Borneo or Sarawak, it was agreed that the British government would mediate and the sultan must abide by any decision thus made.[16] Through this treaty, in fact, the British succeeded in controlling Brunei's foreign relations.[17]

On 17 March 1890, Rajah Charles Brooke unilaterally seized Limbang, proclaiming occupation by Sarawak. This proclamation would only be altered subject to an order issued by the British government offering alternative options to overcoming the issue concerning Limbang. He also promised that he would pay Brunei compensation for the Limbang seizure. Fortresses were erected to safeguard government buildings from any attack.[18] This occupation was later endorsed by the British government despite Sultan Hashim's fierce opposition on the grounds that Limbang was a part of Brunei.

In essence, a majority of the people of Limbang were dissatisfied. Mohammad Kassim, the British consul, stated that only a quarter of the people of Limbang were content to be under the protection of Sarawak, while the majority preferred the administration of the Brunei Sultanate.[19] Sultan Hashim requested the British government to order Brooke to leave Limbang.[20]

The Perjanjian Perlindungan 1888 (Protection Agreement 1888) failed to stem the loss of Bruneian territories; by the end of the nineteenth and early twentieth century, the Brunei Sultanate continued to wane, and its political survival was practically at stake. Then, in 1904, the British government sent Malcolm Steward Hannibal McArthur of the Malayan Civil Service (MCS) to ascertain the situation in Brunei. McArthur reported that Brunei should be given full protection, and its identity and integrity as a sultanate must be preserved.[21] Furthermore, in that year, the British Foreign Office sanctioned the appointment of a British Resident to Brunei, despite a previous disagreement to this proposal due to financial constraints.[22] In order to maintain Brunei's long-term existence and survival, Sultan Hashim signed the Perjanjian Tambahan (Additional Agreement) of 1905/1906 whereby Brunei was prepared to accept a British Resident as an adviser to the sultan in all state matters, with the notable exception of Islamic religious affairs.[23] Following governance under the British Resident (hereafter referred to as the British Residency period), several modern influences and innovations were incorporated into the socioeconomic development of the sultanate. The Resident initiated the move to relocate Brunei's administrative centre, then located in Kampong Ayer, onto land.

The British Resident, originally appointed as an adviser to the sultan, subsequently for all intents and purposes became the highest power in the newly formed public administration. Nevertheless, the Resident introduced modernization to public administration through the creation of government departments such as the police force, Land Office, Department of Works and Customs Office. Although these modernization steps left a positive impact on the socioeconomic development of Brunei, the role of locals as leaders in the governmental sector increasingly diminished, as only British officers headed these new organizations. The Resident did not possess confidence in the ability of Bruneians, regarded as inexperienced, to lead the newly created government departments.[24] Furthermore, the Resident also appeared to have interfered in Islamic affairs, contravening the terms of the 1905/1906 treaty.

Population during the British Residency period

Despite Kampong Ayer being mentioned as the most populous area in Brunei before the introduction of the British Residency administration, no official census was ever conducted to verify this assertion. The inaugural official census of Brunei's population took place in 1911, five years following the introduction of the Residency administration. Thereafter, it was conducted every decade, following the practice of the Commonwealth nations.[25] Table 5.1 shows the population of Brunei according to the censuses of 1911, 1921 and 1931.

The first ever census showed that Brunei Malays and Indigenous people comprised 96.15 per cent of the total population, followed by the Chinese at 3.39 per cent. Most of the Brunei Malays lived in Kampong Ayer, influenced by their livelihood based on rivers and seas, notably fishing and harvesting sea produce.

Although trade relations between Brunei and China began as early as the fifth century, when they traded in luxury goods such as chinaware, silver merchandise, gold and silk, the Chinese had not settled permanently in Brunei. But by the nineteenth century there were some Chinese settlers in northern Borneo, including Brunei. Aside from farming and trading, a large proportion of them worked in gold mines in Sarawak. After Labuan became a British colony in 1846, Chinese labourers were brought in to work in the coal mines on the island. In the early stages, Chinese involvement in the economy of Brunei was exclusively as middlemen in the export and import of goods such as sago, fish and prawns. Some Chinese were also involved in cash cropping.[26]

The Chinese rented housing for their sago trade, along with general and wholesale shops. They also played the role of capital investors or middlemen to fishermen in Kampong Ayer. Chinese trading activities extended beyond Brunei to Labuan and Singapore as exporters of fish and prawns. They enjoyed a strong economic standing due to their dominance in trade and commerce. The small Chinese community in Kampong Ayer carried out trading activities and operated general shops; others traded using *sampan* (small native craft), rowing from one house to another within the environs of Kampong Ayer. Inevitably, they forged good ties with the Malay community.[27]

There was an increase in the presence of Chinese in Brunei when the British brought them from Hong Kong as labourers in the petroleum industry. One of

Table 5.1 Population of Brunei in 1911, 1921 and 1931

Race	1911	1921	1931
Malay and indigenous	20,881	23,938	26,972
Chinese	736	1,434	2,683
Indian	44	37	377
European	20	35	60
Eurasian	2	–	10
Others	35	10	33
Total	21,716	25,454	30,135

Source: *Brunei Annual Report 1941.*

the largest oil wells discovered in 1929 was in Seria, by the British Malayan Petroleum Company (BMPC). The Chinese population expanded due to immigration from Labuan, Jesselton (present-day Kota Kinabalu) and Miri, primarily to seek employment. By 1931, there were 2,683 Chinese, making up 8.9 per cent of Brunei's total population.[28]

During the Residency administration, Indians were brought in as policemen, working closely with the Labuan police force. Moreover, Indian labourers were brought in to overcome the shortage of workers in the rubber plantation sector. The Resident encouraged foreign (especially European) investors to operate rubber plantations aimed at increasing the sultanate's economic resources. The increased number of Indians was quite apparent: in 1911, there were only 44 Indians; two decades later, in 1931, the number rose to 377. This was the result of the robust development of the petroleum industry, in which Indians served as skilled and semi-skilled workers at oil wells in Seria. Because of the small size of the Indian community compared to that of the Chinese, they did not establish schools or temples during the Residency period, unlike their counterparts in British Malaya.

Europeans invested in the petroleum and *ubar* (a type of plant dye) industries and rubber plantations in Brunei. They also served as officers under the British Residency administration. Their numbers, however, remained small: 20 in 1911, 35 in 1921 and 60 in 1931. Besides the civil service, Europeans were professionals, such as doctors and engineers, enjoying high social status.

In 1941, on the eve of the outbreak of the Pacific War (1941–45), the total population of Brunei stood at 40,774.[29] Brunei Malays comprised the bulk of the population, and the majority of them were residents of Kampong Ayer and its environs.

Economy

The people of Kampong Ayer largely depended on maritime activities, especially fishing, as it was regarded as a traditional livelihood inherited through the generations. Other economic activities included handicrafts and trading. This economic pattern remained largely intact through the first phase of the British Residency administration until 1941.

Fishing as a livelihood involved the bulk of the inhabitants of Kampong Ayer during the British Residency period, owing to the ease of access to resources. Fishing was conducted as a means of subsistence, utilizing simple homemade equipment, and the activities were mainly undertaken in rivers or in Brunei Bay. For instance, in order to fish in shallow waters, equipment such as *lintau, kabatan, bubu, rambat* and *selambau* were employed. In deeper waters, the fishermen used *kelong, andang, rawai* and *tugu*. The *lintau, kabatan, kelong* and *bubu* were made from bamboo which was cut to a width of 0.5 centimetres and a length of 2–3 metres. The cut pieces of bamboo were woven or tied together using vines known as *lemiding*. Various items of fishing equipment and *sampan* were utilized to catch fish. The types of fish caught varied, being both small and large, and included prawns, crabs, groupers, sardines, *rumahan* and red snappers. Occasionally, shellfish such as scallops, oysters, mussels and sea snails were also collected.[30]

A variety of handicrafts were conducted by the villagers of Kampong Ayer, including *perahu* (*sampan*)-making, home construction, cloth weaving, mat weaving, food cover weaving, *nipah* palm roof making, and iron, gold, silver and copper forging. These activities lent their names to villages, indicating the types of handicraft and trade that conducted their members (see Table 5.2).

Handicrafts could generally be divided into two categories. The first was the smithing of gold, silver, iron and copper. For example, goldsmiths usually fashioned fine jewelry, and coppersmiths produced kitchenware. The second category

Table 5.2 Names of villages in Kampong Ayer according to the crafts of their communities

	Name of village	*Craft/expertise*
1	Kampong Pandai Emas	Gold- and silversmithing, usually making jewellery and accessories
2	Kampong Pandai Besi	Ironsmithing, usually making weapons such as machetes, knives, *keris* (dagger), axes and spears
3	Kampong Pemariok	Making pots from copper and iron/steel
4	Kampong Burong Pingai, Kampong Lurong Sekuna	Weaving cloth
5	Kampong Kuala Peminyak	Making oils
6	Kampong Menjalin	Making the *balat*, a fishing tool made from bamboo and *lemiding* (vine).
7	Kampong Pebalat	Working as fishermen, using the *balat*
8	Kampong Pemukat	Working as fishermen, using the *pukat*, a fishing tool.
9	Kampong Perambat	Working as fishermen, using the *rambat*, a fishing tool or net
10	Kampong Padaun	Gathering *nipah* fronds to make roofs for homes and *balai* (hall)
11	Kampong Pengatap	Installing roofing
12	Kampong Peramu	Selling foraged wood from the forest to build homes and for other uses
13	Kampong Pakayu	Selling firewood for cooking
14	Kampong Tekoyong	Collecting *tekoyong*, or shells

Sources: D.E. Brown, *Brunei: The Structure and History of a Bornean Malay Sultanate*, *Brunei Museum Journal*, 2(2) (special monograph) (1970); Haji Awang Yahya Haji Ibrahim, 'Beberapa Aspek Mengenai Rumah dan Perumahan di Kampong Ayer' ['A Few Aspects of the Houses and Habitation in Kampong Ayer'], paper presented at International Symposium on Kampong Ayer organized by the Academy of Brunei Studies, Universiti Brunei Darussalam, 6–9 September 1996; Haji Awang Abdul Latif bin Haji Ibrahim, 'Kampong Ayer: Warisan, Cabaran dan Masa Depan' ['Kampong Ayer: Heritage, Challenges and its Future'], paper presented at International Symposium on Kampong Ayer organized by the Academy of Brunei Studies, Universiti Brunei Darussalam, 6–9 September 1996; Haji Abdul Latif bin Haji Ibrahim, 'Variations and Changes in the Names and Locations of the Wards of Brunei's Kampong Ayer over the Last Century', *Brunei Museum Journal*, 2(3) (1971): 56–73.

was non-metal handicrafts, which could be further divided into five groups: cloth-making (such as *songket* weaving); making supplies for home construction, such as roof-making from *nipah* palm fronds; home-building; making fishing equipment, and *perahu-* or *sampan*-making.

Otherwise, there were villagers who were expert in culinary skills such as making *kuih*, or sweet and savoury desserts. Other occupations included *beramu*, or gathering natural resources from the forest and collecting shellfish. Each community's involvement in these different areas of trade was highly specialized to each village, almost exclusively so, and if carried out by other villages, it was on an insignificant scale. This is why the villages were named after the crafts for which they were known. This phenomenon seems to have created an economy of 'one village, one product'. Nevertheless, there were villages that were not named in this way, such as Kampong Lorong Sekuna and Kampong Burong Pingai, which were skilful in weaving *songket*.

However, naming villages after the specialization of their communities gradually dwindled because some villagers resettled on land, while the rest moved to other floating villages. Also, the children of these craftspeople found work in other fields, such as the civil service or the private sector. Those serving the government worked as religious officers and lower-ranking government employees. Others worked at the *ubar* (dye) factory in Subuk, and in the petroleum industry in Seria.

Apart from being involved in fishing and handicrafts, villagers in Kampong Ayer were also engaged in trading activities as a means of livelihood. Trading activities were of two types: regional and local. Regional trade was carried out when Kampong Ayer traders ventured to Limbang in Sarawak, Labuan and North Borneo. Merchants in this category were also known as *nakhoda* (skipper). Their activities contributed to Bruneians being resident in these destinations after marrying local women and settling there.

On the other hand, local trading activities conducted in the Kampong Ayer area and its surroundings were carried out by the *pengalu* and the *padian*, alongside Chinese shopkeepers and/or businessmen. The *pengalu* conducted their trading along the Sungai Brunei, while the *padian* conducted theirs in and around Kampong Ayer waters. Trade merchandise included salted fish, pickled fish and fish jerky, supplied by the fishermen. The *pengalu* also sold *kuih*, especially dry snacks such as *sapit* (wafers), *makanan cincin* (food rings), *madu kasirat* (natural honey) and *kuripit* (flat bread).[31] Trade goods from inland inhabitants consisted mainly of forest produce (camphor, *rotan* and so on) and agricultural harvest products such as rice, vegetables and fruits.[32]

In trading, the *pengalu* would usually use the barter system. Goods not produced in Kampong Ayer, such as fruits and vegetables, would be exchanged for salted fish with peoples from the inland areas. Likewise, goods not produced by inland inhabitants, such as fish, *kuih* and copper handicrafts, would be brought by the *pengalu* on his visits inland. At this time, the *pengalu* served as the connector or middleman between the villagers of Kampong Ayer and the inland communities, supplying food, materials and other necessities. Among the *pengalu*, some were so successful in their trading activities that it enabled them to purchase vast tracts of land in the inland region. During the period of the Residency administration, land could be purchased at relatively low prices. Some among the *pengalu* were bestowed with royal titles, appointed to office as ministers, or became Pehin Menteri Agama (titled religious minister).[33]

The *perahu* or *sampan* used by the *pengalu* were large vessels that had walls and roof awnings to provide shelter against rain and heat. A *pengalu* would usually be assisted by four workers, usually his wife and children, to navigate the *sampan* to its destination.[34] In order to conduct their trading activities, groups of *pengalu* would operate from two bases. The first base was located in present-day Kampong Ujong Klinik, which hosted a group of *pengalu* from Kampong Saba who conducted their trading activities downstream of Sungai Brunei to areas such as Kampong Putat, Pudak, Menunggol, Kupang, and thence to Limbang. The second congregation point was in Kampong Limbongan, where groups of *pengalu* from Kampong Tamoi, Lorong Dalam, Burong Pinggai and Bukit Salat traded in areas such as Kampong Batu Empat, Kilanas, Mulaut, Junjungan and Limau Manis.

The *pengalu*'s merchandise obtained from inland inhabitants, such as fruit and vegetables, besides being sold directly by the *pengalu* to villagers in Kampong Ayer, could also be bought by *padian* traders. These goods would be re-sold in the vicinity of Kampong Ayer. *Padian* trading was conducted exclusively by women travelling from house to house by rowing their *sampan*, also known as a *gubang*. To protect themselves from the elements, they wore large semicircular hats about 60 centimetres in diameter. Known as *saraung bini*, this large hat came to symbolize their identity and categorized its wearer as a *padian*. Besides merchandise obtained from the *pengalu*, the *padian* also sold fish supplied by fishermen and *kuih* supplied by their makers. *Padian* activities centred on Labuhan Kapal (shipping port) or present-day Dermaga Diraja (royal quay), and some areas in Kampong Ayer. The *padian* would meet the *pengalu* and fishermen to obtain goods at *padian* bases.[35] The existence of the *padian* traders in the British Residency period was nothing new within the Kampong Ayer community; it was a continuation and heritage from previous generations since the sixteenth century, as their existence was even recorded by Pigafetta in 1521.[36]

The *padian* trading activities ran from early morning until late in the evening. They were busier during periods of high tide. The *padian* utilized measuring equipment such as scales, *cupak* and *gantang* (measuring cups for quarts, pints or gallons). The *cupak* was made of a coconut shell, whereas the *gantang* was a copper cylinder with a diameter of 18–20 centimetres and a height of 21–25 centimetres.[37] It is apparent that modern influences had yet gain prominence; the traditional economy continued to be dominant as a means to support their livelihood. The economic activities of the people of Kampong Ayer did not seem to cater for large-scale production for a more international market, such as rubber and petroleum. In no way did the Residency administration help with loans for fishermen in Kampong Ayer to improve their lot.

Social relationships

An analysis of the life of the Kampong Ayer community during the British Residency period can be conducted from the perspective of social relations. Social relationships in the Kampong Ayer community were based on strong, close familial and neighbourly ties. This could be seen during special occasions, times of joy and times of sadness, in festivities such as weddings, housewarmings, *mandi berlawat* (baby shower for the first child), *berzikir* (chanting praises to Allah), *khatam* Quran (recitation completion) and *majlis doa selamat* (supplication for safe deliverance), or on the other hand, mournful occasions such as the passing of a beloved. In festivities such as wedding banquets, relatives and neighbours would gather to prepare for such occasions through *memucang-memucang* or *gotong royong* (working collaboratively and collectively). As an example, this type of collaborative work could be witnessed during the making of the *teratak* (hut/house), *menongkat* and repairing of the home of the wedding couple, as well in preparing the feast for guests. During occasions of gaiety or sadness, the community of Kampong Ayer *beraga-agaan* (visit each other), helped by the proximity of their homes. For any occasions, neighbours could easily be informed and could arrive by utilizing the walkways or by *sampan*.[38]

On these special occasions of merriment or mourning, they would gather to communicate using polite and respectful language, especially when addressing and interacting with the older generation. The Malay community of Kampong Ayer was renowned for *awargalat* (courteousness), instilled since youth through teachings, precepts and daily practices. In their everyday speech, they would normally have their own 'titles' by which they addressed one another: *nini* or *tua* (eldest), *tengah* (middle), *amit* and *bungsu* (youngest). Similarly, when speaking with titled individuals, there were specific addresses and language. Such customs and behaviour were practised as a mark of respect in their daily interactions.[39]

Furthermore, the Kampong Ayer community adhered to customs that had been practised for generations. Recalcitrance would only bring shame to one's family. Weddings were highly regarded because they symbolized an important change, a rite of passage in a person's life experienced once in a lifetime. For example, there were the customs of *berbedak* (blessing ceremony by family members using rice flour) and *berpacar* (decorating the hands using henna), to evoke the glow in both the bride and groom – two obligatory customs at wedding festivities.[40]

Education

The social life of the Kampong Ayer community in the British Residency period can also be analysed from the educational perspective. The Residency administration had a deep impact and direct influence on the peoples of Kampong Ayer through the introduction of a formal educational system by the establishment of the Sekolah Rendah Melayu (Malay Primary School) in 1914. Thereafter, Kampong Ayer had two types of educational systems: formal secular and informal religious. The Malay school was needed in order to recruit local youths who could read and write in Romanized Malay in the government bureaucracy.[41]

In the early stage, the Malay school did not receive much support from parents, especially of girls, in Kampong Ayer. The uninhibited mixing of the sexes, even in an educational context, was taboo and greatly discouraged. Nevertheless, the community gradually understood the importance and necessity of sending their children to school. Henceforth, a new breed emerged who became teachers in the Malay schools. Among the pioneers were Marshal Maun and Basir Taha, who succeeded in continuing their studies at the Sultan Idris Teachers' Training College in Tanjung Malim, Perak in the 1930s. Teachers were government officers, and thus were strongly influential on the community. They were considered highly educated and respected by the people in the community. This new generation not only contributed to ensuring that the Kampong Ayer community understood how necessary it was that their children were sent to school to gain worldly knowledge, but also played a role in instilling nationalist sentiments among the people regarding the importance of Brunei attaining political independence.

Religious education, on the other hand, was introduced much earlier to the Kampong Ayer community, carried out by religious scholars, Pehin-Pehin Menteri Agama. Private individuals knowledgeable in Islam also volunteered as religious teachers. Religious classes were conducted in private homes, mosques and the *balai*.[42]

The *balai* educational system emerged because the homes of religious scholars were incapable of catering for the increasing numbers of students. Hence, the *balai* was built in proximity to their homes. The *balai* educational system was mainly conducted in Kampong Ayer, and few existed on the mainland. Religious teachers comprised Bruneian *ulamas* (scholars), mostly the Pehin-Pehin Menteri Agama.[43] Pehin Khatib Muhammad bin Hassan (1860–1941) built a *balai* when his home in Kampong Lurong Sikuna, which later became the centre of Islamic educational activities, was no longer capable of accommodating his ever-increasing number of students.

Likewise, Pehin Datu Imam Abu Bakar bin Abdul Rahman (1880-1937) of Kampong Kianggeh, another floating village, built a *balai* to cater for his large student body.[44] Other Pehin-pehin Manteri Agama who had *balai* included Pehin Dato Imam Haji Mokti (d. 1946) in Kampong Burung Pingai, Pehin Siraja Khatib Haji Abu Hanifah (d. 1956) in Kampong Saba and Khatib Saad bin Juru Apong (d. 1968) in Kampong Pandai Besi.[45] The students of these religious scholars were not limited to the Kampong Ayer community, with some coming from afar. For example, Pehin Khatib Abdul Razak had students from as far away as North Borneo. The proliferation of *balai* did not negate the dissemination of Islamic education in private homes, which continued in parallel in Kampong Ayer. A notable example was that of Tuan Imam Abdul Rahman bin Awang Matserudin (1872–1945), who conducted religious classes in his residence in Kampong Bukit Salat.[46]

The *balai* as a religious educational institution played an important role in spreading the *syiar* (greatness or glory) of Islam in Brunei, not unlike the role played by the *pondok* in Malaya and the *pesantren* in Java in the Dutch East Indies.[47] This *balai* educational system has been in existence since the nineteenth century, or even earlier.[48] It was believed that the *balai* educational system began in Kampong Burung Pingai, thereafter followed by other villages, including Kampong Peramu, Kampong Sungai Kedayan, Kampong Lorong Sikuna and Kampong Saba.[49]

The *balai* educational system had two categories: general and advanced studies. General studies offered lessons on Bruneian Zikir, Ratib Samman, Quran recitation and *hadrah*, and also instructions relating to performing prayer rites. Knowledge in these areas was essential for any Muslim community to be released from the demands of Fardh' Ain (obligatory practices for individual Muslims) and Fardh' Kifayah (obligatory practices for the Muslim community as a whole). However, students who followed these general lessons were not required to be able to write and read Jawi (Arabic letters adapted to the Malay language).[50]

On the other hand, advanced studies required candidates to be able to read and write Jawi. They were taught knowledge in Fiqh, Faraidh, Babun Nikah, Nahu and Qawaid, Tasawuf and Akhlak. Being conversant in these fields allowed students to qualify as a Kadi, Juru Nikah (marital oaths officer) or a teacher.[51] In the *balai* education system, the text references were similar to those in religious educational centres in other parts of the Malay World, for instance *Matla' Badrin*, *Sabilul Muhtadin*, *Furu' Masail*, *Bughyah Al-Tullab*, *Hidayah Al-Salikin* and *Siar Al-Salikin*.[52] The *balai* religious educational system was never conducted in expectation of materialistic returns. The scholars as teachers had no expectations of material rewards from their students, and the students decided whether or not to compensate them. Scholars who taught religious knowledge were spiritually motivated regardless of material gains.

Besides being a centre of religious educational study, the *balai* also supported other religious activities. For example, during the 1940s, in the month of Ramadhan (fasting month), owners of *balai* would hold *tadarus* (Quran recitation) gatherings. Hitherto, *tadarus* gatherings were often held in private homes, prayer halls or mosques. Muslim communities that lived near *balai* were encouraged by the Pehin-Pehin Menteri Agama as the owner of the *balai* to attend and enliven *tadarus* gatherings that usually commenced around 5 p.m. and continued until dusk. For refreshments after the gatherings, it was customary for each of the participants in the *tadarus* to bring a quantity of food to be given as alms by the Muslim community that lived near the *balais*. Giving food such as *kuih* as alms is a common practice among the Muslim community of Brunei, because giving alms in the month of Ramadhan brings the giver great rewards in the hereafter.[53] At times, the *tadarus* gatherings would be held after *tarawih* prayers. In these, refreshments at the end of the gathering would be provided from fish caught using a *kabat* (a type of fish trap) or *lintau* (a trap for prawns) on the same night. The fish caught were mostly *sembilang* (a type of catfish), because this fish would come in at night to feed on prawns that were caught in the *lintau*.[54] At times, these *balai* would also be used as halls for *tahlil* (prayer for the deceased) gatherings, which were customarily held once a year in the month of Syaaban, prior to the commencement of Ramadhan.[55]

According to Mahmud Saedon, the *balai* education system in Brunei greatly contributed to giving rise to the birth of local *ulamas*, or scholars, who had a vast knowledge in *fiqh* in the Malay language, in line with the teachings of Mazhab Syafiee (one of the acknowledged sects of Sunni Muslims). The traditions in education and knowledge were the same as those practised in other parts of the Malay World.[56] These scholars, products of *balai* education, were the generation that would continue efforts to teach and spread Islamic education in Brunei.

Nonetheless, the contribution of the *balai* as a channel for religious knowledge was not all-encompassing among the Muslim community in Kampong Ayer. *Balai* education was exclusively a male domain for both teachers and students, excluding women and girls. Females who excelled at Quran recitation and possessed good religious knowledge relied on studies in private homes, away from interaction with male students.[57] At the same time, not all adult males of Kampong Ayer attended religious educational activities in the *balai*; more often, only those who were interested would attend. Furthermore, there was no ruling at the time that required the Muslim community to commit to study religious education in *balai* – it was all done on a voluntary basis. The role of the *balai* as an educational institution gradually dwindled when Islamic education was introduced in schools, especially after the establishment of the Sekolah Rendah Agama (Religious Primary School) in 1956.

Absence of modern utilities

Modern utilities such as piped water and electricity were conspicuously absent in the life of the Kampong Ayer community during the British Residency period. Kampong Ayer did not yet have access to running water via pipes. In order to obtain their water supply, the people of Kampong Ayer rowed their *sampan* to Subuk to collect water, at the location where the Jalan Residency stands today, at three points where water would stream downhill. Water was collected once or twice a week using containers such as *gerunung*[58] and *bejana-bejana* (pots) were made of clay, and empty tin containers with a piece of stick inserted in the middle for ease of transport.[59]

In the absence of an electricity supply, the people of Kampong Ayer used kerosene lamps, candles and torches, and for cooking they turned to mangrove wood as fuel. Mangrove wood was cut using axes or machetes from nearby mangrove forests and carried home using *sampan*. Thereafter, the wood was further cut, the bark removed, dried under the sun, and finally stacked on the *pantaran* (porch) of the house. Mangrove wood must be fully dried to ease making fire for cooking. Mangrove wood could also be bought from a supplier in Kampong Pakayu, the village specializing in firewood.

The Move to Land Programme

When the British Residency administration was introduced, McArthur was appointed as the Resident. One of his initial plans was to move the centre of administration of the sultanate from Kampong Ayer to the mainland, and at the same time to forbid the construction of homes in the floating village area.[60] This idea of transfer had been proposed by Peter Blundell, an engineer who had served in the *ubar* factory prior to the Residency period, who intended constructing a new township at the *padang* (field) behind the sultan's palace. Kampong Ayer, according to Blundell, was unsuitable as a centre of administration and settlement from the aspect of public health. Infant mortality at the time was high.[61]

Resident McArthur's intention to move Kampong Ayer to the mainland was not only to ease the administration of the government; there were other factors in play. The Residency administration viewed Kampong Ayer as unsuitable for habitation because of public health concerns, concurring with Blundell's opinion, as the area was said to be a breeding ground for mosquitoes that could spread a multitude of diseases. But this argument was spurious, because mosquito-borne diseases were not only limited to the Kampong Ayer community, but also occurred in communities that lived on land.

The close proximity of housing in Kampong Ayer and unplanned house construction could be a recipe for disaster if there was an outbreak of fire. Fire could easily spread rapidly, not only because the houses were close together, but also because they were made of wood, with dried *nipah* fronds as roofs or walls. These materials are highly flammable. But interestingly, during the Residency period, reports of fires occurring in Kampong Ayer were not as frequent as during the end of the twentieth and the early twenty-first centuries. In the later period, Kampong Ayer frequently had fires, often large ones, to the extent that they destroyed scores of homes in a single outbreak.

Although the houses in Kampong Ayer were built using local and inexpensive materials, they exhibited their own unique architectural designs. During the Residency period, *belah bubung* and *tungkup* house designs were very popular. Apart from using *nipah* palm leaves as the roof, the floor of these houses was made of *nibung* (a type of palm resistant to saltwater) and bamboo. The columns were made of hardwood such as *kayu bulian*, *kulimpapa* and *selangan batu*. Other than having a kitchen and bedrooms, each house also had a room (*langgar*) to entertain guests. It was here in the *langgar* that family activities would be conducted, such as teaching and learning to recite the Quran, and hosting various social gatherings. The construction of the house would usually be conducted through *gotong royong*, a collaborative effort by the family and neighbours.[62]

Besides health and safety issues, the Resident wanted to proceed with the programme to move the Kampong Ayer community as a means to improve the economic resources of Brunei. At that time, Brunei had insufficient funding for development expenditure. For example, in 1906, Brunei had funds amounting to 228,173 Sarawak dollars. However, as much as 200,000 Sarawak dollars were borrowed from the Federated Malay States.[63] The Resident viewed the Kampong Ayer settlement as one that was the most populous compared to other places in Brunei. In 1906, the population of Kampong Ayer was estimated at 8,000–10,000 people. According to the census for 1911, the population was 9,767 people, and in 1921 it had dropped to 7,623.[64] It was thought that the potential human resources from this area must be reaped and fully utilized to improve the sultanate's economy. This could be achieved by implementing a project to relocate the Kampong

Ayer community onto land, and later they could become agriculturalists and undertake husbandry that could contribute to increasing the sources of income.

Otherwise, the manpower of Kampong Ayer could not fulfil its potential if it was limited to fisheries, handicrafts and small-scale trade. Agricultural sectors (farming and animal husbandry) were deemed more important and profitable in contributing to efforts to improve the economy during this period. Besides, the relocation project was necessary to increase the population of Brunei Town (present-day Bandar Seri Begawan), the new township located on the mainland. If this move was not implemented, Brunei Town might turn into a lifeless ghost town.

Meanwhile, once committed to this relocation programme, the Residency administration took stern action towards the residents of Kampong Ayer who were reluctant to participate in the transfer. Only those who were directly involved in fishing activities and the *ubar* industry were exempted. Fishing was an important source of income for the economy, as well as fish providing the main food and protein source for the people. The *ubar* industry generated a huge source of income in terms of export duties as well as the mangrove forest concessional payment imposed on the *ubar* factory owners, and also provided employment for Kampong Ayer.[65] The Residency administration granted a grace period until 1911, after which, if many still refused to voluntarily join in this relocation, the government would force the Kampong Ayer community to move to Brunei Town, which by then would already be established on the mainland.[66]

As one of the preliminary measures to siting Brunei Town on the mainland, the Residency administration erected a temporary residential building as the new centre of administration in 1906, notwithstanding the presence of the sultan's palace that remained in Kampong Sultan Lama, one of the villages in Kampong Ayer. In December 1906, construction work on the permanent residential building was begun, and it was completed in July 1907 at a cost of 8,000 Sarawak dollars.[67] This administrative building could be regarded as the foundation for the establishment of Brunei Town, although there are some who believe that the town only came into being in 1908.[68] In 1908, a strip of non-asphalt road slightly less than 2.5 kilometres long was built in the new Brunei Town. Even though there were no cars at that time, a road was necessary to allow ease of transport from one place to another around the town. Prior to this strip of road, there were no structured roads throughout the sultanate, as the socio-cultural and economic lifestyle of the bulk of the population was water-borne.[69]

In 1906, the government established a police force and postal department, hence a police station and a post office building were built.[70] The postal department delivered mail and parcels, and in turn was a source of income for the government through the sale of postage stamps. The police force oversaw security of the Resident, public peace and enforcing the law. This indicates that the Resident was aware that the modernization he had introduced did not have the full support of the people of Brunei, especially the Kampong Ayer community. There was dissatisfaction, to the extent that they had become a threat to the Resident's safety. It was possible that McArthur had in mind the assassination of the Resident to Perak by Dato Maharaja Lela in Pasir Salak in the mid-1870s.[71] Initially,

12 police officers were appointed, and the number increased to 28 (4 Malays and 24 Indians) by 1907. Brunei Town had 14 policemen, Muara and Tutong each had four, and the remaining six were stationed in Temburong. The Indian officers were said to be frequently drunk on duty, and compromised efficiency and discipline in the police force. Consequently, the government enforced rules of conduct forbidding police officers from consuming alcohol while on duty.[72]

The programme identified three relocation sites: Kampong Tumasik, Kampong Sungai Tekuyong[73] and Kampong Sumbiling.[74] In order to attract people to relocate to these areas, the government offered an incentive scheme offering freehold land titles to participants who enrolled in the programme. They were advised to plant coconut and other fruit trees. This meant that for the first time in the sultanate, the common people (*rakyat*) were able to own land, because before 1906, lands in Brunei belonged to the sultan and the nobility, with land status categorized as Sungai Kerajaan, Sungai Kuripan and Sungai Tulin.

Notwithstanding strong opposition from the Kampong Ayer community, a few among them, primarily *pengiran* and the Chinese, warmly accepted the government's call to move to land, appreciating the long-term advantages of living on the mainland. The earliest participants of the relocation project in 1909 were the *pengiran*, members of the Brunei royalty. They pioneered the relocation to Kampong Tumasik. The new site's proximity to the Brunei river allowed the settlers to continue their livelihoods as fishermen while carrying out farming and agricultural activities in line with the government's aspirations. At the same time, the mangrove forest was drained to facilitate development and expansion of the area of Brunei Town.

Although the relocation programme (1906–1920s) received support from only a portion of the population of Kampong Ayer, including the elite, it failed to attract more inhabitants to move onto land, and many remained *in situ*.[75] They opposed the relocation project for a multitude of reasons. One was that they felt proud and comfortable, ingrained in their lives with the culture of living on water that they had inherited through the generations. They felt that if they moved onto land, they would have to change their way of life from fishermen to farmers, which would definitely bring difficulties as it was not easy for them to adapt to a different lifestyle than they had known for generations.[76] Furthermore, the Kampong Ayer community was known for its strong family ties, and relocation to land would have an adverse impact on familial relations because of the large distances between the houses.

On the other hand, there were some village heads who refused to relocate because they feared losing their status. If they relocated to the new settlement on land, their village culture would be different, and it was possible that they would no longer be appointed as village head. Hence, some of them persuaded their fellow villagers not to participate in the relocation project. Owing to the fact that a person appointed as village head was an individual bestowed with titles by the sultan or who was an influential and well-respected elder, his opinion would have a strong influence on his followers. Therefore, when the village head himself refused to be relocated, it was inevitable that many followers would do the same.

This undeniably complicated the government's efforts to attract more members of the Kampong Ayer community to move onto land. In 1906, there were 14 village heads in the whole of Kampong Ayer, and undoubtedly all were influential in remaining *in situ* in their traditional environment.[77]

Conclusion

It is evident that the economic and social aspects of the Kampong Ayer community in the first phase of the British Residency remained strong and steadfast, with traditional elements inherited from past generations as their economic activities – fishing, handcrafting, and trading – localized and supplying the necessities for their daily livelihood. Economic modernization initiatives which were introduced by the Resident in the form of economic production for the international market, such as rubber plantations and the petroleum industries, failed to influence the Kampong Ayer community. Their economic activities remained largely geared to self-consumption and local markets. In the case of education, the Kampong Ayer community sought religious knowledge by traditional methods, learning in mosques and the *balai* institutions. However, after the establishment of the Malay schools in 1914, modernizing influences trickled through such institutions into the community. This was apparent when increasing numbers of parents became more prepared to send their children to school. Under the influence of formal education, a new elite generation, the Malay teachers, emerged. They were largely responsible for ensuring that the Kampong Ayer community understood the importance of sending their children to school to gain knowledge. They also played a role in instilling nationalist sentiments among the Kampong Ayer community. On the other hand, in the programme to relocate the Kampong Ayer community to land, the British Resident faced various challenges and obstacles. Nevertheless, the Residency administration subsequently succeeded in creating a new Brunei township on land that also became the centre of government administration, replacing the role hitherto played by Kampong Ayer. At that time, the government made efforts to provide various modern public facilities, such as government buildings, shops, houses, roads, running water, electricity, schools and mosques, for the purpose of establishing a township on land. As a result of placing a higher priority on development on land, Kampong Ayer came to be merely a part of the identity of Brunei Town that was unable to fully enjoy basic facilities and lagged behind in the developmental and modernization initiatives which were introduced under the Residential administration. In spite of this, most of the people of Kampong Ayer seemed to be unreceptive to the developments and changes that were happening. Consequently, the project to relocate them to land during this period was less successful. Thus today, many of the community members are still permanent residents of Kampong Ayer, and the community has remained relatively traditional in many respects. On one hand, those who wanted to move to land could be considered as trying to adopt modernization elements because they were willing to adapt their lifestyle from life on water to life on land. Moreover, it could also be considered that modernization occurred because the common people were allowed to own state lands, which was hitherto forbidden. However, not all traditional elements of the Kampong Ayer community can be seen as negative or making it difficult to accept modernization, and in fact some of these elements do embody positive values, for example in terms of social relationships such as *berawargalat* and respectful behaviour and disposition. The custom of politeness was not only practised within the community, but was also upheld in interactions with the non-Malay community, such as the Chinese.

Notes

 1 Sabihah Osman, Muhammad Hadi Abdullah and Sabullah Haji Hakip, *Sejarah Brunei Menjelang Kemerdekaan* [*The History of Brunei at the Dawn of Independence*] (Kuala Lumpur: Dewan Bahasa and Pustaka, 1995), pp. 95–109; *Brunei Annual Report* (*BAR*), *1946*, p.8

 2 *Pelita Brunei*, 1 February 1959; *Pelita Brunei*, 29 September 1959.

 3 D.E. Brown, *Brunei: The Structure and History of a Bornean Malay Sultanate. Brunei Museum Journal*, 2(2) (special monograph) (1970), p. 93; Jatswan S. Sidhu, *Sejarah Sosioekonomi Brunei 1906–1959* [The Socioeconomic History of Brunei 1906–1959] (Kuala Lumpur: Dewan Bahasa dan Pustaka, 1995), p. 57.

 4 K.G. Tregonning, 'The Partition of Brunei', *Journal of Tropical Geography*, 2 (1968): 84.

 5 Robert Nicholl, *European Sources for the History of the Sultanate of Brunei in the Sixteenth Century* (Bandar Seri Begawan: Muzium Brunei, 1975), p. 10.

 6 Haji Awg Asbol bin Haji Mail, *Kesultanan Melayu Brunei Abad ke 19 Politik dan Struktur Pentadbiran* [*The Brunei Malay Sultanate in 19th Century: Politics and Administrative Structure*] (Bandar Seri Begawan: Dewan Bahasa dan Pustaka, 2011), pp. 107–12; Pehin Haji Awg Mohd Jamil Al-Sufri, *Tarsilah Brunei: Sejarah Awal dan Perkembangan Islam* [Brunei Inscriptions: Early History and Development of Islam] (Bandar Seri Begawan: Pusat Sejarah Brunei, 1990), pp. 53–4.

 7 A.V.M. Horton, *Report on Brunei in 1904 M.S.H. Mc Arthur*, Monographs in International Studies, Southeast Asia Series, no. 74 (Athens, OH: Ohio University Press, 1987), p. 104; Pengiran Muhammad Yusuf, 'Adat Istiadat Diraja Brunei Darussalam' ['The Royal Customs of Brunei Darussalam'], *Brunei Museum Journal*, 4(3) (1975): 43–108 at 47, 52.

 8 Arthur Louis Keyser, *People and Places: A Life in Five Continents* (London: John Murray, 1922), p. 29; Arthur Louis Keyser, *Trifles and Travels* (London: John Murray, 1923), p. 130; Agreement between Sultan Abdul Mumin, Pengiran Bendahara and Pengiran Digadong with the British North Borneo Company whereby they will not permit any lease or cession of territory north of and including the Limbang river, Muara Damit and Muara Besar, Brunei, 17 Muharram AH 1302 (5 November 1884), FO 12/120; D.E. Brown, 'Sultan Mumin's Will and Related Documents', *Brunei Museum Journal*, 3(2) (1974): 156–70 at 168.

 9 W.H. Treacher, 'British Borneo: Sketches of Brunei, Sarawak, Labuan and North Borneo', *Journal of the Straits Branch of the Royal Asiatic Society*, 20(1) (1889): 13–74 at 52.

10 Consul General Leys to Foreign Office, 14 December 1885, CO 144/59; Frank Swettenham to Marquess of Lansdowne, 25 March 1902, FO 12/120; Brown, 'Sultan Mumin's Will and Related Documents', p. 160.

11 R.E. Stubbs, *Brunei and the Limbang* (Eastern no. 97), printed for the use of the Colonial Office, 1905, p. 7.

12 Ibid., p. 11.

13 The Sarawak dollar, which was equivalent in value to the Straits dollar, was utilized from 1858 to 1953, briefly interrupted by the Japanese occupation (1941–45). It remained at par with the Straits Settlements dollar (pegged at 2s. 4d. sterling in 1906) until 1953, when it was pegged to the Malaya and British Borneo dollar.

14 Spenser St John, Acting Commissioner to the Viscount Palmerston, Foreign Affairs, 1 June 1851, FO 12/9; Consul General Leys to the Marquis of Salisbury, Labuan, 24 February 1887, FO 12/76; *North Borneo Herald*, Official Gazette, no. V, vol. II, 1 November 1884, pp. 1–2.

15 The Sultan of Brunei to Consul General Leys, Brunei, 29 Sapar AH 1304 (27 November 1886), FO 572/18; C.B. Robertson, Memorandum on Admiral Mayne's Question for February 28, Respecting the Cession of Limbang River to Sarawak, 26 February 1886, FO 572/18; The Sultan of Brunei to Her Majesty the Queen, Brunei, 14 Jamadil Akhir AH 1304 (8 February 1887), FO 572/18.

16 Article III of the Protectorate Agreement between Brunei and the British government, Appendix IV, FO 12/130.

17 Stubbs, *Brunei and the Limbang*, p. 16.

18 Ibid., p. 17.

19 A.C. Watson, 'Letters from Brunei: Inche Mahomed's Consular Reports 1866–1890', *Brunei Museum Journal*, 5(4) (1984): 1–90 at 142.

20 Ismail Haji Awg Nordin, 'Sultan Hashim: From Western Points of View' (MA dissertation, University of Hull, 1998), p. 60.

21 Horton, *Report on Brunei*, pp. 135–6.

22 Ibid., p. 23.

23 William George Maxwell and William Summer Gibson, *Treaties and Engagements Affecting the Malay States and* Borneo (London: J. Truscott, 1924), pp. 149–50.

24 *BAR 1907*, pp. 10, 21

25 L.W. Jones, *The Population of Borneo: A Study of the Peoples of Sarawak, Sabah and Brunei* (London: University of London, 1966), p. 17.

26 Haji Awg Asbol bin Haji Mail, *Kesultanan Melayu Brunei Abad ke 19*; Wu Zong Yu. 1994. 'Raja Brunei dalam Sejarah China' ['The King of Brunei in the History of China'], paper presented at International Seminar on the Brunei Darussalam Malay Sultanate organized by the Academy of Brunei Studies, Universiti Brunei Darussalam and Sultan Haji Hassanal Bolkiah Foundation, Bandar Seri Begawan, 13–17 November 1994, p. 1; Yura Halim and Jamil Umar, *Sejarah Berunai* [*History of Brunei*] (Kuala Belait: Brunei Press), p. 11.

27 Pengiran Khairul Rijal bin Pengiran Haji Abdul Rahim, 2007, *Teknologi Menangkap Ikan di Negara Brunei Darussalam 1906–2003* [Fishing Technologies in Negara Brunei Darussalam 1906–2003] (Kuala Lumpur: Penerbit Universiti Malaya), p. 41.

28 *BAR 1955*, p. 31; Tan Pek Leng, 'A History of Chinese Settlement in Brunei', in *Essays on Modern History Brunei* (Bandar Seri Begawan: Universiti Brunei Darussalam, 1992), p. 124; see also *BAR 1955*, p. 32.

29 Pengiran Khairul Rijal, *Teknologi Menangkap Ikan*, p. 33.

30 Interview with Haji Mail bin Haji Bakar, aged 85, at his home, 1 October 2010. He lives at 164D Kampong Setia 'B', one of the villages in Kampong Ayer. His father came from Kampong Saba, another village in Kampong Ayer which was famed for its community's expertise in the *penugu*, a tool to catch fish and prawns. The *lintau* is another tool to catch fish, made from bamboo and resembling the *kelong* in shape. However, the *lintau* was used only in rivers, unlike the *kelong*, which was placed in deeper waters

or at the mouths of rivers. It was able to withstand a month or more of use, depending whether it was producing enough catches, unlike the *kabatan*, which was only set
up overnight, and thereafter moved to another location to harvest new catches. See
also Pengiran Khairul Rijal, *Teknologi Menangkap Ikan*, pp. 42–67; *Kamus Bahasa
Melayu Nusantara* [*The Malay Language Dictionary of the Archipelago*] (Bandar Seri
Begawan: Dewan Bahasa dan Pustaka, 2003), p. 1,628.

31 Rusli bin Murni, 'Mengalu Antara Corak Perniagaan Lama di Brunei' ['Mengalu, One
of the Old Methods of Trading in Brunei'], in *Budaya Bangsa* [*Ethnic Culture*] (Bandar
Seri Begawan: Dewan Bahasa dan Pustaka, 1989), p. 138.

32 Haji Zainuddin bin Haji Hassan, 'Pengalu dan Padian di Brunei: Satu Pengenalan
Ringkas' ['The Pangalu and Padian of Brunei: A Brief Introduction'], *Jurnal Pusaka*, 5
(1996): 177–80.

33 Interview with Dyg Hajah Ismah binti Pehin Khatib Dato Paduka Haji Mohd Said,
aged 58, at her home, 24 May 1993. She lives at 83 Sim 625 Kampong Madewa BF
1120 km 7 Jalan Tutong Negara Brunei Darussalam. She is the daughter of a Menteri
Agama (religious minister). Before moving to the mainland, she lived in Kampong
Pandai Besi, one of the villages in Kampong Ayer.

34 Rusli bin Murni, 'Mengalu', p. 139.

35 Interview with Yang Dimuliakan Pehin Siraja Khatib Dato Paduka Seri Setia Ustaz
Awang Haji Yahya Bin Haji Ibrahim, aged 74, at his home in Kampong Manggis Jalan
Muara Brunei, 2 June 2009. He was one of the earliest Bruneians to receive an MA
degree from Al-Azhar University in Egypt. Before moving to the mainland, he lived
in Kampong Lorong Sekuna, one of the villages in Kampong Ayer. He once held the
office of Deputy Minister of Religious Affairs of Brunei and served as a Sharia Chief
Judge.

36 Nicholl, *European Sources*, p. 10.

37 Haji Zainuddin bin Haji Hassan, 'Pengalu dan Padian', pp. 177–80.

38 Interview with Yang Dimuliakan Pehin Siraja Khatib Dato Paduka Seri Setia Ustaz
Awang Haji Yahya Bin Haji Ibrahim; interview with Haji Kassim bin Serudin, aged 90,
at his home in Kampong Setia 'B', one of the villages in Kampong Ayer, 15 April 2006.

39 Interview with Dato Paduka Dr Haji Abdul Latif bin Haji Ibrahim, aged 65, at his
home in Kampong Mulaut, 15 March 2009. Before moving to the mainland, he lived in
Kampong Lurong Sikuna, Kampong Ayer. He has a PhD from Universiti Kebangsaan
Malaysia, and once held the office of Assistant Director of the Brunei History Centre
and the Director of Sultan Haji Omar Ali Saifuddien Sa'adul Khairi Waddien Memorial,
Prime Minister's Department.

40 Ibid.

41 Madya Haji Asbol bin Haji Mail, Haji Mohamad Yusop Haji Awg Damit and Ampuan
Haji Brahim Ampuan Haji Tengah, *Evolusi dan Tranformasi Kecemerlangan 100
Tahun Pendidikan Negara Brunei Darussalam* [*The Evolution and Transformational
Excellence of Education in 100 Years in Negara Brunei Darussalam*] (Bandar Seri
Begawan: Ministry of Education, 2014), p. 15.

42 There are four definitions of *balai*, according to the Malays in Brunei. Firstly, a *balai*
can be a place to store fishing equipment such as *balat*, *tugu*, *jala*, *pukat* and *lukah*
(fishing nets and traps). It functions as a storage room. Secondly, a *balai* can be a small
industrial workshop for weaving and producing fishing equipment, to make boats or
to process mangrove wood to be made into firewood for cooking. Thirdly, a *balai* can
be a place to study *silat* or martial arts. Finally, a *balai* can be a place to learn and
conduct religious activities. *Balai* such as this are generally owned by scholars who are

Pehin-Pehin Menteri Agama (religious ministers). Thus, the final definition is used in this discussion. Interview with Haji Kassim bin Serudin. See also Abdul Latif bin Haji Ibrahim, 'Peranan Rumah-Rumah Perkumpulan dalam Masyarakat Melayu Brunei' ['The Role of Cluster Houses in the Brunei Malay Community'], in *Ikhtisar Budaya* [*Cultural Highlights*] (Bandar Seri Begawan: Dewan Bahasa dan Pustaka, 1982), p. 83.

43 Bruneian clerics were not necessarily Pehin Menteri Agama. Some of them had the title of *pengiran*, and there were others who were *wazirs*. As an example, a scholar who was a *pengiran* is Maulana Pengiran Haji Abdul Momin bin Pengiran Sabtu. He was said to have studied religion in Mecca around 1800–1820. He had many students from around Kampong Ayer. Maulana Pengiran died around 1880. On the other hand, a Bruneian cleric who was a *wazir* is Pengiran Digadong Pengiran Haji Mohd Salleh bin Pengiran Anak Haji Mohammad (1890–1969). He studied religious knowledge at *balai ulama* Brunei. Because he had a deep knowledge of religion, he was appointed to hold an important position in the religious administration of the Brunei government. In 1940, he was appointed as Kadi Besar, and then in 1948 he was appointed as an adviser in the Sharia Council. He became a member of the Islamic Religious Council in 1955, and a Religious Adviser from 1959 to 1968. See Simat bin Angas, Suhaili bin Haji Hassan and Haji Ismail bin Ibrahim, *Tokoh-tokoh Agama di Brunei Darussalam: Pengenalan Ringkas* [*Religious Figures in Brunei Darussalam: A Brief Introduction*] (Bandar Seri Begawan: Jabatan Muzium-Muzium, 1992), pp. 15, 31–2.

44 Ibid., pp. 21, 28, 50.

45 Mohd Jamil Haji Abas's interview with Mohd Yusof held in the Omar Ali Saifuddien Mosque in Bandar Seri Begawan, Brunei, 5 February 1991. Mohd Jamil was an MA candidate in History Studies at the Universiti Brunei Darussalam.

46 Simat bin Angas et al., *Tokoh-tokoh Agama*, pp. 15, 31–2; Hajah Joriah binti Haji Metali, 'Dato Haji Ahmad', *Pusaka: Berita Jabatan Pusat Sejarah Brunei*, 1 (1988): 62–4 at 18, 40, 63.

47 Mahmud Saedon bin Awg Othman, *Jejak-Jejak, Kumpulan Kertas Kerja* [*Traces: A Compilation of Paperwork*] (Bandar Seri Begawan: Academy of Brunei Studies, Universiti Brunei Darussalam Brunei, 2003), p. 285.

48 Abdul Latif bin Haji Ibrahim, *Brunei Darussalam Rantisan Sejarah dan Budaya* [*Brunei Darussalam History and Traditions*] (Bandar Seri Begawan: Academy of Brunei Studies, Universiti Brunei Darussalam Brunei, 2003), p. 11.

49 Abdul Latif Haji Ibrahim, 'Peranan Rumah-Rumah Perkumpulan', p. 75.

50 Mahmud Saedon, *Jejak-Jejak*, p. 282.

51 *Pendidikan Agama di Negara Brunei Darussalam* [*Religious Education in Negara Brunei Darussalam*] (Bandar Seri Begawan: Department of Islamic Studies, Ministry of Religious Affairs, 1996), pp. 45–6.

52 Mahmud Saedon, *Jejak-Jejak*, p. 286.

53 Interview with Dyg Hajah Ismah binti Pehin Khatib Dato Paduka Haji Mohd Said.

54 Interview with Haji Bungsu bin Jafar, aged 78, at his home at 157D Kampong Setia 'B' Negara Brunei Darussalam, one of the villages in Kampong Ayer, 10 January 2005.

55 Abdul Latif, Rantisan Sejarah dan Budaya, p. 11.

56 Mahmud Saedon, *Jejak-Jejak*, p. 286.

57 Haji Awg Yahya bin Haji Ibrahim, *Sejarah dan Peranan Institusi-institusi Melayu Islam Beraja* [*The History and Role of the Islamic Malay Monarchic Institution*] (Bandar Seri Begawan: Da'wah Islamiah Centre, Brunei Ministry of Religious Affairs, 2000), pp. 30–31.

58 Interview with Dato Paduka Dr Haji Abdul Latif bin Haji Ibrahim. A *gerunung* is a large clay container for storing water.

59 Ibid.

60 *BAR 1910*, p. 15.

61 Peter Blundell was a British engineer who served the *ubar* factory in Brunei town. His book *The City of Many Waters* recounts many stories on the lives of the community in Brunei town in the early twentieth century. Peter Blundell, *The City of Many Waters* (London: J.W. Arrowsmith, 1923), p. 202.

62 Interview with Haji Abu Bakar bin Budin, aged 73, at his home, 21 March 2008. He has experienced living in two villages in Kampong Ayer: first in Kampong Lurong Sikuna and later in Kampong Peramu. After a house fire in 1991, he moved to the Negara Lambak Kanan Housing Programme.

63 *BAR 1907*, p. 5.

64 British Resident, Brunei to High Commissioner, 24 September 1906, CO 144/80; Brown, *Brunei*, p. 50; *BAR 1911*, p. 11; *BAR 1921*, p. 6; Horton, *Report on Brunei*, p. 67.

65 The Island Trading Syndicate was a company involved in the *ubar* industry founded in 1900. See Graham Saunders, *A History of Brunei* (Kuala Lumpur: Oxford University Press, 1994), p. 103.

66 *BAR 1910*, p. 16.

67 A.C. Watson, 'Notes on the History of Bubungan Dua Belas', *Brunei Museum Journal*, 5(2) (1992): 37–104.

68 *BAR 1906*, pp. 13–14; Sidhu, *Sejarah Sosioekonomi Brunei*, pp. 58–9.

69 *BAR 1910*, p. 13.

70 *BAR 1906*, pp. 13–14.

71 Barbara Watson Andaya and Leonard Y. Andaya, *Sejarah Malaysia* [*A History of Malaysia*] (Kuala Lumpur: Macmillan, 1983), p. 188.

72 Haji Duraman Tuah, *Pentadbiran Awam Brunei Darussalam di Period Naungan dan Pemerintahan Sendiri: Satu Kajian* [*Public Administration in Brunei Darussalam in the Period of the Dominion and Self-rule: A Study*] (Bandar Seri Begawan: Brunei Public Services Institute, 2000), pp. 50, 52–3.

73 Currently Kampong Kianggeh.

74 Currently Kampong Sumbiling Lama. See *BAR 1909*, p. 6.

75 Ibid., p. 190.

76 *BAR 1910*, p. 14.

77 In 1967, Kampong Ayer had 35 village heads. See British Resident, Brunei to High Commissioner, 24 September 1906, CO 144/80; Brown, *Brunei*, p. 50, 51; *BAR 1910*, p. 14.

Part III

Islam

6 Women's rights in Brunei under the Islamic Family Law, 1999

Datin Hajah Saadiah binti Datu Derma Wijaya Haji Tamit

Islam is believed to have existed ever since the fourteenth century with the Islamization of Awang Alak Betatar, with the adopted Muslim name Sultan Muhammad Shah, as the first sultan to rule Brunei (1363–1402). Hence, Islamic law is assumed to have been practised by Bruneian society. The laws of *Adat*[1] (Traditional), *Resam*[2] (Customary), *Syarak*[3] (Islamic) and *Hukum Kanun Brunei*[4] (Regulatory) became the reference for the people and guide for the rulers of Brunei and administration of the sultanate.

This practice continued until the introduction of the British Residency system in Brunei in 1906.[5] Co-operative agreements between the Brunei government and the British had an impact on administrative jurisdiction and the judiciary system. In essence, the British slowly eroded the implementation of Islamic laws, directly and indirectly, especially in the jurisdiction of the *Hukum Kanun*, in introducing dual sets of laws, and limited the jurisdiction of Islamic laws related to personal law. This trend continued until Brunei had its own constitution, the Constitution of Brunei Darussalam 1959. This Constitution successfully heightened the status of Islam as the official religion of the country.[6] After Brunei's independence in 1984, the government introduced gradual efforts to Islamize the law.

The implementation of the law in Negara Brunei Darussalam (hereafter Brunei) is divided into two: Civil (Magistrate Court) and Sharia (Sharia Court) laws. Sharia Law is further divided into two: *sharia* (criminal) and *mal* (non-criminal) laws. The *sharia* criminal law encompasses all offences punishable by *hudud*, *qisas* and *takzir*.

These crimes, if committed, will lead the offender to be prosecuted and sentenced by the authorities.[7] On the other hand, *mal* law applies to ownership of property in the legal context. Its jurisdiction under the Sharia Court is applicable to all Muslims resident in Brunei, and this court also has *mal* jurisdiction that encompasses issues related to the family (family law) (see Figure 6.1).

In 1998, Brunei legislated the Sharia Courts Act, Cap. 18. This law raised the jurisdiction and status of the Sharia Court to the same level as the Civil Court. The Sharia Court is divided into three: the Sharia Appellate Court, the Sharia High Court and the Sharia Lower Court.[8] Aside from that, Brunei also enacted a number of laws, including the Islamic Family Law, 1999. This law details provisions related to issues regarding the family institution and the rights of women, especially within marriage and upon divorce.

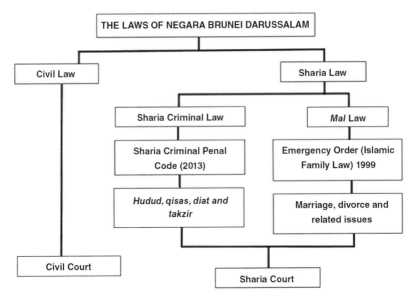

Figure 6.1 The structure of the implementation of laws in Brunei
Source: Author's field research.

Consideration of the Islamic Family Law, 1999 in this chapter focuses on the implementation of *mal* law related to family and marriage. Issues discussed include firstly, the extent to which the implementation of the Islamic Family Law, 1999 upholds the status of women in the family institution, especially regarding the rights of women within marriage in relation to property ownership, protection and so on, and secondly, the strengths and weaknesses that are apparent during the process of claiming the rights of women within marriage.

Islamic family law under the Emergency Order (Islamic Family Law) 1999 and the Family Protection Order, Amendment 2010

The arrival of Islam in the fourteenth century did not merely bring a religion, but brought a civilization that was able to influence and change the Malay World,[9] including Brunei, in the aspects of *aqidah* (faith, religious belief), society, culture, politics, economy, law and others. Following the acceptance and expansion of Islam in Brunei, it also revamped the ideologies and administrative styles of Bruneian rulers, mainly in issues pertaining to law. The development of Islamic law in Brunei went through three periods:

1   Islamic law prior to the arrival of the British (*Adat, Resam, Syarak* and *Hukum Kanun*), pre-1906;

2   Islamic law after the arrival of the British, post-1906: The Muhammadan Laws Enactment (No. 1 of 1912); The Muhammadan Marriages and Divorces Enactment (No. 3 of 1913); Brunei Order in Council 1924 (No. 1 of 1924); The Religious Council, State Custom and Kathi's Court Enactment 1955 (No. 20 of 1955), and the Constitution of Brunei Darussalam 1959;

3   Islamic law after the independence of Brunei in 1984: the Religious Council and Kathi's Courts Act; Chapter 77 of the Laws of Brunei Darussalam; Sharia Courts Act, Cap. 184; Emergency Order (Islamic Family Law) 1999; Halal Meat Act, Cap. 183; Halal Meat Rule, Cap. 183; Islamic Banking Act, Cap. 168; Sharia Courts Evidence Act 2001; Pawnbrokers Order 2001; Islamic Adoption of Children Act 2001; Islamic Family Laws of Rules 2002, and The Sharia Penal Code 2013.

In more recent developments, Brunei has enacted a law related to the family known as the Emergency (Islamic Family Law) 1999 and the Family Protection Order, Amendment 2010. Both these laws have a wider and more encompassing jurisdiction.

Provisions in these laws have heightened the status of women and granted more equality, as well as guaranteeing the rights of women within marriage. These laws are also intended to defend the family institution, namely women, from acts of violence, oppression, abuse and so on. The provisions of these laws as follows.

Emergency Order (Islamic Family Law) 1999

The Muslim family institution is governed by the Emergency Order (Islamic Family Law) 1999, which legislates for specific provisions regarding Islamic family law related to marriage, divorce, alimony, guardianship and other issues related to family life.

The Emergency Order (Islamic Family Law) 1999 is family law that contains provisions which are more explicit and thorough. This order did not wholly abolish provisions contained in the Religious Council and Kathi's Courts Act, Chapter 77 of the Laws of Brunei Darussalam, but merely Parts VI and VII.[10] Revisions were also made to this order in Section 5, Chapter 124, which is the Registration of Marriages Act in subsection (1). The Emergency Order (Islamic Family Law) 1999 contains ten parts.[11]

This law places women on a par with men, for example in the processes of engagement, application for marriage, registration of marriage and equality in the right to possess a marriage certificate, marriage card and *takliq* (dissolution of marriage) certificate. The law also guarantees and provides protection to the wife in terms of her economic welfare. The economic guarantee ordained for the period of the marriage is the compulsory payment of dowry, as well as the provision of alimony for sustenance (food, home, clothing, medical care and so on) from the husband to the wife. The same applies after divorce. There are provisions to guarantee the divorcee's economic situation by way of *mut'ah*, the *iddah* (grace period following divorce) alimony, a place to stay during the period of *iddah*, co-ownership of shared property from the marriage and also alimony for children in the care of a divorced wife.

This law also ensures equality, whereby a wife is able to seek legal recourse should the husband practise polygamy. Furthermore, the law provides social protection to women, such as in the cases of abandonment of the husband or wife, abuse of the husband, wife or children, and the right of the wife to dissolve the marriage by way of *takliq, fasakh* and *khuluq* (divorce).

The Family Protection Order, Amendment 2010

This order, enacted in June 2010, aims to provide protection to victims of domestic violence or abuse. Victims are able to apply for a protective order from the court, clarified as follows: families who have the right to be protected, types of protection available, enforcement officers, the right to compensation, and other related matters.

The case of dharar syar'ie

Dharar syar'ie, from the Islamic family perspective, is defined as a threat towards the wife, physical or mental, especially when it concerns her five fundamental rights that must be protected: religion, life, physical wellbeing, mental health and property. Thus, a threat to her physical wellbeing is considered a violation of her right to protection as granted by Islam. Another example of this is negligence in providing alimony (sustenance), which may affect her mental stability and physical wellbeing. This in turn violates the guarantee of the protection of her life, mental wellbeing and property, which are granted under Islam and the law. This also applies to husbands who are unconcerned about protecting her from any internal or external threat. Such husbands are considered negligent and irresponsible, because they are the rightful protector and the best confidant for grievances, whether internal (worries) or external (other issues of concern).[12]

According to the Protective Order under the Family Protection Order, Amendment 2010, the victims who must be protected are those of *dharar syar'ie*. This includes any acts of the following:[13]

a   intentionally or knowingly causing or attempting to cause a family member to fear harm;
b   inflicting harm on a family member by an act that is known or is supposedly known to cause harm;
c   coercing a family member using violence or threat to participate in any act where he/she has the right not to engage;
d   confining or holding a family member against his/her will;
e   continually disturbing a family member, with the intention to cause hardship, grief or shame, or doing so knowingly to cause possible hardship, grief or shame, or
f   causing destruction or damage to property, or loss of property of a family member, or causing financial loss to a family member.

Family members who have the right to protection

Family members must not only be protected physically, but the head of the family, the husband, must also protect them spiritually, especially their *aqidah* (faith) and *akhlak* (morality), as well as providing for their educational needs, whether worldly or concerning the hereafter. Education at the family level (informal) is the foundation that will produce future generations. If the foundation built does not have a strong basis in religion, monotheistic faith and morals, it will lead to troubled offspring and families. Allah s.w.t ordained for the husband's responsibility to protect his family in the Holy Quran: 'O ye of Faith! Protect yourselves and your families from hellfire, of which fuel consists of humans and stone (idols). . . .'[14]

This Family Protection Order, Amendment 2010 serves as a guide and reference for those who are involved, and victims are able to seek due legal representation and protection. Therefore, members of the family must be given protection so that the offspring born will become wholesome human beings, and so that the lives of the children and family will be better, more harmonious and blessed by Allah s.w.t. In addition, the livelihood of the children will be better protected in terms of sustenance, love, education and overall support. Furthermore, the wife will also receive love, and thus be able to fulfil her responsibilities to the family. Hence, the family and home will be free from fear, anxiety and restlessness, due to the absence of threats of domestic violence.

Right to protection

Dharar syar'ie victims can seek the right to be protected, which includes their right to apply for a Protective Order,[15] an Immediate Protective Order,[16] the right to compensation and the right to receive an Extension Order.

RIGHT TO SEEK FAMILY PROTECTION

Family protection can be sought by *dharar syar'ie* victims, either by the victims themselves, their families or those held responsible by the government to assist these victims. In order to obtain a Protective Order, an application must be made by the concerned family member (victim), enforcement officers, guardians, relatives, agencies responsible for their care or officers appointed by the director of the Department of Community Development (JAPEM, Jabatan Pembangunan Masyarakat) (if the victim is a minor or disabled person).[17] They must file an application and also go through a proceeding under the Sharia Court Civil Procedure Order 2005. Furthermore, they can assist the victim in lodging a report at a police station or take them to hospital if the victim has been injured.

Here, it is further noted that victims (those who are included in the term 'family') can file an application to the court to receive a Protective Order if they are or may be *dharar syar'ie* victims. There are two types of protection that can be sought by these victims: the Protective Order and the Immediate Protective Order.

RIGHT TO PROTECTION UNDER CAP. 60B

The court, after being satisfied that *dharar syar'ie* has been committed or may possibly be committed by any person toward a member of the family, and that the victim needs protection, makes an order to prevent the offender from further doing so.

RIGHT TO IMMEDIATE PROTECTION UNDER CAP. 60C

The right to immediate protection can be sought by a victim who is undergoing or has undergone *dharar syar'ie*. In these situations, the victim can petition the court to issue an Immediate Protective Order to her/him, even in the absence of the respondent (aggressor). For instance, the victim can be temporarily placed in the home of relatives or welfare homes provided by the Ministry of Youth, Welfare and Sports, such as Taman Nurhidayah, Darussakinah and other similar establishments.

RIGHT TO COMPENSATION

Victims of *dharar syar'ie* can apply to the court to be compensated by the respondent (aggressor).[18] The application can be made if the *dharar* has caused bodily harm, destruction or damage to property, loss of property, and financial loss.

RIGHT TO OBTAIN AN EXTENSION ORDER

The court can also issue an Extension Order if deemed necessary to offer further protection to the concerned *dharar syar'ie* victim.[19]

The role of protection

The responsible agencies that provide protection to *dharar syar'ie* victims each have their own roles, including the roles or responsibilities of the enforcement officers, the Ministry of Youth, Welfare and Sports, the Order to Arrest and the prosecution process. These roles are as follows.

ROLES/RESPONSIBILITIES OF ENFORCEMENT OFFICERS

In general, enforcement officers are those who are appointed to execute duties or responsibilities by the law. According to the Protective Order, an enforcement officer may be a police officer or any person expressly appointed by the Director of Community Development or the Director of Sharia Affairs. Enforcement officers also have their own jurisdiction: for example, under this law, a police officer can exercise the power to arrest an abusive husband, remove the *dharar syar'ie* offender or oversee the removal of the offender from the shared residence.

In general, they are responsible for explaining to the victims their right to seek protection from acts of *dharar syar'ie*. Furthermore, they are also responsible for accompanying the victim to their home to collect their belongings, along with carrying out other necessary and important duties to enforce and execute the provisions under the Protective Order (Family Protection Order, Amendment 2010).

THE ROLE AND RESPONSIBILITIES OF THE MINISTRY OF YOUTH,
WELFARE AND SPORTS

The Ministry of Youth, Welfare and Sports is responsible for certifying a place or institution as a shelter home. Hence, the secretary of the ministry is responsible for ordering the removal of the protected person from a residence to a shelter home. The director of JAPEM has the power to place the victim in a shelter home until an application is filed.

The responsibilities of the director of JAPEM include accepting, caring for, looking after the welfare of and providing safety to the victims in a shelter for a determined period.[20] The director is also responsible for appointing, in writing, the enforcement officers to execute the duties under this law[21] and also for providing counselling services to the victims and offenders of *dharar syar'ie,* or their children.[22]

THE ORDER TO ARREST AND THE LITIGATION PROCESS

Under the law, people who commit domestic violence, such as abusive husbands, can be arrested without a warrant by the police, religious inspectors, law enforcement officers or officers appointed by JAPEM. One of the offences that can lead to arrest without a warrant is if the respondent is found to have violated a Protective Order or an Immediate Protective Order, given specific accommodation to the protected person (when there had previously been an order for the respondent to vacate the residence), or approached the victim or entered her/his residence, workplace, school or other location.

The power of the courts under the Sharia Courts Act, Cap. 184

There is a strong relationship between the Bruneian Islamic Family Law and the jurisdiction of the Sharia Courts. This is due to the fact that this law upholds the status and supremacy of the legal system in Brunei, which makes Islam the reference point for its implementation and administration.

On 22 October 1998, the Sultan of Brunei and the Yang Di-Pertuan (Head of State) decreed the Sharia Courts Act, Cap. 184, which is an order enacting certain provisions for the establishment of Sharia Courts, the appointment and powers of Sharia judges, the jurisdiction of the Sharia Courts and other related issues pertaining to proceedings in the Sharia Courts, and also the sighting of the new moon and validation of such a sighting.

The provision in the Sharia Courts Act, Cap. 184 sets out the powers of the Sharia High and Lower Courts in executing the laws regarding marriages, engagements, dissolution of marriages and their implications or effects. These provisions are, as stated under the *mal* (non-criminal) jurisdiction, to hear and decide on all actions and proceedings.[23] Provisions in the Sharia Courts Act, Cap. 184 have abolished provisions in the Religious Council and Kathi's Courts Act, Chapter 77 of the Laws of Brunei Darussalam.[24]

The Sharia Courts have exclusive powers of jurisdiction. In order to avoid any misinterpretations, the Sharia Courts Act, Cap. 184 proclaimed that no court other than a court established under Part II[25] can hear or decide on any claims or proceedings under the jurisdiction of the Sharia Court.[26] Furthermore, the Sharia Courts Act, Cap. 184, established the Sharia Court, comprising the Sharia Lower Court, Sharia High Court and Sharia Appellate Court.[27]

The Sharia Lower, High and Appellate Courts each have their own jurisdictions, responsibilities and authorities, provided and implemented by this order and other written laws. These courts have their own jurisdictions throughout Brunei.[28] These orders also provide jurisdiction to the Sharia Court to try and hear criminal offences committed outside Brunei.[29]

The Sharia High Court has jurisdiction over criminal and *mal* cases. Provisions in the Sharia Courts Act, Cap. 184, Section 15 state that the Sharia High Court must:

a   under its criminal jurisdiction, try any offences that are punishable under any written law, which provides for Sharia criminal offences, under any such written law under the Islamic Family Law or any written law that gives jurisdiction to the Sharia High Court to try any offence, and can adjudge any sentence that is provided within; and

b   under its *mal* jurisdiction, hear and adjudge any action and proceeding related to:

    i   engagement, marriage (including reconciliation), divorce, *khuluq*, *fasakh*, *takliq*, determination of turns (in polygamy), *lian*, *ila'* or any related issues pertaining to the relationship between husband and wife;

    ii   any division of or claims to any property arising from any of the matters mentioned in subsection (i) of this section;

    iii   alimony for sustenance, *ithbat al-nasab* (legality of status) or *hadanah* (guardianship) of children;

    iv   division of or claims to any property co-owned and shared during marriage;

    v   inheritance or gifts at *marad al-maut* (terminal illness);

    vi   gifts (*hibah*) or settlements (*sulh*) made without monetary compensation or value that is adequate for a Muslim;

    vii   *wakaf* or *nazar* (contributions for the community);

    vii   division and inheritance of property, with or without a will;

    ix   determination of the rightful receivers and their respective portions of the deceased Muslim's property or part of it; or

    x   other related matters under the jurisdiction provided by any written law.

Concurrently, the Sharia Lower Courts also have their criminal and *mal* jurisdictions as with the Sharia High Court. However, their powers of execution are limited, as set out in Section 16 of the Sharia Courts Act, Cap. 184. The provisions are as follows:

1   The Sharia Lower Court must:

    a   under its criminal jurisdiction, try any offence that is punishable under any written law, which provides for Sharia Criminal offences, to determine those offences provided, where the maximum sentence does not exceed BND10,000[30] or jail for a period not more than seven years, or both, and can adjudge any sentence that is provided to it;

    b   under its *mal* jurisdiction, hear and adjudge any action and proceeding which the Sharia High Court has been given the authority to hear and adjudge, if the sum or value of such matters contended does not exceed BND500,000 or if its monetary value cannot be estimated.

2   His Royal Highness Duli Yang Maha Mulia Seri Baginda Sultan and the Yang Di-Pertuan can, on the recommendation of the Sharia Chief Judge, from time to time, with a statement in the Government's Proclamation, increase the *mal* jurisdiction of the Sharia Lower Court.

Such is also the case for the Sharia Appellate Court, which also has its own jurisdiction as provided in Section 20 of the Sharia Courts Act, Cap. 184.[31]

Offences that are tried in the Sharia High, Lower and Appellate Courts, which are related to the Islamic Family Law under the Emergency Order (Islamic Family Law) 1999,[32] in the form of *takzir*, if proven guilty is punishable by a fine or a jail term, or both.

On the other hand, offences that are tried in the Sharia High, Lower and Appellate Courts under the Religious Council and Kathi's Court Enactment, Chapter 77 of the Laws of Brunei Darussalam are Sharia criminal offences in the form of *takzir*, punishable by a fine or a jail term, or both.[33]

However, offences that are tried in the Sharia High, Lower and Appellate Courts under the Sharia Courts Act are those related to violation of an order of silence, contempt of the Sharia Court and matters related to the Courts Act.[34]

In analysing the foregoing section, the provisions for the Sharia Court's criminal jurisdiction are narrow and limited in terms of Islamic *sharia* (legal) principles because the sentences meted out for convicted offences are often based on *takzir*, in the form of fines or a jail term, or both. This is despite Brunei's proclamation of implementing the Sharia Criminal Penal Code fully according to Islamic law, based on the Holy Quran and Sunnah. The implementation of this order is not new, because Brunei had in the past implemented Islamic law.

The implementation of Islamic family law in Brunei in relation to the rights of women within marriage

Islamic family laws, especially under the Emergency Order (Islamic Family Law) 1999, have provided rights to women in marriage, specifically regarding the ownership of property, along with other rights. The question discussed here is how far this law is able to guarantee the status of the family institution and other rights of women in marriage, and also after its dissolution. Are women (wives) aware of their rights, and do they have the courage to claim these rights through legal processes?

The right of women to own property in marriage

The first woman was created by Allah s.w.t. as a helper to Adam. It has been inscribed in the history of man that women are of a lower class, weak, contemptible and bearers of misfortune. They can be bought and sold, and are also forced to satisfy the lust of men. They are exposed to oppression, aggression and injustice because men made them victims of discrimination. However, after the arrival of Islam, the status and dignity of women have been heightened, in accord with their positions as mothers and wives.

Islam has allocated special rights to women, such as rights accorded to them in religion, marriage, society, career, politics, property ownership and so on. In order to guarantee these rights, Islam prohibits any provocation or manipulation in the pursuit of negating such rights with the intention of ill-treating women. In this connection, several steps have been taken to prevent these injustices.[35] One of these steps is that taken to protect the rights of women in property ownership during marriage, which are protected by the Emergency Order (Islamic Family Law) 1999. Provisions in this law specifically stipulate the rights of women to property ownership in four periods: prior to marriage, during marriage, after the dissolution of marriage, and after death (of the husband).

Property prior to marriage

Men and women have the same rights to property they owned prior to marriage. The personal property they have owned before marriage is known as default property. This remains their own property until there is dissolution of the marriage, by divorce or death of one of the partners. In the case of death, then the default property becomes an inheritance.

The same goes for engagement customs which involve money or other property prior to the marriage. This has been ordained in the Emergency Order (Islamic Family Law) 1999.[36] If one of the parties, either the groom or bride, refuses to marry without any due reason, that party (whether groom or bride) must return the engagement gifts if they still exist, or provide compensation for their value. Furthermore, if one of the parties has made wedding preparations by advancing any monies, the expenditure must be claimed in court. This also applies to claims for compensation, which can be made by either party, groom or bride, if the other party refuses to satisfy any of the conditions agreed upon during engagement.[37]

In practice, however, very few cases of cancelled engagements are brought to court because most of these cancellations have been settled by traditions or amicable agreement between the two sides of the families involved.

Property during marriage

The Emergency Order (Islamic Family Law) 1999 has made provisions for women for the right of property ownership during marriage. Sections 20 and 58 have ordained a few specific provisions for women, especially with regard to their economic welfare during the full period of marriage, whereby it is compulsory for the husband to give the wife a dowry, expenses or gifts. The dowry may consist of money, property, moveable items or services. According to Othman Ishak, the value of the dowry is as agreed by both parties, and there is no limit in the determination of its value or form.[38] Furthermore, according to Raja Rohana Raja Mamat, the dowry reflects the preparedness of the groom to support and bear the responsibilities of providing for the new family's economic wellbeing after marriage, and as a guarantee to provide for the economic security and rights of the wife.[39] For the future bride, the dowry is a sign of readiness to form a bond. For the bride's family, it is a sign of friendship and a guarantee that their daughter is under the protection of a good provider.

The Emergency Order (Islamic Family Law) 1999[40] has ordained the husband's responsibility in providing sustenance[41] for the wife. The court has the power to order the husband to pay alimony to the wife as long as she does not commit any acts of *nusyuz* (rebellion) or refuses to obey the husband's bidding. Among the acts deemed *nusyuz* are estranging herself from the husband, leaving home without her husband's permission, refusing to move home with her husband, or other reasons which contravene *syarak* (Islamic ordainment). The wife also receives alimony if she has repented from *nusyuz*.

Property after dissolution of marriage

When there has been dissolution of marriage, it does not mean that the responsibilities of the husband towards his children and former wife immediately cease. His responsibility towards their livelihood still continues until a time ordained by *syarak* (Islamic law) and the law (legislated by the government). The Emergency Order (Islamic Family Law) 1999 contains provisions to protect and provide for the economic wellbeing of women who have been divorced. A husband is still responsible for providing the former wife with *mutaah*, alimony during *iddah* (the grace period), a place to live, shared property amassed during marriage and also alimony for the children under the care of his former wife.

(I) *MUTAAH*

Mutaah is in essence a form of goodwill, and is not compulsory. According to Imam Syafie, *mutaah* is a type of property, which may consist of money or material that is compulsory for the husband to give to his former wife when there is a divorce, or when both partners are alive and the dissolution of marriage was not caused by the wife.[42] It has been agreed by religious scholars that on dissolution of a marriage due to death, *mutaah* is not compulsory.[43] The value of *mutaah* is not predetermined, and solely depends on the husband's financial situation. Wealthy husbands are expected to pay according to his financial standing, whereas more average-earning or lesser-earning husbands pay according to theirs.

The giving of *mutaah* by the husband is intended to protect the dignity of the wife and also to compensate her for the divorce. *Mutaah* is intended to indemnify her for the shame she feels after being divorced by her husband, prevent *fitnah* (false accusations), and also as a basis to start life anew on her own.[44]

The Emergency Order (Islamic Family Law) 1999, Section 57 has outlined provisions regarding *mutaah* as follows:

> Aside from her right to petition for alimony, a woman who has been divorced by her husband can also petition from the Court to be given compensation (mutaah), and it can, after hearing both parties and is satisfied that the woman has been divorced, order the husband to pay a sum of money as deemed reasonable and fair according to syarak.

(II) ALIMONY DURING *IDDAH*

It is compulsory for the husband to pay alimony to his wife, whether they are still bonded in marriage or in the period of *iddah*[45] (grace period after divorce), unless when the wife has committed *nusyuz* (rebellion).

Alimony during *iddah* has been ordained in the Emergency Order (Islamic Family Law) 1999.[46] The provisions are as follows:

1   The right of a divorced wife to receive alimony from her former husband under a Court order must cease at the end of the *iddah* period or when the wife has committed *nusyuz*.
2   The right of a divorced wife to receive a gift from her former husband under an agreement must cease when the wife remarries.

An example is the case of *Noresah* v. *Shaffiq*,[47] where the court ordered the plaintiff (wife) to be in *iddah* for three menstrual cycles, and the plaintiff petitioned for *iddah* alimony for the three months to the amount of BND1,200 (BND400 a month). Likewise, in the case of *Hajah Ajijah* v. *Haji Damit*,[48] the court ordered the defendant to pay alimony to the amount of BND900 for three months or BND300 a month during her *iddah*.

(III) ACCOMMODATION

The Emergency Order (Islamic Family Law) 1999[49] further ordains for a wife who has been divorced by her husband the right to a have a place to live, as long as she is in *iddah* or when she is still caring for her children. The provisions are as follows:

1   A woman who has been divorced has a right to live in the house of her normal dwelling as when she was still married, for as long as the husband has not provided suitable alternative accommodation for her.

2   The right to accommodation that is provided in subsection (1) must cease:

    a   when her *iddah* has finished;

    b   when her caring for her child has finished;

    c   when the woman has remarried another man, or

    d   when the woman has committed a clearly contemptible act (*fahisyah*).

(IV) ALIMONY FOR CHILDREN UNDER THE CARE OF THE FORMER WIFE

The father is obligated to provide for the sustenance of his children as ordained by Emergency Order (Islamic Family Law) 1999.[50] These provisions are as follows:

1   Unless there has been an agreement or court order to provide by other means, it is compulsory for a man to provide for the sustenance of his children, whether they are under his care or that of any other person, by providing them with accommodation, clothing, food, medical care and education as deemed reasonable according to his financial ability and lifestyle, or to pay the costs of this.

2   Unless the provisions in subsection (1) apply, it is compulsory for a person who has dependents under *syarak* to provide for the sustenance or contribute to the sustenance of a child if the father of this child is deceased, or if his whereabouts become unknown, or if he is unable to provide for the child's sustenance.

The Emergency Order (Islamic Family Law) 1999[51] has assigned jurisdiction to the court to order the payment of sustenance for a child if it deems fit to do so for the child's benefit. The provisions are as follows:

1   The court may at any time order a father to pay sustenance for the benefit of his children:

    a   if he refuses or is negligent in providing reasonably for the child;

    b   if he completely abandons his wife and children under the care of his wife;

    c   while waiting for the judgment of a proceeding related to the affairs of the husband and wife;

    d   when or after he seeks an order to place the child under the care of any other person.

2   The court has the same jurisdiction to order a person who has dependents under *syarak* to pay alimony or contribute to the alimony for a child if it is satisfied that, according to his ability to do so, is reasonable for the court to order this.

3   An order under subsections (1) or (2) can demand that payment be made to the guardian, caregiver or the trustees of the child.

(V) SHARED PROPERTY DURING MARRIAGE

Shared property during marriage is that which is amassed by the husband and wife during the course of the marriage, resulting from their combined resources or efforts.[52] Shared property in marriage is a concept in Malay traditions that has been acknowledged by the law. In essence, it is not ordained in Islamic Sharia Law, but this provision was created based on the needs that arose in society. Therefore, most of the articles of law related to sharing property in marriage are based on Malay traditions rather than on Islamic *fiqh*.

The provisions of the Emergency Order (Islamic Family Law) 1999[53] concerning shared property during marriage are as follows:

1   The court must have jurisdiction to allow the utterance of *talak* (divorce) or to order divorce, or to order that any asset acquired by any of the parties concerned during the marriage in a combined effort be divided among them so that these assets can be sold and any proceeds divided between these parties.

2   In executing the powers granted to it in subsection (1), the court must consider:

    a   the contributions that have been made by each of the parties in the form of money, property or manpower in gaining those assets;

    b   any debt that is owed by either of the parties which has been incurred for the benefit of both parties;

    c   the needs of their children who have not come of age resulting from the marriage, if any; after making these considerations, the court must divide the assets equally.

3   The court must have jurisdiction to allow the utterance of *talak* or to order divorce, or to order that any asset acquired in the marriage by an effort of a single party be divided among them so that these assets are sold and that any proceeds are divided between the parties.

4   In executing the powers granted to it in subsection (3), the court must consider:

    a   the contributions that have been made by the party that has not acquired the asset to the welfare of the family by maintaining the household or caring for the family;

    b   the needs of their children who have not come of age resulting from the marriage, if any; after making these considerations, the court may divide the assets or proceeds of their sale of a value it deems reasonable. Nevertheless, the party that has acquired these assets by his/her efforts must receive a larger portion.

5   For the purposes of this chapter, the terminology pertaining to assets acquired during marriage includes assets that were previously owned by one party before the marriage that have been sold, with the proceeds used by both parties for the acquisition of more expensive assets during the marriage.

The Emergency Order (Islamic Family Law) 1999[54] has also ordained that a woman who is divorced from her husband or a man who is divorced from his wife may, by petition in court, obtain an order on their former partners regarding the issue of division of shared property.

In the case of *Hajah Amit* v. *Haji Bungsu*,[55] the court granted the petition for shared property filed by the plaintiff. She obtained the right to receive part of the shared property in payment for her services in assisting her former husband in his business dealings. The same applied in the case of *Mastiah* v. *Awang Khamis*,[56] where the former wife petitioned for part of the shared property and claimed that the parcels of land which were registered under her former husband's name were actually hers, because he had changed the ownership to his name after the completion of the sale and purchase. The plaintiff's petition was granted, and the Chief Kathi's Court adjudged according to *syarak* based on her rights, and thus ordered the defendant to return all the parcels of land to the plaintiff.

Property after death

A woman or wife has rights to the inheritance estate that is left by her relation. An inheritance estate is property that is owned by a deceased during his life, which is given to his next of kin, whether in the form of property, deed or any other form included in his ownership after his death.[57] An inheritance estate also means all the property that is left by the deceased which is owned by someone during his/her lifetime and remained as such until he/she dies.[58]

Rights not related to property

Social protection

Husbands cannot commit any acts of aggression, violence or abuse, whether physical or emotional. If convicted of an offence, the husband or wife can be fined not more than BND2,000 or jailed for not more than six months, or both. This is as ordained in the Emergency Order (Islamic Family Law) 1999.[59]

Under the same provisions, it is also ordained that when a husband or wife has appropriated his/her partner's property by way of deception, he/she has committed an offence, and if convicted, is punishable by a fine of not more than BND2,000 or a jail term of not more than six months, or both, and the court must order the return of the property, or if the property no longer exists, its value must be returned to the husband or wife according to *syarak*.

A husband abandoning his wife without any alimony is also a form of ill-treatment. The law has provided a social guarantee to the wife whereby she may wait for him to return, or file a petition to the court to order for the payment of alimony, or apply for a divorce.

An example of such a case is *Alinah* v. *Ali*,[60] where the court granted the petition for *fasakh* or divorce by Alinah (the plaintiff) because her husband was involved in drug abuse. The plaintiff petitioned for divorce was because the defendant had forced her to sell drugs. Another is the case of *Mazuin* v. *Saini*,[61] where the court granted the plaintiff's petition to be divorced from her husband because there was evidence of abuse. He had used a sharp object to strike her.

The right to be released from marital ties (divorce)

Talak (divorce) is a right given to husbands, but this does not mean that women are not accorded their own rights to apply for a divorce. Petitions for divorce must have due reasons that are allowed by *syarak*, because women who ask for divorce from their husbands without valid reasons are not allowed to enter heaven in the hereafter.

Among the methods that can be applied by a wife to dissolve a marriage under the Emergency Order (Islamic Family Law) 1999 are *taklik*,[62] *fasakh*[63] and *khuluk*[64] (compensated *talak*). A wife can file a petition for divorce in court. The court will first hear the petition, and if the wife's plea is granted, the marriage will be dissolved.

An example is the case of *Nur Aryatie* v. *Sofian*.[65] The court granted the petition of divorce through *takliq* because the wife did not receive alimony from her husband for more than four months. Another is *Khatijah* v. *Abd Hamid*,[66] where the court granted the plea for divorce by *takliq* by the plaintiff (wife) because the defendant (husband) had left the plaintiff with no news or alimony for expenses for a period of 11 months.

The right to seek justice

Polygamy or sharing a husband with other wives is allowed by *syarak*, with the condition that the husband must act fairly in terms of turn-taking and payment of alimony. The Emergency Order (Islamic Family Law) 1999[67] ordains that a husband must be fair to his wives. If a husband is found guilty of being unfair, he can be sentenced with a fine of BND2,000 or a jail term of not more than six months, or both.

Furthermore, to avoid abuse of the permission to practise polygamy, the Emergency Order (Islamic Family Law) 1999[68] ordains that any husband who wishes to practise polygamy must first apply for permission from the court. If he does not do so, he can be fined BND2,000 or jailed for not more than six months, or both.

An example is the case of *Mohd Abbas*.[69] The court granted his application to practise polygamy because his wife (the defendant) was unable to conceive. Similarly, in the case of *Zabar*,[70] the court granted his application to practise polygamy because he had the financial means to do so. On the other hand, there have been other applications to practise polygamy which have been rejected by the court. Among the reasons for rejection have been that the applicants were not financially eligible to practise polygamy, and thus should not do so. As a consequence, there have been cases where a wife has filed a petition for divorce because her husband did not treat her fairly in polygamy,[71] for instance *Osman* v. *Siti*[72] and *Yusof* v. *Sialam*.[73]

The law therefore provides a guarantee of justice for women, especially those in a polygamous marriage, so that they are not mistreated.

Hadanah/*guardianship/caregiving*

Under the Emergency Order (Islamic Family Law) 1999,[74] a mother or father has the right to care for a child who is not *mumaiyiz*, whether the mother is still bonded in marriage or has been divorced. This provision clearly provides protection and rights to the child, and the right to care for the child is given to the mother, even after divorce, because the court accords the child's welfare the utmost importance, especially regarding religion, moral guidance and alimony.

Examples include *Judin* v. *Nora*[75] and *Ziziumiza* v. *Hasnah*.[76] In both cases, the court adjudged the right to *hadanah* based on the welfare of the children with regard to guardianship, care, education, safety and so on.

Issues

The legislation of the Emergency Order (Islamic Family Law) 1999 was intended to provide protection, justice and rights to women, especially during the period of marriage and after divorce. Analysis of the provisions in this law clearly shows that the family institution and the rights of women have been guaranteed and protected. The problems that have arisen have not been the result of inadequacies or weaknesses in the current laws, especially the Emergency Order (Islamic Family Law) 1999 and the Family Protection Order, Amendment 2010. The problems and weaknesses were those of the women themselves, which led to their being unable to obtain their lawful rights during marriage and after divorce.

For instance, among the women who have cases involving property or other issues, not all of them have the courage to file petitions in court. This is due to several factors, prominent among which is a low level of education, ignorance of the law, not having an occupation (dependency of livelihood on the husband), threats from the husband, not knowing where or who to report their grievances to, love for their husband, being too trusting of their husband and others, and concern about the consequences that might result for the family, especially the children.

A lower level of education is undoubtedly the main reason why women are unaware of their rights under the law. There have been cases where the couple had married very young, before the age of 15. Such couples would likely have attended only primary or lower secondary school. In these situations, it is difficult for them to be fully aware of their legal rights in marriage or after divorce.

Other women simply do not understand the law and the rights accorded to them during marriage and after divorce. They are unfamiliar with court procedures, the authorities they can forward their grievances to, the availability of counselling services and so on. Such ignorance of the law is one of the reasons why cases presented in court can take a long time to be heard and adjudged.

Not having a job and being full-time housewives (dependence for livelihood on the husband) are also among the factors that lead women to be apprehensive or reluctant to claim their rights under marriage law, because of their dependency on their husbands and fear of losing this perceived security, especially in terms of alimony. Some husbands have also threatened their wives if they try to claim their rights under marriage law by seeking divorce. Some women love their husbands too much or are too trusting of them, which leads them to relinquish claiming their rights under marriage law.

Bruneian women, who are known for being soft-spoken, kind, shy, cultured, loyal and subservient, can easily be taken advantage of by men. This can be disadvantageous for them, because they remain loyal and lack the courage to refuse their husband's wishes, and they will not fight for their rights under marriage law.[77] For example, in cases related to polygamy, a husband must apply to the court for permission to take additional wives. The first wife may be afraid to refuse her husband's wish to practise polygamy, even though she knows her husband is unable to fulfil the requirements permitting a man to practise polygamy as stated in the law and *Hukum Syara'*.

Some women or wives are unable to prove to the court that there have been acts of abuse towards them. One of the reasons is because these women are unaware of the legal procedures required to provide proof of these offences to the court, failing to understand that the law demands solid evidence such as witnesses, police reports and medical examinations.

Concern for the welfare of the children is another deterrent for women who are mothers in seeking redress from the law even though they face an abusive spouse. The adverse consequences of divorce for the children mean that some abused wives do not turn to the courts; instead, they silently endure all the wrongs of their husband for the sake of their children.

Therefore, a number of recommendations to counter the aforesaid weaknesses are proposed, as set out below.

Education

A revision of the formal educational curriculum in government and religious schools must be undertaken, especially for religious education. The educational curriculum, specifically on the subjects of *sharia* and crime, is very important in preparing primary and secondary school pupils by gaining strong, fundamental knowledge. This basic knowledge will be further deepened when they reach upper secondary school and higher education. Education will arm the younger generation with knowledge and further the full implementation of Islamic law, specifically the Sharia Criminal Penal Code and the execution of *mal* law in Brunei.

Free sharia legal representation services

Due to the limited number of lawyers and the high cost of engaging their services, not many court cases employ the services of lawyers, with the exception of criminal cases and the small number of *mal* cases.[78] Thus, the gratis service of a *sharia* lawyer is very important in order to assist women who are ignorant or less knowledgeable about their rights under the law.

Family advice or counselling services

The proposed establishment of family advice services under the Department of Sharia Affairs, Ministry of Religious Affairs aims to resolve family problems by providing advice and guidance about issues related to marriage, dissolution of marriage, polygamy and reconciliation. This family advice service is recommended to help women to become better informed about their rights under family law, either during marriage or after its dissolution.

Billboards and roadshows

The agencies responsible must publicize and hold roadshows about the law for the public, especially women, to foster awareness, disseminate information and promote understanding of the rights of women under marriage law. The mass media, information technology, radio, television, talks, forums and seminars about the law can all play a role in helping the public, especially women, to understand the rights of women under marriage law.

Conclusion

The passing of the Emergency Order (Islamic Family Law) 1999 was intended to provide protection, justice and rights to women, especially during marriage, but also after divorce. An analysis of the provisions in this law clearly exemplifies the guarantee and protection of the family institution and of women. Problems have arisen not because of inadequacies or weaknesses in the current law, especially the Emergency Order (Islamic Family Law) 1999 and the Family Protection Order, Amendment 2010, but because of the problems and weaknesses of the women concerned, which can cause them to lose their rights under family law. The recommendations above need to be given serious consideration by the relevant authorities; but ultimately, it is the women themselves who need to change their mindset and assert their legal rights as provided under the law.

Current developments of women in Brunei are very impressive, especially in the field of education. Women have been entrusted with roles in the administration of the country, to the extent that they are appointed as deputy ministers, secretaries, judges, lawyers, doctors, lecturers, teachers and so on. With this development, it is hoped that women in this country will gain an enlightened awareness of their rights, especially in terms of family law. Those who are well educated could contribute by assisting and raising awareness among other women who are less well informed of their general and specific rights, especially concerning marriage law.

It is hoped that the women of this country will have the awareness and courage to claim their fundamental rights as women – not merely their rights within marriage, but also others, especially in society and in the country as a whole. With knowledge, awareness and the courage to insist on the rights that have been ordained by Islam and the law of the country, the status of women of Brunei could be raised to be on par with that of men, and contribute to the wellbeing of the sultanate.

Notes

1 *Adat* (Tradition) means regulations that are practised over generations by a society, where they become the rules, and thus must be obeyed. *Kamus Bahasa Melayu Nusantara* [*Malay Dictionary of the Archipelago*] (Bandar Seri Begawan: Dewan Bahasa dan Pustaka, 2003), p 13.

2 *Resam* means practices and rituals that subsequently become customs. Teuku Iskandar, ed., *Kamus Dewan* [*The Dewan Dictionary*], new edn (Kuala Lumpur: Dewan Bahasa dan Pustaka, 1992), pp. 1,058–9.

3 *Syarak* means Islamic teachings, commonly known as *Hukum Syarak* (Islamic law). The main source of reference is the Holy Quran and Sunnah (sayings and practices of the Prophet Muhammad s.a.w.). These Islamic teachings encompass *aqidah* (monotheistic belief), *sharia* (religious laws) and *akhlak* (morals). See Haji Mohd Zain Haji Serudin, *Melayu Islam Beraja: Suatu Pendekatan* [*Muslim Malay Monarchy: An Approach*] (Bandar Seri Begawan: Dewan Bahasa dan Pustaka, 1998), p. 11.

4 *Hukum Kanun Brunei*: *Kanun* means laws, regulations and rules; Teuku Iskandar, *Kamus Dewan*, p. 528. *Hukum Kanun Brunei* is the guide to executing the administration in Brunei. Mohd Zain Haji Serudin, *Melayu Islam Beraja*, p. 11. There are two versions of the *Hukum Kanun*: *Hukum Kanun Brunei* and *Undang-undang Adat Brunei Lama* [*Old Bruneian Law and Custom*].

5 In accordance with the Perjanjian Tambahan [Additional Agreement] of 1905/1906, the British Resident was appointed as adviser to the sultan in all state matters except those regarding Islamic religious affairs. Subsequently, for all intents and purposes the Resident became the highest power in the newly formed and modernized public administration of the sultanate. See William George Maxwell and William Summer Gibson, *Treaties and Engagements Affecting the Malay States and Borneo* (London: J. Truscott, 1924), pp. 149–50.

6 The Constitution of Brunei Darussalam 1959, Section 3(1).

7 Richard Card, *Criminal Law*, 13th edn (London: Butterworths, 1995), p. 1.

8 Sharia Courts Act, Cap. 184, Section 6(1).

9 The Malay World covers the greater part of insular Southeast Asia or the Malay Archipelago, comprising the modern nation states of Malaysia, Singapore, Brunei, Indonesia and the Philippines. The term 'Malay World' also include areas where Malay people have migrated and settled; in this context, it stretches westwards as far as East and South Africa and eastwards to the southwest Pacific and northern Australasia.

10 Sections 175, 176, 178(I), 178(2), 179 and 180, which have been abolished.

11 See Appendix 6.1.

12 Mustafa Haji Daud, *Institusi Kekeluargaan Islam* [*The Islamic Family Institution*] (Kuala Lumpur: Dewan Bahasa dan Pustaka, Ministry of Education, Malaysia, 1992), p. 20.

13 Family Protection Order, Amendment 2010, Section 60A.

14 The Holy Quran, Surah At-Tahriem (66): (6).

15 Family Protection Order, Amendment 2010, Section 60B.

16 Ibid., Section 60C.

17 Ibid., Section 60B(2).

18 Ibid., Section 60E.

19 See Appendix 6.2.

20 Family Protection Order, Amendment 2010, Section 60K.

21 Ibid., Section 60(1).

22 Ibid., Section 60(b).

23 See Appendix 6.3.
24 Islamic Religious Council and Kathi's Courts Act, Cap. 77, Sections 45, 46, 47, 48, 49, 50, 50 A, 51, 52, 53, 54, 55, 68, 75, 94 and 198.
25 Part II of the Sharia Courts Act, Cap. 184, establishment and jurisdiction of Sharia Courts.
26 Sharia Courts Act, Cap. 184, Section 5.
27 Ibid., Section 6(1).
28 Ibid., Section 6(2).
29 Ibid., Section 6(3): 'By disregarding subsection (2), the Sharia Court must have criminal jurisdiction on offences conducted outside the country by citizens or permanent residents of Brunei.'
30 All monetary figures are in Brunei dollars (BND); BND1.00 was equivalent to US$0.72 in March 2015.
31 See Appendix 6.4.
32 See Appendix 6.5.
33 See Appendix 6.6.
34 See Appendix 6.7.
35 Datin Dr Hajah Saadiah Datu Derma Wijaya Haji Tamit, *Wanita, Keluarga, dan Undang-undang Di Brunei Darussalam* [*Women, Family and the Law in Brunei Darussalam*] (Bandar Seri Begawan: Dewan Bahasa dan Pustaka, Ministry of Culture, Youth and Sports, 2009), p. 1.
36 Emergency Order (Islamic Family Law) 1999, Section 14(1).
37 Ibid., Section 14(12).
38 Othman b. Hj. Ishak, *Fatwa Dalam Rumahtangga Islam* [*Ordainment of the Muslim Family*] (Kuala Lumpur: Fajar Bakti, 1981), p. 23.
39 M.B. Hooker, *Islamic Law in South East Asia*, translated by Rohani Abd. Rahim, Raja Rohana Raja Mamat and Anisah Che' Ngah (Kuala Lumpur: Dewan Bahasa dan Pustaka, 1991), p. 73.
40 Emergency Order (Islamic Family Law) 1999, Section 61(1) (2)(3).
41 *Nafkah* (alimony) is in essence food, clothing and shelter. Alimony also includes services, medical care, educational needs, religious needs and so on.
42 Al-Shaykh Muhammad al-Khatib al-Sharbiniy, *Mughni al-Muhtaj* [*The Indigent Singer*] (commentary on Imam Nawawi's abridged work of Minhaj al-Talibin) (Cairo: Matba'ah Mustafa al-Babiy al-Halabiy wa Awladuh, AH 1377/1958), p. 241.
43 Al-Nawawiy Abi Zakariyya Yahya b. Sharaf, *Rawdah al-Talibin* (Beirut: Dar al-Kuttub al-Ilmiyyah, AH 1412/1992), p, 636.
44 Mimi Kamariah Majid, *Undang-Undang Keluarga di Malaysia* [*Family Law in Malaysia*] (Kuala Lumpur: Butterworths Asia, 1992), p. 186.
45 *Iddah* is a period of waiting that is compulsory for the wife in order to determine that the woman's womb is clean (from menstruation), she is not conceiving her former husband's child or to comply with Allah's ordainment, or to enable a husband to reconcile with his wife. In other words, *iddah* is a waiting period that is compulsory for a wife who is no longer married to her husband, whether the dissolution of marriage is caused by *talak* or *fasakh* (divorce) or death; Wahbah al-Zuhaiyliy, *al-Fiqh al-Islamiy wa Adillatuh* [*The Understanding of Islamic Jurisprudence*] (Beirut: Dar al-Fikr, AH 1409/1989), 1989) p. 817. *Iddah* for a woman who is divorced and is still menstruating is three full cycles of menses, and three months for a woman who has been through the menopause. For a wife who is pregnant, her *iddah* lasts until she delivers the child, and for a widow, her *iddah* lasts four months and ten days (The Holy Quran, Surah Al-Baqarah 2:228, At-Talaq 65:4, Al-Baqarah 2:234).

46 Emergency Order (Islamic Family Law) 1999, Section 67.
47 MRHS/MAL/TM-01/2004.
48 MRHS/MAL/TM-2/1999.
49 Emergency Order (Islamic Family Law) 1999, Section 74(1)(2).
50 Ibid., Section 75(1)(2).
51 Ibid., Section 76 (1)(2)(3).
52 Haji Md Akhir b. Hj. Yaakub, 'Harta Sepencarian' ['Shared Property in Marriage'], *Jurnal Hukum*, 5(1) (1984): 36–54 at 36–7.
53 Emergency Order (Islamic Family Law) 1999, Section 59 (1)(2)(3)(4)(5).
54 Ibid., Section 60.
55 MKB CM 7/1984, the Chief Kathi's Court, Brunei.
56 Datin Dr Hajah Saadiah Datu Derma Wijaya Haji Tamit, *Pembubaran Perkahwinan Dalam Undang-undang Keluarga Islam Brunei dan Perbandingan Dengan Undang-undang Keluarga Islam Malaysia* [*Dissolution of Marriages under Islamic Family Law in Brunei and its Comparison to Islamic Family Law in Malaysia*] (Bandar Seri Begawan: Dewan Bahasa dan Pustaka, Ministry of Culture, Youth and Sports, 2012), p. 353.
57 Haji Abdul Kadir bin Haji Ismail, *Sistem Pusaka Islam* [*The Islamic Inheritance System*] (Kuala Lumpur: Malaysian Dakwah Islamiah Foundation, 1983), p. 89.
58 Wan Abdul Halim Wan Harun, *Mengurus Harta Pusaka* [*Managing Inheritance Estates*] (Kuala Lumpur: PTS Professional Publishing, 2012), p. 18.
59 Emergency Order (Islamic Family Law) 1999, Section 128 (1)(2)
60 MRHS/MAL/TUT:09/2003.
61 MRHS/KB/MAL/50/2003.
62 Emergency Order (Islamic Family Law) 1999, Section 45.
63 Ibid., Section 46.
64 Ibid., Section 48 (1)(2)(3).
65 MRHS/MAL/TC 08/2001.
66 MRHS/MAL/KB/13/2004.
67 Emergency Order (Islamic Family Law) 1999, Section 129.
68 Ibid., Section 123.
69 TM POL 3/2000.
70 POL/KB/06/2001.
71 Saadiah Datu Derma Wijaya Haji Tamit, *Pembubaran Perkahwinan*, p. 201.
72 MKB 59/94, Kathi's Court Districts of Brunei and Muara.
73 MKB 77/96, Kathi's Court Districts of Brunei and Muara.
74 Emergency Order (Islamic Family Law) 1999, Sections 88–94.
75 MKB 73/95 Kathi's Court Districts of Brunei and Muara.
76 MKB 94/93, Mal: 115/93, Kathi's Court Districts of Brunei and Muara
77 Saadiah Datu Derma Wijaya Haji Tamit, *Wanita, Keluarga dan Undang-undang*, p. 27.
78 Ibid, p. 28.

Part IV
Current concerns

7 Foreign labour in Brunei

Demand, issues and implications

Noralipah binti Haji Mohamed

As a result of the capitalist economy, the movement of people from one place to another is becoming significant. The concept of 'free labour' allows people to move freely, providing they follow policies imposed by each country. This movement of workers as a distinct labour market phenomenon is associated with the rapid transformation of many industrialized nations throughout the world. Host countries which offer job opportunities are preferred by foreign workers. Brunei has considered the importance of importing foreign labour, as the country is facing a shortage of labour. This chapter explores the need for foreign labour as a consequence of colonialism, which transformed the country's economy from subsistence to capitalist industries. However, after independence in 1984, the influx of foreign labour led to a mismatch between local job-seekers' aspirations and the requirements of the economy as a result of changing labour patterns due to economic diversification. The overwhelming presence of foreign workers in Brunei has created economic, social, cultural and political issues and implications. Their positive contributions, on the other hand, are significant in maintaining the country's development growth on an even keel and pace.

Brunei is one of the countries in Asia that has received large numbers of foreign labour. In 2013, the number of foreign workers was estimated at 183, 541.[1] The country's strategic location in Southeast Asia to some extent encourages the influx of foreign labour. Its social and political practices rank the country as a 'welfare state'. Economically, the country has achieved commendable economic performance, largely based on oil and gas production.

Brunei has been regarded as a labour-receiving country since the early twentieth century, with the onset of the oil and gas industries. In the early stages, Brunei received foreign labour from a limited number of countries. But since 1984, following its independence from Britain, the demand for foreign labour increased drastically as the country emphasized industrial economic development. Reasons that influence foreigners to seek employment in another country are numerous. High demand results from the needs of capital for labour – a situation that was inherited from colonialism. Moreover, there are pull and push factors that encourage foreign workers to seek jobs in Brunei. These variables will be analysed in this chapter with cognizance of the historical perspective of labour migration in Brunei and the reasons for foreign workers' arrival. The impact of the influx of foreign labour is apparent in the host or receiving countries. Receiving large numbers of foreign workers comes at a price in terms of issues and their implications, which will also be addressed in this chapter.

Brunei as a labour migration destination

Before the arrival of foreign labour, Brunei's local labour force was primarily engaged in subsistence-based economic activities such as agriculture and fisheries. The arrival of the British in 1906 brought changes to the administration of Brunei. The first strategy was to transform and reorganize the administrative centre of the country, as stated in the *Brunei Annual Report* 1910: 'the country will not be considered to be as modern and developed if its administration is still located and centred off land'.[2]

The British gradually attempted to improve the social life of the people by introducing a modern, secular education system as well as providing modern medical services. Indigenous people served in the administration in low-ranking positions such as office boy.[3]

The British also brought substantial changes to the country's economic condition. The initial focus was to transform the traditional, mainly subsistence-based economic activities to commercial and modern activities such as cutch, coal, rubber and the oil industry. The introduction of these modern industries spurred the influx of foreign labour. Potts has argued that 'the exports of Indians and Chinese coolies are all structural elements of European colonialism in the industrial capitalism'.[4] After the arrival of the British, the country began to recruit large numbers of Chinese and Indian labourers.[5] The concept of 'industrial capitalism' brought by the British facilitated the participation of these labourers. The positive side of the influx of foreign labour was that it contributed to the economic development of the country at a consistent rate. This is evident in the view expressed by Harris that 'as the capitalist economic system spread, migration came to be seen as a means of making up for an inadequate supply of labour in the colonies'.[6]

After Brunei gained independence in 1984, the country developed rapidly. Its economic development, emphasizing industrial progress, forced the country to engage labour not only from underdeveloped countries, but also from developing and developed countries. Table 7.1 shows the numbers in the working population according to the country of origin over three decades, represented by the years 1971, 1981 and 1991.

Table 7.1 shows that in these three decades, Malaysia ranked first in terms of numbers among all the countries that export labour to Brunei. The rapid increase is apparent: the number of workers in 1971 was 22,362, which almost doubled in 1991 with 41,900. Proximity and the favourable currency exchange greatly encouraged labour migration from Malaysia to Brunei.

There was also a drastic increase in Filipino migrant labour to Brunei during 1971–91. Before 1984, there were about 1,298 Filipino workers in Brunei, and by 1991 there had been an eightfold increase to 8,147. The drastically increased numbers of incoming foreign migrant workers since 1984 came not only from Malaysia and the Philippines, but also from other Asian countries.

Table 7.1 Labour population by country of birth, 1971, 1981 and 1991

Country of birth	Nos			%		
	1971	*1981*	*1991*	*1971*	*1981*	*1991*
Brunei	101,511	139,167	184,388	74.5	72.17	70.79
Malaysia	22,362	37,544	41,900	16.41	19.47	16.09
China and Taiwan	5,010	3,038	1,569	3.68	1.58	0.6
United Kingdom	785	2,522	2,075	0.58	1.31	0.8
Nepal	NA	2,394	3,810	NA	1.24	1.46
India, Pakistan, Sri Lanka and Bangladesh	1,586	2,341	4,479	1.16	1.21	1.72
Singapore	1,149	1,792	1,558	0.84	0.93	0.6
Philippines	NA	1,298	8,147	NA	0.67	3.13
Hong Kong	576	551	397	0.42	0.29	0.15
The Netherlands	NA	285	257	NA	0.15	0.1
Thailand	NA	278	6,873	NA	0.14	2.64
Indonesia	NA	235	3,455	NA	0.12	1.33
Korea	520	235	143	0.38	0.12	0.05
Other countries	2,667	1,078	1,418	1.96	0.56	0.53
Not stated	90	74	13	0.07	0.04	0.005
Total	136,256	192,832	260,482	100	100	100

Source: T.S Yean and T.S. Ee, 'Population and Labour Force in Brunei Darussalam: Patterns and Structural Changes', in *Readings on the Economy of Brunei Darussalam*, edited by J. Obben and T.S. Ee (Bandar Seri Begawan: Department of Economics, University of Brunei, 1999), p. 107.

Most of the Thais and Bangladeshis were recruited for the construction industry, while Indonesian and Filipino workers served as domestic helpers. Malaysians, Australians and New Zealanders served as contractors at the higher occupational levels.[7]

The allure of Brunei

The influx of foreign workers to Brunei is largely a consequence of three major factors: the payment of high wages, the availability of jobs, and encouragement by relatives and friends of adopting Brunei as a work destination.

Money matters

As a labour-receiving country, Brunei has attracted over 100,000 foreign workers from various countries.[8] This is due to the current economic situation, which encourages diversity in a attempt to reduce the heavy dependence on oil and gas production. In this connection, two hypotheses are considered: the Harris-Todaro Hypothesis and Schultz's Symmetry Hypothesis.[9]

The Harris-Todaro Hypothesis argues that the main determinants of incoming foreign labour are high expectations in terms of wages and the probability of being hired. On the other hand, Schultz's Symmetry Hypothesis focuses on push and pull factors that are of equal impact, whether in the country of origin or in the destination country. Both hypotheses are applicable to incoming and outgoing migrant labour in Brunei.

The higher value of Brunei's currency (BND) compared to other Southeast Asian countries has been an attractive pull factor for labourers from countries with low currency exchange values. As a result, from the early 2000s, the largest number of foreign labourers have come from Indonesia.[10] The Brunei dollar exchange rate with the rupiah (R) in July 2002 was around BND1.00 = R5,100.[11] In November 2014, the rate was BND1.00 = R9,338 – a most favourable exchange rate for an Indonesian worker repatriating funds to his home village in Indonesia,[12] as a BND200 monthly wage allowed a substantial amount to be sent home. Favourable wages are without any doubt considered to be one of the main attractions according to the Harris-Todaro Hypothesis.

For Filipino workers, the rather high salaries compared to those for their previous jobs elsewhere have encouraged them to favour employment in Brunei. Research conducted in 2001 among 100 randomly collected respondents revealed that 49 per cent earned BND401 per month in their previous employment, while 73 per cent earned the same sum after securing jobs in Brunei.[13] The high wage rate is one of the primary pull factors for Filipino labour migration to the sultanate.

The influx of foreign labour to Brunei is also a result of push factors in source countries where there is a high incidence of unemployment coupled with a high population, leading to competition and scarcity of employment, resulting in poverty. Most foreign labourers in Brunei originate from a home country with a high population. In relation to the Neo-Malthusian theory of population, increases in population will lead to depression of wages, resulting in lower standards of living. Chronic poverty tends to be a major influential factor in the decision to migrate to seek employment abroad.[14]

Apart from the attractive high salaries, the wide gap in wages paid for the same job also features as one of the main reasons for labour migration.[15] This is borne out by neoclassical economic theory, which concludes that 'migrants are expected to go where they can be the most productive, that is, where they are able to earn the highest wages'.[16] For instance, in Brunei, as of early 2015, the minimum monthly wage for a domestic helper is BND450 – far higher than in Indonesia, where a similar job pays BND50 or less per month.[17]

Jobs aplenty

Another contributing factor that influences the movement of people from their home countries is the availability of jobs in the receiving country. A case in point is the demand for foreign labour in the construction industry in Brunei. The availability of positions as labourers and contractors attracts foreign labour to this increasingly expanding industry. Systems theory is applicable here, whereby individual or family decisions that encourage migration are accompanied by other factors, such as market access, income inequality, relative deprivation and social security.[18]

Moreover, it is important to consider that in the majority of cases, the large number of jobs available was the result of a mismatch between local job-seekers and their economic aspirations. A common belief is that Bruneians prefer to work in white-collar jobs,[19] But the validity of this statement remains unsubstantiated without empirical evidence. For certain migrants, their skill level dictates the types of jobs that are available: highly skilled migrants have more options than low-skilled migrants.

Peer pressure

Among the agents of socialization, relatives, friends and peer groups are among the largest pull factors for foreign workers moving to Brunei. It is commonplace in Brunei that if a mother is employed in a certain type of job, her children will also apply for a job within the sultanate. In some cases, workers tend to migrate not only for the job itself, but in search of adventure, exploration and to satisfy curiosity.[20] Moreover, there are also initiatives by embassies of foreign countries in Brunei to organize programmes and projects to attract their countries' citizens to work in Brunei. The Philippines embassy, for instance, runs a programme called Ugnayang Pilipino Bayanihan [Cooperative Filipino Relations] aimed at assisting overseas Filipino workers to acquire new skills to improve their employment status. The programme also conveys a proper understanding of important Bruneian rules and regulations to Filipino workers.

The demand for foreign labour

The need for industrial diversification incorporated in the Fifth National Development Plan (1986–90) and Sixth National Development Plan (1991–95) has resulted in an increase in the number of foreign labourers, particularly in the highly labour-intensive construction industry.[21] Despite population growth, the domestic workforce is unable to meet this high demand for labour.

With a total population of 414,400 in 2010, the demand for labour in Brunei remained high.[22] Such a situation fulfils Carlos's assumption that population growth in the destination country will fuel demand for labour.[23] Table 7.2 indicates that by 2011, the projected required labour force was expected to reach 222,000. In the same year the local labour force was only projected to be 123,000, leading to the expected participation of 99,000 foreign labourers.

Rapid development has forced Brunei to employ large numbers of labourers. Brunei regards human labour power as part of its economic development. Thus, in order to cope with this requirement, the Eighth National Development Plan (2001–2005) focused on providing the local workforce with 'appropriate training and retraining to enhance their productivity'.[24] This is one of the strategies of reducing dependence on foreign labour. As shown in Table 7.3, it was estimated that by 2005, the total number of jobs available would be 163,000 spread

Table 7.2 Estimated labour force requirements in Brunei

Variables	Actual	Projected years			
	1991	1996	2001	2006	2011
Required labour force	110,583	135,000	162,000	191,000	222,000
Local labour	65,408	78,000	92,000	107,000	123,000
Foreign labour	45,175	57,000	70,000	84,000	99,000
% of foreign labour	40.9	42.2	43.2	44.0	44.6

Source: T.S. Ee, and A.A. Haji Hashim, 'Manpower Planning in Negara Brunei Darussalam: Issues and Perspectives', in *Readings on the Economy of Brunei Darussalam*, edited by J. Obben and T.S. Ee (Bandar Seri Begawan: Department of Economics, University of Brunei, 1999), p. 195.

across seven categories, as laid out in the Brunei Darussalam Industrial Structure Statistic, 2001–2005. The largest number were expected to be in the occupational group 'Professionals, technicians and related workers'.

The contribution of foreign workers since the early twentieth century has undoubtedly transformed the physical growth of Brunei. Foreign workers employed in Brunei are mainly contractors.[25]

According to the Labour Department of Brunei Darussalam, the construction industry employs a large number of unskilled foreign workers. In 2003, the number of workers in this industry who held the status of temporary residents reached 24,637.[26] The high demand for unskilled labour is evident in the construction sector. It is also similar in other developed countries such as the US, Spain and the

Table 7.3 Brunei's occupational structure, 2001–2005

Occupational group	2001	2005	Net increase
Administrators and managers	7,250	8,150	900
Professionals, technicians and related workers	34,365	37,490	3,125
Clerical workers	20,880	22,820	1,940
Services, shop, market and related workers	20,735	23,309	2,574
Agricultural, forestry and fishery workers	1,885	4,075	2,190
Production and craftsmen, operators and assemblers and related workers	27,985	31,296	3,311
Labourers, cleaners and equipment, transportation and related workers	31,900	35,860	3,960
Total	145,000	163,000	18,000

Source: Government of Brunei Darussalam, *Eighth National Development Plan 2001–2005*, Economic Planning Unit, Ministry of Finance, p. 64.

UK, where 'some sectors of low productivity agriculture are dependent on them [unskilled labour], so reducing their number might have severe regional economic consequences'.[27] On the other hand, countries that receive migrant labour benefit by gaining low-wage workers who can be sent home in times of economic downturn.[28]

In the context of Brunei, the number of applicants is often much higher than the number of job openings. This is particularly apparent in types of jobs that locals prefer: for instance, in 2003, 2,270 applicants applied for clerical positions, but only 136 were qualified and accepted to fill the 194 positions available. For the position of general labourer, 144 vacancies were offered in 2003; of the 913 applications, only 128 positions were filled by those who met the requirements.[29] The advantages of free education enable locals to attain high levels of education, creating a mismatch with the bulk of unskilled jobs in the labour market.

Manpower participation by countries[30]

By the new millennium, the pattern of foreign workers in Brunei had shifted slightly from the situation in the 1990s. By 2000, Indonesia had overtaken Malaysia as the main labour-exporting country to the sultanate. Although Brunei continued to draw labour from various countries – 106,011 foreign workers from 87 countries – the neighbouring triumvirate of Indonesia, Malaysia and the Philippines accounted for the highest number of workers employed in Brunei. Indonesia had the highest number, with 40,722. Some 19,168 Indonesians were female domestic helpers, reflecting a higher ratio of female workers to male workers. This had been the trend from the late 1980s to the late 1990s, when two-thirds of Indonesian migrants were female. It is obvious that most of these female foreign workers are interested in jobs which are regarded as 'typically female'.[31] Nearly three-quarters of Indonesian female workers are domestic helpers – a proportion not unique to Brunei. Towards the end of 1988, it was recorded that 192,000 Indonesian women had migrated to Saudi Arabia, where the majority served as housemaids in private homes.[32]

Emigrating from their home country is one way for workers to move out of poverty and be able to support their families back home.[33] For some foreign labourers, it is not easy to migrate to other countries to seek work. Kothari outlined the impact of the economic conditions of migrants: 'migration requires a variety of forms of financial expenditure and incurs costs; those without the means cannot migrate'.[34] Kothari considered that 'moving from one place to another has economic and social costs'; they have two options: to remain poor, or to move out of poverty.[35] Job-seeking agencies in their home countries levy high charges, so it is a somewhat risky investment for those who are short of money: many borrow from relatives, promising to repay the debt from their wages abroad. This is considered one of the migration costs that foreign workers have to pay.

Malaysians rank the second highest after Indonesians in terms of the number of foreign workers in Brunei. The favourable currency exchange between the Brunei dollar and the Malaysian ringgit makes the sultanate an advantageous work destination for Malaysian workers. Geographically, East Malaysia shares its boundary with Brunei, and this proximity is another of the attractions. Moreover, both countries share common cultural values and languages, making it easier for East Malaysians to adapt to employment in Brunei.

The Philippines ranks third highest after Indonesia and Malaysia, with 16,393 workers. In total, 391 were employed in the government sector, 11,808 with private companies in various positions, 3,885 as domestic helpers, while 855 were dependants. There has been a fall in the number of Filipino workers employed in Brunei when compared to 1997–99; the number of Filipino workers in 2000 was 23,865, and mainly in the Brunei-Muara District where most of the administration and economic activities takes place.[36] There is little doubt that Filipinos working in foreign countries are an asset to the home economy, and that 'Philippine overseas migration has become a pair of crutches for the local economy. Serving two main objectives – to ease the unemployment situation and to generate foreign incomes to fuel the faltering economy'.[37]

Officially, Filipino workers are classified into five occupational categories: professionals, skilled workers, semi-skilled workers, unskilled workers and domestic helpers.[38] Their main reason for choosing to work in Brunei is their intention to increase earnings in order to support their family back home. The salaries they receive are much higher than in their previous employment.[39]

Most Filipinos working in Brunei are highly educated. In 2001, of a sample of 1,000 Filipinos, 58 per cent of them possessed tertiary-level education, 33.9 per cent secondary-level, and 1.5 per cent only primary level (see Table 7.4).[40] But the need for Filipino employees is usually for domestic work in private households, hence many Filipino housemaids in Bruneian homes are educationally over-qualified for their lowly positions as domestic helpers.

Manpower by industries and occupations

Table 7.5 lists the ten private sector employment categories for the period 2001–2015.

Table 7.4 Educational background of Filipino workers in Brunei based on 100 random samples

Academic level	Male		Female	
	Nos	%	Nos	%
Primary	1	2.9	1	1.5
Secondary	12	34.3	22	33.9
University	21	60	37	56.9
Vocational	1	2.8	4	6.2
Others	—	—	1	1.5
Total	35	100	65	100

Source: Noralipah Mohamed, 'Pekerja Asing di Negara Brunei Darussalam: Kes Kajian Pekerja Filipina' ['Foreign Workers in Negara Brunei Darussalam: A Case Study of Filipino Workers'] (unpublished MS, Bandar Seri Begawan: Universiti Brunei Darussalam, 2001), p. 63.

Table 7.5 Brunei labour statistics, 2001–2005

Private sector employment by industry (no. of persons)	2001	2002	2003	2004	2005
Agriculture, forestry and fishing	3,942	4,235	4,196	4,465	4,832
Production of oil and liquefied natural gas	3,701	3,920	4,215	4,590	4,379
Sawmilling and timber processing	628	701	662	681	673
Other mining, quarrying and manufacturing	16,304	19,098	19,204	21,560	18,508
Construction	27,597	28,667	28,315	27,236	26,900
Wholesale and retail trade	16,537	15,144	16,280	16,740	16,863
Coffee shop, restaurants and hotels	8,404	7,926	9,239	9,582	10,079
Transport, storage and communication	5,232	5,063	5,174	5,122	5,258
Financial, insurance and business services	6,522	6,739	6,854	7,082	7,475
Other community, social and personal service activities	9,505	9,098	10,681	11,413	11,853
All industries	98,372	100,591	104,820	108,471	106,820

Source: Adapted from Table I.3, World Trade Organization, 'Brunei Darussalam: Economic Environment', https://www.wto.org/english/tratop_e/tpr_e/s196-01_e.doc. Accessed 22 August 2015.

Of the categories, 'Construction' accounts for the largest number of workers –26,000–28,000 for the period 2001–2005, constituting some 17 per cent of total employment (2005). In second place is 'Other mining, quarrying, and manufacturing', which accounts for an average of 18,600 workers for the same period, 11 per cent of total employment (2005). The bulk of the unskilled labour force in both categories consists of foreign workers. Brunei is undoubtedly heavily dependent on migrant workers in these sectors. A similar situation is also evident in other major industrial countries, notably Japan. Furthermore, working conditions favour foreign workers and are less popular among locals.[41] One of the main and obvious attractions for foreign labourers in Brunei is the comparatively high wages. One study in the Brunei context found that a fat pay cheque also motivates workers to increase their productivity.[42]

Through its Five-Year National Development Plans, the Brunei government focuses on gradually reducing the number of foreign workers in certain categories at the professional, managerial, semi-professional and technical levels. Moreover, the government has taken further steps to ensure that foreign workers will only comprise one-third of the total labour force by encouraging locals to be positive about the jobs available in various industries.[43] A worrying development from the official standpoint is the overly high dependence of the private sector on foreign labour – an 'estimated 44% of the total working population in 2006'.[44] In other words, it is imperative to change the local mindset to accept that unskilled jobs hitherto dominated by foreign labour are as worthwhile as skilled jobs.

Issues and implications

It is undeniable that the influx of foreign workers to Brunei has contributed to the positive development of the country. The workforce shortages caused by the small population of the sultanate have given rise to great employment opportunities for foreign workers. Brunei's population in 2006 was estimated at around 383,000, with the foreign workforce accounting for some 20 per cent of the total.[45] Moreover, the mismatch between jobs and the country's aspirations towards industrial development outside the oil and gas sector is one of the factors that has resulted in increasing numbers of foreign labourers. The influx and presence of foreign workers has implications for Brunei, both at on individual basis and at national level. The issues are varied and spread across the social, cultural, economic and political milieu.

Issues

There is no doubt that the influx of foreign workers in Brunei has come at a price – there have been downsides alongside the advantages it has brought. Not only has the presence of large numbers of foreign workers had an adverse impact on the economy, it has also resulted in social and cultural issues and has even possessed political undertones. Brunei as the host country needs to address and resolve various issues that may have long-term effects and implications for the sultanate as a whole.

Economic issues

One of the major issues caused by the influx of foreign workers to Brunei is high dependency on a foreign workforce. This is particularly apparent in industries that do not fulfil local job-seekers' aspirations. The shortage of unskilled labourers in particular has forced employers to recruit large numbers from outside the country. Brunei does not enforce a levy on employers who import foreign labour, unlike West Asian (Middle East) countries, Singapore, Hong Kong, China or Taiwan, where strict levies are imposed on companies hiring foreign workers, serving as a deterrent.[46]

The government continually emphasizes the imperative of reducing local unemployment rates by encouraging the participation of locals, particularly at the professional level. This was one of the objectives highlighted in the Brunei Darussalam Eighth National Development Plan (2001–2005). The large numbers of foreign workers in low-skilled jobs had increased the proportion of locals employed at upper levels, not unlike the situation experienced in Europe in the 1960s, and similarly in Canada, Australia and the US. This 'distributional impact' provides an advantageous edge to locals with higher levels of academic qualifications.[47]

While the number of foreign workers is high, the unemployment rate also tends to be high. According to official indicators for 2014, the number of unemployed stood at 18,815, or 9.3 per cent.[48] Undeniably, the availability of jobs suitable for unemployed locals remained inadequate. The impact from the economic diversification strategy – which emphasizes diversification via industrialization, industrialization via privatization and privatization via Bruneization – indicates that the country is increasingly moving towards active participation in the competitive economic world. The government recognizes that the country faces a number of obstacles, notably 'the need to foster a strong independent work ethic and high managerial motivation amongst Bruneians'.[49] The government has also emphasized that local social and Islamic values need not hinder any economic activities as long as they adhere to fundamental ethical practices:

> How to preserve social and Islamic values and adjust to commercial realities in a modern competitive world is important. It should be noted, however, that Islam is not inconsistent with commercial activity and trade. Indeed, it has been suggested that originally, conversion to Islam in Southeast Asia was in part because Islam was associated with traders, e.g., the Arabs, and because it was adopted by better-off commercial groups in Southeast Asia.[50]

The concept of Bruneization has also been stressed within the private sector. Brunei Shell Companies, as the biggest private sector employer, initiated a programme giving locals the opportunity to fill positions. By 2000, the participation of locals had increased to 24 per cent from 22 per cent in 1996, and during the same period there was a 2 per cent decrease in the proportion of foreign workers in Brunei.[51] The government's initiative in introducing the Employees Trust Fund (ETF) to the government sector in 1993, and thereafter the private sector in 1994, was one of the key factors that motivated locals to be interested in work in the private sector.

Social and cultural issues

Brunei's perspective on development incorporates essential values. High economic growth undermined by myriad social problems and political instability is meaningless. As the workforce is regarded as one of the agents of development, it is important for the government to highlight the importance of national values to both local and foreign workers. Table 7.1 has highlighted that foreign labourers migrating to Brunei come from a multitude of countries, each with their own sociocultural backgrounds and beliefs. At the individual level, a foreign worker needs to undergo a process of adaptation to the new physical and sociocultural environment in Brunei.

The wide differences between the culture of the country of origin and the host country creates cross-class community.[52] Consequently, Brunei is facing the same cultural integrity threat as besieged Malaysia faced.[53] Hitherto, social problems or serious crimes are rare in Brunei. As Islam is the official religion of the country, Islam's all-encompassing characteristics are given utmost importance and priority in Brunei's 'appropriate' development, where its policies are based on Islamic principles. The influx of foreign workers, however, has contributed to increasing crime rates, not unlike countries such as Malaysia.[54]

A major concern posed to contemporary Brunei by the influx of foreign labourers is the increase in offences against the country's law and order. For instance, the Police Department of Brunei Darussalam recorded that Filipino workers were often involved in robbery and murder. Between 1990 and 2000 there was a twofold increase in offences against the Immigration Act among Filipinos (see Table 7.5). Brunei proscribes all forms of gambling activities, but is increasingly facing the involvement of foreign workers in this vice.

Almost every country confronts this seemingly insurmountable issue despite continuous operations against illegal migrants. Chronic violations have led the Brunei government to amend the immigration laws with the imposition of a heavy penalty of imprisonment of not less than three months but not exceeding two years, and a minimum of three strokes of the cane.[55]

Currently, there is a trend for migrant labourers to obtain permanent resident status by marrying local women. The process allowing foreigners to become naturalized citizens is rather lenient, either involving passing an examination or five years of residence and marriage to a Brunei citizen. Consequently, 200 foreigners were naturalized in November 1999.[56] This trend is particularly rife among those of the same culture, values and religious practices. De Carvalho considers intermarriage as a major index of integration, but notes that some countries discourage male foreign workers from marrying local women, with any violation resulting in revocation of the work permit, and deportation.[57]

Table 7.6 Filipinos convicted of offences in Brunei in 1990 and 2000

	Type of offence	*1990*			*2000*		
		Male	*Female*	*Total*	*Male*	*Female*	*Total*
01	Causing injury				2		2
02	Stealing	10	1	11		1	1
03	Stealing car				1		1
04	Owning obscene film	1	1	2		2	2
05	Gambling Act	17	3	20	6	16	22
06	Immigration Act	13	14	27	30	23	53
07	Customs and Excise Act	1	1	2		1	1
08	Drug Abuse Act	2	1	3	3	1	4
09	Fisheries Act				21		21
10	Women Protection Act					1	1
11	Murder	3		3			
12	Robbery	2		2			
13	Corruption	2	1	3			
14	Maiden Protection Act 1972	1	4	5			
15	Forestry Act	3		3			
Total		55	26	81	63	45	108

Source: Noralipah Mohamed, 'Pekerja Asing di Negara Brunei Darussalam: Kes Kajian Pekerja Filipina' ['Foreign Workers in Negara Brunei Darussalam: A Case Study of Filipino Workers'] (unpublished MS, Bandar Seri Begawan: Universiti Brunei Darussalam, 2001), p. 51.

Political issues

Brunei has clear guidelines for agreements made with foreign workers employed in the sultanate. In practice, there is no union activity despite trade unions being legal as long as they are registered with the government and prohibited from association with the International Labour Organization. Thus: 'There is no provision in the laws that underpins the right to collective bargaining', according to the ILO, but 'An individual contract is required between an employer and a worker, and trade union activities are not allowed to violate these individual labour contracts.'[58] Furthermore:

> Although all workers including government employees can join and form trade unions (excluding military personnel, police officers and prison guards) the government neither facilitates nor encourages the establishment of unions. In addition, collective bargaining has no legal basis in the country and strikes are illegal. The country's oil sector accounted for all three of Brunei's registered unions, of which 5% of the industry's workforce was unionized. However, all three unions were inactive. Wages and benefits were set by market conditions.[59]

Any strike action is illegal, and wage and benefit packages are based on market conditions. Labourers are not allowed to voice their grievances in public. Although foreign workers had been briefed prior to their arrival, there was apparently an incident in the late 1990s when factory workers held a small strike to voice dissatisfaction towards their employer.

Moreover, under the Labour Department of Brunei Darussalam, a Complaint Section has been established to hear of grievances of foreign labourers who have been mistreated by their employers. Any complaints or problems raised fall under Labour Enactment No. 11, 1954. Most cases, however, have been minor infractions. More serious cases require further investigation by the Labour Department.

Brunei celebrates its homogeneous society, emphasizing the similarities between the various ethnic groups. The Chinese and Indian communities that have settled in Brunei have their own communal organizations. Community representatives are appointed to the administration of the country. Since the administration juxtaposes traditional and modern elements, community representatives are honoured with titles by the sultan.

In other countries, the influx of foreign workers has led to the creation of a form of communal identity despite their being granted citizenship of the country where they have settled. This is usually apparent in their business activities. In these countries, the settlement of a Chinese community, for instance, is apparent through the emergence of a 'Chinatown', and likewise the Indian community may give rise to an 'India Street'. Notwithstanding the absence of 'Chinatowns' or 'India Streets', foreign communities in Brunei try to form their own clusters of businesses in their localities. The Indian cluster of businesses is focused on Jalan Serusop, a newly developed business area some distance from the city centre of Bandar Seri Begawan. Chinese settlers, on the other hand, have gravitated to the vicinity of Jalan Subok, a mere stone's throw from the city centre.

Foreigners entering Brunei have to pass through one of five major immigration posts. Although all of these boundaries are fully under control, the country still faces the bane of an influx of illegal migrants as well as smugglers of non-halal items. Brunei is confronting the decision of whether to strengthen existing border control points, or to heighten surveillance of the other routes used by illegal migrants that run through dense forests.[60]

Implications

As a destination country for migrant workers, Brunei has borne the positive and negative implications of this influx. The country has had to make sacrifices in order to ensure sustainable development that can take advantage of the benefits of foreign workers. Brunei, sharing commonalities with neighbouring Southeast Asian countries, is the preferred destination for migrant workers in the region. Within Brunei, the sultanate has benefited from a human resource development strategy that has led to a flexible labour supply. Undoubtedly, the influx of foreign labour has contributed to sustainable economic growth in Brunei.

Implications of human resource development strategies

Realizing that Brunei is heavily dependent on foreign labour, the government has planned strategies to promote the development of local employees. The Seventh National Development Plan (1996–2001) emphasized expanding local human resource development. The sultan expressed these intentions in an address in 1997: 'to support our industrial strategy, other aspects like Human Resources Development, should be given continuous attention, especially in the fields of skills and training, aimed at producing skilled, efficient and dedicated manpower'.[61]

The importance of human resource development continued to be highlighted in the Eighth National Development Plan (2002–2005), where the focus was on the participation of all stakeholders in both the public and private sectors. In addition, seed funding of BND200 million was allocated to the Human Resource Development Fund under the Eighth National Development Plan.[62] The government itself could afford to promote human development without the involvement of the private sector. The priority was to improve the level of education of the population, both in terms of quality and quantity. As a result, Brunei attained a 93 per cent literacy rate. Universiti Brunei Darussalam is the only university in the country that has set up an Entrepreneurship Development Unit to 'provide comprehensive assistance, particularly to those inspired to become entrepreneurs or to participate in small and medium enterprises'.[63]

Sustaining economic growth

It is apparent that a host country gains much from the influx of foreign labourers, especially in the form of sustaining its economic growth. Economic indicators such as GDP have proven that from year to year, the country has made great achievements.

In receiving-labour countries like Brunei, migrant workers have contributed significantly to economic growth. The garment industry, which hires large numbers of foreign workers, became the second largest export earner after oil and gas. In 2007, clothing was among the three main export commodities that contributed to the country's income, along with oil and liquefied natural gas. In 2006, the industry exported BND207.7 million worth of clothing, but this fell to BND175.6 million in 2007.[64] Japan and Indonesia remained the major export market, accounting for some 60 per cent of total exports.[65]

Moreover, the influx of foreign labour has assisted Brunei to increase its workforce. Foreign workers are needed to fill jobs that are shunned by local employees, particularly in labour-intensive industries. The flexible supply of labour is not only advantageous to the construction industry, but facilitates the attainment of some infrastructure projects such as roads, sanitation and other public works.

Remittance is also one of the sources of government revenue. The value of Brunei's currency is greater compared to the currencies of other ASEAN countries and on par with the Singapore dollar, hence undoubtedly highly advantageous in terms of remittance. The higher the number of foreign labourers, therefore, the more benefits accrue to Brunei in terms of currency exchange.

Conclusion

As a result of capitalism, the need for wage labour and the free movement of labour has spread throughout the world. Colonialism has played a major role in spreading the need for labour. The former form of slave labour is no longer applicable, and has been replaced by the concept of free labour. People are free to move and work wherever they choose, subject to the policies (immigration, work permits, domicile and so on) imposed by the host country. Although the demand for labour is primarily decided by the market, state intervention is still needed to control the pattern of migration in each country.

The movements of people from one place to another, or from one country to another, are caused by many factors. Rising population trends lead to a high demand for jobs in an individual country. A large population in a labour-exporting country can serve as a major push or pull factor, spurring migrants' movements from one place to another. Pressures that tend to compel a person to leave one place and move to another are considered push factors. On the other hand, attraction of an area that encourage migration from one place to another, are categorized as pull factors.

Brunei was a British protectorate from the late nineteenth century to the last quarter of the twentieth century. The British played an important role in initiating the transformation of the country's subsistence economy to a form of capitalist economy. The British also dominated the country's sources of income. The impact of colonialism had influenced the country's need for labour, particularly in the oil and gas sectors.

Brunei's need for immigrant labour was born from the mismatch between local job-seekers' aspirations and the requirements of the diversified and restructured economy. Following independence in 1984, emphasis on diversifying the economy has resulted in a shift in the pattern of labour demands, from the needs of the oil industry to the need for labour in the construction and manufacturing industries. This has created many jobs which do not match the aspirations of local job-seekers. Before 1984, the country stressed the importance of education to its citizens, and with the benefit of free education, local people were educated to a comparatively high level, with a minimum of a high school certificate. In line with the policy of Bruneization, locals are favoured over foreigners in terms of job recruitment. Professional, skilled and semi-skilled levels of occupation are gradually being taken over by locals. However, the bulk of the unskilled levels of occupation in industries such as construction have drawn scant interest from local inhabitants. Consequently, Brunei has had no option but to recruit thousands of foreign workers.

The impact of an influx of foreign workers is clear in the receiving countries. In hiring large numbers of foreign workers, Brunei has faced a host of issues – economic, social, cultural and political – and their respective implications. It is a non-negotiable price that Brunei has had to pay in order to maintain sustainable development, achieve economic diversification and wean itself off over-dependence on oil and gas.

Notes

1 Dk. Siti Redzaimi Pg. Hj. Ahmad, 'Gaji Pekerja Asing, Tempatan Sama Rata', *Pelita Brunei*, 20 November 2014. http://www.pelitabrunei.gov.bn/nasional/item/11089-gaji-pekerja-tempatan-asing-sama-rata. Accessed 22 August 2015.
2 *Brunei Annual Report (BAR)* 1910, p. 15.
3 Ibid.
4 L. Potts, *The World Labour Market: A History of Migration* (London: Zed Books, 1990), p. 204.
5 Noralipah Mohamed, 'Pekerja Asing di Negara Brunei Darussalam' ['Foreign Workers in Negara Brunei Darussalam'] (unpublished MS, Bandar Seri Begawan: Universiti Brunei Darussalam, 2001), p. 23.
6 Nigel Harris, *The New Untouchables: Immigration and the New World Worker* (London: I.B. Tauris, 1995), p. 2.
7 T.S. Yean and T.S. Ee, 'Population and Labour Force in Brunei Darussalam: Patterns and Structural Changes', in *Readings on the Economy of Brunei Darussalam*, edited by J. Obben and T.S. Ee (Bandar Seri Begawan: University of Brunei, 1999), p. 108.
8 *Statistics on Total Foreign Workers in the Public Sector, Companies, Domestic Helpers and their Dependents* (valid until 2003), Department of Labour, Brunei Darussalam.
9 M.R.D. Carlos, 'On the Determinants of International Migration in the Philippines: An Empirical Analysis', *International Migration Review*, 36(1) (2002): 81–102 at 84–5.
10 *Statistics on Total Foreign Workers*.
11 *Brunei Darussalam Statistical Yearbook 2002*, Department of Economic Planning and Development, Brunei Darussalam, p. 99.
12 According to the XE Currency Converter: http://www.xe.com/currencyconverter.
13 Noralipah Mohamed, 'Pekerja Asing', p. 66.
14 Uma Kothari, *Migration and Chronic Poverty*, Working Paper no 16 (Manchester: Institute for Development Policy and Management, Chronic Poverty Research, University of Manchester, 2002), p. 6.

15 A.H.M. Zehadul Karim et. al., *Foreign Workers in Malaysia* (Kuala Lumpur: Utusan Publications and Distributors, 1999), p. 18.
16 Hein de Haas, *The Determinants of International Migration: Conceptualising Policy, Origin and Destination Effects*, Working Paper 32 (Oxford: International Migration Institute, University of Oxford, 2011), p. 9.
17 Informal interview by the author conducted with several foreign domestic helpers in Brunei.
18 De Haas, *The Determinants of International Migration*, p. 10.
19 H.H.M.A. Maricar, 'ASEAN Workers in Brunei Darussalam's Development', paper presented at the Southeast Asian Geography Association Fourth International Conference on Geography and the Development of the Southeast Asian Region and the Seventh National Geographic Seminar of Thailand, Chiang Mai, Thailand, 1996, p. 13.
20 Zehadul Karim et al., *Foreign Workers in Malaysia*, pp. 62–4.
21 T.S. Ee and Hj. A.A. Hashim, 'Manpower Planning in Negara Brunei Darussalam: Issues and Perspectives', in *Readings on the Economy of Brunei Darussalam*, edited by J. Obben and T.S. Ee (Bandar Seri Begawan: Department of Economics, University of Brunei, 1999), p. 185.
22 *Brunei Darussalam Key Indicators*, Department of Statistics, Department of Economic Planning and Development, Prime Minister's Office. http://www.depd.gov.bn/download/BDKI2011.pdf. Accessed 4 September 2015.
23 Carlos, 'On the Determinants of International Migration in the Philippines'.
24 Government of Brunei Darussalam, *Eighth National Development Plan 2001–2005*, Economic Planning Unit, Ministry of Finance, p. 47.
25 According to Stalker, there are five types of migrants: settlers, contract workers, professionals, unauthorized workers, and asylum seekers and refugees. Contract workers are admitted to other countries on the understanding that they will stay only for a specific period constituting the length of their contract; some are seasonal workers, and others will be on longer-term contracts lasting a year or more. Peter Stalker, *The Work of Strangers: A Survey of International Labour Migration* (Geneva: International Labour Office, 1994), p. 4.
26 *Statistics of Total Foreign Workers*.
27 Bob Sutcliffe, 'Crossing Borders in the New Imperialism', in *Socialist Register 2004: The New Imperial Challenge*, edited by Leo Panitch and Colin Leys (London: Merlin Press, 2004), p. 269.
28 Wilfred J. Ethier, 'International Trade and Labor Migration', *The American Economic Review*, 75(4) (1985): 691–707 at 691.
29 Noralipah Mohamed, 'Pekerja Asing'.
30 Unless stated otherwise, statistical data cited in this section are for 2000, drawn from *Statistics of Total Foreign Workers*.
31 S. Castle, and M.J. Miller, *The Age of Migration: International Population Movements in the Modern World* (New York: Guilford Press, 1998), p. 150.
32 R. Skeldon, 'International Migration within and from the East and Southeast Asian Region: A Review Essay', *Asian and Pacific Journal*, 1(1) (1992): 19–63 at 41.
33 Kothari, *Migration and Chronic Poverty*, p. 7.
34 Ibid., p. 13.
35 Ibid., p. 7.
36 The other districts are Belait, Temburong and Tutong.
37 Piyasari Wickramasekera, *Asian Labour Migration: Issues and Challenges in an Era of Globalization*, International Migration Papers 57 (Geneva: International Labour Office, 2002), p. 8.

38 The categorization was made by the Labour Division, Embassy of the Philippines in Brunei Darussalam.
39 Noralipah Mohamed, 'Pekerja Asing', pp. 57–60.
40 Ibid., p. 62.
41 H. Komai, *Migrant Workers in Japan* (London: Kegan Paul International, 1993), p. 100.
42 S. Arief, *The Brunei Economy* (East Balmain, Australia: Southeast Asia Research and Development Institute, 1986), p. 319.
43 Government of Brunei Darussalam, *Eighth National Development Plan 2001–2005*, p. 59.
44 World Trade Organization (WTO), 'Brunei Darussalam: Economic Environment'. https://www.wto.org/english/tratop_e/tpr_e/s196-01_e.doc. Accessed 22 August 2015.
45 Ibid.
46 Wickramasekera, *Asian Labour Migration*, p. 12
47 David Held and Anthony McGrew, eds, *Global Transformation: Politics, Economics and Culture*, 22nd edn (Cambridge: Polity Press, 2003), p. 324.
48 *Brunei Darussalam Key Indicators 2014 Half Release 1: Half Year*, Department of Economic Planning and Development of Brunei Darussalam, p. 5.
49 C.A. Tisdell, 'Brunei's Quest for Sustainable Development: Diversification and Other Strategies', in *Readings on the Economy of Brunei Darussalam*, edited by J. Obben and T.S. Ee (Bandar Seri Begawan: Department of Economics, University of Brunei, 1999), p. 209.
50 Ibid.
51 Government of Brunei Darussalam, *Eighth National Development Plan 2001–2005*, p. 52.
52 Held and McGrew, *Global Transformation*, p. 336.
53 Zehadul Karim et al., *Foreign Workers in Malaysia*, pp. 68–9.
54 For instance, see Hamzah Abdul Rahman et al., 'Negative Impact Induced by Foreign Workers: Evidence in Malaysian Construction Sector', *Habitat International*, 36 (2012): 433–43.
55 'Brunei Imposes Caning on Immigration Offenders', Corpun file 12783, BruneiDirect. Com, 15 February 2004. http://www.corpun.com/bnj00402.htm. Accessed 4 September 2015.
56 'Malaysia, Singapore, Indonesia', *Migration News*, 7(2) (February 2000). https://migration.ucdavis.edu/mn/more.php?id=2033. Accessed 4 September 2015.
57 D. de Carvalho, *Migrants and Identity in Japan and Brazil: The Nikkeijin* (London: Routledge, 2003), p. 41.
58 *Brunei Darussalam – Country Baselines under the ILO Declaration Annual Review (2000–2008): Freedom of Association and the Effective Recognition of the Right to Collective Bargaining (FACB)*, 2008. http://www.ilo.org/declaration/follow-up/annualreview/archiveofbaselinesbycountry/WCMS_DECL_FACB_BNR/lang--en/index.htm. Accessed 4 September 2015.
59 'Brunei Darussalam', *Worldmark Encyclopedia of Nations* (2007). Encyclopedia.com. http://www.encyclopedia.com/topic/Brunei_Darussalam.aspx. Accessed 22 August 2015.
60 Held and McGrew, *Global Transformation*, p. 322.
61 Government of Brunei Darussalam, *Seventh National Development Plan 1996–2001*, Economic Planning Unit, Ministry of Finance.

62 'Policy Measures for Youth Development and Human Resources Development in Brunei Darussalam', information paper presented at the Symposium on Globalization and the Future of Youth in Asia, 2–3 December 2004, Tokyo. http://www.ilo.org/public/english/region/asro/tokyo/conf/2004youth/downloads/brunei.pdf. Accessed 22 August 2015.

63 Government of Brunei Darussalam, *Eighth National Development Plan 2001–2005*, p. 51.

64 'Brunei Darussalam Economic Review: Outlook and Recent Economic Developments', *Brunei Economic Bulletin*, 5 (May 2008): 1–29 at 11. http://www.bruneiresources.com/pdf/economicbulletin0508.pdf. Accessed 22 August 2015.

65 Ibid., p. 12.

8 Fishing in Brunei

Developments of the fishing industry in the post-independence period, 1984–2000s

Pengiran Khairul Rijal bin Pengiran Haji Abdul Rahim

Fishing undoubtedly was and still is an important industry and major source of economic livelihood and protein for the peoples of Negara Brunei Darussalam. This chapter presents an overview of Brunei's fishing industry since independence and over the following three decades. It charts developments and progress in the fishing industry, provides a detailed overview of the domestic fishing industry, including the various government-driven programmes, and evaluates the country's high dependency on the importation of fishery resources, weaknesses of the local processing sector, and the marketing aspects of fishery resources.

Brunei is a maritime country located in the northwestern part of Borneo Island. It has a land area of 5,765 km² and 130 km of coastline fronting the South China Sea. The total marine territorial area is estimated at about 38,600 km², covering the Brunei Fisheries Limits.[1] Of the total area, so far only about 4,600 km² have been explored; the unexplored waters are very deep, ranging from 800 to 3,000 metres. The coastal waters are characterized by narrow continental shelves with a total area of about 8,600 km².[2]

Brunei's fish fauna is typical of the fish communities in Southeast Asian waters, with high diversity. About 500 species of fish and invertebrates have been reported from the catch of various fishing gears used in Brunei waters. Two main resource groups are targeted by fishing operations: demersal and pelagic species. Overall, the total fishery resources in Brunei waters are estimated at about 21,300 metric tons (mt), with a value of BND112 million in terms of potential yield, based on surveys conducted by the Department of Fisheries in recent years. The bulk of the resources comprise demersal species, amounting to about 12,500 mt, while the pelagic species are estimated at about 8,800 mt. 'Demersal' refers to fish and invertebrates that spend most of their life on or near the sea bottom, accounting for the bulk of the catch, numbering about 400 out 500 species. About 100 species occur regularly in bottom trawl catches, include slipmouth, goatfish, bream, croaker, grunt, lizardfish, sea catfish and mojarra, to name but a few. 'Pelagic', on the other hand, refers to species that spend most of their adult lives in the water columns away from the shore or sea bed. Less diverse than the demersal, there are about 100 pelagic species. The pelagic catch is divided into two major groups: small and large. Small pelagic species include roundscad, mackerel, anchovy, herring, jack, butterfish and cobia, while the large pelagic species are yellowfin tuna, bigeye tuna, billfish, skipjack, shark, wolf herring, barracuda and bonito.[3]

Fishing in Brunei waters is divided into two parts. The first is the shallow estuarine waters and in Brunei Bay, where fishing activity is usually conducted from December to February, when the northeast monsoon winds are sweeping the South China Sea. This is what local fishermen called the *iraga* season, when the northeast winds blow firmly and dominantly.[4] The second lies in the sea area off the South China Sea, where fishing activity is divided into four zones according to the types of boat or vessel and the engine power used. Zone 1 extends 0–3 nautical miles (nm) offshore, and is exclusively for small-scale fishermen with small boats, only operating using traditional fishing gears. Zone 2 extends 3–20 nm offshore, and is operated by vessels with inboard engines (hereafter inboard fishing vessels) not exceeding 350 horsepower and with a gross tonnage of 60 tons or over. Zone 3 extends 20–45 nm offshore, and is open to purse seiners with engines of 351–600 horsepower and a gross tonnage of 60.1–150 tons. Zone 4 extends 45–200 nm offshore, and is open to larger vessels such as purse seiners and tuna long liners with engines of more than 600 horsepower and gross tonnage of over 150 tons. [5] Figure 8.1 shows the disposition of this zonal system.

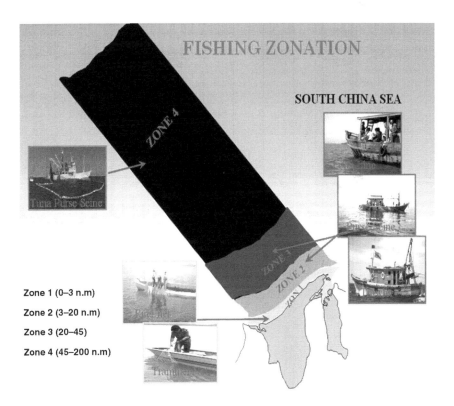

Figure 8.1 Fisheries zonation map

Brunei is the only country in Southeast Asia that has more part-time than full-time fishermen. In 2008, there were 5,191 registered fishermen; only 1,150 (22 per cent) were full-time fishermen, and the remaining 4,041 (78 per cent) were part-time.

The number of licensed boats and fishing vessels totalled 3,214 units in 2008. Of this number, 2,894 units (90 per cent) were vessels with outboard motors (hereafter outboard fishing vessels), 280 (9 per cent) were fishing vessels with no engine, and the remaining 40 (1 per cent) were inboard fishing vessels. Almost all outboard fishing vessels and vessels with no engine operate in rivers and coastal waters (Zone 1) using simple tools like traps (fish pots, crab pots, shrimp pots, palisade traps, tidal weirs, barrier nets and conical or funnel inter-tidal traps), amounting to a total of 41,119 units; nets (portable cast nets, stick-held nets, beach seines, small beach seines with no cod-end, mini-purse seines, ring nets, surface gill nets, drift gill nets, bottom-set gill nets, crab gill nets, trammel nets, encircling gill nets, scoop nets and push nets) accounted for a total of 8,717 units, and hooks (mounted on simple hand-lines, poles and lines, multiple handlines, longlines, bottom-set longlines, troll lines and vertical longlines) totalled 7,806 units. Inboard fishing vessels mainly operate in areas beyond 3 nm offshore (Zones 2, 3 and 4). Of the 40 vessels that were registered in 2008, 20 were bottom trawlers and beam trawlers, 10 operated ordinary purse seines and luring purse seines with lights, and the remainder used other methods such as drift/tuna longlines, crab pots and diving equipment.

The fishing industry in Brunei plays an important role as the main supplier of the cheapest source of protein and dietary resources. The demand for fisheries foodstuff products has increased over the years along with the increase in population. The average estimated annual needs for fishery resources amount to more than 15,000 mt, representing one of the highest worldwide per capita consumptions of fish, estimated at about 47 kg per year. In order to meet the demand for fishery resources, Brunei has implemented several measures to develop the fishing industry, particularly in the capture fisheries sector.

Developments and progress in the fisheries industry

After Brunei's independence, the fishing industry not only served as the cheapest protein supplier, but also as one of the Brunei's main sustainable resources, which is expected to play a role in accelerating the government's efforts to diversify the economy. Therefore, the government pays full attention to the fishing industry as one of the non-oil sectors that is expected to contribute to national income. Not only does the government play a vital role through its high commitment and direct involvement in the fishing industry, it has become the main force driving its development and progress. This is because almost all the efforts and changes in the fishing industry are the responsibility of the government, whereas the role played by the private sector and investors in developing of the fishing industry takes the form of financial loans and some co-operation and transfers of modern technology in fishing operations.

The efforts of the government are clearly illustrated by the implementation of several initiatives based on fishing industry development goals, whose main aim is to increase the productivity of fisheries.[6] The government wants to improve the fisheries industry in order to meet domestic demands for fish, reducing the dependence on imports, which has been increasing each year.

The implementation of the fishing industry development programme has taken place in three main stages. The first consisted of basic preparations for expanding the fishing industry to commercial levels, as stated in the Fourth (1980–84) and Fifth (1986–90) National Development Plans (NDPs). This was followed by efforts to improve the fishing industry through the provision of integrated services to facilitate and support the development of the industry, as embodied in the Sixth (1991–95) and Seventh (1996–2000) NDPs. Subsequently, the Eighth (2001–2005) NDP focused on attracting more foreign direct investment, the application of new technologies in the fishing industry, and expanding market exploration and the export trade.[7]

The determination of the government to achieve the goal of improving its fisheries is clearly visible in the implementation of research on fishery resources with the potential to serve as pioneering steps in developing the sector. Important research has been conducted by the Department of Fisheries, in collaboration with other institutions such as the Southeast Asian Fisheries Development Centre (SEAFDEC) and the International Coastal Living Aquatic Resources Management (ICLARM), including investigation of fishery resources in Brunei, the country's coastal environmental profile, the management plan for the coastal zone of Brunei, and a fish utilization study.[8] The results of this research have been used as guidance in the formulation and implementation of several policies and development programmes for the fishing industry. For example, research conducted on fishery resources and their potential showed that the industry could generate revenues worth BND200 million a year: BND112 million from the assets, BND71 million from the aquaculture sector, and the remaining BND17 million from the processing sector.

Based on this, commercialization of the fishing industry through the use of completely motorized fishing vessels fitted with modern equipment such as a compasses, radar, echo sounders and VHF transceivers in the exploitation of fishery resources in the deep offshore areas was deemed necessary to achieve the objective of improve landing outcomes. Thus, a fleet of eight powered fishing vessels, consisting of four trawlers, two purse seiners and two drift longliners, was licensed to start operations in 1984. Six years later, in 1990, a vessel operating fish pots was added, which was followed the next year by the licensing of a diving vessel and vessels using fishing technology called the *rantau* (drift gill net) (see Table 8.1).

The government's efforts to develop the fishing industry to a commercial level have focused on two elements: commercial-scale and small-scale fisheries. The development of commercial-scale fisheries involved the deployment of inboard fishing vessels in offshore areas, using trawl nets, purse seines, drift longlines, fish pots and other equipment. Small-scale fisheries involve the use of outboard fishing vessels with artisanal gears such as trammel gill nets, ring nets, fish traps, handlines, deep-water fish corrals and intertidal fish traps. In an effort to develop the commercial-scale and small-scale fisheries, the government has divided the fishing area into four zones, aiming to ensure that both can be carried out in a more organized manner (see Figure 8.1).

Table 8.1 Number of registered inboard fishing vessels in Brunei, 1984–2008

	Trawler	Purse seine	Hook and line	Traps	Others	Total
1984	4	2	2	0	0	8
1985	4	4	1	0	0	7
1986	4	7	0	0	0	11
1987	4	5	1	0	0	10
1988	5	5	0	0	0	10
1989	8	3	0	0	0	11
1990	10	3	2	1	0	16
1991	11	3	2	2	2	20
1992	10	3	1	2	2	18
1993	13	4	1	3	1	22
1994	17	3	2	2	2	26
1995	18	1	1	1	0	21
1996	23	1	3	3	5	35
1997	26	0	2	2	2	32
1998	22	1	4	5	7	39
1999	22	1	5	3	4	35
2000	21	2	16	9	3	51
2001	25	2	14	6	4	51
2002	25	5	12	6	3	51
2003	20	4	8	5	2	39
2004	22	4	6	5	1	38
2005	20	7	8	6	2	43
2006	19	7	5	0	3	34
2007	20	8	5	0	2	35
2008	20	10	2	0	8	40

Sources: *Brunei Darussalam Statistical Yearbook* (Bandar Seri Begawan: Department of Economic Planning and Development, Prime Minister's Office, Brunei Darussalam, 2000–2008); *Brunei Darussalam Statistical Yearbook* (Bandar Seri Begawan: Statistics Division, Department of Economic Planning and Development, Ministry of Finance, 1984–99).

In addition, the government is also trying to develop small-scale fisheries on a commercial basis by encouraging small-scale fishermen to establish fishing companies. Although such companies are locally managed and manned, they can also hire foreign workers. This situation has created two categories of small-scale fisheries: independent and those run by companies. Independent operations are often run out by the fishermen themselves, whereas companies often use foreign workers. Small-scale fisheries companies are different from commercial-scale inboard fishing vessel operations, as the companies conduct fishing operations in Zone 1, using two to eight outboard fishing vessels.

To promote the success of commercial-scale and small-scale fisheries, the government has introduced financial assistance schemes through the local banks, called the Enterprise Facilitation Scheme (EFS) and Microcredit Finance Scheme (MFS), to help fishermen to run companies. Commercial-scale fisheries can obtain loans of up to BND5 million through the EFS and small-scale fisheries can obtain loans of up to BND50,000 through the MFS for the purchase of equipment such as fibreglass vessels, outboard engines and fishing gears.[9]

Another important role of the government consists of providing material assistance to operators of commercial-scale and small scale fisheries. In commercial-scale fisheries, the government has been supplying raw materials for trawler and purse seine nets, to reduce the burden on entrepreneurs of purchasing nets from external suppliers that can only supply in large quantities. Moreover, to ensure that purse seiners and drift longliners can increase their catches and landings, the government has built artificial reefs to facilitate fishing operations,[10] and supplied cool boxes to facilitate the storage of the catch.[11]

The determination of the government to improve results in the landing of fishery resources is also reflected in the opportunities that are open to foreign investors and entrepreneurs to make investments and undertake joint ventures in the commercial fishing industry. In addition to increasing revenue landings, joint ventures are also expected to contribute benefits such as the transfer of modern technology, creating jobs and additional revenue from landings for export markets. However, in the early stages, local operators were not ready to fulfil several criteria in terms of finances, experience and technology required to form joint venture companies with foreign investors and entrepreneurs.[12] This led to failures in implementation despite encouraging responses from investors and foreign businesses.

In early 1993, these efforts came to fruition when investors from the Philippines, together with a local company, established a joint venture fishing company called Silangan Enterprise. The company conducted fishing operations in Zone 3 using purse seines. The following year, another joint venture fishing company, IDICO, was established by local entrepreneurs with investors from South Korea, deploying trawlers in Zone 3.[13] Then two companies from the People's Republic of China, Luen Thai Fishing Venture Ltd and Shenzhen Haiyuan Company Ltd, set up joint ventures with the local companies Mas Sugara Fishing Venture Private Ltd and Semaun Seafood Ltd. The joint venture companies began their operations in 1999 using trawlers, gillnets and longlines in Zone 3 and zone 4.[14] In 2001 and 2002, investments from abroad increased with the participation of several investors and businesses from Vietnam.[15]

Meanwhile, in small-scale fisheries, the government introduced the use of advanced and more efficient fishing technologies, including nets made from synthetic materials. At the same time, the government also introduced the use of fishing vessels made of fibreglass, which proved more durable and safer. In addition, the government has also promoted the use of trailers for conveying fishing vessels from fishermen's houses to jetties.[16] This enabled vessels to be stored safely, whereas previously the vessels had usually been left on the beaches.

The next step taken by the government to develop small-scale fisheries was through the construction of artificial reefs made from tyres, abandoned oil rigs, galvanized pipes and concrete arranged into a triangular pyramid.[17] This major project was initiated in 1985, and continues to this day, when almost the entire border area between Zone 1 and Zone 2 consists of artificial thresholds. Construction of these thresholds aims to provide a haven for food, breeding and protection of fishery resources, to help small-scale fisheries to increase their catches, and also to prevent the use of trawlers in Zone 1, as it is restricted to small-scale fisheries.[18] It is also intended to provide alternative areas for those who have been affected by the law banning fishing within 500 metres of oil facilities.[19]

In addition, the government also provided small-scale fishermen with modern electronic aids such as Global Positioning System (GPS) receivers and fish finders, saving time by helping fishermen to find productive areas.[20] The government also provides training and workshops to instruct fishermen in the use these tools.[21] Currently, almost all small-scale fishermen who use fish pots and handlines rely on GPS systems and fish finders.

Apart from the measures described above, the government has directed attention to the development of the fishing industry at the landing stage through the construction of several facilities and landing complexes. In 1985 and 1986, two landing facilities have been built in the district of Belait along with another two in Brunei Muara to cater for inboard fishing vessels. The complexes have basic amenities such as fish unloading areas, jetties for berthing, ice factories, cold rooms, net stores and barns for repairing nets. In addition, the government has also set up a central processing, storage and distribution facility near the fish landing areas in Brunei Muara district. This is equipped with a cold room and fish processing area for fish to be used as fertilizer or fish feed, hence reducing the amount of fish with no market value.

For small-scale fishermen who utilize outboard fishing vessels, the government has built several concrete jetties to enable loading of supplies and catches, along with slipways for boats. Currently, a total of 16 jetties have been built throughout the country. The construction of jetties has enabled small-scale fishermen to increase their use of outboard fishing vessels. A pontoon was built at the fish landing complex in Belait district to enable small-scale fishermen to moor their vessels and unload their catches.

The focus on the development of the fishing industry is also evident at the marketing stage. Fish markets have been built in several strategic locations, such as at boat jetties or in densely populated areas. Currently, there are seven fish markets in the country, located in Gadong, Jerudong, Muara, Belait, Seria, Tutong and Bangar. Almost all the fish markets are adjacent to landing areas, making it easier for fishermen to sell their catches or transfer them to other markets. These fish markets provide basic facilities such as fish benches and refrigerated fish stores.

The government has introduced a five-point plan to encourage entrepreneurs to run integrated fisheries companies. This programme focuses on integrating the catch and aquaculture sector with the processing sector, marketing and support services in order to market the fish that have been landed or produced. Hence, catches that are unsuitable for the domestic market can be channelled to the processing sector to become products for downstream fisheries.

These governmental programmes have enhanced the development of the fishing industry, as is evident in the increased contribution of the fishing industry to the gross domestic product (GDP) and enhanced revenue from landings of fish.

The contribution of the fishing industry to GDP has increased greatly, from BND12.3 million in 1984 to BND46.9 million in 2008 – almost a fourfold increase. The highest contribution was recorded in 2005, amounting to BND86.4 million (see Table 8.2).

In terms of revenue from landings of fish, in 1985 the fishing industry landed a total of 2,763 mt, worth BND14.26 million, and by 2008 this had increased to

Table 8.2 Contribution of the fisheries sector to gross domestic product at current year prices, 1984–2008

	GDP	Fisheries sector	
	(BND million)	*(BND million)*	%
1984	9,064	12.3	0.1
1985	8,787	13.2	0.2
1986	5,303	11.8	0.2
1987	5,891	14.0	0.2
1988	5,357	16.4	0.3
1989	5,823	19.4	0.3
1990	6,381	22.9	0.4
1991	6,394	25.7	0.4
1992	6,817	28.0	0.4
1993	6,634	31.9	0.5
1994	6,243	33.2	0.5
1995	6,710	35.7	0.5
1996	7,213	37.2	0.5
1997	7,716	40.3	0.5
1998	6,778	43.2	0.6
1999	7,796	39.1	0.5
2000	10,346.0	43.5	0.4
2001	10,035.4	48.7	0.5
2002	10,463.4	52.0	0.5
2003	11,424.2	74.7	0.7
2004	13,305.8	76.1	0.6
2005	15,864.1	86.4	0.5
2006	18,225.7	64.9	0.4
2007	18,458.4	56.5	0.3
2008	20,397.9	46.9	0.2

Sources: Department of Statistics, Department of Economic Planning and Development, Brunei Darussalam, *Perencanaan Kemajuan Jangka Panjang Negara Brunei Darussalam* [*Long-term Progress Planning of Negara Brunei Darussalam*] (Bandar Seri Begawan: Department of Economic Planning and Development, 2008); Government of Brunei Darussalam, *Brunei Darussalam Annual National Accounts 2000–2004* (Bandar Seri Begawan: Department of Statistics, Department of Economic Planning and Development, Prime Minister's Office, February 2006); Government of Brunei Darussalam, *Brunei Darussalam Annual National Accounts 2006 and 2007* (Bandar Seri Begawan: Department of Statistics, Department of Economic Planning and Development, Prime Minister's Office, 2008).

15,576 mt, with a value of BND85.09 million. In 2006, landings reached 16,924 mt, worth BND87.77 million – the highest quantity and value of landings during this period (see Table 8.3). However, 78.9 per cent (13,356 mt) of the total landings in that year (16,925 mt) were from small-scale fisheries. Table 8.3 clearly shows that commercial-scale fisheries landings had yet to reach 5,000 mt, and the quantities landed are often volatile. The highest landing ever achieved was 4,230 mt in 1997. The contrasts with small-scale fisheries, as their landings increased from 2,395 mt in 1985 to 11,604 mt in 2008. Thus, the fisheries development programme implemented by the government was more successful in small-scale fisheries, which employ many more fishermen than commercial-scale fisheries.

The main factor leading to the poor performance of commercial-scale was the number of licensed inboard fishing vessels. For example, licensing of inboard fishing vessels increased from 8 in 1984 to 51 in 2000 and 2002, but fell back to 40 in 2008 (see Table 8.1). This was caused by several problems faced by the operators of the commercial-scale fisheries, including poor management, less effective use of cash flow, the limited number of operations, some of them only partially inoperative, inexperience, lack of financial resources, damage to engines, and inefficient labour and marketing of catches.[22] Furthermore, the trawlers that were widely used had to discard 50–70 per cent of their landings because they had no market value.

The effectiveness of the fisheries development programme in small-scale fisheries can be seen in encouraging developments such as increases in the numbers of registered fishermen, fishing vessels, licensed fishing equipment and small-scale fishing companies. The number of fishermen registered with the Fisheries Department increased from 2,692 in 1984 to 5,191 in 2008. However, 50–80 per cent of these were part-time fishermen who also had permanent jobs in the public or private sector. For example, in 2008 there were 4,041 part-time fishermen, compared with 1,150 full-time fishermen (see Table 8.4). The use of trailers has encouraged more people to engage in fishing activities during weekends and holiday periods.

The number of fishing vessels licensed outboard fishing vessels increased from 1,576 in 1984 to 2,894 in 2008, with a peak of 3,208 vessels in 2004. This increase was due to the introduction of vessels that made of fibreglass. The number of non-powered fishing vessels also increased, from 11 in 1984 to 280 in 2008 (see Table 8.5), due to the introduction of regulations requiring the licensing of all fishing vessels, even those not using engines. Regular patrols are carried out by licensing enforcement officers to ensure that the rules are followed.

The increase in the number of fishing vessels is associated with an increased number of small-scale fishing companies, mostly utilizing two to eight fishing boats. This was evident when the number of small-scale fishing companies with only seven vessels in 1984 increased to 438 in 2007 (see Table 8.6). This drastic increase was the result of MFS financial assistance that helped fishermen to set up small-scale fishing companies.[23] At the same time, the growth in the number of small-scale fishing companies led to an increase in the number of foreign fishermen engaged in fishing activities, from 39 in 1985 to 706 in 2008,

Table 8.3 Total production of Brunei capture fisheries, 1984–2008

	Quantity (metric tons)				Value (BND million)			
	Commercial	Company	Private	Total	Commercial	Company	Private	Total
1984	n.d.	n.d.	n.d.	n.d.	n.d.	n.d.	n.d.	16.26
1985	368	2,395		2,763	n.d.	n.d.	n.d.	14.26
1986	627	2,209		2,836	n.d.	n.d.	n.d.	19.45
1987	584	3,212		3,796	n.d.	n.d.	n.d.	26.45
1988	1,007	2,080		3,087	n.d.	n.d.	n.d.	18.54
1989	1,015	1,985		3,000	n.d.	n.d.	n.d.	16.94
1990	2,370	3,215		5,585	n.d.	n.d.	n.d.	24.43
1991	3,970	3509		7,479	n.d.	n.d.	n.d.	26.18
1992	3,978	4,072		8,050	n.d.	n.d.	n.d.	28.17
1993	3,225	3,215	1,038	7,478	5.81	16.96	3.59	26.36
1994	3,033	3,813	2,169	9,015	5.10	21.61	12.29	39.00
1995	3,412	3,168	1,836	8,416	5.67	17.95	10.41	34.03
1996	3,895	3,081	1,472	8,448	6.46	17.46	8.34	32.26
1997	4,230	1,676	799	6,705	6.68	9.46	4.53	20.67
1998	4,103	3,819	1,945	9,867	6.57	21.64	11.02	39.23
1999	3,007	3,861	2,756	9,624	5.06	22.33	11.49	38.88
2000	5,492	2,626	2,458	10,576	5.48	11.74	15.13	32.35
2001	3,500	2,769	4,075	10,344	6.81	15.43	23.68	45.92
2002	3,069	4,665	6,163	13,897	6.87	21.04	33.10	61.01
2003	3,177	6,055	5,310	14,542	7.43	44.34	21.53	73.30
2004	3,353	7,465	4,864	15,682	8.26	32.98	43.87	85.11
2005	4,211	7,449	4,437	16,097	10.8	45.03	29.52	85.35
2006	3,568	8,474	4,882	16,924	9.21	45.81	32.75	87.77
2007	3,997	8,019	3,294	15,310	10.17	41.72	31.40	83.29
2008	3,972	8,233	3,371	15,576	9.85	43.64	31.60	85.09

Sources: Department of Fisheries, Brunei, *Brunei Darussalam: A Study of the Market for Fish and Fish Products in Hong Kong, Taiwan, Singapore and Australia*, vol. 2, Final Report (Bandar Seri Begawan: Statistics Division, Economic Planning Unit, Ministry of Finance, June 1993); Narong Ruangsivakul et al., eds, *Fishing Gears and Methods in Southeast Asia: Brunei Darussalam*, vol. 5 (Bandar Seri Begawan: Department of Fisheries, Brunei Darussalam and SEAFDEC Training Department, 2007).

Note: n.d. – no data.

Table 8.4 Total number of fishermen, 1984–2008

	Full-time fishermen					Part-time fishermen					Totals
	BM	TUT	BEL	TEMB	Total	BM	TUT	BEL	TEMB	Total	
1984	381	61	80	6	528	1,700	125	122	217	2,164	2,692
1985	337	109	112	—	558	1,268	85	98	60	1,511	2,069
1986	470	75	141	—	686	1,267	123	116	60	1,566	2,252
1987	337	120	66	—	523	1,542	157	179	71	1,949	2,472
1988	337	66	111	—	514	1,426	107	151	67	1,751	2,265
1989	394	53	125	—	572	984	118	126	76	1,304	1,876
1990	337	81	108	—	526	1,042	116	101	115	1,374	1,900
1991	400	80	106	2	588	932	100	84	111	1,227	1,815
1992	406	73	100	—	579	1,090	102	97	123	1,412	1,991
1993	714	107	167	4	992	1,560	157	181	158	2,056	3,048
1994	635	106	230	2	973	1,122	163	190	98	1,573	2,546
1995	637	87	163	—	887	980	125	138	131	1,374	2,261
1996	324	59	124	—	507	493	73	63	33	662	1,169
1997	559	102	173	2	836	594	134	106	52	886	1,722
1998	477	92	94	—	663	597	127	76	44	844	1,507
1999	496	113	75	—	684	604	98	99	79	880	1,564
2000	659	167	103	10	939	761	94	156	120	1,131	2,070
2001	726	98	94	7	925	654	104	128	121	1,007	1,932
2002	967	83	120	4	1,174	860	110	80	220	1,270	2,444
2003	989	123	141	11	1,264	1,716	191	230	266	2,403	3,667
2004	1,104	105	173	14	1,396	2,067	316	697	334	3,414	4,810
2005	830	122	173	9	1,134	1,342	225	786	370	2,723	3,857
2006	1,001	113	150	20	1,284	1,381	197	614	364	2,556	3,840
2007	1,258	174	197	21	1,650	2,383	336	698	474	3,891	5,541
2008	844	145	137	24	1,150	2,474	337	646	584	4,041	5,191

Source: Department of Fisheries, Brunei Darussalam.
Key: BM – Brunei Muara District; TUT – Tutong District; BEL – Belait District; TEMB – Temburong District.

Table 8.5 Number of registered outboard and non-powered fishing vessels, 1984–2008

	Outboard	*Non-powered*	*Total*
1984	1,576	11	1,587
1985	1,124	10	1,134
1986	1,392	8	1,400
1987	1,452	6	1,458
1988	1,202	68	1,270
1989	1,291	9	1,300
1990	1,317	5	1,322
1991	1,799	16	1,815
1992	1,298	8	1,306
1993	1,172	7	1,179
1994	970	8	978
1995	838	5	843
1996	710	6	716
1997	637	6	643
1998	834	6	840
1999	852	5	857
2000	1,025	16	1,041
2001	1,037	6	1,043
2002	1,391	15	1,406
2003	2,149	24	2,173
2004	3,204	380	3,584
2005	2,531	175	2,706
2006	2,360	158	2,518
2007	3,058	312	3,370
2008	2,894	280	3,174

Sources: *Brunei Darussalam Statistical Yearbook* (Bandar Seri Begawan: Statistics Division, Department of Economic Planning and Development, Ministry of Finance, Brunei Darussalam, 1984–99); *Brunei Darussalam Statistical Yearbook* (Bandar Seri Begawan: Department of Economic Planning and Development, Prime Minister's Office, Brunei Darussalam, 2000–2008).

whereas the involvement of local fishermen only increased from 24 in 1985 to 266 in 2008 (see Table 8.6 and Figure 8.2). It was evident that 60–80 per cent of small-scale fishing companies were using foreign fishermen. Foreign fishermen play an important role in small-scale fishing companies' efforts to improve their landing results.

This has led to increases in revenue. In 2006–2008, 50 per cent of total landings revenue was generated by small-scale fishing companies (see Table 8.3), indicating that small-scale fishing companies are the most important element of the fishing industry. Nonetheless, the number of small-scale fishing companies declined sharply by over 100 per cent to 201 in 2008 as a result of the moratorium on enforcement of transferring small-scale fishing companies from Zone 1 to Zone 2.[24]

As well as dominating catching and landing activities, small-scale fishing companies have also cornered the marketing sector, where most of the landings are

Table 8.6 Number of companies and fishermen in small-scale fisheries, 1984–2008

	Companies					Fishermen		
	BM	TUT	BEL	TEMB	Total	Local	Foreign	Total
1984	5	2	—	—	7	n.d.	n.d.	n.d.
1985	4	6	—	—	10	24	39	63
1986	5	3	—	—	8	30	62	92
1987	5	6	—	—	11	33	72	105
1988	3	7	5	—	15	28	72	100
1989	4	6	5	—	15	58	84	142
1990	3	6	5	—	14	68	100	168
1991	3	5	3	—	11	75	146	221
1992	3	6	6	—	15	79	131	210
1993	4	8	5	—	17	85	140	226
1994	4	9	10	—	23	84	200	284
1995	5	9	6	—	20	87	249	336
1996	8	9	9	—	26	108	229	337
1997	9	13	8	—	30	111	236	347
1998	11	13	9	—	33	120	273	393
1999	28	13	7	—	48	132	319	451
2000	46	13	10	—	69	113	288	401
2001	62	15	10	—	87	159	470	629
2002	109	16	10	—	135	181	677	858
2003	95	13	14	2	124	226	478	704
2004	175	15	16	2	208	193	500	693
2005	230	14	14	—	258	210	565	775
2006	259	46	40	—	345	315	735	1,050
2007	356	46	36	—	438	240	524	764
2008	132	42	27	—	201	266	706	972

Source: Department of Fisheries, Brunei Darussalam and Labour Department, Brunei Darussalam.
Key: n.d. – no data; BM – Brunei Muara District; TUT – Tutong District; BEL – Belait District; TEMB – Temburong District.

marketed by small-scale fishing companies. This demonstrates that the control of Chinese traders of the business of marketing before Brunei's independence has been transferred successfully to local residents who run small-scale fishing companies. Many local small-scale fishing companies have their own sales benches that allow them to market their own landings. Several small-scale fishing companies also have delivery trucks that allow fish landings to be transported to locations distant from the landing area.

The increase in the number of fishermen and small-scale fishing companies has also led to increases in the number of licensed fishing gears: from 4,904 in 1984 to 57,642 in 2008. This impressive growth applies to all categories of fishing equipment, involving traps, nets and hooks. Of these three categories, handset hooks have shown the most drastic increase, from 1,555 in 1984 to 41,119 in 2008. Equipped trap nets and licensed equipment have also increased, from 1,830 and 1,519 units respectively in 1984 to 7,806 and 8,717 units respectively

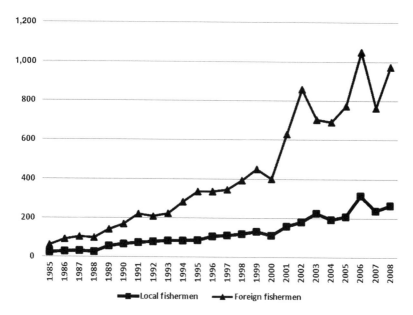

Figure 8.2 Comparison of local and foreign fishermen in small-scale companies
Source: Labour Department, Brunei Darussalam.

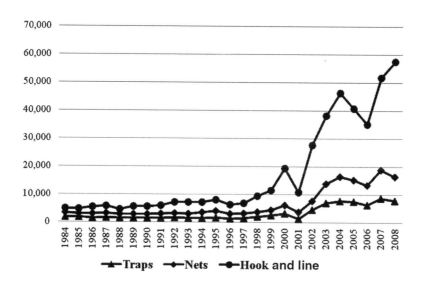

Figure 8.3 Licensed fishing gears, 1984–2008

Sources: *Brunei Darussalam Statistical Yearbook* (Bandar Seri Begawan: Statistics Division, Department of Economic Planning and Development, Ministry of Finance, Brunei Darussalam, 1984–99); *Brunei Darussalam Statistical Yearbook* (Bandar Seri Begawan: Department of Economic Planning and Development, Prime Minister's Office, Brunei Darussalam, 2000–2008).

in 2006 (see Figure 8.3). In addition, the availability of construction materials sold in stores has also contributed to an increase in the number of fishing gears.

Although the development of small-scale fishing companies is encouraging, it has had a negative impact on the potential of fishery resources in Zone 1. According to the Fisheries Department, the potential of fishery resources in Zone 1 has dropped by 43 per cent owing to excessive fishing, the use of gillnets of 6–25 millimetres diameter that exceeded the maximum limit, the increasing use of electronic aids such as GPS and fish finders, and the commercialization of small-scale fisheries by small-scale fishing companies.[25]

In order to reduce the potential reduction of fishery resources, the government imposed a Moratorium on Fishing Operations in Zone 1 on 1 January 2008, including the transfer of small-scale fishing companies from Zone 1 to Zone 2, placing new part-time fishermen and new applicants in Zone 2, and freezing the issuing of licenses for several types of fishing gears and those that exceeded the maximum limits.[26]

Furthermore, to increase the income from fishery resources in line with the current development of the fishing industry, the government has stepped up efforts to improve and expand the advanced aquaculture and processing sectors. In the aquaculture sector, over the years the government has opened many fish maintenance areas to carry out verification operations in offshore fish farming, along with diversification of cultivated species fishery resources such as shellfish, crabs and freshwater fish. In the processing sector, the government has encouraged the establishment of more processing companies, carried out research, and has developed programmes to commercialize products, diversify income from products, provide assistance in improving the quality and attractiveness of products, and promote the domestic and export markets.

The range of efforts that have been implemented in both the aquaculture and processing sectors have led to growth in production, which in the aquaculture

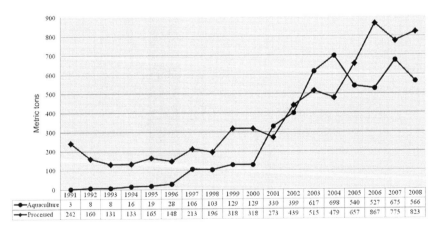

Figure 8.4 Total production of aquaculture processed seafood products, 1991–2008

Source: Department of Fisheries, Brunei Darussalam.

sector increased tremendously from a mere 3 mt in 1991 to 566 mt in 2008 (see Figure 8.4), while the processing sector increased from 242 mt in 1991 to 823 mt in 2008. Although production in both these sectors has improved, it is still not able to meet the demand for domestic fish, which is constantly increasing.

Figure 8.5 shows the supply of food from local fisheries during 1985–2000, which only met about 32–40 per cent of the total demand, while 2005 showed better results of 57 per cent, decreasing to 47 per cent in 2008. Thus, the imports of fish are necessary to compensate for Brunei's inability to meet the demand for fish from local resources.

This situation is aggravated because consumption of fish per capita increased from 37 kg in 1985 to 49 kg in 2008 (Figure 8.5). This is due to the increase in health awareness among the population. Most people have recognized that fish are

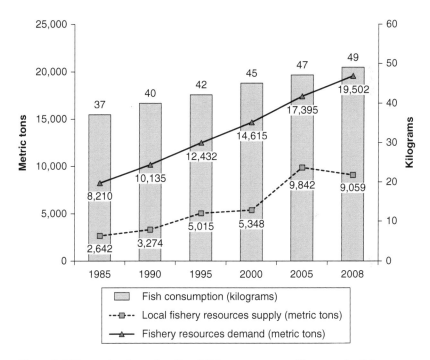

Figure 8.5 Demand and supply of local fishery resources with per capita fish consumption, 1985–2008

Sources: Khoo Hong Woo et al., 'Capture Fisheries', in *The Coastal Environmental Profile of Brunei Darussalam: Resource Assessment and Management Issues*, edited by Chua Thia-Eng et al. (Manila: Fisheries Department, Ministry of Development, Brunei Darussalam and International Center for Living Aquatic Resources Management, 1987), pp. 90–91; Geronimo T. Silvestre and Hj. Matdanan Hj. Jaafar, 'Brunei Darussalam Capture Fisheries: A Review of Resources, Exploitation and Management', in *The Coastal Resources of Brunei Darussalam: Status, Utilization and Management*, edited by Geronimo T. Silvestre et al. (Manila: International Center for Living Aquatic Resources Management and Department of Fisheries, Ministry of Industry and Primary Resources, Brunei Darussalam, 1992), pp. 22–3 and 173.

Table 8.7 Quantity and value of imported fishery resources

	Fresh		Processed						Others		Total	
			Frozen		Dried		Canned					
	Quantity	Value	Quantity	Value	Quantity	Value	Quantity	Value	Quantity	Value	Quantity	Value
1987	1,828	11,934	1,510	3,001	282	1,892	1,026	5,678	644	4,302	5,290	26,807
1990	3,695	23,265	1,848	3,357	544	1,957	963	5,911	842	5,850	7,892	40,340
1995	5,225	33,686	2,427	9,109	634	3,669	1,153	6,277	314	2,745	9,753	55,486
2000	2,690	16,740	1,328	5,605	658	2,808	1,307	6,421	414	2,104	6,397	33,678
2005	2,598	11,276	2,498	9,771	662	5,587	1,296	6,085	442	1,934	7,496	35,225
2008	2,070	8,819	3,065	13,688	487	3,354	2,151	9,187	481	1,878	8,254	37,669

Sources: Government of Brunei, *Annual Statistics of External Trade* (Bandar Seri Begawan: Department of Customs and Excise, 1987–2008); *Brunei Darussalam Statistical Yearbook* (Bandar Seri Begawan: Statistics Division, Department of Economic Planning and Development, Ministry of Finance, Brunei Darussalam, 1984–99); *Brunei Darussalam Statistical Yearbook* (Bandar Seri Begawan: Department of Economic Planning and Development, Prime Minister's Office, Brunei Darussalam, 2000–2008).

Note: Quantities are in metric tons; values are in BND000.

a source of protein leading to fewer health problems, because tests have shown that the amount of cholesterol in fish is far less than that in meat, especially red meat.

The increase in local production has led to reductions in imports of fresh fish. This is evident in comparing the significant increase in total imports of fresh fish from 1,828 mt in 1987 to 5,225 mt in 1995 with the reduction to 2,070 mt in 2008 (see Table 8.7). However, the demand for processed fisheries products, whether frozen, dried or canned, has remained high. Total imports of frozen fishery products increased from 1,510 mt in 1987 to 3,065 mt in 2008. Dried fishery products imports increased from 282 mt to 487 mt in 2008, and imports of canned fisheries products increased from 1,026 mt in 1987 to 2,151 mt in 2008. This amounted to an increase in the total imports of fish from 5,290 mt in 1987 to 8,254 mt in 2008 (Table 8.7). Therefore the goal of providing adequate supplies of food based on domestic fisheries without the need to rely on imports remained unattainable, with 48 per cent of fish being imported in 2008.

Importation of fishery resources

In the period 1987–2008, the quantity of imports of fishery resources increased by around 56 per cent, from 5,290 mt to 8,254 mt (Table 8.7). Table 8.7 shows an increase in the quantity of imports of all forms of fishery resources. Fresh fish increased from 1,828 mt in 1987 to 2,070 mt in 2008, with the highest quantity recorded in 1995, a total of 5,225 mt. Processed fish, in the form of frozen, dried and canned products, also increased from 2,818 mt in 1987 to 5,703 mt in 2008. Of these processed fish, frozen products showed the highest increase, from 1,510 mt in 1987 to 3,065 mt in 2008.

The growth in imports of fresh fish is due to the inability of the local fishing industry to meet increasing demand. Although the fishing sector has managed to increase landing revenue, not all the species landed may be accepted by the local population, meaning that most are used for fertilizer. Also there are fish that are not yet known or explored, and are regarded as extraordinary species. Moreover, some species of fish may be too big, ugly and scary-looking, too colourful or poisonous, among other defects. Approximately 40 per cent of landings every year cannot be marketed to meet the demands of the growing population.

Moreover, the willingness of suppliers and exporters from neighbouring countries like Sabah, Sarawak and the Federal Territory of Labuan Malaysia to supply fresh fish at cheaper prices has also led to growth in the quantity of imports of fresh fish. In the early stages of this period, most of the fish were supplied fresh from Miri, Sarawak, because of the availability of road transport. Typically, importers and wholesalers of fish from Brunei would depart early in the morning, usually at dawn, to ensure they arrived in Miri as early as possible to collect the catches being landed, then brought them back to be marketed in Brunei that same morning.[27]

Fresh fish from Sabah, Labuan Federal Territory and several districts in Sarawak in close proximity to Brunei, like Limbang and Lawas, are exported by Malay entrepreneurs from Lawas and the Federal Territory of Labuan by sea using outboard-powered boats. These are usually 9–12 metres long and 2–2.5

metres wide, equipped with two outboard engines of 60 or 75 horsepower. In one trip, they can deliver 1–2 mt of fish.[28] Due to the very high demand for fish in Brunei, most of the Malay entrepreneurs transport them from Kota Kinabalu, Kudat and Sandakan Sabah using trucks by road, which are then unloaded into boats to be exported to Brunei.[29]

In addition, some wholesalers and fish *tauke* (or *towkay*) of Brunei also go to Lawas themselves using small outboard-powered vessels to obtain fresh fish through unofficial channels. Most of them enter the Lawas area without valid travel documents, and appear to be unconcerned because most of the Marine Police and Marine Department officers on patrol recognize them and understand their intentions. Trade activities between the Bruneian contractors and employers and fishermen or Malay entrepreneurs in Lawas district are conducted in cottages, usually erected on the river banks or on the estuary.[30] A number of wholesalers and fish *tauke* from Brunei also meet with businessmen and fishermen at sea. They usually arrive in the area around 8 or 9 a.m. and return by 10 or 11 a.m.[31] As these imports are illegal, they are not declared to the Customs and Excise Departments of Brunei or Malaysia, which is why the fresh fish declared in 1987 only amounted to approximately 315 mt, while imports sold in fish markets nationwide totalled approximately 1,828 mt.

Payment in the fisheries trade is not primarily through cash alone. There is a system of exchange utilizing oil and fresh fish. Fish *tauke* and wholesalers of Brunei will bring oil supplies and sell them to the fishermen at a relatively low price. Each barrel contains 35 litres and as sold for BND15, which is about BND0.43 per litre. Fish wholesalers and fish *tauke* will usually bring with them about ten barrels of oil. Furthermore, a number of Bruneian wholesalers and fish *tauke* also provide financial loans to fishermen of Lawas district to enable them to buy outboard engines and fishing equipment. Payment of financial assistance is done through credit, whereby the wholesalers and fish *tauke* take a cut of the price of fish imported. In addition, they provide fishing equipment such as trammel nets at BND13 per unit.[32] This indicates that this fishery trade has created forms of capitalist relationships, with the wholesalers of Brunei and fish *tauke* as capital investors and the fishermen as producers of fishery resources.

However, the trade by sea began to decrease as land transport links between Brunei and Sabah began to improve in mid-1989.[33] With the availability of land transport, Bruneian wholesalers and fish *tauke* and entrepreneurs from the region started to move away from the use of the outboard-powered vessels to various types of conveyance, such as lorries, vans, four-wheel drive vehicles, and the latest development, double-cab vehicles. This change has been due to convenience and cost-effectiveness in terms of the cost of oil, the quantity of fishery resources, and the process of loading and unloading. For instance, the cost of oil using only road vehicles totalled approximately BND40, compared to BND100 for outboard vessels boats, since lorries can deliver up to 4 mt of fish, compared to only 2 mt using outboard vessels. Since fish obtained from Kudat, Sandakan and Kota Kinabalu can be sent directly to Brunei without having to be loaded onto boats and unloaded again, this help saves time and energy.[34]

Table 8.8 Types of vehicles used by Brunei companies to import fresh fisheries resources from Sabah

	Name of company	Vehicle registration nos	Type of vehicle
1	Syarikat POKSS Hj. Ali & Anak-anak	KP5891	Double-cab
2	MAHR Berjaya Enterprise	KB6970	Double-cab
3	Syarikat Perikanan Hj. Matusin bin Hj. Omar & Anak-Anak	KN2454	Double-cab
4	Leeway Sdn. Bhd.	KA6006	Urvan
5	Syarikat Aminuddin bin Haji Abas & Anak-Anak	QME74 SAA8375V QAF8375	Pickup Pickup Pickup
6	ZHM Enterprise	QLA5667 QMJ5667	Pickup Pickup
7	Razeh Enterprise	SAA7254A	Double-cab
8	Syarikat Ruzeknan & Adik-Beradik	SAA3989G	Double-cab
9	Syarikat Jaafar bin Haji Daim dan Anak-Anak	SAA5011T SK6434 QMH6447	Pickup Double-cab Double-cab
10	Syarikat Matyassin bin Hj. Yusof	QL7722	Pickup
11	Syarikat HA Sumali dan Adik Beradik	SAA8053T SAA1115J SAA9629R	Pickup Pickup Double-cab
12	Perusahaan Shahrin bin Haji Mega	QLA5899 QLA7299	Pickup Pickup
13	Syarikat Hj. Hamidon bin Hj. Nassar	SAA7753U QMH6017 QL7722 QML5667 SAA9629R	Pickup Pickup Pickup Double-cab Double-cab
14	Syarikat Ahmadnoor bin Hj. Sarbini	SD3619D	Double-cab
15	Syarikat Usaha Hj. Ahmad bin Hj. Chuchu & Anak-Anak	QLA9977	Pickup
16	Hj. Arman Enterprise	QML5667	Double-cab
17	Syarikat Hisada	QSM7181	Double-cab
18	OCH Enterprise	QL7723	Pickup
19	Syarikat Musfalina Enterprise	SAA1115J	Pickup

Source: Author's fieldwork.

The change to direct road transport made Sabah a major supplier of fresh fish, replacing Miri district. Approximately 2,335 mt (86 per cent) of fresh fish are supplied from Sabah – a very high quantity compared to imports by road from Sarawak (Miri and Bintulu) of approximately 106 mt (4 per cent). Fish imported

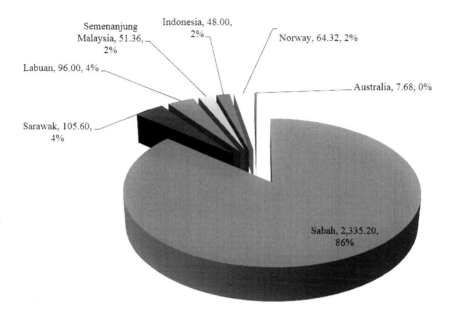

Figure 8.6 Origin of imported fishery resources
Source: Author's fieldwork.

by sea from Labuan Federal Territory amount to approximately 96 mt (4 per cent), and imports from Peninsular Malaysia, Singapore and Indonesia using air transport total approximately 164 mt (6 per cent) (see Figure 8.6).

The growth in the quantity of imports of fresh fish from Sabah is also closely linked to the increasing number of foreign vehicles used in that trade. Table 8.8 shows that the 23 foreign vehicles were involved, compared to only four that were registered in Brunei. In Sarawak (Miri and Bintulu), only four vehicles were registered in Brunei, and a single foreign vehicle was involved.

Importation of fresh fish from Sabah is mostly controlled by fish exporters from Lawas district using the name of the fish wholesaler and fish *tauke* of Brunei. Fish exporters from Lawas district are responsible for all matters concerning the supply of fish to Bruneian wholesalers and fish *tauke*. The types of vehicles used in this trade consist of 15 (65 per cent) lorries and 9 (33 per cent) double-cab vehicles (Table 8.8). This indicates that all the vehicles involved are small in size compared to other locations such Peninsular Malaysia and Thailand, where container lorries are utilized.[35]

In the 1990s, exporters from Lawas district only obtained their fresh fish from the fisheries centre in Kota Kinabalu. However, in order to procure fish of better quality and at more competitive prices, exporters have to venture to fish markets and fishing centres in Kudat and Sandakan themselves. The trip to Kudat takes about nine hours and that to Sandakan takes about twelve hours, compared to around four hours to Kota Kinabalu. Because fishing boats in Kudat and Sandakan may land their catches as early as 2 a.m., they need to depart from Lawas at 5 p.m. to reach Kudat district and 2 p.m. to reach Sandakan district in time.

Only fish that command high market prices in Brunei will be bought, such as *tenggiri* (Spanish mackerel), *merah* (*Lutjanidae/Lutijanus* spp.), *barah-barahan* (*Lutjanus johni*), *putih* (*Pampus argenteus*), *kerosi bali* (*Nemipterus japonicus*), *balanak* (*Liga vaigienis*), *rumahan bini* (*Rastrelliger brachysoma*), *kuasi* (*Anodonstoma chacunda*), shrimp (*Penaeus* sp.), squid (*Loligo* spp.) and crab (*Portunus pelagicus*).

Typically, each lorry will carry six to eight barrels of fish, and each barrel can accommodate 500–700 kg. Vans and double-cab vehicles can only carry one barrel of fish of around 1,000 kg. Therefore, a lorry can transport about 4 mt, while a double-cab vehicle or van only around 1 mt on each trip. Deliveries of fish to Brunei leave at 5 or 6 p.m., to co-ordinate with the 6 a.m. opening time of the Merapuk-Sindumin immigration post at the border between the states of Sabah and Sarawak. The journey from the Merapuk-Sindumin immigration post to Brunei takes about four hours, so the produce will reach Brunei's fish markets by 10 a.m.[36]

Unloading of fish can only be done after obtaining permission from the Bruneian fish wholesalers or fish *tauke* that are conducting the imports. The exporters alone handle the loading and unloading, while the business of marketing is handled by the fish wholesalers and fish *tauke*. Not all the fish are sold at Gadong's fish market; they are also supplied to the fish markets in Belait and Tutong, supermarkets, hotels and restaurants, governmental and private organizations, including hospitals, universities, colleges, military barracks, fishery processing plants, oil plants and airlines. Whenever deliveries arrive, the wholesalers and fishmongers scramble to obtain the fresh fish. The Gadong fish market also serves as a distribution centre or wholesale market for fishery resources in Brunei.

Due to this time-consuming process of importation, only a small number of wholesalers and fish *tauke* of Brunei organize their own supplies of fish. They usually only import fish from Lawas district and Kota Kinabalu through their regular exporters, using only small vans and double-cab vehicles (Table 8.8). Fish wholesalers and fish *tauke* dealing in imports from Lawas district may leave at 6 a.m. and return around 2 or 3 p.m. Imports of fish from Kota Kinabalu will usually wait overnight before being transported to Brunei. However, there are also fish wholesalers and fish *tauke* who go in the morning and return in the evening. Because they use vehicles that are registered in Brunei, they can continue supplying imported fish to fish markets, supermarkets, restaurants, hotels and so on.

Apart from land and sea transport, a proportion of fresh fish from Kuala Lumpur, Kuching, Kota Kinabalu, Singapore and Indonesia are imported by air. Due to the high cost of this, most such imports are destined for airlines, hotels and restaurants. Air importation for the purpose of selling is only carried out by some of the leading supermarkets in Brunei, such as Supa Save Supermarket and Hua Ho Department Store. For example, the cost of importing approximately 554 kg of fresh salmon from Singapore by air can be as much as BND2,484. On average, in

2009 the cost of imports by air amounted to BND4.50 per kg.[37] Fresh salmon and trout are the most abundant species imported by air, from Norway, the Netherlands, Australia, Singapore, Indonesia, Peninsular Malaysia, Sabah and Sarawak.[38] This is due to the high demand for both these fish from European workers in Brunei, as witnessed by the fact that supermarket shelves may be cleared of these products within two hours of their going on display. In fact, half of European workers make early reservations for such fish. The growth in demand is also due to the existence of several Japanese restaurants that serve sushi, in which salmon and trout can be the main ingredient.[39]

From 2003, the importation of fresh live shellfish from Peninsular Malaysia began to be carried out by air. Fresh and live clams are packed neatly into sacks before being put into plastic containers of 1.9 by 1.1 by 0.7 metres, each container holding about 50 kg. The imports arrive three times a week.[40] Cost of importing shellfish amounted to only BND565.83 for 238 kg of fresh live mussels that were on average only worth BND1.10 per kg.[41]

In 2008, a number of fish such as fresh red snapper (*Lutjanidae/Lutijanus* spp.), *duai putih* (*Pampus argenteus*) and *duai hitam* (*Formio niger*) began to be imported from Jakarta using air transport. Among the factors that led fish wholesalers to shift to importing from Jakarta was the cheaper price of fish. For instance, the overall cost of importing 1,000 kg of red snapper (*Lutjanidae/Lutijanus* spp.), *duai putih* (*Pampus argenteus*) and *duai hitam* (*Formio niger*) was BND3,158.57. Out of this total cost, the fish only accounted for BND1,506.60, while the remaining cost was for transportation.[42] On average, the price of fish is only BND1.50 per kg, compared to the cost of transportation of BND1.65 per kg.

The increasing ease of importation, has lowered the price of imported fresh fish. In 1987, the value of 1,828 mt of fresh fish amounted to approximately BND11,934,000. In 2008, this value has decreased to approximately BND9,562,000 for a total of 2,242 mt. The average price of imported fresh fish declined by 35 per cent from BND6.53 per kg in 1987 to BND4.26 per kg in 2008. This price reduction is one of the factors that has influenced the increase in quantity of imports of fresh fish.

The weakness of the local processing sector in producing satisfactory products has been one of the factors that has increased the importation of processed fish. In 2008, this sector was only able to produce approximately 823 mt, meeting only about 14 per cent of the total demand, which amounted to 5,703 mt. The bulk of the production was fish crackers, while the greatest demand has been for frozen processed products.[43]

The increase in the quantity of imports of frozen fish was due to the cheaper selling prices in the local market than for fresh fish. For example, frozen *tenggiri* (Spanish mackerel), *putih* (*Pampus argenteus*) and *rumahan bini* (*Rastrelliger brachysoma*) only cost BND6.50, BND4.20 and BND2.80 per kg respectively. In fresh form, these fish were priced at BND8, BND7 and BND5 respectively.[44] Their lower prices led to increased demand for fish among Brunei's population, especially foreign workers in the construction and manufacturing sectors.

The increase in imports of frozen fish was also caused by the growth in the number of catering services for wedding events, thanksgiving feasts, funerals and so on, which led price competition among them. Some catering services that offer lower prices than others usually use frozen products, as they cost less than fresh fish.[45]

This increase was also due to the growth in the number of grilled fish stalls. Total sales of grilled fish were usually 25–30 kg a day, increasing to 50 kg at weekends.[46] Similarly to catering services, price competition has led to more reliance on frozen fish products.

Most of the frozen fish products are imported from Thailand, Peninsular Malaysia, Singapore, the Philippines, Vietnam, Myanmar, Hong Kong, India, Norway and the US. Frozen fish are usually imported in large quantities. Importation is only carried out by sea using standard refrigerated 20-foot or 40-foot shipping containers. A 20-foot container can accommodate approximately 15 mt and a 40-foot container approximately 30 mt. For storage and offloading facilities, frozen fish are stored in paper boxes or bags of various sizes, depending on the species. When the container arrives at the port, it is transferred to a container lorry to be delivered to the importing company's premises. The frequency of importation depends on the capacity and level of sales of the dealer. For example, Cerah Sdn. Bhd. imports between four to five containers in a month, amounting to 50–60 mt of frozen fish,[47] while TGT Sdn. Bhd. only imports two containers in a month, amounting to 20–40 mt.[48]

There have also been increases in quantities of imports of fisheries in canned and dried form, from 1,026 mt of canned fish in 1987 to 2,151 mt in 2008, and from 282 mt of dried fish in 1987 to 487 mt in 2008. Canned sardines are the most highly sought by Brunei's population because they are easy to prepare and are delicious. The quantity of imports increased by 70 per cent, from 335 mt in 1987 to 568 mt in 2008.[49] Dried shrimp, dried anchovies, dried fish and salted fish are the most highly demanded commodities in the domestic market. Almost the entire quantity of imports of dried fish consists of these commodities. The increase in imports of both canned and dried fish was due to relatively low production from the canning factory and the absence of a fish drying factory in Brunei. The only fish canning factory in Brunei belongs to Sabli Food Industries (B) Sdn. Bhd. Meanwhile, drying fish is carried out on a small scale in homes for daily consumption, with any excess being sold at the local food market or in the village. Drying fish is currently an underdeveloped cottage industry.

Canned fish are imported by sea using standard 20-foot and 40-foot shipping containers. Canned food items are imported along with other items in tins or bottles. The methods of importation and delivery of canned fish are similar to those for frozen fish. Most canned fish are imported from Peninsular Malaysia, Singapore and the Philippines. Almost all dried fish imports come from neighbouring Sabah and Sarawak by road and sea. Most dried fish transportation is conducted by traders from Sabah and Sarawak, with Bruneian fish wholesalers and importers placing orders via telephone or Short Message Service (SMS).

Unlike other fishery resources, imports of dried fish are in low quantities, each batch amounting to 200–500 kg, and only rarely exceeding 1,000 kg. Dried fish are usually stored in plastic containers or bags, paper sacks or boxes of various sizes. Each sack or plastic container/bag only contains 4.5–9 kg, allowing them to conveyed to market using saloon cars, four-wheel drive vehicles and vans. For shipments by sea, suppliers and exporters use small outboard-powered boats which also carry passengers between Brunei and Sabah and Sarawak. Dried fish are sent to distributors in Tamu Kianggeh and Bandar Seri Begawan.

Marketing of fishery resources

The rapid developments taking place in the fishing industry, particularly in small-scale fisheries, have reduced the control of Chinese investors in marketing fishery products. Following independence, almost the entire business of marketing fishery products was dominated by a few entrepreneurs and Malay traders who became wholesalers/purveyors and fish *tauke*. Consequently, Chinese investors turned to the marketing of processed fish, mainly frozen products imported from overseas suppliers.

Changes in the control of marketing have also changed the flow of fresh fish from the fish markets to other selling outlets. In the early period, which began in 1987, approximately 91 per cent of the total landings were sold in fish markets across the country to meet demand from Brunei's residents, with only about 3 per cent being exported. The remaining 6 per cent was consumed by the fishermen themselves and also marketed at the village level to meet the demands of the rural population who did not engage in fishing activities (Table 8.9).

However, in 2008, the marketing flow changed significantly. Sales of fish were no longer concentrated in the fish markets, but switched to other places such as supermarkets, sales desks in villages, the food preparation sector (hotels and

Table 8.9 Marketing flow of local and imported fishery resources

	Local						Imported				
	Total	Fish market		Other location		Export		Total	Fish market		Other location	
	mt	mt	%	mt	%	mt	%	mt	mt	%	mt	%
1987	2,278	2,071	91	146	6	61	3	1,828	1,828	100	0	0
1990	3,351	1,865	56	1,409	42	77	2	3,695	3,695	100	0	0
1995	5,050	956	19	4,040	80	54	1	5,225	5,225	100	0	0
2000	6,346	1,668	26	3,894	61	1,127	8	2,690	2,690	100	0	0
2005	9,658	2,577	27	7,623	79	356	4	2,598	2,288	88	310	12
2008	9,346	1,378	15	8,157	87	853	9	2,070	1,215	59	855	41

Sources: Government of Brunei, *Annual Statistics of External Trade* (Bandar Seri Begawan: Department of Customs and Excise, 1987–2008); *Brunei Darussalam Statistical Yearbook* (Bandar Seri Begawan: Statistics Division, Department of Economic Planning and Development, Ministry of Finance, Brunei Darussalam, 1984–99); *Brunei Darussalam Statistical Yearbook* (Bandar Seri Begawan: Department of Economic Planning and Development, Prime Minister's Office, Brunei Darussalam, 2000–2008).

Note: mt – metric tons.

restaurants), governmental and private organizations (hospitals, universities, colleges, military barracks, the fish processing industry, the oil industry and airlines) or sold directly to consumers. The proportion of fish sold in fish markets declined from 91 per cent in 1987 to 15 per cent in 2008. Fishery resource exports have not undergone great changes: from 1987 to 2008, the percentage of fish exported to the international market increased by only 6 per cent (Table 8.9).

The situation is different for fish marketed by supermarkets, governmental organizations, the private sector (cafeterias of oil companies) and food preparers (restaurants, cafes, food stalls) as well as for fishermen, who have witnessed substantial increases from merely 6 per cent in 1987 to 87 per cent in 2008 (Table 8.9). This increase was due to the illegal selling of fresh fish in villages which made it easier for consumers to obtain fresh fish every day. In addition, many supermarkets that previously only sold processed fish began to sell fresh fish. This increase in the number of outlets selling fresh fish was closely associated with the growth in demand for fish due to the increasing population.

Furthermore, the receipt of cash payments from supermarkets, the food preparation sector and private institutions was one of the factors that led to changes in the marketing trends. The fishermen mostly prefer to sell their catches to those who will pay in this way rather than to fish market vendors, who mostly pay by credit.[50] Typically, fish market vendors will only pay for the fish that were supplied after they have been sold. When sales are slow, they usually cannot afford to pay the fishermen. The impact of this situation has led to decreases in the supply of fish to fish markets. To overcome this, the fish sellers obtain their fresh supplies from neighbouring Sarawak, Sabah and Labuan.

By the 2010s, these changes also applied to the marketing flow of imported fresh fish. Imported fresh fish that were previously only sold in fish markets have started to appear in other outlets. In 2005, approximately 12 per cent of total imports of fresh fish were marketed to other outlets, rising to 41 per cent by 2008.

The marketing of fresh fish, either local or imported, is no longer concentrated in fish markets, but has switched to other fish sale outlets, as demonstrated by the very significant decrease from 5,178 mt sold in fish markets in 1984 to 2,593 mt in 2008 (see Table 8.10).

Marketing of locally processed fish also concentrated on exporting to overseas markets, as it gave greater returns than in the domestic market. However, the export market only began to be considered commercially around 1997, after the establishment of a processing company. Since its inception, the company has managed to export approximately 291 mt of processed fish to Singapore, Malaysia, Hong Kong and Japan. By the late 2000s, there were 12 commercial fish processing companies producing a variety of products, but exports of processed fish had only increased by 7 per cent to 312 mt in 2008.[51]

Almost the entire importation of processed fish is dominated by distributor companies, which therefore control all the marketing of these resources. Two marketing patterns are practised by these companies. The first is marketing through large-scale reservations placed by supermarkets, restaurants, hospitality companies, airlines and catering companies. Normally bookings are placed by

Table 8.10 Local and imported fresh fishery resources marketed in fish markets, 1984–2008

	Local		Imported		Total	
	Quantity	Value	Quantity	Value	Quantity	Value
1984	2,133	12,721	3,045	17,592	5,178	30,313
1985	2,401	13,838	3,085	19,490	5,486	33,328
1986	2,187	11,924	2,085	13,557	4,272	25,481
1987	2,071	10,322	1,828	11,934	3,899	22,256
1988	1,548	10,225	2,523	16,538	4,071	26,763
1989	1,826	11,403	3,489	23,190	5,315	34,593
1990	1,865	11,268	3,695	23,265	5,560	34,533
1991	1,570	9,294	3,447	18,908	5,017	28,202
1992	1,684	8,752	3,512	20,505	5,196	29,257
1993	1,727	8,886	4,967	26,955	6,694	35,841
1994	862	5,329	5,215	32,142	6,077	37,471
1995	956	6,280	5,225	33,686	6,181	39,966
1996	1,438	6,975	4,336	29,283	5,774	36,258
1997	1,273	7,929	3,934	26,547	5,207	34,476
1998	1,946	9,570	3,283	20,676	5,229	30,246
1999	2,262	10,278	2,752	17,222	5,014	27,500
2000	1,668	8,988	2,690	16,740	4,358	25,728
2001	1,597	8,847	3,026	18,046	4,623	26,893
2002	2,059	10,803	3,087	17,094	5,146	27,897
2003	2,226	11,785	2,668	13,463	4,894	25,248
2004	2,520	13,463	2,428	13,438	4,948	26,901
2005	2,577	14,386	2,288	13,861	4,865	28,247
2006	2,161	12,794	1,761	11,374	3,922	24,168
2007	1,520	9,118	1,100	7,192	2,620	16,310
2008	1,378	8,330	1,215	8,090	2,593	16,420

Source: Government of Brunei, *Annual Statistics of External Trade* (Bandar Seri Begawan: Department of Customs and Excise, 1987–2008); *Brunei Darussalam Statistical Yearbook* (Bandar Seri Begawan: Statistics Division, Department of Economic Planning and Development, Ministry of Finance, Brunei Darussalam, 1984–99); *Brunei Darussalam Statistical Yearbook* (Bandar Seri Begawan: Department of Economic Planning and Development, Prime Minister's Office, Brunei Darussalam, 2000–2008).

Notes: Quantities are in metric tons; values are in BND000.

telephone, facsimile and e-mail, while payments are made through the company's bank account, and delivery is provided free of charge. The second is direct marketing to grilled fish sellers, food stall owners and other such outlets. For instance, a grilled fish seller will go in person to the company's distribution centre to make the purchase. In contrast to the first pattern, direct marketing payments are in cash only, and no delivery service is provided.

Conclusion

To ensure effective development of the country, the Brunei government has stepped up its efforts to develop the non-oil sectors of the economy, namely industrial, services, agriculture, forestry and fisheries. The government's development policy has opened up opportunities for an increasing number of foreign workers to engage in economic activity in the sultanate's non-oil sectors. The presence of foreign workers has also increased the population, leading in turn to a growth in demand for food, including fish products.

In order to meet the increasing demand for fish, the fisheries industry needed to be improved in order to combat increases in imports. The government has been behind a major drive in planning and implementing fisheries programmes, covering the production stage, landing and marketing. One of the important initiatives has been the commercialization of the fishing industry through the use of powered vessels equipped with modern technologies. This has led to the establishment of two categories of fisheries in Brunei: commercial-scale and small-scale.

Due to problems involving management, finance and limited operations, as well as labour and marketing, commercial-scale fisheries were unable to produce the desired improvements. Although the government had opened up opportunities for any foreign investors and entrepreneurs to invest and form joint ventures in the fishing industry, this was unable to increase the quantity of landings. Faced with this situation, the government tried to commercialize small-scale fisheries by establishing small-scale fishing companies. Through several financial assistance schemes, the number of small-scale fisheries has grown drastically. Unlike commercial-scale fisheries, small-scale fisheries have been able to improve their landings every year. A large proportion of the overall landings during this period were produced by small-scale fisheries – quite unusual in the fishing industry, because in other countries most landings are by commercial-scale fisheries that use powered vessels. This suggests that small-scale fisheries are the most important element in the fishing industry of Brunei.

However, this increase in landings is largely attributable to foreign fishermen who have come to work in small-scale fisheries. Therefore, their involvement in the fishing industry following independence was essential to increase the yield of landings. Most of the locals were part-time fishermen, fishing only on weekends or public holidays. Brunei is the only country in Southeast Asia that has more part-time fishermen than full-time fishermen: there are three times as many part-time fishermen as full-time ones.

Encouraging the development of small-scale fisheries has reduced the influence of Chinese investors. The approach the government has adopted through financial assistance schemes to establish and support small-scale fisheries has made the government and the banks competitors to Chinese investors. Therefore, the role of Chinese investors as lending institutions has begun to be taken over by the government and banks. The control of Chinese investors over marketing has been eroded by small-scale fisheries companies, causing the Chinese investors to switch to the importation and marketing of frozen and canned fish.

However, despite the government's encouragement for the small-scale fisheries and their success in increasing landings, it has still not been possible to meet the increasing domestic demand for fish every year because almost half the fish landed have not been suitable for the market. Although the government has paid attention to the development of the aquaculture sector, its production has not been able to overcome the shortfall. Further development of small-scale fisheries and the aquaculture sector could contribute to reducing the quantity of fresh fish imports. The increase in demand has not only been for fresh fish, but also for frozen, dried and canned products. The slow development of the processing sector has led Brunei to rely almost entirely on imports of processed fish from foreign countries like Singapore, Malaysia, Thailand, Philippines, India and Norway. This dependence on fish imports has persisted from the post-independence period to the present – undoubtedly an unhealthy state of affairs, but a reality that has yet to be successfully addressed.

Notes

1 Ajamain bin Hj. Sawal, 'Future Fisheries Management Strategy for Brunei' (Master's thesis, Humberside Polytechnic, 1990), p. 1.
2 Narong Ruangsivakul et al., eds, *Fishing Gears and Methods in Southeast Asia*, vol. 5, *Brunei* (Bandar Seri Begawan: Department of Fisheries, Brunei Darussalam and SEAFDEC Training Department, 2007), p. 2.
3 Narong et al., *Fishing Gears and Methods in Southeast Asia*, vol. 5, *Brunei*, p. 2.
4 Mohammad Raduan bin Mohd Ariff and Amaluddin Bakeri, 'Hubungan Perdagangan Sumber Perikanan Sarawak-Negara Brunei: Kajian Kes Daerah Perikanan Limbang dan Lawas' ['Sarawak–Brunei Commercial Relations in Fisheries Resources: Case Study of the Districts of Limbang and Lawas'], *Jurnal Jabatan Pengajian Asia Tenggara*, 4 (1998): 108–29 at 109.
5 Narong et al., *Fishing Gears and Methods in Southeast Asia*, vol. 5, *Brunei*, p. 2.
6 Jabatan Perikanan, Brunei, 'Pencapaian Jabatan Perikanan Dari 1984 hingga 2003 dan Perancangan Strategik bagi Tempoh 20 Tahun Mendatang' ['Achievements of the Fisheries Department from 1984 until 2003 and Strategic Planning for the Next Twenty Years'], 2004, p. 6.
7 Ibid.
8 Ibid, p. 10.
9 Brosur Bank Islam Brunei Berhad, *Skim Pembiyaan Pengusaha Kecil dan Sederhana* [*Payment Scheme for Small and Medium Industries*] (Bandar Seri Begawan: Bank Islam Brunei Berhad, 2014).
10 *Laporan Tahunan 2002* [*Annual Report 2002*], Kementerian Perindustrian dan Sumber-Sumber Utama [Ministry of Industry and Primary Resources], Negara Brunei Darussalam, 2003, p. 74.
11 Jabatan Perikanan [Department of Fisheries], Kementerian Perindustrian dan Sumber-Sumber Utama [Ministry of Industry and Primary Resources], Brunei, *Suara Perikanan* [*Sound Fisheries*], January–June 2006, p. 15.

12 Jabatan Perikanan, Brunei, 'Pencapaian Jabatan Perikanan', p. 13.

13 Ibid, p. 20.

14 *Pelita Brunei*, 6 October 1999, p. 5; *Borneo Bulletin*, 26 November 1999, p. 8.

15 Jabatan Perikanan, Brunei, 'Pencapaian Jabatan Perikanan', p. 20.

16 Pg. Khairul Rijal Pg. Hj. Abdul Rahim, *Teknologi Menangkap Ikan di Negara Brunei 1906–2003* [*Fishing Technologies in Negara Brunei Darussalam 1906–2003*] (Kuala Lumpur: Penerbit Universiti Malaya, 2007), p. 189.

17 *Pelita Brunei*, 1 July 1998, p. 12.

18 Jabatan Perikanan [Department of Fisheries], Kementerian Perindustrian dan Sumber-Sumber Utama [Ministry of Industry and Primary Resources], Brunei, *Kejayaan Takat Tiruan* [*Artificial Reef*], n.d., p. 1.

19 *Laporan Tahunan 2002*, p. 74.

20 Jawatankuasa Tertinggi Penerbitan Buku Perjalanan Negara Brunei Memasuki Alaf Baru [Supreme Committee for the Book Publication of the Development of Brunei in the New Millennium], *Perjalanan Negara Brunei Memasuki Alaf Baru* [*The Development of Brunei in the New Millennium*]. Jabatan Percetakan Kerajaan, Brunei, 1999, p. 64.

21 *Borneo Bulletin*, 18 June 1998, p. 3.

22 Ajamain, 'Future Fisheries Management Strategy for Brunei', pp. 41–2; Jabatan Perikanan, Brunei, 'Pencapaian Jabatan Perikanan', p. 21; *Pelita Brunei*, 11 October 1995, p. 12.

23 Khairul Rijal, *Teknologi Menangkap Ikan di Negara Brunei*, p. 191.

24 Divisyen Perkembangan dan Pengurusan Perikanan Marin [Development and Management of Marine Fisheries Division], Jabatan Perikanan [Department of Fisheries], Kementerian Perindustrian dan Sumber-Sumber Utama [Ministry of Industry and Primary Resources], Negara Brunei, Pelaksanaan, *'Moratorium' Ke Atas Operasi Menangkap Ikan Zon 1* [*Implementation of 'Moratorium' on Fishing Operations in Zone 1*], Negara Brunei, June 2007, p. 4.

25 Ibid., pp. 1–3.

26 Ibid,, p. 4.

27 Mohammad Raduan Mohd Ariff and Amaluddin Bakeri, 'Hubungan Perdagangan Sumber Perikanan Sarawak-Negara Brunei: Kajian Kes Daerah Perikanan Miri' ['Sarawak–Brunei Commercial Relations in Fisheries Resources: Case Study of the Districts of Miri'], *Jurnal Jabatan Pengajian Asia Tenggara*, 6 (2001): 1–28.

28 Interview with fish suppliers and exporters Awang Mohen bin Haji Mohamad, Awang Haji Latif bin Haji Damit and Awang Haji Abdul Kadir bin Akob, 9 June 2009; interview with fish supplier and exporter Rashid bin Haji Dullah, 18 May 2009.

29 Interview with fish suppliers and exporters Awang Mohen bin Haji Mohamad and Awang Haji Latif bin Haji Damit, 9 June 2009.

30 Mohammad Raduan bin Mohd Ariff, *Petempatan Kampung Air di Pulau Borneo: Satu Kajian Perbandingan* [*The Settlement of Kampung Air in Borneo Island: A Comparative Study*], Monograf Akademi Pengajian Brunei, no. 2 (Bandar Seri Bagawan: Akademi Pengajian Brunei, Universiti Brunei, 2005), pp. 43–6; Mohammad Raduan and Amaluddin Bakeri, 'Hubungan Perdagangan Sumber Perikanan' (1998), pp. 108–29.

31 Interview with fish supplier and exporter Haji Matserudin bin Haji Kahar, 10 June 2009.

32 Mohammad Raduan, *Petempatan Kampung Air di Pulau Borneo*, p. 45.

33 Interview with fish supplier and exporter Awang Mohen bin Haji Mohamad, 9 June 2009.

34 Ibid.
35 Mohammad Raduan and Amaluddin Bakeri, 'Hubungan Perdagangan Sumber Perikanan' (2001), p. 22.
36 Interview with fish suppliers and exporters Rosli bin Taha, Muhammad bin Haji Abu Bakar, Awang Ajmain bin Haji Yusof and Noraji bin Adun, 28 May 2009.
37 *Air Waybill, Royal Brunei Airline*, 5 May 2009.
38 Interview with Assistant Superintendent of Customs Awang Haji Emran bin Tali, 2 May 2009.
39 Interview with Excapade Restaurant Manager Mr David, 6 May 2009.
40 Interview with fish supplier and exporter Awang Haji Jamudin bin Haji Piut, 5 May 2009.
41 *Air Waybill, Royal Brunei Airline*, 1 May 2009.
42 *Air Waybill, Royal Brunei Airline*, 5 May 2009.
43 Interview with Assistant Senior Fisheries Officer Awang Haji Asli bin Haji Raub, 6 October 2009.
44 Interview with Manager of Cerah Sdn. Bhd. Awang Aminuddin bin Abdullah Teo, 7 May 2009.
45 Interview with Manager of Teguh Mesra Company Dayang Chong Saw Yong, 8 May 2009.
46 Interview with grilled fish seller Awang Ursan bin Abu Salem, 4 January 2010.
47 Interview with Manager of Cerah Sdn. Bhd. Awang Aminuddin bin Abdullah Teo, 7 May 2009.
48 Interview with Manager of TGT Sdn. Bhd. Tan To Ling, 22 May 2009.
49 Data from Department of Economics and Development, Brunei.
50 Interview with fish wholesaler and importer Awang Haji Hamidon bin Haji Nasar, 28 May 2009.
51 Data from Department of Economic Development, Brunei.

Appendices

Appendix 6.1

Emergency Order (Islamic Family Law) 1999

1 terminology and interpretations, Caps 1–7;
2 marriage, Caps 8–23;
3 registration of marriage, Caps 24–32;
4 excerpts of laws and provisions related to marriage vows and registration of marriage, Caps 33–9;
5 dissolution of marriage, Caps 40–60;
6 alimony for wife, children and others, Caps 61–87;
7 Section 7 covers the care of children (*hadanah*), Caps 88–94, and guardianship of people and estates, Caps 95–112;
8 excerpts of Caps, 113–22;
9 punishments, Caps, 123–39;
10 general issues, Caps 140–47.

Sharia laws must be implemented if there are no provisions, exceptions, annulments or amendments, Cap. 5, Section 124.

Appendix 6.2

Family Protection Order, Amendment 2010

The right to receive an Extension Order

i ordering to prohibit the respondent (the *dharar* aggressor) from provoking;

ii ordering the exclusive right to dwelling for the applicant (order to remove the respondent from the residence);

iii prohibiting the respondent from approaching the protected person (shared residence, alternative residence, workplace, school, institution or other location), or making contact (via letter, telephone or other means) without the presence of an enforcer;

iv allowing the applicant to enter the premises, accompanied by an enforcement officer to collect personal belongings;

v allowing the applicant the use of transport;

vi ordering the applicant, respondent or their children to attend counselling with an officer appointed by the director of JAPEM or a person ordered by the court;

vii ordering to place the respondent in an allocated alternative residence.

Appendix 6.3

***Mal* jurisdiction of the Sharia Courts under the
Sharia Courts Act, Cap. 184**

i   engagement, marriage (including reconciliation), divorce, *khuluk*, *fasakh*, *cerai takliq*, determination of turns (in polygamy), *lian, ila'* or any related issues pertaining to the relationship between husband and wife;
ii any division of or claims to any property arising from any of those matters mentioned in subsection (i) of this section;
iii alimony for sustenance, *ithbat al-nasab* (legality of status) or the care of children (*hadanah*);
iv division of or claims to any property co-owned and shared during marriage.[1]

Appendix 6.4

Jurisdiction of the Sharia Appellate Court under the Sharia Courts Act, Cap. 184

1 The Sharia Appellate Court must have jurisdiction to hear and adjudge any appeal on any judgments made by the Sharia High Court in executing its specific jurisdiction.

2 When an appeal is made regarding a judgment made by the Lower Sharia Court that has been adjudged by the Sharia High Court, the Sharia Appellate Court can, at the request of an applicant, give its consent to any queries regarding law, for the benefit of the public, that arose from the appeal, and if the judgment of the Sharia High Court affected the result of the appeal, be brought forward to the Sharia Appellate Court to be decided.

3 When permission is granted by the Sharia Appellate Court, it must hear and adjudge permissible queries to be referred to for its decision, and make any order possible that has been made by the Sharia High Court, and as it deems just to resolve the appeal.

The Sharia Appellate Court has jurisdiction to regulate and revise, as ordained by Section 21 of the Emergency Order (Sharia Courts), 1998. The provisions are as follows:

1 The Sharia Appellate Court must have jurisdiction to regulate and revise the Sharia High Court, and can, if found necessary to serve justice, either under its own initiative or at the request of any party or concerned person, at any level regarding any issue or proceeding, either *mal* or criminal in the Sharia High Court, request and examine any related record and can issue any orders necessary to serve justice.

2 When the Sharia Appellate Court requests records under subsection (1), all proceedings in the Sharia High Court related to the issue or the specific proceeding must be temporarily suspended pending further instructions from the Sharia Appellate Court.

The Sharia Appellate Court consists of members who are appointed, as ordained by Sections 22 and 23 of the Emergency Order (Sharia Courts), 1998. The provisions are as follows:

1   An appeal in the Sharia Appellate Court must be heard and adjudged by a Chair and any two Sharia Appellate Court Judges, as decided by the Sharia Chief Judge.[2]

2   The Sharia Chief Judge can appoint any Sharia High Court Judge to be a member of the Sharia Appellate Court in any particular proceeding as the Sharia Chief Judge deems necessary.

3   The two people appointed to the Sharia Appellate Court under subsections (1) and (2) must not include the Sharia Judge who had heard or made judgment regarding the case being appealed.

4   The Sharia Chief Judge must chair every proceeding in the Sharia Appellate Court, and if it is found that he/she is unable to carry out his/her duties, the Sharia Chief Judge appoints the judge who is highest in rank among the Sharia Appellate Court Judges to be the Chair. An appeal must be decided according to the vote of the majority of the members of the Sharia Appellate Court.[3]

Appendix 6.5

**Offences that can be tried in the Sharia High Court,
Lower Court and Appellate Court under the
Emergency Order (Islamic Family Law) 1999:**

a   Failure to be present in front of the registrar to register a marriage which occurred outside the country within six months after entering the country is punishable by a fine of not more than BND1,000 or a jail term of not more than three months, or both.[4]

b   Marriage officiants who violate the provision in Cap. 15 are punishable by a fine of not more than BND1,000 or a jail term of not more than three months, or both, and for the second or consecutive offences, a fine of not more than BND2,000 or a jail term of not more than six months, or both.[5]

    a   Coercing someone or prohibiting a man from marrying after he reaches the age of 18, or a woman after she has reached the age of 16, attracts a fine of not more than BND2,000 or a jail term of not more than six months, or both.[6]

    b   False admission or declaration to obtain permission is punishable by a fine of not more than BND2,000 or a jail term of not more than six months, or both.[7]

    c   Officiating marriages without permission attracts a fine of not more than BND2,000 or a jail term of not more than six months, or both.[8]

    d   (a) Officiating marriages without permission as provided in Cap. 18, permission to marry outside the country:

         (b) not having two reliable witnesses attracts a fine of not more than BND2,000 or a jail term of not more than six months, or both;[9]

         (c) a person who marries in violation of the provision in Cap. 11 (related to marriages) can be sentenced to a fine or a jail term of not more than six months, or both.[10]

    e   Any party to a marriage which does not register a reconciliation of marriage as ordained by subsection (10) has committed an offence punishable by a fine of not more than BND1,000 or a jail term of not more than three months, or both.[11]

f   Practising polygamy without permission attracts a fine of not more than BND2,000 or a jail term of not more than six months, or both.[12]

g   Divorce outside the court without its permission attracts a fine of not more than BND2,000 or a jail term of not more than six months, or both.[13]

h   (1) Being intentionally negligent or not making a report attracts a fine of not more than BND2,000 or a jail term of not more than six months, or both.[14]

  (2) Being intentionally negligent or not making a report or not submitting an application or not informing or not signing any necessary documents attracts a fine of not more than BND2,000 or a jail term of not more than six months, or both.[15]

i   Making a false report to the registrar attracts a fine of not more than BND2,000 or a jail term of not more than six months, or both.[16]

j   A husband or wife who does not comply with the court's order to reconcile is subject to a fine of not more than BND2,000 or a jail term of not more than six months, or both.[17]

k   (1) Oppressing a husband or wife attracts a fine of not more than BND2,000 or a jail term of not more than six months, or both.[18]

  (2) Expunging a husband or wife of his/her property by deception attracts a fine of not more than BND2,000 or a jail term of not more than six months, or both, and the court must order the return of the property, or if the property no longer exists, its equivalent value, to the husband or wife according to *syarak* law.[19]

l   A husband who treats his wife unjustly according to *syarak* law is subject to a fine of not more than BND2,000 or a jail term of not more than six months, or both.[20]

m   A wife who intentionally disobeys her husband's orders according to *syarak* law after being advised by a Sharia Judge is subject to a fine of not more than BND500, or for the second and consecutive offences, a fine of not more than BND1,000.[21]

n   Becoming apostate due to disliking the husband or wife as an excuse to annul the marriage is punishable by a jail term of not more than five years.[22]

o   (1) The offence of living with a wife who has been officially divorced without a valid *rujuk* (reconciliation) utterance is punishable by a fine of not more than BND1,000 or a jail term of not more than three months, or both.[23]

  (2) Divorcing a wife without her knowledge and yet continuing to live with her attracts a fine of not more than BND2,000 or a jail term of not more than six months, or both.[24]

  (3) A divorced wife conspiring to live with her husband without valid reconciliation is subject to the penalties set out in Section 132.[25]

r   In cases of intentional failure to comply with an order, if it concerns the payment of any sums, the sums must be paid according to the law. If the order is for monthly payment and there is an intentional failure to comply with this order, the offender can be jailed for not more than one month for every monthly payment that has not yet been paid. The same applies to failure to comply with an order other than for monthly payment, which attracts a jail term of not more than one year.[26]

s   Contempt of court under the Islamic Family Order 1999 attracts a fine of not more than BND2,000 or a jail term of not more than six months, or both.[27]

t   In the case of a marriage which violates any provision in this order, the offender is subject to a fine of not more than BND2,000 or a jail term of not more than six months, or both.[28]

u   Failure to comply with an order to detain income/salary and so on attracts a fine of not more than BND5,000 or a jail term of not more than one year, or both.[29]

v   Failing to fulfil an agreement attracts a fine of not more than BND2,000 or a jail term of not more than six months, or both.[30]

w   Attempting and conspiring to commit any offence under this order attracts the same sentence as ordained for the offence itself.[31]

x   Sentences not ordained for any matter that violates or fails to comply with anything under this order attract a fine of not more than BND2,000 or a jail term of not more than six months, or both. The offender can be sentenced to jail if the fine is not paid, but it is not more than half of the ordained jail sentence for such an offence, or seven days' jail if the sentence is only a fine.

Appendix 6.6

**Offences that can be tried in the Sharia High
Court, Lower Court and Appellate Court under
the Religious Council and Kathi's Courts Act,
Cap. 77 of the Laws of Brunei Darussalam**

a   Failing to attend Friday mass prayer for males aged 15 or above is not an
    offence by any person if:

    1   his attendance is hindered by rain;
    2   his residence is more than 3 miles from the nearest road to a mosque, or
    3   he has been exempted from attending the mosque by a mosque official of
    the constituency where he usually resides or by reason of illness or is not
    present in his usual area of residence.

The sentence for this offence is a fine of BND100, for a second offence a fine
BND200, and for third or consecutive offences, a fined of BND500.[32]

b   Selling, buying or consuming *yang* alcoholic beverages or other drinks pro-
    hibited by *syarak* attracts a fine of BND500, for the second offence BND750,
    and for the third and consecutive offences BND1,000.[33]
c   Eating food or smoking in daytime in public during the month of Ramadhan,
    other than by those who are exempted by *syarak*, attracts a fine of BND500, for the
    second offence BND750, and for the third or consecutive offences BND1,000.[34]
d   An employer is considered to have conspired if his employee sells anything
    prohibited as ordained in Caps 172 and 173, except when it is proven that the
    offence was committed without his permission, knowledge or consent and
    that he has taken reasonable steps to prevent it. The sentence is the same as
    that for the offence itself.[35]
e   A Muslim man who has committed an offence of *khalwat*, or close proximity,
    is subject to a jail term of one month or a fine of BND1,000, or a jail term of
    two months or a fine of BND2,000 for the second or consecutive offences.[36]
f   A Muslim woman who conspires to commit *khalwat* is subject to a jail term
    of 14 days or a fine of BND500, or a jail term of one month or a fine of
    BND1,000 for the second and consecutive offences.[37]

g   A Muslim woman who conspires to commit *khalwat* with any non-Muslim man is subject to the same sentence as under subsection (2).[38]

h   Engaging in illicit sexual relations with those prohibited to be married under *syarak* attracts a sentence for men of a jail term of five years, and for women a jail term of one year.[39]

i   Engaging in illicit sexual relations is punishable by a jail term of six months or a fine of BND5,000.[40]

j   Invalid conversion to Islam is punishable by a jail term of one month or a fine of BND1,000.[41]

k   Being intentionally negligent in conducting official duties attracts a jail term of three months or a fine of BND2,000.[42]

l   Leaking confidential information is punishable by a jail term of three months or a fine of BND2,000.[43]

m   Constructing mosques or contributing for such acts in contravention of the law attracts a fine of BND10,000, and the court can, subject to any rights of third parties, order the demolition of the building.[44]

n   Teaching religious education without written permission from the council is punishable by a jail term of one month or a fine of BND1,000.[45]

o   Preaching cult teachings is punishable by a jail term of three months or a fine of BND2,000.[46]

p   Pronouncing *fatwa*, other than by a *mufti* or a person acting under power ordained by this Act, is punishable by a jail term of three months or a fine of BND2,000.[47]

q   Publishing, broadcasting, selling or importing into the country books or documents containing any content against *syarak* or Islamic teachings or containing any invalid *fatwa* is punishable by a jail term of six months or a fine of BND4,000 and confiscation of the books or documents.[48]

r   Perverting the Holy Quran is punishable by a jail term of one month or a fine of BND8,000.[49]

s   Contempt towards any religious authority is punishable by a jail term of one month or a fine of BND1,000.[50]

t   Contempt towards Islam is punishable by a jail term of six months or a fine of BND4,000.[51] (section 77: s. 191)

u   Not paying the *fitrah* (personal) alms is punishable by a jail term of 14 days or a fine of BND1,000.[52]

v   Inciting others to abandon religious duties is punishable by a jail term of six months or a fine of BND4,000.[53]

w   Attempting and conspiring to commit these offences attracts the same sentence as the offence itself.[54]

x   Non-Muslims who conspire under Caps 172 and 173 are punishable by a fine of BND400, or BND800 for the second or consecutive offences.[55]

y   Non-Muslims who conspire to commit any offence under this Act apart from the offences in Cap. 172 are sentenced according to the conditions in Part V of the Criminal Penal Code.[56]

Appendix 6.7

**Offences that are heard in the Sharia High Court,
Lower Court and Appellate Court under the
Sharia Courts Act, Cap. 184**

a   Violating an order of silence attracts a fine of not more than BND5,000 or a jail term of not more than one year, or both.[57]

b   Contempt towards the Sharia Court attracts the following sentences:

  1   a fine of not more than BND2,000 or a jail term of not more than six months, or both for cases in the Sharia Lower Court;

  2   in the Sharia High and Appellate Courts, a fine of not more than BND100 or a jail term of not more than one year, or both.[58]

Finally, offences heard in the Sharia High Court, Sharia Lower Court and Sharia Appellate Court under the Sharia Court *Mal* Procedure Order, 2005 are as follows:

a   Contempt of court attracts a jail term of not more than six months or a fine of not more than BND2,000.[59]

Notes

1   Sharia Courts Act, Cap. 184, Section 15(b) (i)(ii)(iii)(iv).
2   Ibid., Section 22.
3   Ibid., Cap. 184, Section 23.
4   Emergency Order (Islamic Family Law) 1999, Section 33.
5   Ibid., Section 34.
6   Ibid., Section 35.
7   Ibid., Section 36.
8   Ibid., Section 37.
9   Ibid., Section 38.
10   Ibid., Section 38.
11   Ibid., Section 52.
12   Ibid., Section 123.
13   Ibid., Section 24.
14   Ibid., Section 125.

15 Ibid., Section 125.
16 Ibid., Section 125.
17 Ibid., Section 127.
18 Ibid., Section 128.
19 Ibid., Section 128.
20 Ibid., Section 129.
21 Ibid., Section 130.
22 Ibid., Section 131.
23 Ibid., Section 132.
24 Ibid.
25 Ibid.
26 Ibid., Section 133.
27 Ibid., Section 134.
28 Ibid., Section 135.
29 Ibid., Section 136.
30 Ibid., Section 137.
31 Ibid., Section 138.
32 The Religious Council and Kathi's Court Act, Cap. 77, Section 171.
33 Ibid., Section 172.
34 Ibid., Section 173.
35 Ibid., Section 174.
36 Ibid., Section 171(1).
37 Ibid., Section 171(2).
38 Ibid., Section 171(3).
39 Ibid., Section 178(1).
40 Ibid., Section 178(2).
41 Ibid., Section 181.
42 Ibid., Section 182.
43 Ibid., Section 183.
44 Ibid., Section 184.
45 Ibid., Section 185.
46 Ibid., Section 186.
47 Ibid., Section 187.
48 Ibid., Section 188.
49 Ibid., Section 189.
50 Ibid., Section 190.
51 Ibid., Section 191.
52 Ibid., Section 192.
53 Ibid., Section 193.
54 Ibid., Section 194.
55 Ibid., Section 195.
56 Ibid., Section 196.
57 Sharia Courts Act, 7A (3).
58 Sharia Courts Act, 7A, Section 28 (A).
59 Sharia Court *Mal* Procedure Order 2005, Section 220.

Bibliography

Archival materials

The National Archives, Kew, United Kingdom

Acting Consul General Treacher to Earl Granville, Brunei, 19 March 1885, CO 144/60.

Agreement between Sultan Abdul Mumin, Pengiran Bendahara and Pengiran Digadong with the British North Borneo Company whereby they will not permit any lease or cession of territory to the north of and including the Limbang river, Muara Damit and Muara Besar, Brunei, 17 Muharram AH 1302 (5 November 1884), FO 12/120.

Article III of the Protectorate Agreement between Brunei and the British government, Appendix IV, FO 12/130.

British Resident, Brunei to High Commissioner, 24 September 1906, CO 144/80.

Consul General Leys to Foreign Office, 14 December 1885, CO 144/59.

Consul General Leys to the Marquis of Salisbury, Labuan, 24 February 1887, FO 12/76.

Robertson, C.B. Memorandum on Admiral Mayne's Question for 28 February, Respecting the Cession of Limbang River to Sarawak, 26 February 1886, FO 572/18.

St John, Spenser, Acting Commissioner to the Viscount Palmerston, Foreign Affairs, 1 June 1851, FO 12/9.

Sultan of Brunei to Consul General Leys, Brunei, 29 Sapar AH 1304 (27 November 1886), FO 572/18

Sultan of Brunei to Governor Sir F. Weld, Brunei, 15 Ramadhan AH 1304 (7 June 1887), FO 12/77.

Sultan of Brunei to Her Majesty the Queen, Brunei, 14 Jamadil Akhir AH 1304 (8 February 1887), FO 572/18.

Swettenham, Frank to Marquess of Lansdowne, 25 March 1902, FO 12/120.

Official publications

Brunei Annual Report, 1906–46.

Brunei Darussalam – Country Baselines under the ILO Declaration Annual Review (2000–2008): Freedom of Association and the Effective Recognition of the Right to Collective Bargaining (FACB), 2008. http://www.ilo.org/declaration/follow-up/annualreview/archiveofbaselinesbycountry/WCMS_DECL_FACB_BNR/lang--en/index.htm. Accessed 4 September 2015.

Brunei Darussalam, Government of. *Annual Statistics of External Trade* (Bandar Seri Begawan: Department of Customs and Excise, 1987–2008).

Brunei Darussalam, Government of. *Brunei Darussalam Annual National Accounts 2000–2004* (Bandar Seri Begawan: Department of Statistics, Department of Economic Planning and Development, Prime Minister's Office, February 2006).

Brunei Darussalam, Government of. *Brunei Darussalam Annual National Accounts 2006 and 2007* (Bandar Seri Begawan: Department of Statistics, Department of Economic Planning and Development, Prime Minister's Office, 2008).

Brunei Darussalam, Government of. *Eighth National Development Plan 2001–2005*. Economic Planning Unit, Ministry of Finance.

Brunei Darussalam, Government of. *Seventh National Development Plan 1996–2001*. Economic Planning Unit, Ministry of Finance.

Brunei Darussalam Industrial Structure, 2001–2005. Department of Labour, Brunei Darussalam.

Brunei Darussalam Key Indicators 2014 Half Release 1: Half Year. Department of Economic Planning and Development, Brunei Darussalam.

Brunei Darussalam Statistical Yearbook (Bandar Seri Begawan: Statistics Division, Department of Economic Planning and Development, Ministry of Finance, 1984–99).

Brunei Darussalam Statistical Yearbook (Bandar Seri Begawan: Department of Economic Planning and Development, Prime Minister's Office, Brunei Darussalam, 2000–2008).

Brunei Department of Religious Affairs. *Brunei*. Dakwah Islamiah Centre, 1981.

Department of Fisheries, Brunei. *Brunei Darussalam: A Study of the Market for Fish and Fish Products in Hong Kong, Taiwan, Singapore and Australia*, vol. 2, Final Report. Bandar Seri Begawan: Statistics Division, Economic Planning Unit, Ministry of Finance, June 1993.

Department of Statistics, Department of Economic Planning and Development, Brunei Darussalam. *Annual National Accounts* 2000–2004, 2006 and 2007.

Department of Statistics, Department of Economic Planning and Development, Brunei Darussalam. *Perencanaan Kemajuan Jangka Panjang Negara Brunei Darussalam* [*Long-term Progress Planning of Negara Brunei Darussalam*]. Bandar Seri Begawan: Department of Economic Planning and Development, 2008.

Divisyen Perkembangan dan Pengurusan Perikanan Marin [Development and Management of Marine Fisheries Division], Jabatan Perikanan [Department of Fisheries], Kementerian Perindustrian dan Sumber-Sumber Utama [Ministry of Industry and Primary Resources], Negara Brunei, Pelaksanaan. *'Moratorium' Ke Atas Operasi Menangkap Ikan Zon 1* [*Implementation of 'Moratorium' on Fishing Operations in Zone 1*], Negara Brunei, June 2007.

Jabatan Perikanan [Department of Fisheries], Kementerian Perindustrian dan Sumber-Sumber Utama [Ministry of Industry and Primary Resources], Brunei. *Kejayaan Takat Tiruan* [*Artificial Reef*], n.d.

Jabatan Perikanan [Department of Fisheries], Kementerian Perindustrian dan Sumber-Sumber Utama [Ministry of Industry and Primary Resources], Brunei. *Suara Perikanan* [*Sound Fisheries*], January–June 2006.

Jawatankuasa Tertinggi Penerbitan Buku Perjalanan Negara Brunei Memasuki Alaf Baru [Supreme Committee for the Book Publication of the Development of Brunei in the New Millennium]. *Perjalanan Negara Brunei Memasuki Alaf Baru* [*The Development of Brunei in the New Millennium*]. Jabatan Percetakan Kerajaan, Brunei, 1999.

Khoo Hong Woo et al. 'Capture Fisheries'. In: *The Coastal Environmental Profile of Brunei Darussalam: Resource Assessment and Management Issues*, edited by Chua Thia-Eng et al. Manila: Fisheries Department, Ministry of Development, Brunei Darussalam and International Center for Living Aquatic Resources Management, 1987.

'Labour Act, 1954, Enactment No. 11 of 1954'. *Government Gazette*, State of Brunei.

Laporan Tahunan 2002 [Annual Report 2002]. Kementerian Perindustrian dan Sumber-Sumber Utama [Ministry of Industry and Primary Resources], Negara Brunei Darussalam, 2003.

Negara Brunei Darussalam Preliminary Report of the 2002 Economic Census. Department of Economic Planning and Development (JPKE), Brunei Darussalam, Prime Minister's Office, 2003.

Negara Brunei Darussalam Vital Statistics 2001: Preliminary Report of the 2002 Economic Census. Department of Economic Planning and Development, Brunei Darussalam.

Population and Housing Census (BPP) 2011 Report. Bandar Seri Begawan: Department of Economic Planning and Development, 2012.

Silvestre, Geronimo T. and Hj. Matdanan Hj. Jaafar. 'Brunei Darussalam Capture Fisheries: A Review of Resources, Exploitation and Management'. In: *The Coastal Resources of Brunei Darussalam: Status, Utilization and Management*, edited by Geronimo T. Silvestre et al. (Manila: International Center for Living Aquatic Resources Management and Department of Fisheries, Ministry of Industry and Primary Resources, Brunei Darussalam, 1992).

Statistics on Availability of Jobs According to Occupation and Sex, 2003. Department of Labour, Brunei Darussalam.

Statistics on Employees by Industries, Occupation and Sex, 2003. Department of Labour, Brunei Darussalam.

Statistics on Total Foreign Workers in the Public Sector, Companies, Domestic Helpers and their Dependents (valid until 2003). Department of Labour, Brunei Darussalam.

Statistics on Total Job Registration According to Occupation and Sex, 2003. Department of Labour, Brunei Darussalam.

Statistics on Total of Employees by Industries. Occupation and Sex, 2003. Department of Labour, Brunei Darussalam.

Stubbs, R.E. *Brunei and the Limbang* (Eastern no. 97). Printed for the use of the Colonial Office, 1905.

Unpublished manuscripts

Jabatan Perikanan, Brunei. 'Pencapaian Jabatan Perikanan Dari 1984 hingga 2003 dan Perancangan Strategik bagi Tempoh 20 Tahun Mendatang' ['Achievements of the Fisheries Department from 1984 until 2003 and Strategic Planning for the Next Twenty Years'], 2004.

Noralipah Mohamed, 'Pekerja Asing di Negara Brunei Darussalam: Kes Kajian Pekerja Filipina' ['Foreign Workers in Negara Brunei Darussalam: A Case Study of Filipino Workers']. Unpublished MS. Bandar Seri Begawan: Universiti Brunei Darussalam, 2001

Journal articles and book chapters

Abdul Latif bin Haji Ibrahim, Haji. 'Variations and Changes in the Names and Locations of the Wards of Brunei's Kampong Ayer over the Last Century', *Brunei Museum Journal*, 2(3) (1971): 56–73.

Adelaar, Alexander K. 'Where Does Malay Come From? Twenty Years of Discussions about Homeland, Migrations and Classifications', *Bijdragen tot de Taal-, Land- en Volkenkunde*, 160 (2004): 1–30.

Archaeological Work in Sarawak: With Special Reference to Niah Caves. Sarawak Museum Occasional Paper no. 1. Kuching: Vanguard Press, 1980.

Azim, P. 'The Ageing Population of Brunei Darussalam, Trends and Economic Consequences', *Asia Pacific Population Journal*, 17(1) (2002): 29–54.

Bain, I. 'South-east Asian', *International Migration*, 36(4) (1998): 553–85.

Ball, R and N. Piper. 'Globalisation and Regulation of Citizenship: Filipino Migrant Workers in Japan', *Political Geography*, 21 (2002): 1,013–34.

Barker, Graeme et al. 'Foraging–farming Transitions at the Niah Caves, Sarawak, Borneo', *Antiquity*, 85 (2011): 492–509.

Bellwood, Peter. 'Formosan Prehistory and Austronesian Dispersal'. In: *Austronesian Taiwan: Linguistics, History, Ethnology, Prehistory*, rev. edn, edited by David Blundell. Taipei: Shung Ye Museum; Berkeley: Phoebe A. Hearst Museum, University of California, 2009, pp. 336–64.

Bellwood, Peter and Matussin bin Omar. 'Trade Patterns and Political Developments in Brunei and Adjacent Areas, A.D. 700–1500', *Brunei Museum Journal*, 4 (1980): 155–79.

Bellwood, Peter and Peter Koon. '"Lapita Colonists Leave Boats Unburned!" The Question of Lapita Links with Island Southeast Asia', *Antiquity*, 63 (1989): 613–22.

Blust, Robert. 'Austronesian Culture History: The Window of Language'. In: *Prehistoric Settlement of the Pacific*, edited by W.H. Goodenough. Philadelphia, PA: American Philosophical Society, 1996, pp. 28–35.

Blust, Robert. 'The Austronesian Homeland: A Linguistic Perspective', *Asian Perspectives*, 26 (1984–85): 45–68.

Braddell, Roland. 'A Note on Sambas and Borneo', *Journal of the Malayan Branch of the Royal Asiatic Society*, 22(4) (1949): 1–15.

Brahim bin Ampuan Haji Tengah, Ampuan Haji. 'Manuskrip Syair Awang Semaun: Kajian dan Manfaatnya kepada Orang Brunei' ['Manuscript of Syair Awang Semaun: Its Study and Benefit to the People of Brunei'], *Jurnal Darussalam*, 10 (2010): 73–83.

Braveboy-Wagner, Jacqueline Anne. 'The English-speaking Caribbean States: A Triad of Foreign Policy'. In: *Small States in World Politics*, edited by Jeanne A.K. Hey. Boulder, CO: Lynne Rienner, 2003, pp. 31–52.

Brown, D.E. 'Hiranyagarbha – the Hindu Cosmic Egg – and Brunei's Royal Line', *Brunei Museum Journal*, 4 (1980): 30–37.

Brown, D.E. 'Sultan Mumin's Will and Related Documents', *Brunei Museum Journal*, 3(2) (1974): 156–70.

Carlos, M.R.D. 'On the Determinants of International Migration in the Philippines: An Empirical Analysis', *International Migration Review*, 36(1) (2002): 81–102.

Castle, S. 'New Migration in the Asia-Pacific Region: A Force for Social and Political Change', *International Social Science Journal*, 50(2) (1998): 215–27.

Cator, G.E. 'Brunei', *Asiatic Review*, 35 (1939): 736–44.

Chaffee, John. 'Muslim Merchants and Quanzhou in the Late Yuan–Early Ming: Conjectures on the Ending of the Medieval Muslim Trade Diaspora'. In: *The East Asian Mediterranean: Maritime Crossroads of Culture, Commerce and Human Migration*, edited by Angela Schottenhammer. Wiesbaden: Otto Harrassowitz, 2008, pp. 115–32.

Chen Da-sheng. 'A Brunei Sultan in the Early 14th Century: Study of an Arabic Tombstone', *Journal of Southeast Asian Studies*, 23 (1992): 1–13.

Chia, Stephen. 'Archaeological Evidence of Early Human Occupation in Malaysia'. In: *Austronesian Diaspora and the Ethnogenesis of People in [the] Indonesian Archipelago: Proceedings of the International Symposium*, edited by Truman Simanjuntak, Ingrid Harriet, Eileen Pojoh and Muhamad Hisyam. Jakarta: LIPI, 2006, pp. 239–60.

Chin, Lucas. 'Trade Pottery Discovered in Sarawak from 1948 to 1976', *Sarawak Museum Journal*, 25 (1977): 1–7.

Christie, Jan Wisseman. 'Javanese Markets and the Asian Sea Trade Boom of the Tenth to Thirteenth Centuries A.D.', *Journal of the Economic and Social History of the Orient*, 41 (1998): 344–81.

Christie, Jan Wisseman. 'On Po-ni: The Santubong Sites of Sarawak', *Sarawak Museum Journal*, 34 (1985): 77–89.

Christie, Jan Wisseman. 'State Formation in Early Maritime Southeast Asia: A Consideration of the Theories and the Data', edited by Jan Wisseman Christie, *Bijdragen tot de Taal-, Land- en Volkenkunde*, 151 (1995): 235–88.

Christie, Jan Wisseman. 'The Sanskrit Inscriptions Recently Discovered in Kedah, Malaysia'. In: *Modern Quaternary Research in Southeast Asia*, edited by Gert-Jan Bartstra and Willem Arnold Casparie. Rotterdam: A.A. Balkeme, 1990, pp. 39–53.

Christie, Jan Wisseman. 'Trade and the Santubong Iron Industry'. In: *Southeast Asian Archaeology 1986: Proceedings of the First Conference of the Association of Southeast Asian Archaeologists in Western Europe*, edited by Ian Glover and Emily Glover. Oxford: British Archaeological Reports, International Series 561, 1986, pp. 231–40.

Collins, James T. 'Sumbangan Dialek Brunei dalam Pengkajian Sejarah Bahasa Melayu' ['The Contribution of the Brunei Dialect in the Study of the History of Malay Language']. In: *Tinggal Landas ke Abad 21 [Takeoff to the 21st Century]*. Bandar Seri Begawan: Dewan Bahasa dan Pustaka, 1994, pp. 62–75.

Doherty, C. et al. 'Archaeological Investigations at Songai Santubong, Kuching, Sarawak, 2006', *Sarawak Museum Journal*, 63 (2007): 65–94.

Duraman, H.I. 'Achieving Sustainable Development in an Oil-dependent Economy: The Case of Brunei Darussalam'. In: *Readings on the Economy of Brunei Darussalam*, edited by J. Obben and T.S. Ee. Bandar Seri Begawan: Department of Economics, University of Brunei, 1999, pp. 158–99.

Ee, T.S. and A.A. Haji Hashim. 'Manpower Planning in Negara Brunei Darussalam: Issues and Perspectives.' In: *Readings on the Economy of Brunei Darussalam*, edited by J. Obben and T.S. Ee. Bandar Seri Begawan: Department of Economics, University of Brunei, 1999, pp. 158–99.

Ethier, Wilfred J. 'International Trade and Labor Migration', *The American Economic Review*, 75(4) (1985): 691–707.

Everett, Harold H. and John Hewitt. 'A History of Santubong, an Island Off the Coast of Sarawak', *Journal of the Straits Branch of the Royal Asiatic Society*, 51 (1909): 1–30.

Findlay, A.M. et. al. 'Migration Transition or Migration Transformation in the Asian Dragon Economies?' *International Journal of Urban and Regional Research*, 22(4) (1998): 643–63.

Franke, Wolfgang and Ch'en T'ien-fan. 'A Chinese Inscription of A.D. 1264, Discovered Recently in Brunei: A Preliminary Report', *Brunei Museum Journal*, 3 (1973): 91–9.

Green, Jeremy and Rosemary Harper. 'Maritime Archaeology in Thailand: Seven Shipwrecks'. In: *Proceedings of the Second Southern Hemisphere Conference on Maritime Archaeology 1983*, edited by W. Jeffery and J. Amess. Adelaide: South Australia Department of Environment and Planning and the Commonwealth Department of Home Affairs and Environment, 1983, pp. 153–74.

Griswold, A.B. 'The Santubong Buddha and its Context', *Sarawak Museum Journal*, 11 (1962): 363–71.

Hall, Kenneth R. 'Sojourning Communities, Ports-of-trade, and Commercial Networking in Southeast Asia's Eastern Regions, c. 1000–400'. In: *New Perspectives on the History and Historiography of Southeast Asia: Continuing Explorations*, edited by Michael Arthur Aung-Thwin and Kenneth R. Hall. London: Routledge, 2011, pp. 56–74.

Harrisson, Barbara. 'A Classification of Archaeological Trade Ceramics from Kota Batu, Brunei', *Brunei Museum Journal*, 2 (1970): 114–88.

Harrisson, Tom. 'The Golden Hoard of Limbang', *Brunei Museum Journal*, 1 (1969): 57–71.

Harrisson, Tom. 'The Ming Gap and Kota Batu, Brunei', *Sarawak Museum Journal*, 8 (1958): 273–7.

Harrisson, Tom and Barbara Harrisson. 'Kota Batu in Brunei', *Sarawak Museum Journal*, 7 (1956): 283–319.

Harrisson, Tom and Barbara Harrisson. *The Prehistory of Sabah. Sabah Society Journal*, 4 (special monograph) (1971).

Hamzah Abdul Rahman et al. 'Negative Impact Induced by Foreign Workers: Evidence in Malaysian Construction Sector', *Habitat International*, 36 (2012): 433–43.

Hashim Haji Hamid, Haji. 'Malay Islamic Monarchy: An Extension of Brunei History', *Jurnal Darussalam*, 1 (1992): 77–87.

Hey, Jeanne A.K. 'Introducing Small State Foreign Policy'. In: *Small States in World Politics*, edited by Jeanne A.K. Hey. Boulder, CO: Lynne Rienner, 2003, pp. 1–12.

Horton, A.V.M. 'Brunei Rebellion (December 1962): A Cry for Change'. In: *Southeast Asia: A Historical Encyclopedia, from Angkor Wat to East Timor*, vol. I, edited by Ooi Keat Gin. Santa Barbara, CA: ABC-CLIO, 2004, pp. 278–9.

Hussainmiya, B.A. 'The Malays of Brunei Darussalam and Sri Lanka', *Southeast Asia: A Multidisciplinary Journal*, 10 (2010): 65–78.

Jacques, Claude. '"Funan", "Zhenla": The Reality Concealed by These Chinese Views of Indochina'. In: *Early South East Asia: Essays in Archaeology, History, and Historical Geography*, edited by R.B. Smith and W. Watson. New York: Oxford University Press, 1979, pp. 371–9.

Joriah binti Haji Metali, Hajah. 'Dato Haji Ahmad', *Pusaka: Berita Jabatan Pusat Sejarah Brunei*, 1 (1988): 62–4.

Kamarulzaman Askandar, Jacob Bercovitch and Mikio Oishi. 'ASEAN Way of Conflict Management: Old Patterns and New Trends', *Asian Journal of Political Science*, 10(2) (2002): 21–42.

Karim bin Pengiran Haji Osman, Pengiran. 'Further Notes on a Chinese Tombstone Inscription of A.D. 1264', *Brunei Museum Journal*, 8 (1993): 1–10.

Kershaw, Roger. 'The Last Brunei Revolt? A Case Study of Microstate (In)security', *Internationales Asienforum*, 42(1–2) (2011): 107–34.

King, V.T. 'What is Brunei Society? Reflections on a Conceptual and Ethnographic Issue', *South East Asia Research*, 2 (1994): 176–98.

Kurz, Johannes L. 'Boni in Chinese Sources from the Tenth to the Eighteenth Century', *International Journal of Asia-Pacific Studies*, 10(1) (2014): 1–32.

Kurz, Johannes L. 'Pre-modern Chinese Sources in the National History of Brunei: The Case of Poli', *Bijdragen tot de Taal-, Land- en Volkenkunde*, 169 (2013): 213–43.

Lim Jock Hoi. 'Achieving the AEC 2015: Challenges for Brunei Darussalam'. In: *Achieving the ASEAN Economic Community 2015: Challenges for Member Countries and Businesses*, edited by Sanchita Basu Das. Singapore: Institute of Southeast Asian Studies, 2012, pp. 21–36.

Lynch, Marc. 'Abandoning Iraq: Jordan's Alliances and the Politics of State Identity', *Security Studies*, 8(2–3) (1999): 347–88.

Matassim bin Haji Jibah. 'Notes on Tombstones Recently Found in Brunei', *Brunei Museum Journal*, 5 (1982): 19–36.

Matussin Omar. 'A Note on the Stone Wall and Earthen Causeway at Kota Batu', *Brunei Museum Journal*, 5 (1983): 27–50.

Matussin Omar and P.M. Shariffuddin. 'Distribution of Chinese and Siamese Ceramics in Brunei', *Brunei Museum Journal*, 4 (1978): 59–65.

Maxwell, Alan. 'Headtaking and the Consolidation of Political Power in the Early Brunei State'. In: *Headhunting and the Social Imagination in Southeast Asia*, edited by Janet Hoskins. Stanford, CA: Stanford University Press, 1996, pp. 90–126.

McKinnon, E. Edwards. 'Buddhism and the Pre-Islamic Archaeology of Kutei'. In: *Studies in Southeast Asian Art: Essays in Honor of Stanley J. O'Connor*, edited by Nora A. Taylor. Ithaca, NY: Southeast Asia Program, Cornell University, 2000, pp. 217–40.

McKinnon, E. Edwards. 'The Sambas Hoard: Bronze Drums and Gold Ornaments Found in Kalimantan in 1991', *Journal of the Malaysian Branch of the Royal Asiatic Society*, 67 (1994): 9–28.

Md Akhir b. Hj. Yaakub, Haji. 'Harta Sepencarian' ['Shared Property in Marriage'], *Jurnal Hukum*, 5(1) (1984): 36–54.

Mehmet, Ozay and M. Tahiroglu. 'Globalization and Sustainability of Small States', *Humanomics*, 19(1) (2003): 45–58.

Mohammad Raduan bin Mohd Ariff and Amaluddin Bakeri. 'Hubungan Perdagangan Sumber Perikanan Sarawak-Negara Brunei: Kajian Kes Daerah Perikanan Limbang dan Lawas' ['Sarawak–Brunei Commercial Relations in Fisheries Resources: Case Study of the Districts of Limbang and Lawas'], *Jurnal Jabatan Pengajian Asia Tenggara*, 4 (1998): 108–29.

Mohammad Raduan Mohd Ariff and Amaluddin Bakeri. 'Hubungan Perdagangan Sumber Perikanan Sarawak-Negara Brunei: Kajian Kes Daerah Perikanan Miri' ['Sarawak–Brunei Commercial Relations in Fisheries Resources: Case Study of the Districts of Miri'], *Jurnal Jabatan Pengajian Asia Tenggara*, 6 (2001): 1–28.

Mohammad Yusuf, Pengiran. 'Adat Istiadat Diraja Brunei Darussalam' ['The Royal Customs of Brunei Darussalam'], *Brunei Museum Journal*, 4(3) (1975): 43–108.

Mohd Jamil al-Sufri. 'Sultan Sharif Ali', *Jurnal Darussalam*, 1 (1992): 6–33.

Morshidi, A.M. and S.A. Siddiqui. 'Causes and Implications of the Declining Population Growth Rate in Brunei Darussalam'. In: *Readings on the Economy of Brunei Darussalam*, edited by J. Obben and T.S. Ee. Brunei Darussalam: University of Brunei Darussalam, 1999, pp. 132–57.

Mustaffa Omar. 'Bisaya: Suatu tinjauan ringkas' ['Bisaya: A Brief Overview'], *Brunei Museum Journal*, 9 (1993): 17–28.

Nicholl, Robert. 'A Study of the Origins of Brunei', *Brunei Museum Journal*, 7 (1990): 20–31.

Nicholl, Robert. 'Brunei Rediscovered: A Survey of Early Times', *Brunei Museum Journal*, 4 (1980): 219–37.

Nicholl, Robert. 'Notes on the Early Toponymy of Brunei', *Brunei Museum Journal*, 3 (1975): 123–30.

Nicholl, Robert. 'Some Problems in Brunei Chronology', *Journal of Southeast Asian Studies*, 20(2) (1989): 175–95

Noor Azam Haji-Othman. 'English and the Bilingual Bruneian'. In: *English in South East Asia: Challenges and Changes*, edited by Kate Dunworth. Perth, Australia: Curtin University of Technology, 2007, pp. 59–70.

Nothofer, Bernd. 'The Languages of Brunei Darussalam'. In: *Papers in Austronesian Linguistics*, vol. 1, edited by H. Steinhauer. Canberra: Australian National University Press, 1991, pp. 151–76.

Nothofer, Bernd. 'The Network of Malay Isolects in Borneo: A Preliminary Analysis'. In: *Proceedings of the International Seminar on Brunei Malay Sultanate 13–17 November 1994*, edited by Hj. Mohd Taib Osman and Hj. Abdul Latif Hj. Ibrahim. Tungku Link: Academy Pengajian Brunei, Universiti Brunei Darussalam, 1996, pp. 460–71.

O'Connor, Stanley J. 'Tom Harrisson and the Ancient Iron Industry of the Sarawak River Delta', *Journal of the Malaysian Branch of the Royal Asiatic Society*, 50 (1977): 4–7.

Ooi Keat Gin. 'The Cold War and British Borneo: Impact and Legacy 1945–63'. In: *Southeast Asia and the Cold War*, edited by Albert Lau. London: Routledge, 2012, pp. 102–32.

Othman bin Haji Mat Don, Awang. 'Brunei KM XVII–XIX: An Analysis of the History of its Decline', *Jurnal Darussalam*, 10 (2010): 84–105.

Pearson, Richard, Li Min and Li Guo, 'Quanzhou Archaeology: A Brief Review', *International Journal of Historical Archaeology*, 6 (2002): 23–59.

Rusli bin Murni. 'Mengalu Antara Corak Perniagaan Lama di Brunei' ['Mengalu, One of the Old Methods of Trading in Brunei']. In: *Budaya Bangsa [Ethnic Culture]*. Bandar Seri Begawan: Dewan Bahasa dan Pustaka, 1989, pp. 137–43.

Sandin, Benedict. 'The Bisayah of Limbang', *Sarawak Museum Journal*, 19 (1971): 1–19.

Sanib Said. 'Pembentukan kerajaan Brunei lama: Teori penghijrahan dari Sumatera' ['The Establishment of Old Brunei Government: Migration Theory from Sumatra'], *Jurnal Darussalam*, 1 (1992): 88–100.

Sanib Said. 'The Establishment of the Old Brunei Government: A Migration Theory from Sumatra', *Jurnal Darussalam*, 1 (1992): 88–100.

Sarnagi Punchak. 'Bisaya Ethnography: A Brief Report', *Sarawak Museum Journal*, 40 (1989): 37–46.

Schottmann, Sven Alexander. '"Melayu Islam Beraja": The Politics of Legitimisation in a Malay Islamic Monarchy', *RIMA: Review of Indonesian and Malaysian Affairs*, 40(2) (2006): 111–39.

Sharifuddin, P.M. and Abdul Latif bin Haji Ibrahim. 'The Genealogical Tablet (Batu Tarsilah) of the Sultans of Brunei', *Brunei Museum Journal*, 3(2) (1974): 253–64.

Shariffuddin, P.M. and Robert Nicholl. 'A Possible Example of Ancient Brunei Script', *Brunei Museum Journal*, 3 (1975): 116–22.

Sharma, Arvind. 'The Interpretation of a Sanskrit Inscription in the Ancient Script of Brunei', *Journal of the Malaysian Branch of the Royal Asiatic Society*, 52 (1979): 99–101.

Skeldon, R. 'International Migration within and from the East and Southeast Asian Region: A Review Essay', *Asian and Pacific Journal*, 1(1) (1992): 19–63.

Southworth, William A. 'Sailendras: A Javanese Buddhist Dynasty'. In: *Southeast Asia: A Historical Encyclopedia, from Angkor Wat to East Timor*, vol. 3, edited by Ooi Keat Gin. Santa Barbara, CA: ABC Clio, 2004, pp. 1,167–8.

Stalker, Peter. *The Work of Strangers: A Survey of International Labour Migration*. Geneva: International Labour Office, 1994.

Stark, Miriam. 'From Funan to Angkor: Collapse and Regeneration in Ancient Cambodia'. In: *After Collapse: The Regeneration of Complex Societies*, edited by G. Schwartz and J. Nichols. Tucson, AZ: University of Arizona Press, 2006, pp. 144–67.

Sutcliffe, Bob. 'Crossing Borders in the New Imperialism', in *Socialist Register 2004: The New Imperial Challenge*, edited by Leo Panitch and Colin Leys. London: Merlin Press, 2004, pp. 261–80.

Sweeney, P.L. Amin. 'Silsilah Raja-Raja Berunai' ['The Family History of the Kings of Brunei'], *Journal of the Malaysian Branch of the Royal Asiatic Society*, 41(2) (1968): 1–82.

Takong Amit. 'A Discussion on Vital Information about the Existence of the Old Brunei Government Based on Local, Arabic and Chinese Sources', *Beriga*, 19 (April–June 1988): 47–66.

Tan Pek Leng. 'A History of Chinese Settlement in Brunei'. In: *Essays on Modern History of Brunei*. Bandar Seri Begawan: Universiti Brunei Darussalam, 1992, pp. 100–136.

Thambipillai, Pushpa. 'Brunei Darussalam and ASEAN: Regionalism for a Small State', *Asian Journal of Political Science*, 6(1) (1998): 80–94.

Tisdell, C.A. 'Brunei's Quest for Sustainable Development: Diversification and Other Strategies'. In: *Readings on the Economy of Brunei Darussalam*, edited by J. Obben and T.S. Ee. Bandar Seri Begawan: Department of Economics, University of Brunei, 1999, pp. 199–225.

Treacher, W.H. 'British Borneo: Sketches of Brunei, Sarawak, Labuan and North Borneo', *Journal of the Straits Branch of the Royal Asiatic Society*, 20(1) (1889): 13–74.

Tregonning, K.G. 'The Partition of Brunei', *Journal of Tropical Geography*, 2 (1968): 83–9.

Treloar, F.E. 'Chemical Analysis of Iron, Iron Slag and Pottery Remains of the Prehistoric Iron Industry of the Sarawak River Delta', *Sarawak Museum Journal*, 26 (1978): 125–33.

Trimble, Joseph E. and Ryan Dickson. 'Ethnic Identity'. In: *Encyclopedia of Applied Developmental Science*, edited by Celia B. Fisher and Richard M. Lerner. Thousand Oaks, CA: Sage, 2005, pp. 415–20.

Vickery, Michael. 'Funan Reviewed: Deconstructing the Ancients', *Bulletin de l'Ecole française d'Extrême-Orient*, 90 (2003): 101–43.

Wade, Geoff. 'An Earlier Age of Commerce in Southeast Asia, 900–1300 CE', *Journal of Southeast Asian Studies*, 40 (2009): 221–65.

Wade, Geoff. 'Po-luo and Borneo – a Re-examination', *Brunei Museum Journal*, 6 (1986): 13–35.

Wai Toon Han. 'Notes on Bornean Camphor Imported to China', *Brunei Museum Journal*, 6 (1985): 1–31.

Wan Kong Ann. 'Examining the Connection between Ancient China and Borneo through Santubong Archaeological Sites', *Sino-Platonic Papers*, 236 (2013): 1–18.

Wang Gungwu. 'The Nanhai Trade: A Study of the Early History of Chinese Trade in the South China Sea', *Journal of the Malayan Branch of the Royal Asiatic Society*, 31 (1958): 1–135.

Warr, C.G. and E.W.S. Yin. 'Geographies of Displacement: The Karenni and the Shan across the Myanmar–Thailand Border', *Singapore Journal of Tropical Geography*, 23(1) (2002): 93–122.

Watson, A.C. 'Letters from Brunei: Inche Mahomed's Consular Reports 1866–1890', *Brunei Museum Journal*, 5(4) (1984): 1–90.

Watson, A.C. 'Notes on the History of Bubungan Dua Belas', *Brunei Museum Journal*, 5(2) (1992): 37–104.

Yean, T.S. and T.S. Ee. 'Population and Labour Force in Brunei Darussalam: Patterns and Structural Changes'. In: *Readings on the Economy of Brunei Darussalam*, edited by J. Obben and T.S. Ee. Bandar Seri Begawan: Department of Economics, University of Brunei, 1999, pp. 100–131.

Zainie, Carla and Tom Harrisson. 'Early Chinese Stonewares Excavated in Sarawak, 1947–67', *Sarawak Museum Journal*, 15 (1967): 30–90. Zainuddin bin Haji Hassan, Awang Haji. 'Old Brunei: An Early Analysis', *Jurnal Darussalam*, 7 (2007): 114–36.

Zainuddin bin Haji Hassan, Haji. 'Pengalu dan Padian di Brunei: Satu Pengenalan Ringkas' ['The Pangalu and Padian of Brunei: A Brief Introduction'], *Jurnal Pusaka*, 5 (1996): 177–80.

Books

Abdul Kadir bin Haji Ismail, Haji. *Sistem Pusaka Islam* [*The Islamic Inheritance System*]. Kuala Lumpur: Malaysian Dakwah Islamiah Foundation, 1983.

Abdul Latif bin Haji Ibrahim. *Brunei Darussalam Rantisan Sejarah dan Budaya [Brunei Darussalam History and Traditions*]. Bandar Seri Begawan: Academy of Brunei Studies, Universiti Brunei Darussalam Brunei, 2003.

Ahmad Ibrahim and Mahmud Saedon Awang Othman. *Ke arah Islamisasi Undang-Undang Di Malaysia* [*Towards Islamization of the Law in Malaysia*]. Kuala Lumpur: Malaysian Dakwah Islamiah Foundation, 1988.

Air Waybill, Royal Brunei Airline, 1 May 2009; 5 May 2009.

Al-Marhum Sultan Haji Omar Ali Saifuddien Sa'adul Khairi Waddien Dalam Kenangan [*In Memory of Al-Marhum Sultan Haji Omar Ali Saifuddien Sa'adul Khairi Waddien*]. Brunei: Department of Broadcasting and Information, Prime Minister's Department, 1995.

al-Nawawiy Abi Zakariyya Yahya b. Sharaf. *Rawdah al-Talibin*. Beirut: Dar al-Kuttub al-Ilmiyyah, AH 1412/1992.

al-Sharbiniy, al-Shaykh Muhammad al-Khatib. *Mughni al-Muhtaj* [*The Indigent Singer*] (commentary on Imam Nawawi's abridged work of Minhaj al-Talibin). Cairo: Matba'ah Mustafa al-Babiy al-Halabiy wa Awladuh, AH 1377/1958.

Andaya, Barbara Watson and Leonard Y. Andaya. *Sejarah Malaysia* [*A History of Malaysia*]. Kuala Lumpur: Macmillan, 1983.

Arief, S. *The Brunei Economy*. East Balmain, Australia: Southeast Asia Research and Development Institute, 1986.

Asbol bin Haji Mail, Haji Awg. *Kesultanan Melayu Brunei Abad ke 19 Politik dan Struktur Pentadbiran* [*The Brunei Malay Sultanate in the 19th Century: Politics and Administrative Structure*]. Bandar Seri Begawan: Dewan Bahasa dan Pustaka, 2011.

Asbol Haji Mail, Haji Awg, Haji Mohamad Yusop Haji Awg Damit and Ampuan Haji Brahim Ampuan Haji Tengah. *Evolusi dan Tranformasi Kecemerlangan 100 Tahun Pendidikan Negara Brunei Darussalam* [*The Evolution and Transformational Excellence of Education in 100 Years in Negara Brunei Darussalam*]. Bandar Seri Begawan: Ministry of Education, 2014.

Beharell, A. *Unemployment and Job Creation*, London, Macmillan, 1992.

Bellwood, Peter. *Prehistory of the Indo-Malaysian Archipelago*, rev. edn. Honolulu, HI: University of Hawai'i Press, 1997.

Bernard, Timothy, ed. *Contesting Malayness: Malay Identity across Boundaries*. Singapore: Singapore University Press, 2004.

Bilcher, Bala. *Thalassocracy: A History of the Medieval Sultanate of Brunei Darussalam*. Kota Kinabalu: School of Social Science, University of Malaysia Sabah, 2005.

Blundell, Peter. *The City of Many Waters*. London: J.W. Arrowsmith, 1923.

Blust, Robert. *The Austronesian Languages*, rev. edn. Canberra: Asia-Pacific Linguistics Research School of Pacific and Asian Studies, Australian National University, 2013.

Brahim bin Ampuan Haji Tengah, Ampuan Haji. *Traditional Brunei Literature: A Discussion of Genre and Theme*. Bandar Seri Begawan: Dewan Bahasa dan Pustaka Brunei, 2010.

Brosur Bank Islam Brunei Berhad, *Skim Pembiayaan Pengusaha Kecil dan Sederhana* [*Payment Scheme for Small and Medium Industries*]. Bandar Seri Begawan: Bank Islam Brunei Berhad, 2014.

Brown, D.E. *Brunei: The Structure and History of a Bornean Malay Sultanate. Brunei Museum Journal*, 2(2) (special monograph) (1970).

Card, Richard. *Criminal Law*, 13th edn. London: Butterworths, 1995.

Castle, S. and M.J. Miller. *The Age of Migration: International Population Movements in the Modern World*, New York: Guilford Press, 1998.

Cheng Te-k'un. *Archaeology in Sarawak*. Cambridge: W. Heffer and Sons for University of Toronto Press, 1969.

Chhabra, B.C. *Expansion of Indo-Aryan Culture during Pallava Rule (as Evidenced by Inscriptions)*. Delhi: Munshi Ram Manohar Lal, 1965.

Chin, Lucas. *Ceramics in the Sarawak Museum*. Kuching: Sarawak Museum, 1988.

Clynes, Adrian. *Brunei Malay: An Overview*. Occasional Papers in Language Studies, vol. 7. Tungku Link: Department of English Language and Applied Linguistics, Universiti Brunei Darussalam, 2001.

Coe, Michael D. *Angkor and the Khmer Civilization (Ancient Peoples and Places)*. New York: Thames and Hudson, 2003.

Collins, James T. and Awang Sariyan, eds. *Borneo and the Homeland of the Malays: Four Essays*. Kuala Lumpur: Dewan Bahasa dan Pustaka, 2006.

de Carvalho, D. *Migrants and Identity in Japan and Brazil: The Nikkeijin*. London, Routledge, 2003.

de Casparis, J.G. *Indonesian Palaeography: A History of Writing in Indonesia from the beginning to c. A.D. 1500*. Leiden: E.J. Brill, 1975.

de Haas, Hein. *The Determinants of International Migration: Conceptualising Policy, Origin and Destination Effects*, Working Paper 32. Oxford: International Migration Institute, University of Oxford, 2011.

Duraman Tuah, Haji. *Brunei Darussalam: Nation Building Based on Melayu Islam Beraja (Malay Islamic Monarchy Philosophy)*. Gadong, Negara Brunei Darussalam: Civil Service Institute, Prime Minister's Office, n.d. [2002?].

Duraman Tuah, Haji. *Pentadbiran Awam Brunei Darussalam di Period Naungan dan Pemerintahan Sendiri: Satu Kajian* [*Public Administration in Brunei Darussalam in the Period of the Dominion and Self-rule: A Study*]. Bandar Seri Begawan: Brunei Public Services Institute, 2005.

Easter, David. *Britain and the Confrontation with Indonesia, 1960–66*. London: Tauris Academic Studies, 2004.

Emmers, Ralf. *Cooperative Security and the Balance of Power in ASEAN and the ARF*. London: RoutledgeCurzon, 2003.

Gordon, D.M. *Theories of Poverty and Underemployment*. London: Lexington Books, 1972.

Gunn, Geoffrey C. *History Without Borders: The Making of an Asian World Region, 1000–1800*. Hong Kong: Hong Kong University Press, 2011.

Hall, Kenneth R. *A History of Early Southeast Asia: Maritime Trade and Societal Development, 100–1500*. New York: Rowman & Littlefield, 2011.

Harris, Nigel. *The New Untouchables: Immigration and the New World Worker*. London: I.B. Tauris, 1995.

Harrisson, Tom. *The Malays of South-west Sarawak before Malaysia: A Socio-ecological Survey*. London: Macmillan, 1970.

Harrisson, Tom and Stanley J. O'Connor Jr. *Excavations of the Prehistoric Iron Industry in West Borneo*, Data Paper no. 72, 2 vols. Ithaca, NY: Cornell University Southeast Asia Program, 1969.

Harun Abdul Majid. *Rebellion in Brunei: The 1962 Revolt, Imperialism, Confrontation, and Oil*. London: I.B. Tauris, 2007.

Held, David and Anthony McGrew, eds. *Global Transformation: Politics, Economics and Culture*, 22nd edn. Cambridge: Polity Press, 2003.

224   *Bibliography*

Heng, Derek. *Sino-Malay Trade and Diplomacy from the Tenth through the Fourteenth Century*. Athens, OH: Ohio University Press, 2009.

Hooker, M.B. *Islamic Law in South East Asia*. Translated by Rohani Abd. Rahim, Raja Rohana Raja Mamat and Anisah Che' Ngah. Kuala Lumpur: Dewan Bahasa dan Pustaka, 1991.

Horton. A.V.M. *Report on Brunei in 1904 M.S.H. Mc Arthur*, Monographs in International Studies, Southeast Asia Series, no. 74. Athens, OH: Ohio University, 1987.

Horton, A.V.M. *The British Residency in Brunei, 1906–1959*. University of Hull, Centre for South-East Asian Studies, Occasional Paper no. 6, 1984.

Hussainmiya, B.A. *Sultan Omar Ali Saifuddin III and Britain: The Making of Brunei Darussalam*. Singapore: Oxford University Press, 1995.

James, Harold and D. Sheil-Small. *The Undeclared War: The Story of Indonesian Confrontation, 1962–1966*. London: Leo Cooper, 1971.

Jamil al-Sufri. *History of Brunei in Brief*, 2nd edn. Bandar Seri Begawan: Brunei History Centre, Ministry of Culture, Youth and Sports, 2000.

Jones, L.W. *The Population of Borneo: A Study of the Peoples of Sarawak, Sabah and Brunei*. London: University of London, 1966.

Jones, Matthew. *Conflict and Confrontation in South East Asia, 1961–1965: Britain, the United States, and the Creation of Malaysia*. Cambridge: Cambridge University Press, 2001.

Jordaan, R.E. and B.E. Colless. *The Mahārājas of the Isles: The Śailendras and the Problem of Śrīvijaya*. Leiden: Department of Languages and Cultures of Southeast Asia and Oceania, University of Leiden, 2009.

Kamus Bahasa Melayu Nusantara [The Malay Language Dictionary of the Archipelago]. Bandar Seri Begawan: Dewan Bahasa dan Pustaka, 2003.

Karim bin Pg. Haji Osman, Pengiran. ed. *Songai Limau Manis: Tapak Arkeologi Abad ke 10–13 Masihi [Songai Limau Manis: Archaeological Site of the 10th–13th Century AD]*. Bandar Seri Begawan: Muzium Brunei, 2004.

Keyser, Arthur Louis. *People and Places: A Life in Five Continents*. London: John Murray, 1922.

Keyser, Arthur Louis. *Trifles and Travels*. London: John Murray, 1923.

Khairul Rijal bin Pg. Haji Abdul Rahim, Pg. *Teknologi Menangkap Ikan di Negara Brunei Darussalam 1906–2003 [Fishing Technologies in Negara Brunei Darussalam 1906–2003]*. Kuala Lumpur: Penerbit Universiti Malaya, 2007.

King, Victor T. *The Peoples of Borneo*. Oxford: Blackwell, 1993.

Komai, H. *Migrant Workers in Japan*. London: Kegan Paul International, 1993.

Kothari, Uma. *Migration and Chronic Poverty*, Working Paper no. 16. Manchester: Institute for Development Policy and Management, Chronic Poverty Research, University of Manchester, 2002.

Lieberman, Victor. *Strange Parallels: Southeast Asia in Global Context, c. 800–1830*, vol. 1, *Integration of the Mainland*. Cambridge: Cambridge University Press, 2003.

Mackie, J.A.C. *Konfrontasi: The Indonesia–Malaysia Dispute, 1963–1966*. Kuala Lumpur: Oxford University Press, 1974.

Mahmud Saedon Awang Osman, Haji. *Pelaksanaan dan Pentadbiran Undang-Undang Islam di Negara Brunei Darussalam: Satu Tinjauan [The Implementation and Administration of Islamic Law in Negara Brunei Darussalam: A Review]*. Bandar Seri Begawan: Dewan Bahasa dan Pustaka, 1996.

Mahmud Saedon bin Awg Othman. *Jejak-Jejak, Kumpulan Kertas Kerja [Traces: A Compilation of Paperwork]*. Bandar Seri Begawan: Academy of Brunei Studies, Universiti Brunei Darussalam Brunei, 2003.

Matussin Omar. *Archaeological Excavations in Protohistoric Brunei*. Bandar Seri Begawan: Muzium Brunei, 1981.

Maxwell, William George and William Sumner Gibson. *Treaties and Engagements Affecting the Malay States and Borneo*. London: J. Truscott, 1924.

Miles, R. *Capitalism and Unfree Labour: Anomaly or Necessity?* London: Tavistock Publications, 1987.

Milner, Anthony. *The Malays*. Oxford: Wiley-Blackwell, 2008.

Mimi Kamariah Majid. *Undang-Undang Keluarga di Malaysia* [*Family Law in Malaysia*]. Kuala Lumpur: Butterworths Asia, 1992.

Mohd Jamil al-Sufri, Hj. *Chatatan Sejarah Perwira dan Pembesar Brunei* [*A Historical Record of Bruneian Heroes and Dignitaries*]. Bandar Seri Bagawan: Dewan Bahasa dan Pustaka, 1973.

Mohammad bin Pengiran Haji Abd. Rahman, Pengiran Haji. *Islam in Brunei Darussalam*. Bandar Seri Begawan: Dewan Bahasa dan Pustaka Brunei, 1992.

Mohammed Jamil al-Sufri, Pehin. *Tarsilah Brunei: Sejarah awal dan perkembangan Islam* [*Brunei Inscriptions: Early History and the Development of Islam*], rev. edn. Bandar Seri Begawan: Pusat Sejarah Brunei, 2001.

Mohammad Raduan bin Mohd Ariff. *Petempatan Kampung Air di Pulau Borneo: Satu Kajian Perbandingan* [*The Settlement of Kampung Air in Borneo Island: A Comparative Study*]. Monograf Akademi Pengajian Brunei no. 2. Bandar Seri Bagawan: Akademi Pengajian Brunei, Universiti Brunei, 2005.

Mohammad Tahir bin Abdul Ghani. *Hikayat Datuk Merpati*. Kuala Lumpur: Dewan Bahasa dan Pustaka, 1989.

Mohd Jamil al-Sufri. *Brunei Darussalam: A Malay Islamic Monarchic Country*. Bandar Seri Begawan: Pusat Sejarah Brunei, 2007.

Mohd Jamil al-Sufri, Pehin Haji Awg. *Tarsilah Brunei: Sejarah Awal dan Perkembangan Islam* [*Brunei Inscriptions: Early History and Development of Islam*]. Bandar Seri Begawan: Pusat Sejarah Brunei, 1990.

Mohd Yaakub Hj. Johari, Bison Kurus and Janiah Zaini, eds. *BIMP-EAGA Integration: Issues and Challenges*. Kota Kinabalu: Institute for Development Studies, 1997.

Mohd Zain Haji Serudin, Haji. *Melayu Islam Beraja: Suatu Pendekatan* [*Malay Muslim Monarchy: An Approach*]. Bandar Seri Begawan: Dewan Bahasa dan Pustaka, 1998.

Munoz, Paul M. *Early Kingdoms of the Indonesian Archipelago and the Malay Peninsula*. Singapore: Editions Didier Millet, 2006.

Mustafa Haji Daud. *Institusi Kekeluargaan Islam* [*The Islamic Family Institution*]. Kuala Lumpur: Dewan Bahasa dan Pustaka, Ministry of Education, Malaysia, 1992.

Narong Ruangsivakul et al., eds. *Fishing Gears and Methods in Southeast Asia*, vol. 5, *Brunei Darussalam*. Bandar Seri Begawan: Department of Fisheries, Brunei Darussalam and SEAFDEC Training Department, 2007.

Nicholl, Robert. *European Sources for the History of the Sultanate of Brunei in the Sixteenth Century*. Bandar Seri Begawan: Muzium Brunei, 1975.

Ooi Keat Gin. *Historical Dictionary of Malaysia*. Lanham, MD: Scarecrow Press, 2009.

Ooi Keat Gin. *Of Free Trade and Native Interests: The Brookes and the Economic Development of Sarawak*. Kuala Lumpur: Oxford University Press, 1997.

Ooi Keat Gin. *Post-war Borneo, 1945–1950: Nationalism, Empire, and State-building*. London: Routledge, 2013.

Ooi Keat Gin. *The Japanese Occupation of Borneo*. London: Routledge, 2011.

Pendidikan Agama di Negara Brunei Darussalam [*Religious Education in Negara Brunei Darussalam*]. Bandar Seri Begawan: Department of Islamic Studies, Ministry of Religious Affairs, 1996.

Othman bin Haji Ishak. *Fatwa Dalam Rumahtangga Islam* [*Ordainment in the Muslim Family*]. Kuala Lumpur: Fajar Bakti, 1981.

Pham, P.L. *Ending 'East of Suez': The British Decision to Withdraw from Malaysia and Singapore 1964–1968*. Oxford: Oxford University Press, 2010.

Pigafetta, Antonio. *First Voyage Round the World by Magellan, Translated from the Accounts of Pigafetta, and Other Contemporary Writers*. London: Hakluyt Society, 1874.

Porritt, Vernon L. *British Colonial Rule in Sarawak, 1946–1963*. Kuala Lumpur: Oxford University Press, 1997.

Porritt, Vernon L. *The Rise and Fall of Communism in Sarawak 1940–1990*. Clayton, Australia: Monash Asia Institute, 2004.

Potts, L. *The World Labour Market: A History of Migration*. London: Zed Books, 1990.

Pryor, R.J. *Migration and Development in South-East Asia*. Kuala Lumpur: Oxford University Press, 1979.

Ranjit Singh, D.S. *Brunei 1839–1983: The Problems of Political Survival*. Singapore: Oxford University Press, 1991.

Saadiah binti Datu Derma Wijaya Haji Tamit, Datin Hajah. *Pembubaran Perkahwinan Dalam Undang-undang Keluarga Islam Brunei dan Perbandingan Dengan Undang-Undang Keluarga Islam Malaysia* [*Dissolution of Marriages under Islamic Family Law in Brunei and its Comparison to Islamic Family Law in Malaysia*]. Bandar Seri Begawan: Dewan Bahasa dan Pustaka, Ministry of Culture, Youth and Sports, 2012.

Saadiah binti Datu Derma Wijaya Haji Tamit, Datin Hajah. *Wanita, Keluarga, dan Undang-undang Di Negara Brunei Darussalam* [*Women, Family and the Law in Negara Brunei Darussalam*]. Bandar Seri Begawan: Dewan Bahasa dan Pustaka, Ministry of Culture, Youth and Sports, 2009.

Sabihah Osman, Muhammad Hadi Abdullah and Sabullah Haji Hakip. *Sejarah Brunei Menjelang Kemerdekaan* [*The History of Brunei at the Dawn of Independence*]. Kuala Lumpur: Dewan Bahasa dan Pustaka, 1995.

Sanib bin Hj. Said et al. *Dahulu Terasing Kini Terjalin: Bahagian Limbang-Daerah Limbang dan Lawas* [*Divided in the Past, Enjoined at the Present: Limbang Division-Limbang and Lawas District*]. Sarawak: Pejabat Residen Bahagian Limbang, 2009.

Saunders, Graham. *A History of Brunei*. Kuala Lumpur: Oxford University Press, 1994.

Shukri Zain et al. *The Malay Islamic Monarchy: A Closer Understanding*. Bandar Seri Begawan: National Supreme Council of the Malay Islamic Monarchy Brunei Darussalam, 2013.

Sidhu, Jatswan S. *Sejarah Sosioekonomi Brunei 1906–1959* [*The Socioeconomic History of Brunei 1906–1959*]. Kuala Lumpur: Dewan Bahasa dan Pustaka, 1995.

Simat bin Angas, Suhaili bin Haji Hassan and Haji Ismail bin Ibrahim. *Tokoh-tokoh Agama di Brunei Darussalam: Pengenalan Ringkas* [*Religious Figures in Brunei Darussalam: A Brief Introduction*]. Bandar Seri Begawan: Jabatan Muzium-Muzium, 1992.

Tarling, Nicholas. *Britain, the Brookes and Brunei*. Kuala Lumpur: Oxford University Press, 1971.

Teuku Iskandar, ed. *Kamus Dewan* [*The Dewan Dictionary*], new edn. Kuala Lumpur: Dewan Bahasa dan Pustaka, 1992.

Teuku Iskandar. *Malay Classical Literature Throughout the Century*. Bandar Seri Begawan: Universiti Brunei Darussalam, 1995.

Tibbetts, G.R. *A Study of the Arabic Texts Containing Material on South-East Asia*. Leiden: Brill, 1979.

Turnbull, C.M. *A Short History of Malaysia, Singapore and Brunei*. Singapore: Graham Brash, 1981.

Van der Bijl, Nicholas. *The Brunei Revolt, 1962–1963*. Barnsley: Pen & Sword Military, 2012.

Wahbah al-Zuhayliy. *al-Fiqh al-Islamiy wa Adillatuh* [*The Understanding of Islamic Jurisprudence*]. Beirut: Dar al-Fikr, AH 1409/1989.

Wan Abdul Halim Wan Harun. *Mengurus Harta Pusaka* [*Managing Inheritance Estates*]. Kuala Lumpur: PTS Professional Publishing, 2012.

Wickramasekera, Piyasari. *Asian Labour Migration: Issues and Challenges in an Era of Globalization*, International Migration Papers 57. Geneva: International Labour Office, 2002.

Wolters, O.W. *Early Indonesian Commerce: A Study of the Origins of Srivijaya*. Ithaca, NY: Cornell University Press, 1967.

World Bank. *World Development Report 2004: Making Services Work for Poor People*. Washington, DC: Oxford University Press, 2003.

Wright, L.R. *The Making of British Borneo*. Hong Kong: Hong Kong University Press, 1988.

Wright, Thomas. *The Travels of Marco Polo, the Venetian: The Translation of Marsden Revised, with a Selection of His Notes*. Whitefish, MT: Kessinger Publishing, 2004.

Yahya bin Haji Ibrahim, Haji Awg. *Sejarah dan Peranan Institusi-institusi Melayu Islam Beraja* [*The History and Role of the Islamic Malay Monarchic Institution*]. Bandar Seri Begawan: Da'wah Islamiah Centre, Brunei Ministry of Religious Affairs, 2000.

Yakub Othman, P.M. *Brunei Darussalam – Challenges for Economic Diversification: Economic Diversification within the Context of National Development Planning in Brunei*. Saarbrücken, Germany: Lambert Academic Publishing, 2012.

Yura Halim and Jamil Umar. *Sejarah Berunai* [*History of Brunei*]. Kuala Belait: Brunei Press, 1958.

Zaini Haji Ahmad, Haji, ed. *Partai Rakyat Brunei/The People's Party of Brunei: Selected Documents/Dokumen Terpilih*. Petaling Jaya: Institute of Social Analysis, n.d. [1987?].

Zehadul Karim, A.H.M. et. al. *Foreign Workers in Malaysia*. Kuala Lumpur: Utusan Publications and Distributors, 1999.

Proceedings and working papers

Abdul Latif bin Haji Ibrahim. 'Peranan Rumah-Rumah Perkumpulan dalam Masyarakat Melayu Brunei' ['The Role of Cluster Homes in the Brunei Malay Community']. In: *Ikhtisar Budaya* [*Cultural Highlights*]. Bandar Seri Begawan: Dewan Bahasa dan Pustaka, 1982.

Abdul Latif bin Haji Ibrahim, Haji Awang. 'Kampong Ayer: Warisan, Cabaran, dan Masa Depan' ['Kampong Ayer: Heritage, Challenges and its Future']. paper presented at International Symposium on Kampong Ayer organized by the Academy of Brunei Studies, Universiti Brunei Darussalam, 6–9 September 1996.

Maricar, H.H.M.A. 'ASEAN Workers in Brunei Darussalam's Development'. Paper presented at the Southeast Asian Geography Association Fourth International Conference on Geography and the Development of the Southeast Asian Region and the Seventh National Geographic Seminar of Thailand, Chiang Mai, Thailand, 1996.

Wu Zong Yu. 1994. 'Raja Brunei dalam Sejarah China' ['The King of Brunei in the History of China']. Paper presented at International Seminar on the Brunei Darussalam Malay Sultanate organized by the Academy of Brunei Studies, Universiti Brunei Darussalam and Sultan Haji Hassanal Bolkiah Foundation, Bandar Seri Begawan, 13–17 November 1994.

Yahya Haji Ibrahim, Haji Awang. 'Beberapa Aspek Mengenai Rumah dan Perumahan di Kampong Ayer' ['A Few Aspects of the Houses and Habitation in Kampong Ayer']. Paper presented at International Symposium on Kampong Ayer organized by the Academy of Brunei Studies, Universiti Brunei Darussalam, 6–9 September 1996.

Internet sources

Abdul Malik Omar. 'How Singapore and Brunei Became Friends', *The AMO Times*, 15 May 2014. http://amotimes.com/tag/brunei-and-singapore-abiding-ties-of-close-neighbours. Accessed 22 August 2015.

Applied History Research Group. *Peopling North America: Population Movements & Migration*. University of Calgary Applied History Research Group, 2001. http://www.ucalgary.ca/applied_history/tutor/migrations/Fhome.html. Accessed 2 December 2003.

ASEAN Secretariat. 'Declaration of ASEAN Concord II (Bali Concord II)', 7 October 2003. http://www.asean.org/news/asean-statement-communiques/item/declaration-of-asean-concord-ii-bali-concord-ii-3. Accessed 22 August 2015.

Asia Economic Institute. 'Brunei and Oman: Strengthening Bilateral Relations', n.d. http://www.asiaecon.org/special_articles/read_sp/12237. Accessed 20 August 2014.

'Brunei Darussalam', *Worldmark Encyclopedia of Nations*, 2007. Encyclopedia.com. http://www.encyclopedia.com/topic/Brunei_Darussalam.aspx. Accessed 22 August 2015.

'Brunei Darussalam Economic Review: Outlook and Recent Economic Developments', *Brunei Economic Bulletin*, 5 (May 2008): 1–29. http://www.bruneiresources.com/pdf/economicbulletin0508.pdf. Accessed 22 August 2015.

Brunei Darussalam Key Indicators. Department of Statistics, Department of Economic Planning and Development, Prime Minister's Office. http://www.depd.gov.bn/download/BDKI2011.pdf. Accessed 4 September 2015.

'Brunei Darussalam's Information Paper: Policy Measures for Youth Development and Human Resources Development in Brunei Darussalam'. Information paper presented at the Symposium on Globalization and the Future of Youth in Asia, 2–3 December 2004, Tokyo. http://www.ilo.org/public/english/region/asro/tokyo/conf/2004youth/downloads/brunei.pdf. Accessed 22 August 2015.

'Brunei Imposes Caning on Immigration Offenders', Corpun file 12783, BruneiDirect. Com, 15 February 2004. http://www.corpun.com/bnj00402.htm. Accessed 4 September 2015.

Embassy of Brunei Darussalam and Mission to the European Union, Belgium. 'Sultan to Attend OIC Summit', 14 August 2012. http://bruneiembassy.be/sultan-to-attend-oic-summit/. Accessed 22 August 2015.

Fernandez, Edwin. 'Brunei Military Official Visits Troops Monitoring Ceasefire of PH Gov't, MILF', *Inquirer Global Nation*, 14 July 2014. http://globalnation.inquirer.net/107908/brunei-military-official-visits-troops-monitoring-ceasefire-of-ph-govt-milf. Accessed 22 August 2015.

'Friendship Bridge a Symbol of Close M'sia-Brunei Ties', *Borneo Post Online*, 9 December 2013. http://www.theborneopost.com/2013/12/09/friendship-bridge-a-symbol-of-close-msia-brunei-ties/. Accessed 22 August 2015.

Irfan Mohammed. 'Brunei Studying Kingdom's Implementation of Shariah', *Arab News*, 14 February 2014. http://www.arabnews.com/news/525641. Accessed 22 August 2015.

Lee Hsien Loong. 'Brunei and Singapore: Abiding Ties of Close Neighbours', *Straits Times*, 29 October 2012. http://www.straitstimes.com/st/print/566078. Accessed 22 August 2015.

Leong Shen-li. 'A Tale of Two Blocks', *The Star Online*, 2 May 2010. http://www.the-star.com.my/story.aspx/?file=%2f2010%2f5%2f9%2fnation%2f6188182. Accessed 22 August 2015.

'Malaysia, Singapore, Indonesia', *Migration News*, 7(2) (February 2000). https://migration.ucdavis.edu/mn/more.php?id=2033. Accessed 4 September 2015.

Ministry of Defence, Singapore. 'SAF and Other Militaries Conclude the ADMM-Plus HADR/ MM Exercise', 20 June 2013. http://www.mindef.gov.sg/imindef/press_room/official_ releases/nr/2013/jun/20jun13_nr.html#.U8T6Jq2KDoY. Accessed 22 August 2015.

Ministry of Foreign Affairs and Trade, Brunei Darussalam. 'Brunei Darussalam Country Brief', n.d. http://dfat.gov.au/geo/brunei-darussalam/pages/brunei-darussalam-coun-try-brief.aspx. Accessed 22 August 2015.

Ministry of Foreign Affairs, Arab Republic of Egypt. 'Egypt's Relations with ASEAN Countries', 4 March 2006. http://www.mfa.gov.eg/English/EgyptianForeignPolicy/ EgyptianAsianRelation/News/Pages/NewsDetails.aspx?Source=6781921f-3993-444a-859e-ee26ce851de8&newsID=b81c8bfc-cae6-46ff-9efb-d46d90870230. Accessed 22 August 2015.

Ministry of Foreign Affairs of Japan. 'Japan and Brunei: 30 Years of Diplomatic Relations', January 2014. http://www.bn.emb-japan.go.jp/jbyear2014/jb2014_bro-chure.pdf. Accessed 22 August 2015.

Ministry of Foreign Affairs of the People's Republic of China. 'Premier Li Keqiang Holds Talks with Sultan Haji Hassanal Bolkiah of Brunei, Stressing to Further Uplift Level of China-Brunei Strategic Cooperation', 11 October 2013. http://www.fmprc.gov.cn/mfa_ eng/topics_665678/lkqzlcxdyldrxlhy_665684/t1088909.shtml. Accessed 22 August 2015.

Mitsubishi Corporation. 'Brunei LNG Project Strengthening Ties with a Resource-rich Country to Ensure Stable, Long-term Energy Supplies'. http://www.mitsubishicorp. com/jp/en/mclibrary/evolving/vol01/page3.html. Accessed 22 August 2015.

Monetary Authority of Singapore. 'Currency Interchangeability Agreement – Brunei Notes and Coins'. http://www.mas.gov.sg/currency/currency-interchangeability-agreement-with-brunei.aspx. Accessed 22 August 2015.

Parameswaran, Prashanth. 'China, Brunei: Ties that Bind', *Asia Times Online*, 9 November 2012. http://www.atimes.com/atimes/China_Business/NK09Cb01.html. Accessed 22 August 2015.

Sea Around Us Project. 'EEZ Waters of Brunei Darussalam'. http://www.seaaroundus.org/ eez/96.aspx. Accessed 22 August 2015.

Shields, Daniel L. 'Working with Brunei to Get the Rebalance Right', *The Ambassadors Review*, Spring 2014. http://s3.amazonaws.com/caa-production/attachments/462/C_ Pages20to22_Shields.pdf?1399575078. Accessed 22 August 2015.

Siti Redzaimi Pg. Hj. Ahmad, Dk. 'Gaji Pekerja Asing, Tempatan Sama Rata', *Pelita Brunei*, 20 November 2014. http://www.pelitabrunei.gov.bn/nasional/item/11089-gaji-pekerja-tempatan-asing-sama-rata. Accessed 22 August 2015.

Waleed P.D. Mahdini. 'Brunei Joins OIC Call for Conflict Resolution', 16 May 2007. http://www.bt.com.bn/classification/frontpage/2007/05/16/brunei_joins_oic_call_for_ conflict_resolution. Accessed 22 August 2015.

Wardi Buntar. 'Brunei 8th UNIFIL Team Off to Lebanon', *The Brunei Times*, 5 July 2012. http://www.bt.com.bn/news-national/2012/07/05/brunei-8th-unifil-team-lebanon. Accessed 22 August 2015.

World Trade Organization. 'Brunei Darussalam: Economic Environment'. https://www. wto.org/english/tratop_e/tpr_e/s196-01_e.doc. Accessed 22 August 2015.

Newsprint

Azlan Othman. 'His Majesty Visits Tsunami-hit Aceh', *Borneo Bulletin*, 2 February 2005.

Borneo Bulletin, 18 June 1998; 26 November 1999.

Goh De No. 'Brunei Owns Blocks J and K, Says Abdullah', *The Brunei Times*, 1 May 2010.

'Japan to Provide Energy Tech Aid to Brunei', *Jiji Press*, 13 May 2013.

North Borneo Herald, Official Gazette, no. V, vol. II, 1 November 1884.

Pelita Brunei, 1 February 1959; 29 September 1959; 11 October 1995; 1 July 1998; 6 October 1999.

Zareena Amiruddin. 'Brunei's Financial Aid to Tsunami Victims is Well Spent', *The Brunei Times*, 25 December 2010.

Theses and dissertations

Ajamain bin Hj. Sawal. 'Future Fisheries Management Strategy for Brunei', Master's thesis, Humberside Polytechnic, 1990.

Alas, Yabit. 'The Reconstruction of Pre-Dusun and the Classification of its Descendants', MA thesis, University of Hawai'i, 1994.

Brown, Roxanna. 'The Ming Gap and Shipwreck Ceramics in Southeast Asia', PhD thesis, University of California, Los Angeles, 2004.

Ismail Haji Awg Nordin. 'Sultan Hashim: From Western Points of View', MA dissertation, University of Hull, 1998.

Karim bin Pengiran Haji Osman, Pengiran. 'The Evidence of Oriental Ceramics and Earthenware Distributions in Brunei Darussalam as an Aid in Understanding Protohistoric Brunei', PhD thesis, University of Southampton, 1997.

Masnon bt. Haji Ibrahim, Hajah. 'Perlaksanaan Undang-Undang Keluarga Islam di Brunei dan Perbandingannya dengan Undang-Undang Keluarga Islam di Sarawak' ['The Implementation of Islamic Family Law in Brunei and its Comparison to the Islamic Family Law in Sarawa, Malaysia']. MA thesis, Universiti Kebangsaan Malaysia, 1988.

Swain, Nicholas D. 'The Foreign Policy of Small States: A Comparison of Bhutan and Brunei', MA thesis, University of Hong Kong, 1991.

Index

Note: Page references in **bold** refer to the Glossary; *f*, *t* and 'n' refer to figures, tables and notes.